Launching the Imagination

A Comprehensive Guide to Basic Design

Launching the Imagination

A Comprehensive Guide to Basic Design

first edition

Mary Stewart

Launching the Imagination:
A Comprehensive Guide to Basic Design
is dedicated to Janet Ballweg, who got
the job started, and to Cynthia Ward,
who made sure it got done.

McGraw-Hill Higher Education

*A Division of The **McGraw-Hill** Companies*

LAUNCHING THE IMAGINATION: A COMPREHENSIVE GUIDE TO BASIC DESIGN
Published by McGraw-Hill, an imprint of The McGraw-Hill Companies, Inc. 1221 Avenue of the Americas, New York, NY, 10020. Copyright © 2002 by The McGraw-Hill Companies, Inc. All rights reserved. No part of this publication may be reproduced or distributed in any form or by any means, or stored in a database or retrieval system, without the prior written consent of The McGraw-Hill Companies, Inc., including, but not limited to, in any network or other electronic storage or transmission, or broadcast for distance learning. Some ancillaries, including electronic and print components, may not be available to customers outside the United States.

This book is printed on acid-free paper.

2 3 4 5 6 7 8 9 0 KGP/KGP 0 9 8 7 6 5 4 3 2

ISBN   0-07-230355-7

Editorial director: *Phillip A. Butcher*
Sponsoring editor: *Joe Hanson*
Developmental editor: *Cynthia Ward*
Senior marketing manager: *David Patterson*
Lead project manager: *Mary Conzachi*
Production supervisor: *Susanne Riedell*
Senior designer: *Pam Verros*
Media producer: *Shannon Rider*
Lead supplement producer: *Cathy L. Tepper*
Photo research coordinator: *Ira C. Roberts*
Photo researchers: *Elsa Peterson Ltd. and Photosearch, Inc.*
Cover design: *Jenny El-Shamy*
Interior design: *Pam Verros*
Typeface: *10.5/14 Palatino*
Compositor: *GTS Graphics, Inc.*
Printer: *Quebecor World Kingsport*
Cover Image Credits:
[1]   Käthe Kollwitz. *Self-Portrait in Profile, Facing Left, I.* 1889. Lithograph, 5-7\8 × 5-7/8"
        (15 × 15 cm). Unsigned. Staatliche Kunstsammlungen der DDR. Kupferstichkabinett
        Dresden.
[2]   Poster: *"Master Harold" ... and the Boys.* Poster. The Department of Theater Arts, California
        State University, Los Angeles, David McNutt, 1985.
[3]   Bella Coola mask representing the sun from British Columbia. Before 1897. Wood,
        diameter 24 3/4". American Museum of Natural History, New York. Transparency
        2104(2) Courtesy Department of Library Services, American Museum of Natural History.
[4]   Auguste Rodin. *The Kiss.* 1886–1898. Marble. Over life size. Rodin Museum, Paris.
[5]   Bart Forbes. *Landmark.* 1999. Oil on canvas, 14" w × 19" d (35.6 × 48.3 cm). From
        Frogfolio 10, Dellas Graphics, Syracuse, NY. © Bart Forbes, 2001.
[6]   Nancy Crow. *Double Mexican Wedding Rings 1.* © 1988. Hand quilted by Marie Moore.
        72 × 720 (183 × 183 cm). Photo: J. Kevin Fitzsimons.

Library of Congress Control Number: 2001097904

www.mhhe.com

Mary Stewart is currently an Associate Professor and the Foundation Coordinator in the Northern Illinois University School of Art. She also serves as the Regional Coordinator Advisor for Foundations in Art: Theory and Education, a professional organization devoted to excellence in college-level teaching. A long-time member of the Syracuse University Foundation Program, she has taught Two-Dimensional Design, Three-Dimensional Design, and Drawing for over twenty-five years. As an artist, Stewart uses the dialogs of Plato as a beginning point for visual narratives using drawing, visual books, and computer graphics.

The Design Continuum

My fascination with design dates back to 1980, the year I taught my first two-dimensional design course. As a graduate student at Indiana University, I had been teaching drawing since 1977. The transformation of perceptual reality into effective illusion was the main concern in basic drawing, and I knew many ways to accomplish this goal. It was far more difficult to determine either the form or the content for a course in design. In researching the subject, I discovered a dizzying array of skills to master and concepts to explore.

Auditing the courses of two master teachers raised even more questions. The first, taught by Professor William Itter, was derived from the approach developed by his teacher, Joseph Albers. Professor Itter's course was methodical, systematic, and highly analytical. The second course, taught by Professor David Hornung, offered a thorough investigation of unity and variety through an exploration of patterns in art and life. His approach was exuberant, synthetic, and often irreverent. Despite significant differences in their assignments, both teachers presented substantial design information effectively.

In developing my own course, I concluded that a comprehensive approach to design required exuberance as well as analysis and that rambunctiousness was the natural partner to rigor. Design is equally a noun and a verb. It offers a problem-solving process as well as a well-crafted product. Because the ideas and approaches to design are ever-changing, the educational possibilities are infinite. Thus, when McGraw-Hill invited me to write a new design book, I was determined to present substantial information in the liveliest possible way.

A Flexible Framework

Launching the Imagination: A Comprehensive Guide to Basic Design offers a clear, concise, and comprehensive overview of the elements, principles, and problem-solving processes for courses in two-, three-, and four-dimensional design, and concept development. The book covers all of the topics common to foundations courses and found in other textbooks; however, I have attempted to refine, distill, and update the presentation of this core material. Over six hundred images from a wide variety of sources illustrate these points in a clear and engaging manner. A special effort has been made to include the broadest possible range of images, including examples from photography, design and the media arts, as well as traditional fine arts. *Launching the Imagination* showcases contemporary art, so that first-year students (many of whom are concurrently studying art history) have a fuller view of the art world they will be entering. The stylistic range is broad and the examples are drawn from many cultures.

Launching also includes many unique features:

- For the first time, four-dimensional design is presented as a unique and complex design dimension in its own right. Time has always been an essential aspect of art, from the narrative paintings of the Renaissance to a contemporary photographer's awareness of the decisive moment. New technologies such as video, film, and computers continually expand the potential uses of time in art. Six major aspects of time are discussed in Chapter 10, narrative and non-narrative aspects are addressed in Chapter 11, and interdisciplinary arts are discussed in Chapter 12.

- *Launching the Imagination* is the only foundations text that includes an extensive discussion of concept development and creativity, including specific critical thinking and problem-solving strategies, time-management techniques, and a thorough discussion of critiques.

- Profiles are special two-page spreads, found in every chapter, which highlight interviews with living artists and designers. Through these interviews, students learn about the working processes, career choices, obstacles overcome, and criteria for excellence of a remarkable group of masters in the field. These interviews help students see connections between basic design and professional practice while providing an introduction to potential careers.

- Each chapter ends with a point-by-point summary, a list of key words, a brief list of recommended readings, and at least five key questions. These questions are designed to help students analyze their studio works in progress, rather than solely relying on a final critique for input.

A glossary, extensive bibliography, and comprehensive index provide further information and help readers access sections of the book of particular interest.

Unified in a single text, yet separated into four clearly defined divisions, *Launching the Imagination: A Comprehensive*

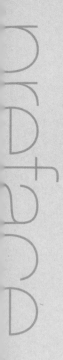

Guide to Basic Design offers teachers enormous flexibility in creating courses which combine traditional ideas with timely innovations.

A Pedagogical Support System

In addition to the integrated pedagogy highlighted above, each copy of *Launching the Imagination* is packaged with Launching the Imagination's *Core Concepts in Art* CD-ROM, which features over 70 interactive exercises illustrating such fundamental elements as line, shape, and color; narrated video segments on a wide range of media; study resources correlated to each chapter; a research and Internet guide; and a study skills section offering practical advice on succeeding at college.

Instead of providing extensive exercises in the text, *Launching the Imagination* is accompanied by an extensive Instructor's Manual. Advice on course construction, critique skills, and technical resources is included, along with over fifty terrific assignments.

Finally, *Launching the Imagination* is supported by a dynamic Website featuring additional studio exercises, Web-based resources for students and teachers, and interactive problems for further study. The address for this site is www.mhhe.com/launching

Acknowledgments

It has been quite a job and I've received a lot of help from my colleagues. At Northern Illinois University, School of Art Chair Adrian Tió has been relentlessly optimistic and highly supportive. From Syracuse University, I would like to thank Paul Nielsen and Sarah McCoubrey, who chaired the Art Foundation Department during this project, and were consistently helpful. Peter Forbes, Jude Lewis, Stephen Carlson, and Stan Rickel offered their encouragement and lots of help, and librarians Randall Bond and Terence Keenan provided prompt, gracious, and insightful advice on my many research questions. Mat Kelly, Ben Marra, and Akiyo Okura acted as my assistants at various points—each contributed ideas as well as energy to the book. I would particularly like to thank Jason Chin for commenting at length on many chapters, and Trisha Tripp and Cally Iden, whose critiques appear in chapter six. Colorado College, where I worked as a scholar-in-residence in January 2000, also provided valuable support. I would especially like to thank Kate Leonard, who arranged my visit, librarian Leroy Smith, who created a storyboard Website for my students, and Carl Reed, whose advice substantially improved the three-dimensional design section of this book.

I would like to thank the following artists and designers who contributed so generously to the Profiles which accompany each chapter:

Ken Botnick	*Graphic Designer*
Nancy Callahan	*Artist*
Bob Dacey	*Illustrator*
Diane Gallo	*Writer*
Sharon Greytak	*Filmmaker*
Ann Baddeley Keister	*Weaver*
Heidi Lasher-Oakes	*Sculptor*
David MacDonald	*Ceramicist*
Rodger Mack	*Sculptor*
Bonnie Mitchell	*Internet Artist*
Rick Paul	*Sculptor*
Ken Stout	*Painter*
Jerome Witkin	*Painter*
Phillia Yi	*Printmaker*

I am also grateful for the advice of the following reviewers, who responded thoughtfully to the project in various stages of development. Their opinions, suggestions, criticisms, and encouragement helped shape the book:

Scott Betz	*Weber State University*
Jeff Boshart	*Eastern Illinois University*
Peter Brown	*Ringling School of Art and Design*
Brian Cantley	*California State University, Fullerton*
Laurie Beth Clark	*University of Wisconsin, Madison*
Michael Croft	*University of Arizona*
John Fillwalk	*Ball State University*

David Fobes	*San Diego State University*
Albert Grivetti	*Clarke College*
Imi Hwangbo	*University of Louisville*
Michelle Illuminato	*Bowling Green State University*
Ann Baddeley Keister	*Grand Valley State University*
Margaret Keller	*St. Louis Community College*
Dan Lowery	*Southwestern Illinois College*
Karen Mahaffy	*University of Texas at San Antonio*
Richard Moses	*University of Illinois*
Gary Nemcosky	*Appalachian State University*
Helen Maria Nugent	*Art Institute of Chicago*
Rick Paul	*Purdue* University
Ron Saito	*California State University, Northridge*
Karen Schory	*Johnson County Community College*
Susan Slavick	*Carnegie Mellon University*
Paul Wittenbraker	*Grand Valley State University*
William Zack	*Ball State University*

Finally, the McGraw-Hill team has been knowledgeable, supportive, and unfailingly enthusiastic. Sponsoring Editor Joe Hanson was wonderfully encouraging, and strongly committed to the design of this book as well as its content. Development Editor Cynthia Ward, Editorial Director Phil Butcher, Designers Keith McPherson and Pam Verros, Production Manager Mary Conzachi, and Marketing Manager David Patterson were highly accessible and wonderfully supportive throughout. Christine Baker, Editorial Project Manager for GTS Publishing Services, offered clear production guidelines and kept the whole project on track. And, Picture Researchers Elsa Peterson and Judy Brody of Elsa Peterson Ltd. did a great job with my many requests and obscure sources: without their detective work, I could never have included such a wide range of images in this book.

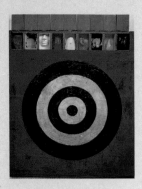
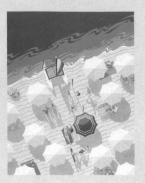
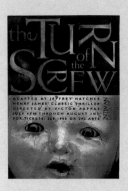
two-dimensional design

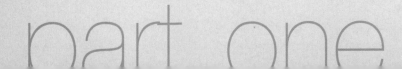

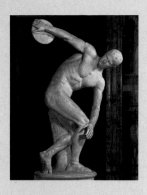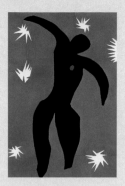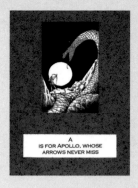

A
IS FOR APOLLO, WHOSE
ARROWS NEVER MISS

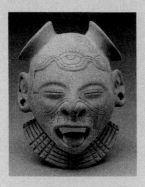

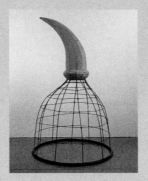

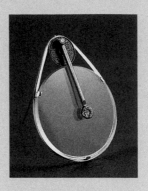

three-dimensional design

part three

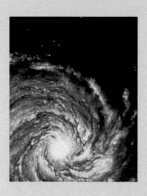
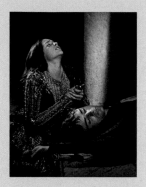
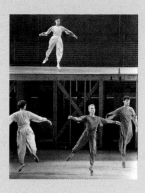

time design

part four

Introduction
Beginner's Mind, Open Mind

You are ready to embark on a marvelous journey. New technologies and exhibition venues offer dazzling new ways to produce, perform, and publicize visual ideas. Contemporary sculpture has expanded to include performance art and installations (i.1), and metalsmiths now use everything from plastics to precious metals to create inventive small-scale sculptures (i.2). Graphic designers develop many forms of visual communication, from shopping bags and exhibitions (i.3) to Websites, logos, and brochures. Film and video, the most popular forms of public storytelling worldwide, are becoming increasingly integrated with the Internet, which promises to extend visual communication even further (i.4). And, as a result of the extensive experimentation

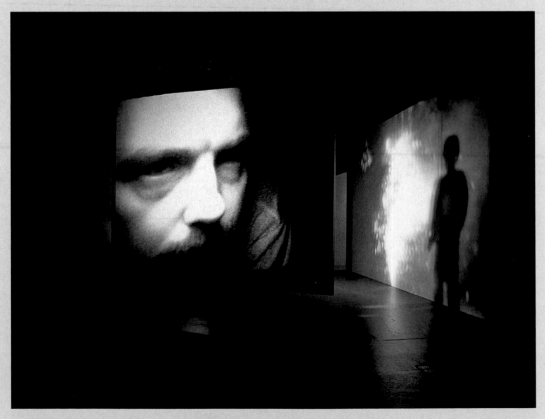

i.1 Bill Viola, *Slowly Turning Narrative*, 1992. Bill Viola's *Slowly Turning Narrative* consists of a large, rotating screen onto which moving images are projected. One side of the screen is a mirror, which reflects distorted images back into the room.

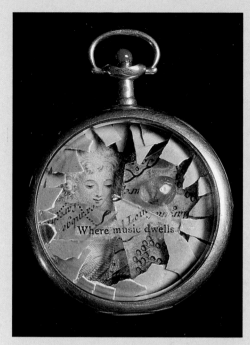

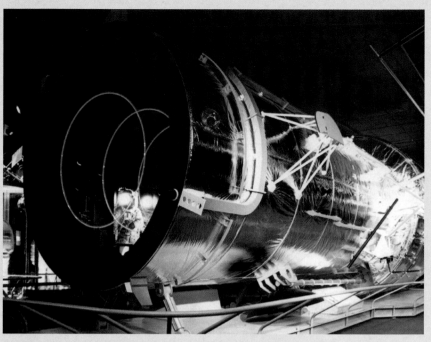

i.2 Keith E. LoBue, *Where the Music Dwells,* 1993. A broken pocket watch can become an evocative artwork when images and words are added.

i.3 Bill Cannan & Co., NASA's Participating Exhibit at the 1989 Paris Air Show. To suggest the mystery of space travel and highlight individual displays, this NASA exhibition used dramatic pools of light within a mysterious dark setting.

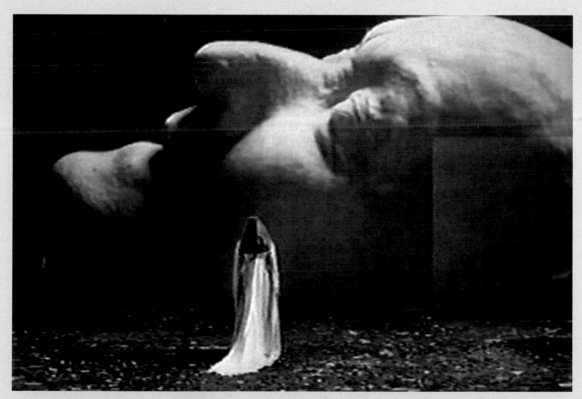

i.4 Hans-Jürgen Syberberg, *Parsifal,* 1982. Syberberg combined live actors with oversized projections of dreamlike landscapes in his filmic interpretation of Richard Wagner's opera.

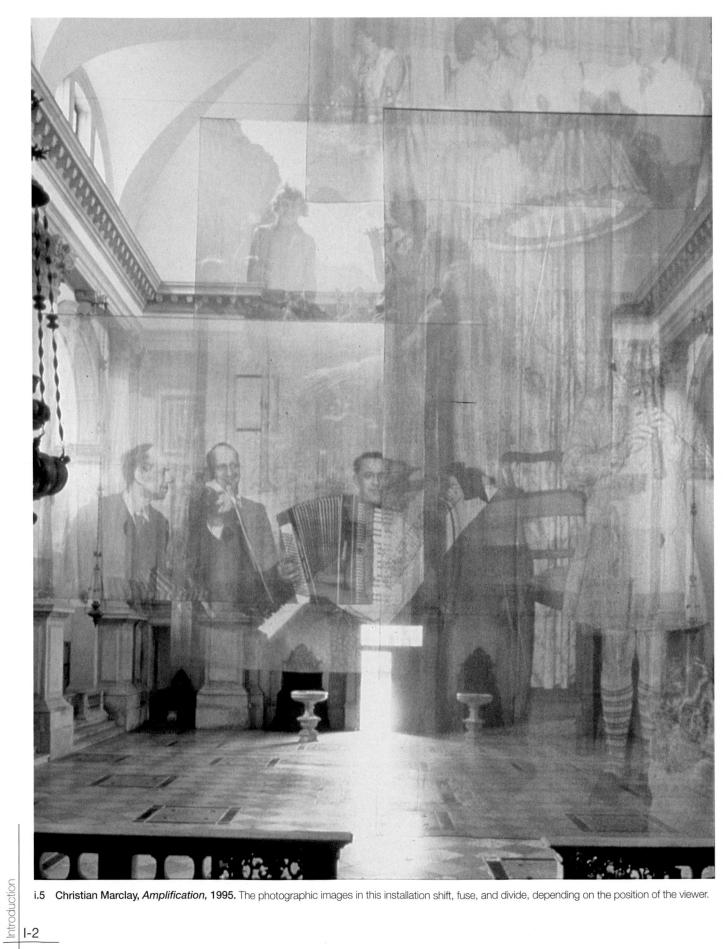

i.5 **Christian Marclay,** *Amplification,* **1995.** The photographic images in this installation shift, fuse, and divide, depending on the position of the viewer.

with expression and abstraction in the twentieth century, the traditional arts of painting, printmaking, and photography (i.5) now offer expanded opportunities for introspective thinking and the development of a personal vision. The opportunities for exploration are endless. It is a great time to be studying art and design!

A journey of a thousand miles begins with one step. As a beginner, your first steps are especially important. Free of the preconceptions or habitual patterns that often paralyze more advanced students, beginners enter the learning experience with an open mind and an intense desire to learn. With no reputation to defend, they can more easily make the mistakes that are so essential to learning. Having taught students at all levels (from freshmen to graduate students and beyond), I have found that beginners of any age are the most courageous students by far. The open, unencumbered "beginner's mind" is wonderfully receptive and resilient. As a result, remarkable changes occur during the first year of study.

Defining the Basics

Launching the Imagination is designed to supplement and support a variety of introductory courses. These courses provide a general overview of studio art and often serve as prerequisites for many specific majors, ranging from advertising design to sculpture and video. Because it is impossible to teach the specific skills required for all these majors in one year, first-year courses focus on general knowledge and essential skills. These **foundation** classes are designed to provide the base on which more advanced study can be built.

Most schools divide this essential information into a variety of drawing and design courses. Drawing helps us develop a heightened awareness of the visual world and gives us many ways to translate our observations into images. At the foundation level, "design" refers to all other types of visual organization, from photography and collage to cardboard constructions and simple Websites. *Launching the Imagination* is devoted to all aspects of basic design.

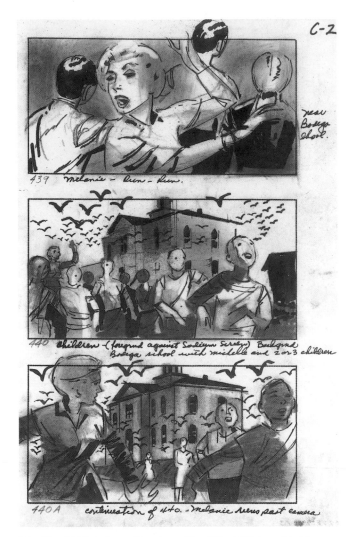

i.6 **Harold Michelson, Storyboard for Alfred Hitchcock's** *The Birds.* Storyboards are used to plan the sequence of events and compose the specific shots in a film. Alfred Hitchcock, who began his career as an artist, preplanned his films with exacting care.

Defining Design

The ideas and implications of basic design are extensive and complex. The compositions created by fine artists and the designs used in the applied arts are all derived from the same raw material. As a verb, design can be defined four ways:

- To plan, delineate, or define, as in designing a building.

- To create a deliberate sequence of images or events, as in developing a film storyboard (i.6).

- To create a functional object, as in product design (i.7).

- To organize disparate parts into a coherent whole, as in composing a brochure (i.8).

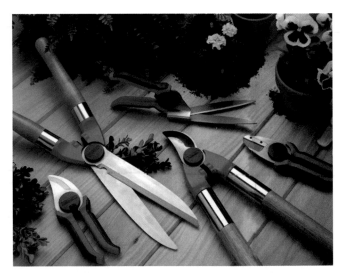

i.7 **Designworks/USA, Home Pro Garden Tool Line.** These five gardening tools are all based on the same basic combination of handle, blades, and simple pivot. Variations in proportion determine their use.

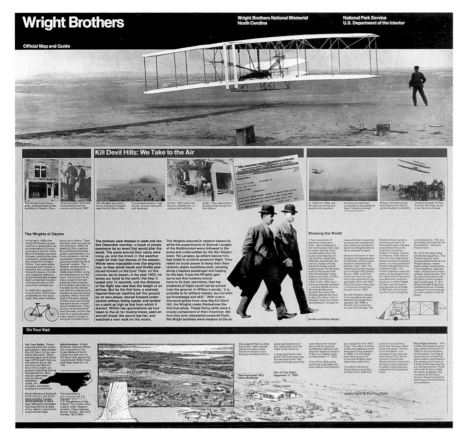

i.8 Bruce Geyman, Brochure for the National Park Service. Graphic designers often work with words and images equally. Blocks of text are carefully integrated into the visual composition.

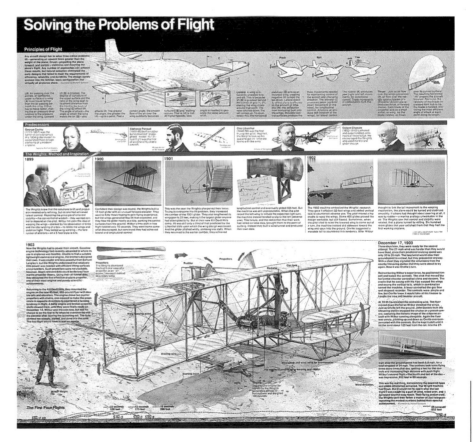

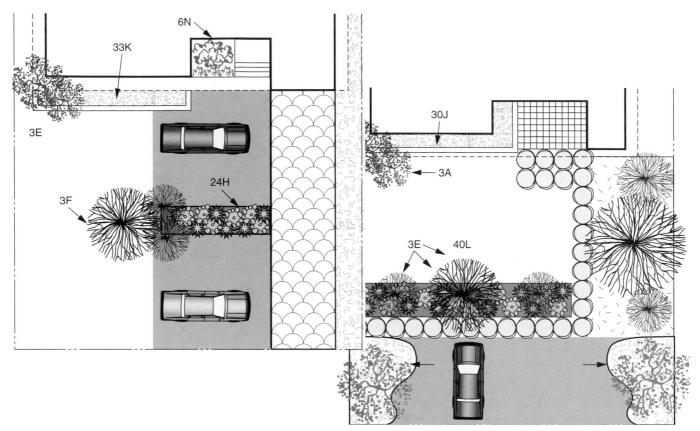

i.9 Garden Design. An extensive layout is generally used for planning a garden. Matching the plants to the soil conditions, setting, climate, and overall intent saves money and improves results. In this case, the design is not an artwork in itself, but rather a plan of action.

As a noun, design may be defined as

- A plan or pattern, such as the layout for a garden (i.9).

- An arrangement of lines, shapes, colors, and textures into an artistic whole, as in the composition of a painting or sculpture (i.10).

Design is deliberate. Rather than hope for the best and accept the result, artists and designers explore a wide range of solutions to every problem, then choose the most promising option for further development. Even when chance is used to generate ideas, choices are often made before the results are shown. Design creates a bridge between artistic intention and compositional conclusion. As painter Joseph Albers noted, "To design is to plan and to organize, to order, to relate and to control."

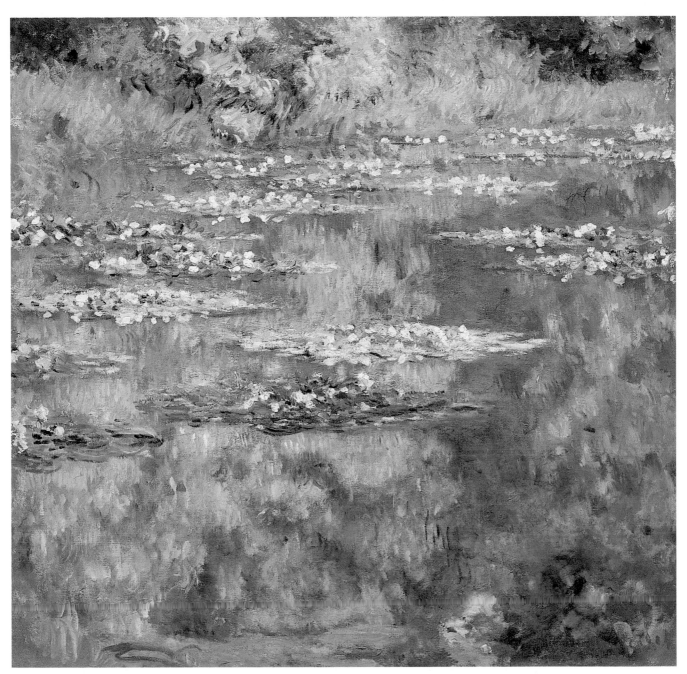

i.10 **Claude Monet,** *Waterlily Pond (Le Bassin des Nymphéas),* **1904.** Impressionist Claude Monet moved to the village of Giverny in 1883 and built an extensive water garden. The waterlilies he grew there inspired his last major series of paintings. Monet combined lines, shapes, textures, and colors to create a compelling illusion of a shimmering space.

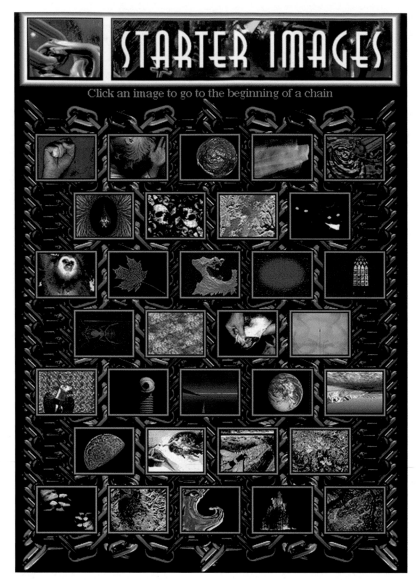

i.11A **Bonnie Mitchell,** *Chain Art* **Index Web Page.** Working with collaborators from around the world, Mitchell explores communication, cultural influences, and creativity in her projects.

Design Fundamentals

The title of this book defines its purpose. Painter Ken Stout has described the purpose of a foundation program clearly and simply. He says:

Imagine that each of your students is a rocket sitting on a launching pad. Each one has plenty of fuel and is ready to fly. As a foundation teacher, it is your job to fire them up, to get them off the ground. It is their job to keep the process going and to fly to the furthest reaches of their imagination.

The first year is indeed a launching pad. To help ignite your imagination, I have woven the following four themes into every chapter in this book.

Visual Communication Is Fundamental

Through the study of art, we can learn about ourselves and the world around us. For computer graphics master Bonnie Mitchell, the Web provides endless opportunities for innovation and expression. It all began with *Chain Art* (i.11) in 1992, at the very beginning of the Internet explosion. Mitchell sent an e-mail to six people, inviting their participation. They forwarded the message to many others, all around the globe. The respondents were then divided into 22 groups, and each received an incomplete starter image. One team member completed the image, which was then sent to another team member for further elaboration. This process continued until each team member completed a variation, producing a total of 136 images. All were shown on Mitchell's Website. Through this project, Mitchell and her collaborators explored their own ideas about creativity and learned about the creative processes of others. Using a new technology, they transformed personal expression into global communication.

Indeed, mastering the basics of visual communication is another reason to study art. The traditional Western emphasis on verbal communication is rapidly expanding. New technologies encourage us to integrate words, and images in Websites, books, and magazines. Some ideas are best expressed in words, while others can only be conveyed through images. This creates new applications for art and design in every field of knowledge, from anthropology to zoology.

Concepts Feed Communication

A concept may be defined as a well-developed thought. By developing rich concepts, we set the stage for the development of inventive objects and images. Dull concepts, on the other hand, generally result in dull images. In any foundation course, we often see predictable solutions to predictable problems. These include the use of a jagged red line to convey anger, or a skull and a pool of blood to suggest death. Each of these choices is usually effective—but rarely inspiring. We've seen it all before. By developing new approaches and new ideas, we can personalize our communication and make our messages memorable.

Developing concepts is just as much work as developing technical skills. As is the case with any new task, your first efforts at concept development may be frustrating. Initially, your ideas may seem foolish or inadequate. A willingness to explore and experiment is essential. With a combination of hard work and a sense of adventure, your ideas will improve rapidly. To help in this process, Chapter Five provides two major problem-solving strategies and many examples of concept development.

Concept + Composition = Communication

Developing a great idea is only half the battle. To reach an audience, the idea must be communicated visually, through composition. Composition may be defined as "the combination of multiple parts into a harmonious whole." For example, a simple musical composition consists of an arrangement of multiple notes to create melodies and harmonies that are sung or played in a particular rhythm.

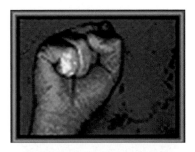
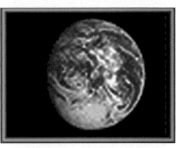
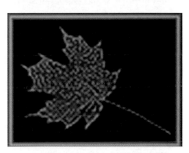
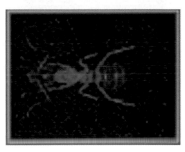

i.11B *Chain Art*, details.

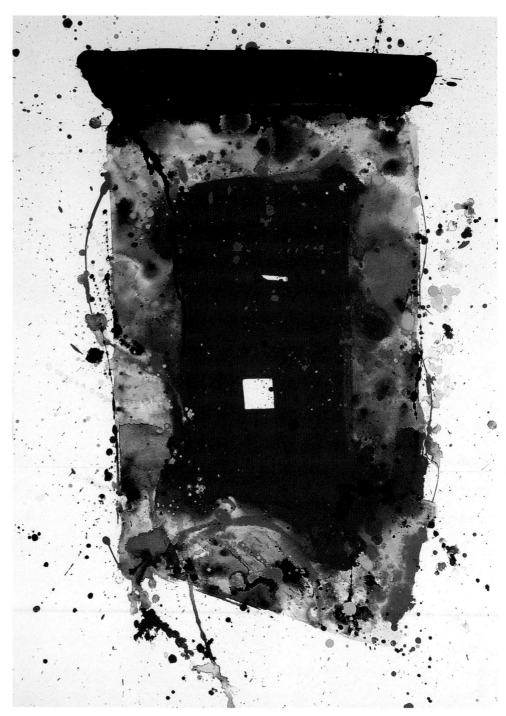

i.12 Sam Francis, *Flash Point*, 1975. Surrounded by explosive energy, the white square in the center of this painting provides a unifying focal point.

Two-dimensional compositions are constructed from lines, shapes, textures, values, and colors that have been arranged to create a unified whole (i.12). Lines, planes, volumes, masses, and space are the most basic components of a three-dimensional composition (i.13). Time design, including video, photography, performance, kinetic sculpture (i.14),

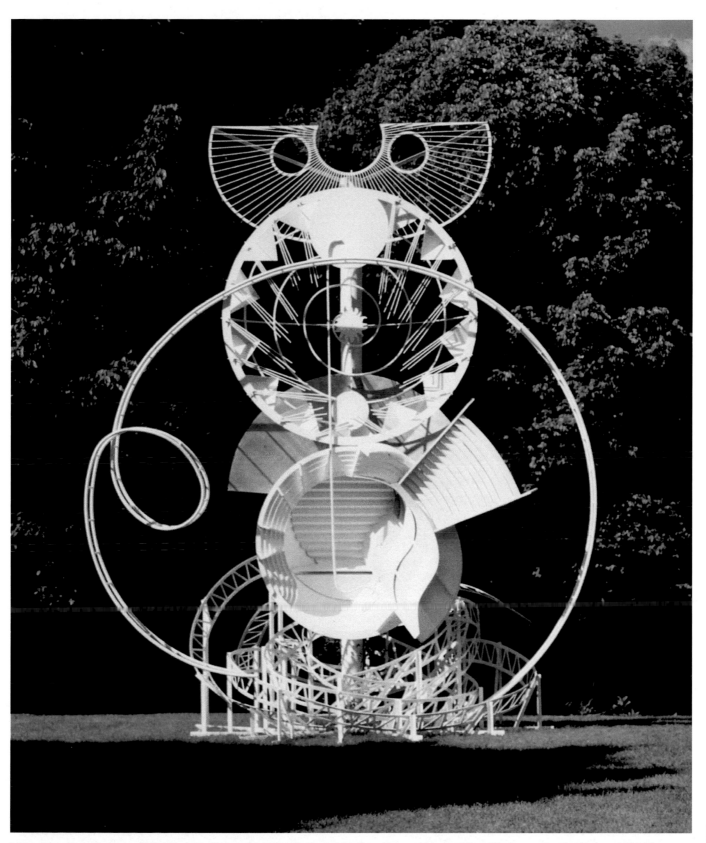

i.13 Alice Aycock, *Tree of Life Fantasy: Synopsis of the Book of Questions Concerning the World Order and/or the Order of Worlds,*
1990–92. Inspired by the double-helix structure of DNA and by medieval illustrations representing the entrance to paradise as a spinning hole in the sky, Aycock has combined a linear structure with a series of circular planes and a lot of open space. The resulting sculpture is as open and playful as a roller coaster.

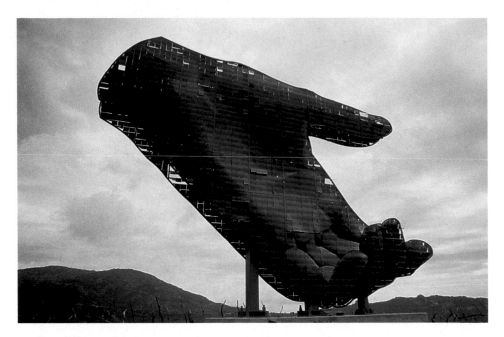

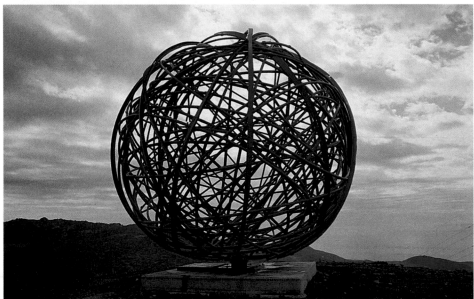

i.14 **Todd Slaughter,** *Mano y Balo* **(details), 1997.** Constructed using over one thousand movable panels, the monumental hand appears and disappears as the wind blows.

and the book arts (i.15), is based on the juxtaposition of images and events. A great idea never saved a bad painting. Art and design are visual forms of communication: without careful composition, a great idea may be lost.

Developing a wide range of solutions to every problem is the quickest way to master composition. Small, quick studies are often used to explore the

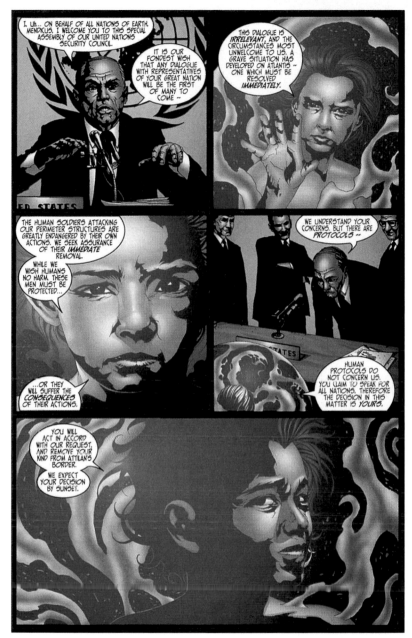

i.15   Paul Jenkins and Jae Lee, from *Inhumans:* "First Contact," March 1999.
Comic books, like films, rely on development of characters, use of "camera" angles, and the organization of multiple images.

possibilities. By translating a mental image into a rough sketch, you can immediately see whether the idea has potential. Furthermore, the best way to have a good idea is to have a lot of ideas. If you explore only one idea, you are far less likely to produce an inventive image. By selecting the best rough composition from 20 sketches, you will have a good beginning point for your final design.

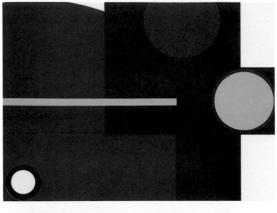

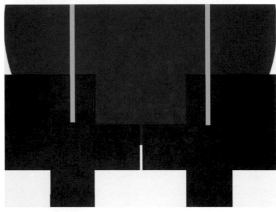

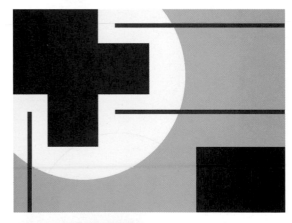

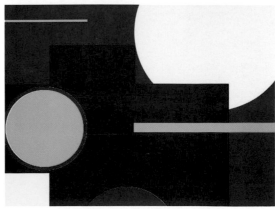

While the compositions created by experienced artists and designers may convey all sorts of complex ideas, at the foundation level composition is often distilled down to **pure form.** Form may be defined as the physical manifestation of an idea. For example, Sam Francis' painting in Figure i.12 is formed by a small square surrounded by an irregular rectangular shape. A series of circles and curving lines creates the sculptural form of *Tree of Life Fantasy* (i.13) by Alice Aycock. Form is created whenever the elements of design are combined.

Translating elusive ideas and emotions into tangible form is one of the greatest challenges for any artist or designer. Simply inventing various ways to balance a circle, cross, and line provides a heightened understanding of basic visual relationships (i.16). When we tackle composition at such a fundamental level, we have only the elements and principles of design as companions. We cannot rely on our brilliant ideas or eloquent explanations to get us out of a compositional jam.

Critical Judgment Supports Creative Thinking

Imagine yourself ruby mining in North Carolina. It is a sunny day and you are surrounded by rolling hills. To your right is a series of pits, half full of mud. To your left, a stream has been directed into a wooden trough. Benches and open trays with wire mesh on the bottom face the trough. You start by shoveling mud into two buckets, then head to the trough to wash it out in the flowing water. When the mud is removed, small bits of gravel remain in the washing tray. If you are lucky, you may find rubies, sapphires, or garnets in this gravel.

However, you will only find these treasures if you know where to look. Except for its six-sided shape, an uncut ruby looks like any other stone. Likewise, determining which ideas and images have the most potential requires a trained eye. You must be able to spot the compositional gems while

i.16 Mary Stewart, *Formal Relationships* (Exercise), 2001. The relationships between the parts and the whole determine the visual quality of a design. To explore a wide range of relationships, artists and designers often complete many small studies before developing more elaborate work.

discarding the compositional gravel. Critiques, or group discussions of artwork, are the most common means by which such visual thinking is developed. By describing an image, comparing it to the other artworks on display, identifying its greatest strengths, or proposing alternative solutions, you can learn a great deal about composition and communication.

Putting It All Together

In the pages that follow, the ideas presented in this introduction are explored in depth. Over 600 images supply visual examples from many cultures and in all areas of art and design. Fourteen interviews with living artists provide insight into the creative process.

Reading this book, however, is just the first step. True understanding comes through your own efforts combined with the direction your teachers can provide. Remember that basic drawing and design courses provide the foundation on which all subsequent courses are built. You are only a beginner once in your entire life: this is not a rehearsal. By using your time well, you really *can* get the rocket off the launching pad.

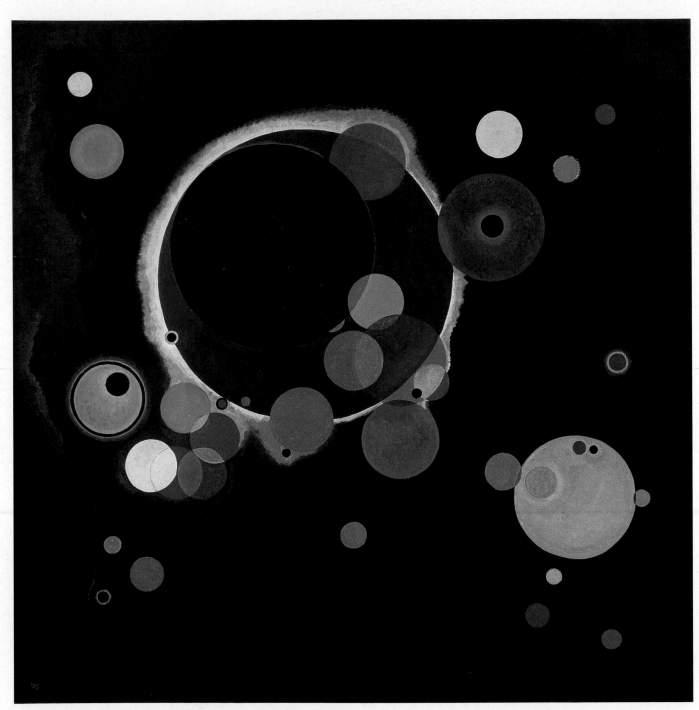

Wassily Kandinsky, *Several Circles,* **1926.** Oil on canvas, 55¼ × 55⅜ in. (140.3 × 140.7 cm).

Two-Dimensional Design

The careful observation required for drawing, the understanding of color required for watercolor painting, and the craftsmanship required for metalsmithing can increase awareness of ourselves and our world. On a personal level, making art heightens our attention, engages our emotions, and provides a sense of accomplishment. Creating objects and images is engrossing and exhilarating. These personal rewards make art one of the most popular hobbies.

The professional artist or designer must translate these personal insights into public communication. No one will pay for the production of meaningless images. The ideas and emotions a professional wishes to express must engage an audience, whether the communication occurs in the silence of a museum or in the chaos of a city street.

This ability to communicate visually is developed through years of study plus relentless practice. Artists and designers must develop their visual awareness, develop engaging ideas, and master various techniques. Fully committed to their work, they spend hours in the studio, refining ideas and inventing alternative solutions to visual problems.

A journey of one thousand miles begins with one step. In the chapters that follow, we will begin by defining several basic elements and principles of design and explore their expressive qualities. Chapter One focuses on the basic elements of two-dimensional design. Chapter Two is devoted to the characteristics and compositional impact of color. Chapter Three is devoted to the organization of all the elements of design into increasingly complex compositions. These readings, combined with studio assignments, can help you build the base of visual knowledge needed for art and design at a personal as well as a professional level.

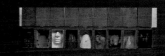

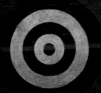

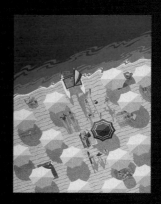

chapter one

Two-Dimensional Design:
Elements

Line, shape, texture, value, and color are the building blocks from which two-dimensional designs are made. Just as oxygen and hydrogen are powerful both individually and when combined as H_2O , so the visual elements are powerful both individually and in combination. In this chapter we explore the unique characteristics of line, shape, texture, and value, and then analyze their uses in art and design. Color, the most complex visual element, is discussed in Chapter Two. In Chapter Three, the design elements are combined to create complex compositions.

Line

Defining Line

Line is one of the simplest and most versatile elements of design. Line may be defined as

- A point in motion (1.1A).

- A series of adjacent points (1.1B).

- A connection between points (1.1C).

- An implied connection between points (1.1D).

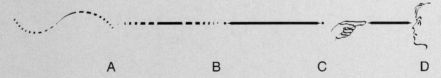

    A   B   C   D

1.1 Despite its apparent simplicity, line can be created in many ways and can play many roles in a design.

    The inherent dynamism of line is embodied in the first definition. Lighter and more fluid than any of the other visual elements, line can add a special energy to a design. To retain this enegy, the line must be substantially longer than it is wide. The remaining three definitions emphasize the connective power of line. Simply by drawing a line, we can create a bridge between separate visual elements.

Types of Line

Actual Lines

As shown in Figure 1.2, a wide variety of lines can be produced using graphite, markers, or brushes. Many drawings are entirely composed from lines. In Figure 1.3, Eleanor Dickinson used **contour lines** to describe both the inner and outer edges of a woman's hands. In Figure 1.4, Rembrandt used a chalk line to define the spheres and cylindrical volumes from which the moving figures are made. Because it uses such basic forms to communicate visual information, this type of drawing is often called a **volume summary.** Rico Lebrun's **gesture drawing** of a hand (1.5) combines contour, volume, and movement. More concerned with action than anatomical detail, this drawing captures the movement of the muscular hand.

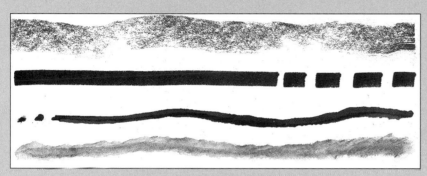

1.2 Every tool produces a distinctive line.

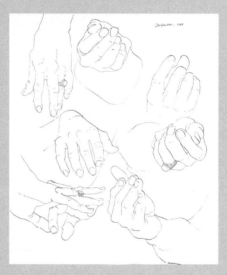

1.3   Eleanor Dickinson, *Study of Hands,* **1964.** Pen and ink, 13⅛ × 10⅛ in. (34 × 26 cm).

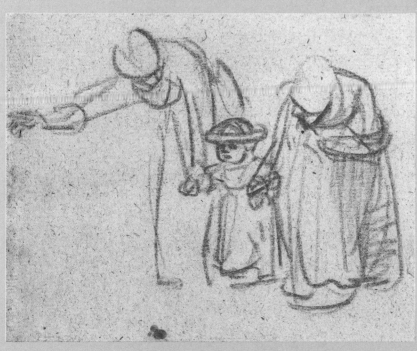

1.4   Rembrandt van Rijn, *Two Women Helping a Child to Walk,* **c. 1635–37.** Black chalk.

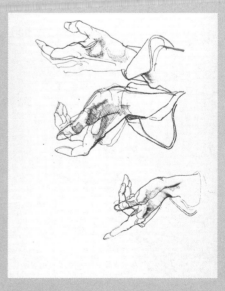

1.5   Rico Lebrun, *Hand,* **1964.** Pen and ink.

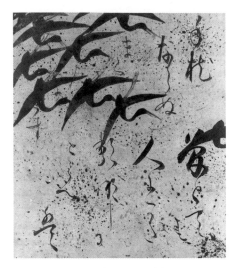

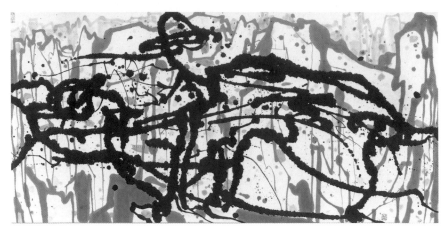

1.7 Wu Guanzhong, *Pine Spirit,* 1984. Chinese ink, color on paper, 2 ft 3⅝ in. × 5 ft 3½ in. (70 × 140 cm).

1.6 Attributed to Tawaraya Sôtatsu, calligraphy by Hon'ami Koetsu, *Flying Cranes and Poetry,* Edo period (1615–1868). Ink on gray-blue paper, gold flecked, 7⅝ × 6⅜ in. (19 × 16 cm).

Calligraphic lines can add even more energy to a drawing or a design. The word *calligraphy* is derived from two Greek words: *kalus,* meaning "beautiful," and *graphein,* meaning "to write." Like handwriting, the calligraphic line is personal, eloquent, and highly expressive. In Figure 1.6, words and images are combined in a celebration of flight. In this image, painter Tawaraya Sôtatsu and calligrapher Hon'ami Koetsu used variations in line weight and velocity to suggest the graceful motion of birds. This exploration of movement is pushed even further in *Pine Spirit,* by Wu Guanzhong (1.7) Fluid ink lines record the movement of the artist's hand while simultaneously creating an abstract landscape. There is a wonderful economy in each

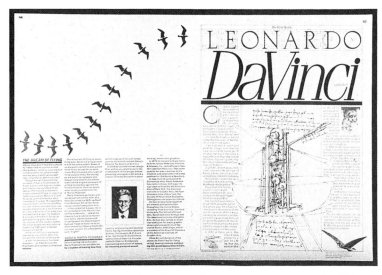

1.8 B. Martin Pedersen, Page Layout: Leonardo da Vinci, March 1982.

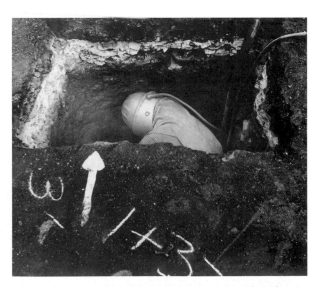

1.9 Minor White, *Sandblaster,* San Francisco, 1949. Gelatin silver print, 10⁷⁄₁₆ × 11⁷⁄₁₆ in.

of these drawings: like poetry, the story is fully told using minimal means.

Implied Lines

Given enough clues, the human mind will combine separate visual parts by filling in the missing pieces. This inclination for **closure** is so strong that connections will be made even when lines are **implied,** rather than drawn. Broken lines become continuous. In B. Martin Pedersen's Leonardo da Vinci layout (1.8), closure creates an elegant curve while breaks in the line emphasize the energy of flying birds. Visual bridges are built. The actual arrow in Minor White's photograph (1.9) extends by implication to connect the worker's helmet to the numbers in the foreground. Compositional structure may be revealed. In Alfred Leslie's *The Killing Cycle* (1.10), the single woman in the lower left corner is connected to the four figures in the upper right by the dead man on the diagonal board. Bent arms and legs create even more diagonal lines.

In *Design Basics,* David Lauer describes an especially elegant form of closure as "lost and found" contours.[1] Some paintings can easily be reduced to a clear, concise line drawing. In other paintings, the edges of volumes are less clearly defined, causing figure and ground to merge. Both approaches are used in *The Killing Cycle,* as the top four figures are clearly delineated while the lower two figures begin to merge with the surrounding space. This effect is even more pronounced in Caravaggio's *The Deposition* (1.11A), from which Leslie derived his inspiration. A line drawing of this image has many gaps, as details are lost in the shadows (1.11B). Used skillfully, this loss of definition becomes a strength rather than a weakness. Connections made through closure can stimulate the viewer's imagination and increase visual impact.

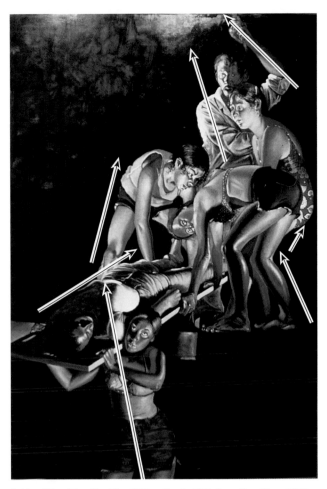

1.10 Alfred Leslie, *The Killing Cycle (#5): Loading Pier*, 1975. Oil on canvas, 9 × 6 ft (2.7 × 1.8 m).

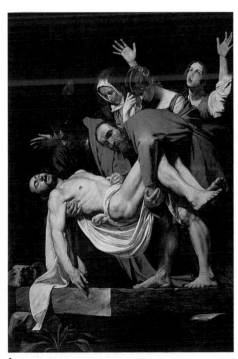

A

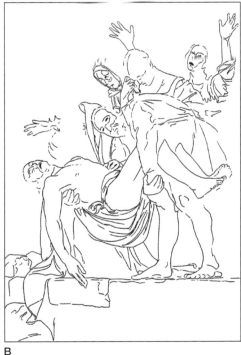

B

1.11 Caravaggio, *The Deposition*, 1604. Oil on canvas, 9 ft 10⅛ in. × 6 ft 7⅞ in. (3 × 2.03 m).

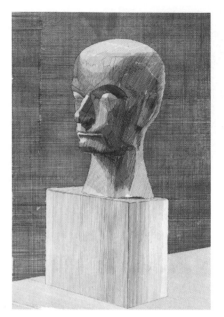

1.12 Jacques Villon, *Baudelaire*, c. 1918. Etching, printed in black, plate 16⁵/₁₆ × 11 in. (41.4 × 28 cm).

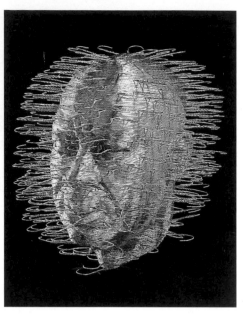

1.13 David Mach, *Eckow*, 1997. Coathangers, 2 ft 2¼ in. × 1 ft 11½ in. × 2 ft 5½ in. (67 × 60 × 75 cm).

Line Networks

When grouped together, multiple lines and line networks can further describe volume and suggest space. **Hatching,** a technique often used in printmaking and drawing, produces a range of grays through straight parallel lines. Even a wider range of grays can be produced through **cross-hatching,** which creates networks of lines. Jacques Villon's portrait of the poet Charles Baudelaire (1.12) is divided into faceted planes, with layers of lines providing both the structure and the shadows. Each set of lines emphasizes the angularity of the plane it defines, and each plane adds to the illusion of the three-dimensional head. **Cross contours,** created through curving parallel lines, can create an even more powerful illusion of dimensionality. By bending coat hangers into the curves and depressions defining the head (1.13), David Mach has created a type of topographic map. These lines form an actual sculpture, which has been photographically reduced to create the two-dimensional image shown here. By combining hatching, cross-hatching, and cross contour in *Head of a Satyr* (1.14), Michelangelo carved out an image that clearly describes the curves and planes of the head while retaining the energy of the liveliest gesture drawing.

Expressive Uses of Line

Lines can contain, define, dissect, or combine elements within a composition. Each aspect of line is equally important. Two lines dominate Barnett Newman's *Stations of the Cross: Lema Sabachthani, The First Station* (1.15). The hard black line is as emphatic as a mathematical equation. Despite its great height, this line gains stability through its position along the left edge of the painting. In contrast, the line on the right is agitated and exposed, surrounded by open space rather than being supported by a firm edge. In this painting, Newman sought to convey both

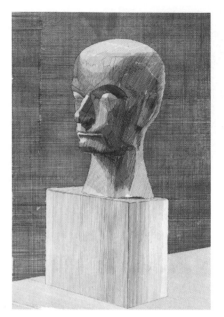

1.14 Michelangelo, *Head of a Satyr*, c.1620–30. Pen and ink over chalk, 10⁵/₈ × 7⁷/₈ in. (27 × 20 cm).

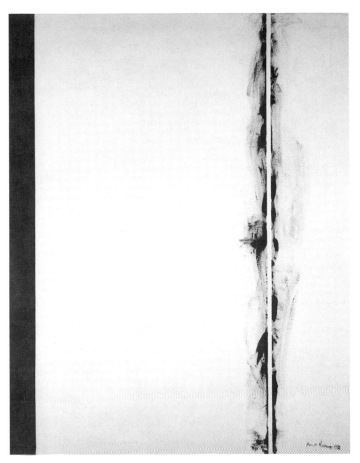

1.15 Barnett Newman, *Stations of the Cross: Lema Sabachthani, The First Station*, 1958. Magna on canvas, 6 ft 5⅞ in. × 5 ft ½ in. (1.98 × 1.54 cm).

1.16 Ad by Citizens Against Cocaine Abuse: "The average high induced by cocaine lasts thirty minutes. The average death induced by cocaine lasts slightly longer." Art Director & Designer: Gary Goldsmith, Copywriter: Neal Gomberg, Agency: Goldsmith/ Jeffrey, Client: Citizens Against Cocaine Abuse.

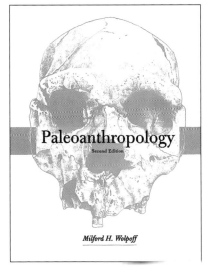

1.17 Crispin Prebys, Cover of *Paleoanthropology*, 2nd ed., by Milford H. Wolpoff, 1999. Drawing of a skull.

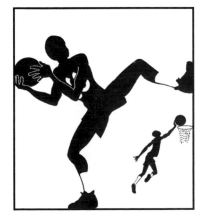

1.18 In this drawing, the edges of the format create a strong boundary.

spiritual strength and human suffering using the most minimal means possible.

In an ad for an antidrug campaign, Gary Goldsmith used a similar economy of line (1.16). When combined with a sentence describing the brevity of a cocaine high and a sentence suggesting the finality of death, the boundary between the narrow white line and the large black rectangle becomes the boundary between life and death.

Lines also can be used to expand or compress an image. The bold horizontal line in Crispin Prebys's textbook cover design (1.17) provides an anchor for the title while visually expanding the design. Like a time line, the cover image seems to continue right into the book. On the other hand, a compressive force at the edge of the composition is opposed by the explosive force of the basketball players in Figure 1.18. Asymmetrical balance and spatial exaggeration add to the effect and convey the message that these players are really pushing the limits.

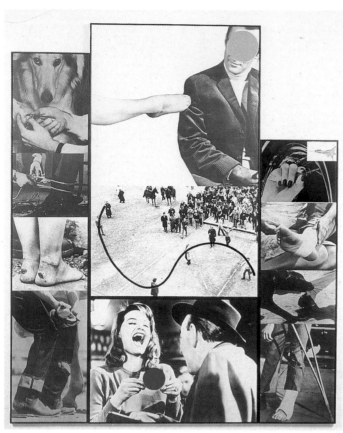

1.19 **John Baldessari,** *Heel,* **1986.** Black-and-white photographs with oil tint, oil stick and acrylic, mounted on board, 8 ft 10½ in. × 7 ft 3 in. (2.7 × 2.2 m).

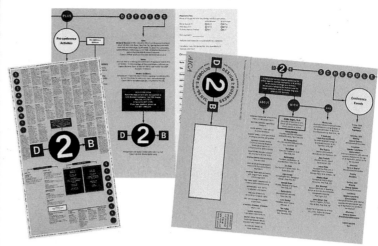

1.20 Brochure from an American Institute of Graphic Arts conference "Design 2 Business, October 5–6 '96 NYC."

Lines can serve many purposes at once. In John Baldessari's *Heel* (1.19), a curving red line near the center of the painting connects the people on the plaza, while the vertical and horizontal black lines simultaneously contain and connect nine different images of heels. In an advertisement for the American Institute of Graphic Artists (1.20), two vertical dotted lines highlight the speaker's schedule, while a horizontal line dissects the "design to business" logo. Inside the brochure, an arrow line connects the D, 2, and B, reinforcing the same theme. Even the columns of text can be read as lines. Despite their apparent simplicity, lines bring both power and grace to these two compositions.

Shape

Defining Shape

A **shape** is created when

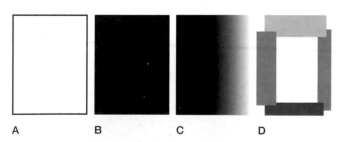

1.21 Any form of enclosure can create a shape.

- A line connects to enclose an area (1.21A).

- An area of color or texture is defined by a clear boundary (1.21B, 1.21C).

- An area is surrounded (1.21D).

In two-dimensional design, a shape that seems three dimensional is called a **volume.** This illusion of space is generally created using lighting.

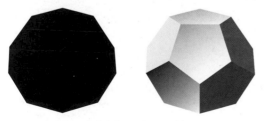

1.22 Variations in lighting can transform a shape into an illusory volume.

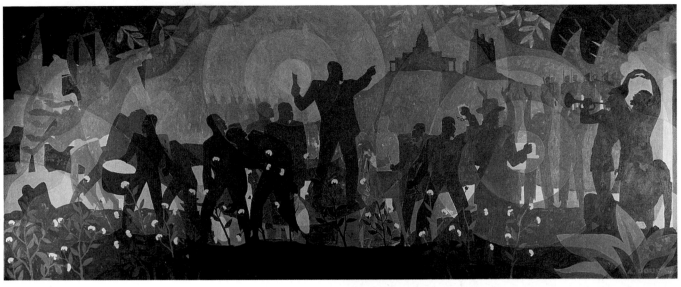

1.23 Aaron Douglas, *Aspects of Negro Life: From Slavery Through Reconstruction*, 1934. Oil on canvas, 5 ft × 11 ft 7 in. (1.52 × 3.5 m).

Through lighting, a three-dimensional solid can be defined on a flat surface using a series of **values,** or gray tones. In drawing, continuous values are used to create **shading,** or **gradation.** For example, in Figure 1.22, an angular shape becomes a faceted polyhedron through variations in lighting.

Both shape and volume can be used to create a compelling composition. In Aaron Douglas' *From Slavery Through Reconstruction* (1.23), overlapping shapes and transparent targets create an energetic panorama. We can almost hear the speaker in the center and feel the movement of the crowd.

In Rivera's *Detroit Industry* (1.24), shading and perspective have been added to increase the illusion of space. The overlapping shapes have been methodically organized in a structure known as one-point perspective (which is discussed at length in Chapter Three). The use of shading gives the men and machinery a three-dimensional look.

Graphic designers are equally aware of the unique power of both flat shapes and dimensional volumes. In a cover for *Ulysses* (1.25), Carin Goldberg used crisp, simple shapes to create a dramatic design. The primary colors of red, yellow, and blue combined with the tilted text block immediately attract attention. Krystyna Skalski and John Jinks used a very different approach in their cover for a mystery novel (1.26). Every shape is gradated to suggest a light

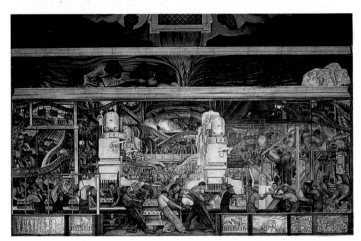

1.24 Diego M. Rivera, *Detroit Industry, north wall*, 1932–33. Fresco, 17 ft 8½ in. × 45 ft (5.4 × 13.7 m).

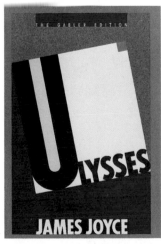

1.25 Cover of *Ulysses*, by James Joyce, 1986. Designer: Carin Goldberg.

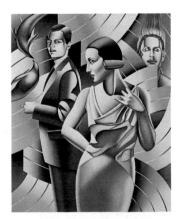

1.26 Cover image from *The Penguin Pool Murder*, a Hildegarde Withers Mystery, by Stuart Palmer. Art Director & Designer: Krystyna Skalski, Illustrator: John Jinks.

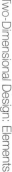

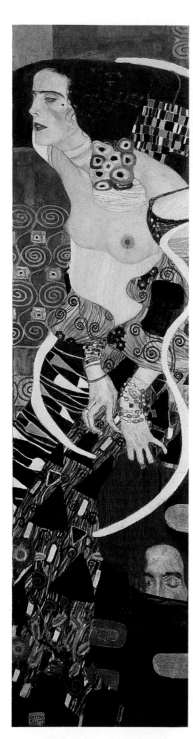

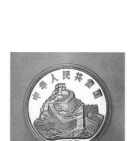
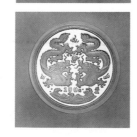

1.27 Gustav Klimt, *Salomé*, **1909.** Oil on canvas, 70⅛ × 18⅛ in. (178 × 46 cm).

source and create the illusion of space. Both approaches are appropriate to the literary content. Many readers consider *Ulysses* one of the most complex novels ever written: any suggestion that the corrected text may increase clarity could be welcome. On the other hand, twisting plots and surprise endings delight the readers of mystery novels. For them, simplicity is rarely a virtue.

Flat shapes have been combined with dimensional volumes in Gustav Klimt's *Salomé* (1.27). In this horrific tale from the *New Testament*, John the Baptist, held prisoner in the palace, has rejected the sexual advances of Salomé, the king's niece. After she performs a stunning dance, the delighted king grants her a single wish. In revenge, Salomé asks for the head of the prophet John. Klimt's painting is dominated by the beautiful Salomé whose curled fingers clutch the suspended head of the prophet. Flat patterns and color surround the volumetric figures, while two curving lines add a sinuous energy to the center of the design.

Types of Shape

The **format,** or outer edge of a design, provides the first shape in the composition. For example, the circular shape of the 100-yuan coin substantially affects the dragon composition on the front and the landscape on the back (1.28). Likewise, the tall rectangle used for Klimt's *Salomé* compresses the sordid drama into a narrow, vertical shape, while the long horizontal rectangles used by Douglas and Rivera provide a broad panorama.

Postive and Negative

As shown in Figure 1.29A, this basic compositional shape is often called the **negative shape,** or **ground,** while any shape added to this compositional playing field is called a **positive shape,** or **figure.** Depending on the location within the ground, the figure can become dynamic or static, leaden or buoyant (1.29 B–D).

1.28 1988 silver coin from China, worth 100 Yuan, obverse & reverse.

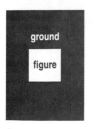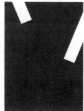

A   B   C   D   1.29

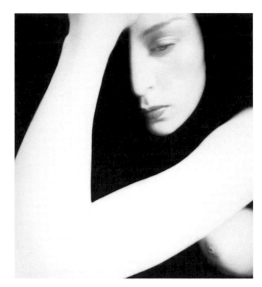

1.30 Bill Brandt, *Nude*, 1952. Gelatin silver print.

When the figure and ground are equally well designed, every square inch of the image becomes engaged. In Bill Brandt's photograph (1.30), the dark negative shapes define the positive figure while the brightly lit arm, face, and breast define the edges of the dark ground. In a cubist painting, such as Georges Braque's *Man with a Guitar* (1.31), the figure and ground often merge and shift, constantly activating the space inside and outside the musician. In such paintings, the simple fixed viewpoint of Newtonian physics and traditional perspective have been shattered. Echoing Einstein, the cubists dissolved matter to create compositional energy.

Figure/ground reversal creates another kind of force, as first the positive then the negative shapes command attention. M. C. Escher was a master of figure/ground reversal, as shown in this fragment from *Metamorphosis II* (1.32). Bees change into hexagons that soon change into lizards. Shifts between the black and white shapes continually animate the 13-foot-long composition.

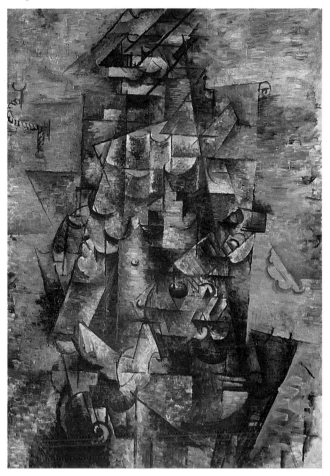

1.31 Georges Braque, *Man with a Guitar*, 1911–12. Oil on canvas, 45¾ × 31⅞ in. (116.2 × 80.9 cm).

1.32 M. C. Escher, part of *Metamorphosis II*, 1939–40. Woodcut in black, green, and brown, printed from twenty blocks on three combined sheets, 7½ × 153⅜ in. (19 × 390 cm).

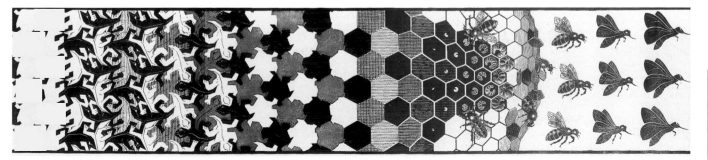

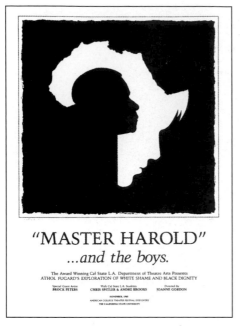

1.33 David McNutt, *"Master Harold" . . . and the Boys,* 1985. Poster.

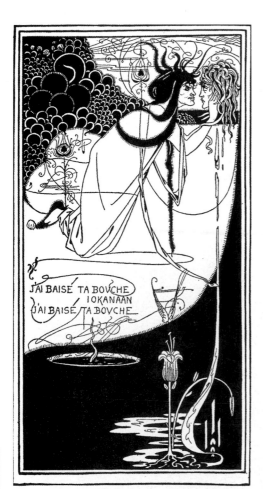

1.35 Aubrey Beardsley, *Salomé with the Head of John the Baptist,* 1894. Line block print, 11 × 6 in. (27.9 × 15.2 cm).

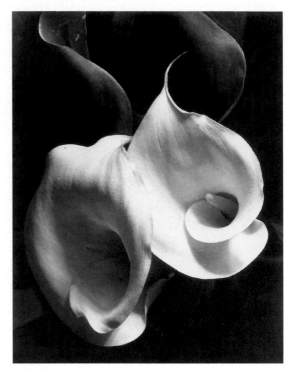

1.34 Imogen Cunningham, *Two Callas,* c. **1929.** Gelatin silver print.

Figure/ground reversal is often used to create mutiple interpretations using minimal shapes. In Figure 1.33, David McNutt uses a single white shape on a black ground to create the head of a master and a servant within the outline of Africa. Used to advertise a South African play, the poster immediately communicates a basic human relationship within a specific cultural context.

Rectilinear/Curvilinear

Rectilinear shapes are dominated by straight lines and angular corners, while curves and flowing lines create **curvilinear shapes,** as shown in this photograph by Imogen Cunningham (1.34). Simple rectilinear shapes, such as squares and rectangles, are highly cooperative. When placed within a standard format, they easily lose their identity and become part of a unified design. Curvilinear shapes, especially circles, are often less cooperative. They retain individuality even when they are partially concealed by other shapes.

Aubrey Beardsley combined rectilinear and curvilinear shapes to create his *Salomé with the Head of John the Baptist* (1.35). The rectilinear format is strongly defined by three repeated lines. Within

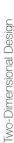

this boundary, curving black and white shapes create a complex composition that is dominated by the bubble pattern in the upper left corner, Salomé with John's head in the right corner, and a flower at the bottom edge. Packed with lines and shapes, this drawing captures many aspects of a complex story.

A very different combination of rectilinear and curvilinear shapes activates Robert Rauschenberg's *Brace* (1.36). The central image of three baseball players is surrounded by agitated rectangles to the right, left, and bottom, while a solid line extends from the catcher to the top edge. Bold, curving brush strokes add power to the painting. Occupying only a small fraction of the composition and surrounded by vigorously painted shapes, the circle *still* dominates the design: we have to keep our eyes on the ball!

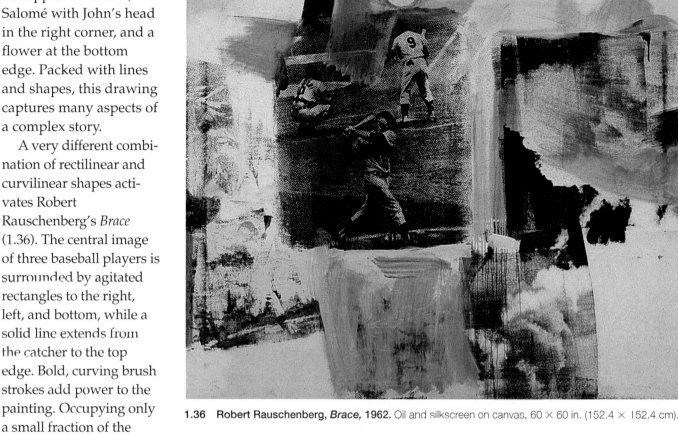

1.36   Robert Rauschenberg, *Brace*, 1962. Oil and silkscreen on canvas, 60 × 60 in. (152.4 × 152.4 cm).

Geometric/Organic

Geometric shapes are distinguished by their crisp, precise edges and mathematically consistent curves. They dominate the technological world of architecture and industry and also appear in crystalline structures and natural growth patterns, such as the spiral. In Valerie Jaudon's *Tallahatchee* (1.37), geometric shapes provide a clarity, harmony, and universality comparable to a mathematical equation. **Organic shapes** are more commonly found in the natural world of plants and animals, sea and sky. As shown in Helen Frankenthaler's *Interior Landscape* (1.38), organic shapes can bring an unpredictable energy in a design.

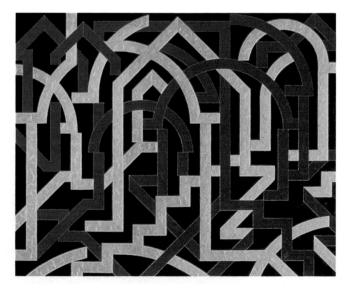

1.37   Valerie Jaudon, *Tallahatchee*, 1984. Oil and gold leaf on canvas, 6 ft 8 in. × 8 ft (2 × 2.4 m).

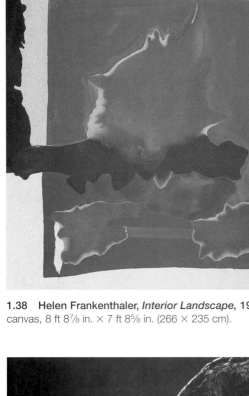

1.38 Helen Frankenthaler, *Interior Landscape*, **1964.** Acrylic on canvas, 8 ft 8⅞ in. × 7 ft 8⅝ in. (266 × 235 cm).

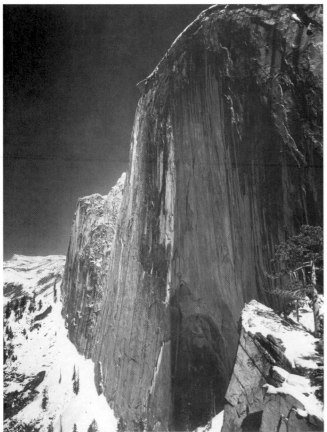

1.39 Ansel Adams, *Monolith, The Face of Half Dome, Yosemite Valley.* Photograph.

Two-Dimensional Design

Representational, Nonobjective, and Abstract Shapes

Representational or **descriptive shapes** are derived from specific subject matter and strongly based on perceptual reality. For example, in Ansel Adams' *Monolith, The Face of Half Dome, Yosemite Valley* (1.39), every toehold on the steep cliff is clearly defined. Indeed, Adams' photograph gains its power from the clarity of its description. **Nonobjective shapes** such as circles, squares, and triangles are **pure forms,** created without reference to specific subject matter. Between these two extremes, **abstract shapes** are derived from a visual source, but are so transformed that they bear little resemblance to the referent. As a result, the abstracted cliff in Moskowitz's *Seventh Sister* (1.40) becomes a universal representation of a vertical surface as well as a painting of a particular cliff.

When working descriptively, the artist gains meaning through the reference to reality. Drawing from their own experience, viewers can expand on the visual information presented. When nonobjective shapes are used, the energy in the design must come from the visual relationships created. Compositional relationships such as the orientation of shapes, interaction of color, and the use of the format edge must now generate all of the impact.

Working abstractly, the artist can retain the power of association while accentuating visual dynamics. By reducing the factory structure to a series of interlocking verticals, circles, and diagonals, Charles Demuth created a graceful abstraction of an architectural space in Figure 1.41. Likewise, while Cartier-Bresson's *Valencia* (1.42) is photographically descriptive, its power is based on a complex composition as well as on specific content. Sharply focused and framed by the window, the policeman's face dominates the foreground. Squeezed between the target shapes and the wall on the left, the boy turns toward us apprehensively. The dissected target is balanced by the monocle on the right and the boy's face on the left. Horizontal rectangles compress three of the four corners of the composition. The resulting interplay of shapes creates a complex dialog between childhood fears and adult authority.

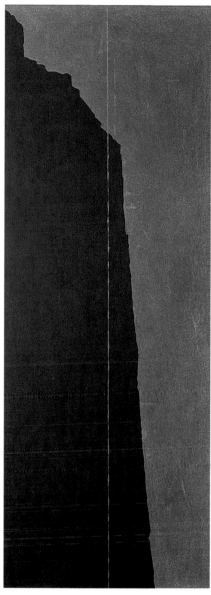

1.40 Robert Moskowitz, *Seventh Sister,* **1982.** Oil on canvas, 108 × 39 in. (274.3 × 99 cm).

Degrees of Definition

Definition is the degree to which a shape is distinguished from both the ground area and the other shapes within the design. **High definition,** creates strong contrast between shapes and tends to increase clarity and immediacy of communication. For this reason, the diagrams used in this book generally use black figures on a white ground. **Low-definition** shapes, including gradations, transparencies, and soft-edged shapes, can increase the complexity of the design and often encourage multiple interpretations.

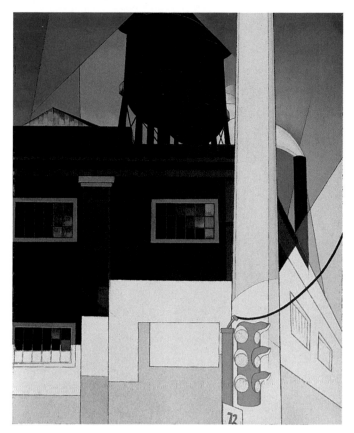

1.41 Charles Demuth, . . . *And the Home of the Brave,* **1931.** Oil on composition board, 29¹/₂ × 23⁵/₈ in. (74.8 × 59.7 cm).

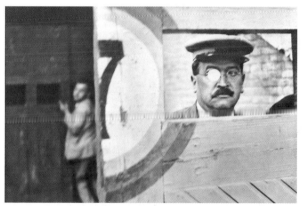

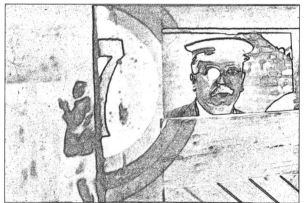

1.42 Henri Cartier-Bresson, *Valencia,* **1933.** Photograph.

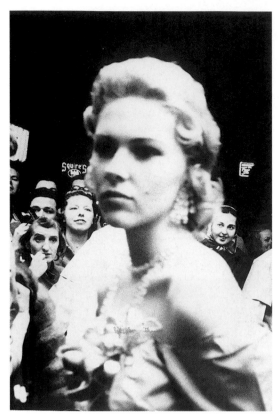

1.43 Robert Frank, *Movie Premiere, Hollywood,* from *The Americans,* **1955–56.** Gelatin silver photograph, 12½ × 8⅜ in. (31.75 × 21.27 cm).

Definition is an inherent quality in photography. In addition to variations in focus, the photographer can choose finer-grained film and slick paper for a sharper focus and coarser-grained film and matte paper for a softer focus. Variations in definition can change meaning. In *Movie Premiere, Hollywood* (1.43), Robert Frank reverses our expectations, both spatially and conceptually. He focuses on the faces of the worshiping crowd rather than on the somber actress, who seems trapped by her fans. The meaning of the photograph shifts from a Hollywood cliché to an exploration of the darker side of fame.

Definition also plays an important role in drawing. Many mediums, including graphite and charcoal, can be used to create strong, clear lines as well as soft, fuzzy shapes. In Sidney Goodman's *Man Waiting* (1.44), this effect enhances the illusion of space while simultaneously creating a sense of mystery. The darker, more clearly defined shapes in the upper torso seem to push toward us while the legs, hips, and chair dissolve into the background.

Expressive Uses of Shape

The shape of each page plays a major role in Claire Van Vliet's design for *Aunt Sallie's Lament* (1.45). A square cover, dominated by a diamond shape, sets the stage for this tale of an old woman's lost love. Bits of dialog appear on the pages, contrasting her broken heart with her friends' joyous weddings. As the book and the story unfold, the diamond-shaped pages gradually accumulate to form the image of a completed quilt.

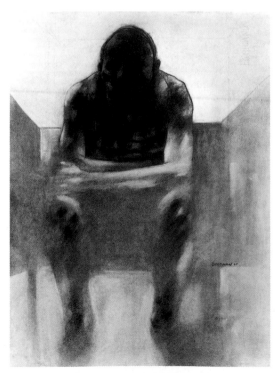

1.44 Sidney Goodman, *Man Waiting,* **1961.** Charcoal on paper, 25⅝ × 19⅛ in. (65.1 × 48.7 cm).

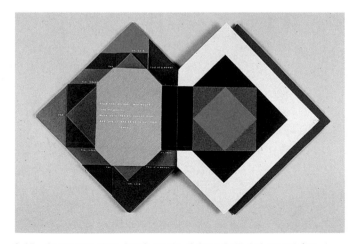

1.45 Claire Van Vliet, book cover of *Aunt Sallie's Lament,* by Margaret Kaufman. Chronicle Books, 1993.

A series of concentric circles creates the target shape that dominates Jasper Johns' *Target with Plaster Casts* (1.46). Nine figurative fragments line the upper edge. Equally attracted to the body parts above and the target below, we enter a visual combat zone as soon as we encounter this painting. To add further complexity, scraps of newspaper were embedded in the colored wax from which the painting was constructed. This **collage** (an image constructed from fragments initally designed for another purpose) adds a verbal undercurrent to a powerful visual image.

Collage plays an even bigger role in Romare Bearden's *The Dove* (1.47). The outer edges of each photographic fragment create one set of shapes. The textures and volumes within each of these fragments create a second set of shapes. Through the combination of the cut and photographic edges, Bearden has created a complex pattern of shifting shapes.

Texture

Defining Texture

The surface quality of a two-dimensional shape or three-dimensional volume is called **texture. Tactile texture** can actually be felt. **Visual texture** can be created using multiple shapes or through the simulation of physical texture. Texture creates a bridge between two- and three-dimensional design. Through an appeal to our sense of touch, it creates a unique connection between image and audience.

Creating Texture

Texture can be created in four major ways.

First, each material has its own textural quality. The

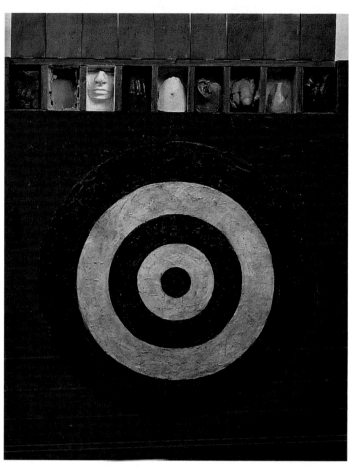

1.46 Jasper Johns, *Target with Plaster Casts*, 1955. Encaustic and collage on canvas with objects, 51 × 44 × 2½ in. (129.5 × 111.8 × 6.4 cm).

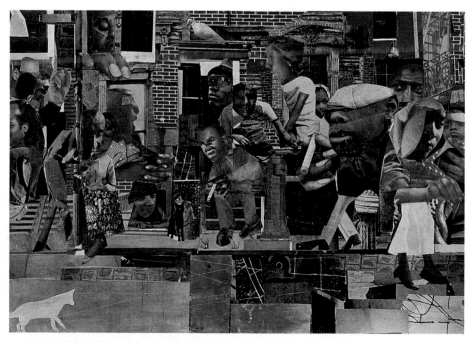

1.47 **Romare Bearden, *The Dove*, 1964.** Cut-and-pasted paper, gouache, pencil, and colored pencil on cardboard. 13⅜ × 18¾ in. (34 × 47.5 cm).

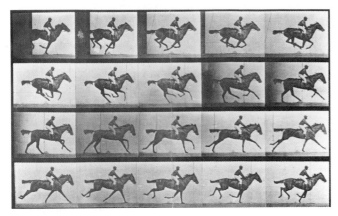

1.48 Eadweard Muybridge, *Galloping Horse, Motion Study—Sallie Gardner, owned by Leland Stanford, running at 1.40 gait over the Palo Alto track, June 19, 1878*. Collotype print, 9³⁄₁₆ × 12 in. (23.5 × 30.5 cm).

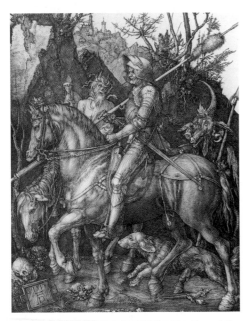

1.49 Albrecht Dürer, *The Knight, Death and the Devil*, 1513. Engraving, 11 × 14 in. (28 × 36 cm).

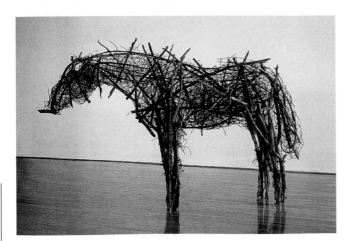

1.50 Deborah Butterfield, *Large Horse #4*, 1979. Steel, wire, sticks, 77 × 124 × 33 in. (195 × 315 × 84 cm).

smooth surface of Eadweard Muybridge's photograph (1.48) invites us to concentrate on the illusion of the galloping horse rather than on the reality of the paper on which it is printed. Albrecht Dürer's engraving of a horse (1.49) is more strongly textured. The embossed ink and the masterful cross-hatching give the print a wonderful texture. Using chicken wire and strips of wood, Deborah Butterfield created an extremely textural sculpture for her *Large Horse* (1.50). In contrast to the animal's passive pose, every surface of its body is highly agitated.

Second, physical variations in a surface can create powerful textures even when the artwork is primarily two dimensional. Constructed from scraps of canvas, zippers, and welded steel, Lee Bontecou's collage (1.51) extends more than an inch from the wall. The dark, open ovals invite entry into an even more extensive world, which seems to exist below the surface.

Third, texture can be created through multiplication of individual marks or shapes. In Figure 1.52, African-American painter Glenn Ligon repeatedly stenciled the phrase "I feel most colored when I am thrown against a sharp white background." As the density of the words increases, the words begin to fuse together, creating variations in the visual texture while reducing verbal clarity.

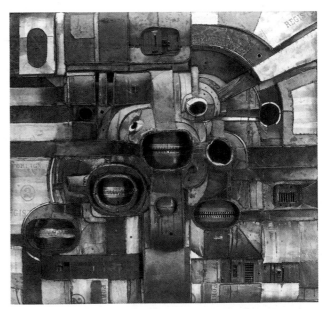

1.51 Lee Bontecou, *Untitled*, 1964. Welded steel with canvas, 6 ft × 6 ft 10 in. × 1 ft 6 in. (1.82 m × 2.1 m × 46 cm).

1.52 Glenn Ligon, *Untitled (I feel most colored when I am thrown against a sharp white background)*, **1990.** Oilstick and gesso on wood, each panel 6 ft 6 in. × 30 in. (2 m × 76.2 cm).

Finally, texture can be created through an invented pattern that simulates a textured surface. Belgian artist René Magritte was a master of textural illusion. In *The Red Model II* (1.53), a pair of shoes metamorphose into the bare feet that rest on the sharp gravel ground. Two coins and a scrap of newspaper complete the scene. In the background, a wooden wall presents an even more convincing illusion. Here, representation is used to raise a series of questions rather than to supply simple answers.

Expressive Uses of Texture

Textural Density and Orientation

Density and **orientation** are important aspects of both visual and actual texture. Finer marks, tightly packed, can suggest spatial distance while larger marks tend to advance spatially. In Douglas Smith's illustration of a prison (1.54), texture has been combined with perspective to create a convincing illusion of space. The lines of mortar between the bricks all point toward the truck in the center, while the bricks themselves diminish in size as the distance increases.

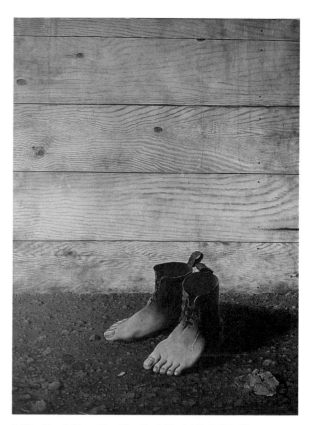

1.53 René Magritte, *The Red Model II*, **1937.** Oil on canvas, 72 × 53½ in. (183 × 136 cm).

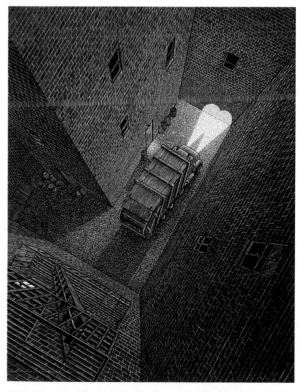

1.54 Douglas Smith, *No Turning*, **1986.** Scratchboard and watercolor, 11½ × 15 in. (29.2 × 38.1 cm).

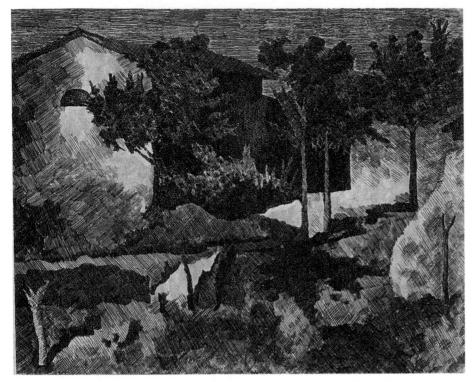

A very different use of texture animates Giorgio Morandi's *Paesaggio del Poggio* (1.55). The marks made are relatively uniform in size. A pattern of horizontal marks brings stability to the sky, while a series of intersecting diagonals activates the vegetation in the foreground. Areas of light and dark have been created through cross-hatching. The recurrent orientation of marks helps to unify the image.

Illusory Texture and Trompe L'Oeil

Through careful observation and painstaking work, artists can create a remarkably convincing textural illusion.

Illusory texture adds weight to shapes and can suggest three-dimensional volume. In Charles Sheeler's *Feline Felicity* (1.56), texture has been used in three ways. First, the fur of the

1.55 Giorgio Morandi, *Paesaggio del Poggio (View of Poggio)*, **1927.** Etching on copper, 15 × 16⅛ in. (38.1 × 41.1 cm).

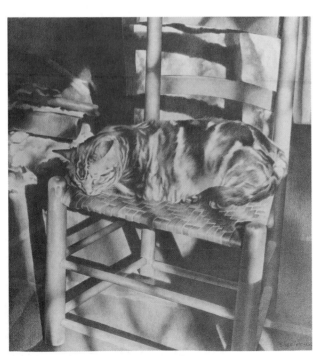

1.56 Charles Sheeler, *Feline Felicity,* 1934. Black crayon on paper, 22 × 18 in. (55.9 × 45.7 cm).

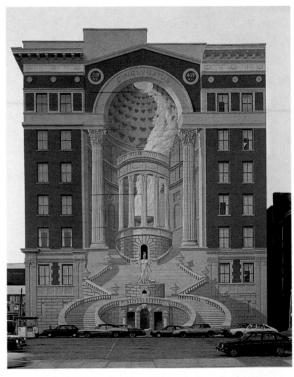

1.57 Richard Haas, *trompe l'oeil* mural on Brotherhood Building, Cincinnati, OH.

cat is distinguished from the wood of the chair by the drawing of the texture. Second, the cat's texture adds volume; this is clearly a substantial, well-fed animal. Third, by drawing on a textured sheet of paper with conte crayon, Sheeler unifies the whole image with a subtle, pervasive texture.

Taken to an extreme, illusory texture can so resemble reality that a deception occurs. By replicating architectural details, Richard Haas created an amazing dialog between illusion and reality in Figure 1.57. *Trompe l'oeil*, the French term meaning "to fool the eye," can become simply an exercise in technical virtuosity, or it can significantly alter our understanding of reality. In large scale, as on a city wall, a trompe l'oeil painting can actually appear to extend an architectural space.

Marks and Meanings

Every mark an artist makes can add to or subtract from the composition as a whole. When the texture is random or discordant, the composition will suffer. When the texture is deliberate and appropriate, the composition will improve. For example, each brush stroke in Ben Marra's *Self-Portrait* (1.58) describes a different facet of the face. Just as a sculptor carves out a portrait in plaster, so Marra has carved out this portrait in paint.

In Van Gogh's *The Starry Night* (1.59), the texture of oil paint serves three distinct purposes. First, it creates an invented texture that simulates the tactile surface of the trees in the foreground. Second, it brings great energy to every painted shape: we feel the wind; we become mesmerized by the glowing whirlpools of light. Finally, we become connected to the artist himself. His hand is clearly evident in every mark. He speaks to us with each brush stroke made.

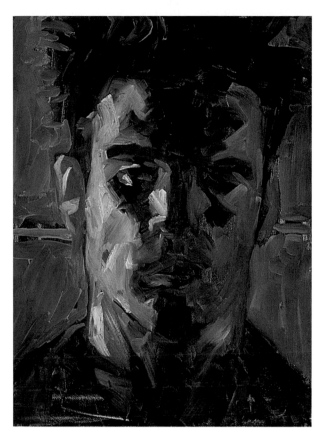

1.58 Benjamin Marra, *Self-Portrait*, 1998. Oil, 8½ × 11 in. (21.6 × 28 cm).

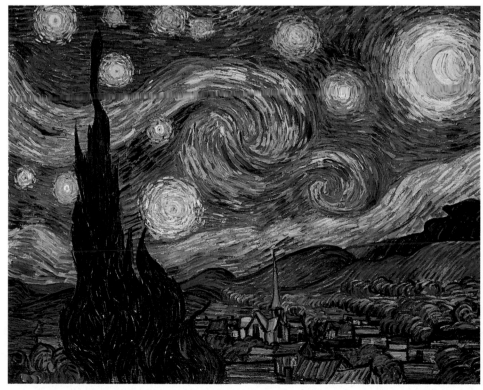

1.59 Vincent Van Gogh, *The Starry Night*, 1889. Oil on canvas, 29 × 36½ in. (73.7 × 92.1 cm).

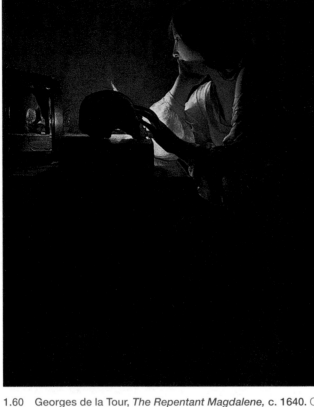

1.60   Georges de la Tour, *The Repentant Magdalene,* c. 1640. Oil on canvas, 44½ × 36½ in. (113 × 93 cm).

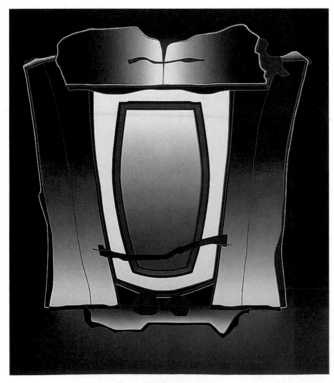

1.62   Deborah Remington, *Capra,* 1974. Oil on canvas, 6 ft 4 in. × 5 ft 7 in. (1.93 × 1.7 m).

Value

Defining Value

Value is determined by the relative lightness or darkness of a surface. The context in which an object is placed is crucial. In *The Repentant Magdalene* (1.60) by Georges de la Tour, the flame of a single candle illuminates a darkened room. The same candle, placed outdoors, would become nearly invisible on a sunny day.

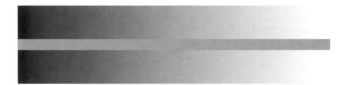

1.61

A **value scale,** consisting of a series of gradated values demonstrates this effect (1.61). A solid gray line, extending from left to right, is clearly defined when it is placed on a black background. As it crosses over the middle grays and into the white area, it appears to darken. In the center, it merges with the gray background. As shown in Deborah Remington's *Capra* (1.62), the glowing effect created by gradual changes in value can add expansive power to a painting.

Value and Volume

When a full range of values is used, two-dimensional shapes can be transformed into illusionistic volumes that suggest three-dimensional forms. Figure 1.63 shows the transformation of a flat circle into an illusionist volume. We begin with a simple outline, then add the **attached shadows,** or values, that directly define the basic form. Addition of a **cast shadow** in the third image grounds the sphere, while a separation between the shadow and the sphere creates a floating effect.

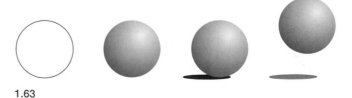

1.63

This illusion of space is so convincing that sculptural forms can appear to rise from a two-dimensional surface. The earliest oil painters used **grisaille,** or a gray underpainting, to define volume. Color was then added to this dimensional matrix using transparent layers of paint. In *The Ghent Altarpiece* (1.64), Jan van Eyck used both grisaille painting and full color. The statues painted at the bottom of the image are defined with gray, while color has been added to the kneeling figures in red. Subtle variations in value give all the figures a remarkable illusion of space.

Expressive Uses of Value

Darker values tend to sink while lighter values tend to rise. In Charles Demuth's . . . *And the Home of the Brave* (see 1.41), the dark values that dominate the upper half of the painting tend to compress the lighter values at the bottom. The tension between these forces of light and dark adds energy to the austere painting.

Ray K. Metzker used a very different distribution of value to energize *Philadelphia* (1.65). Surrounded by darkened buildings in a silent city, the commuters huddle together under the brightly lit bus shelter like actors in a mysterious play.

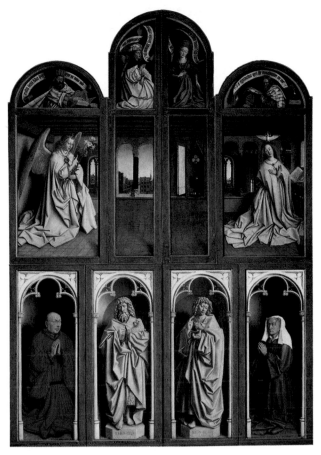

1.64 Jan van Eyck, *The Ghent Altarpiece* (closed), completed **1432.** Oil on panel, approx. 11 ft 6 in. × 7 ft 7 in. (3.5 × 2.33 m).

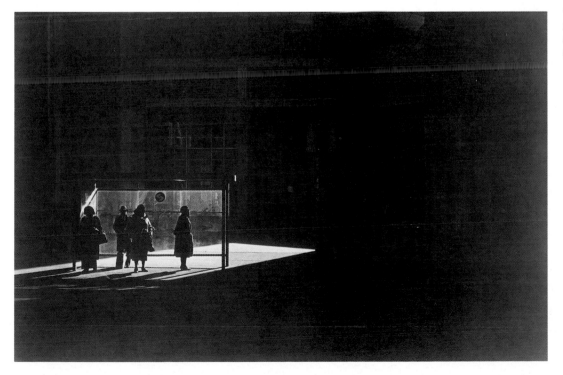

1.65 Ray K. Metzker, *Philadelphia,* **1963.** Gelatin silver print on paper, 6⅛ × 8¾ in. (15.4 × 22.3 cm).

Value is also used by landscape painters to create an illusion of space. The distribution of values in Thomas Moran's *Noon-Day Rest in Marble Canyon* (1.66) is typical. The darker, more clearly defined shapes in the foreground gradually fade until the cliffs in the background are more suggestive than definite. As we will see in Chapter Three, this effect is one of the simplest ways to create the illusion of space.

Value and Lighting

Filmmakers and set designers are especially aware of the expressive uses of value. Working with a wide range of lights, including sharply defined **spotlights** and more diffused **floodlights,** they can increase or decrease the illusion of space, emphasize an object or an action, and influence our emotional response to a character.

Four common forms of lighting are shown in Figure 1.67. As described by Herbert Zettl in *Sight, Sound, Motion: Applied Media Aesthetics*, a **key light** is the primary source of illumination. Placing this light at a 45-degree angle can enhance the illusion of space. Addition of a **backlight** separates the actor from the background and adds definition. When a **fill light** is added, the contrast between light and dark becomes less harsh, and the actor may appear less formidable. In dance performances, **side lighting** is often used to increase drama while enhancing dimensionality.

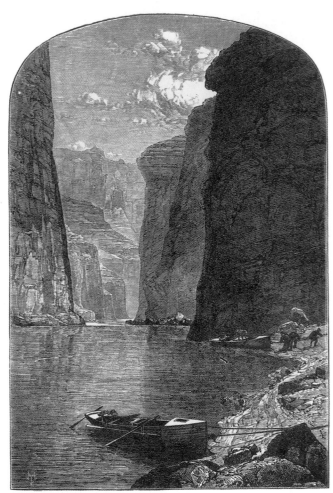

1.66 Thomas Moran, *Noon-Day Rest in Marble Canyon,* from *Exploration of the Colorado River of the West,* by J. W. Powell, 1875. Wood engraving after an original sketch by Thomas Moran, 6½ × 4⅜ in. (16.5 × 11 cm).

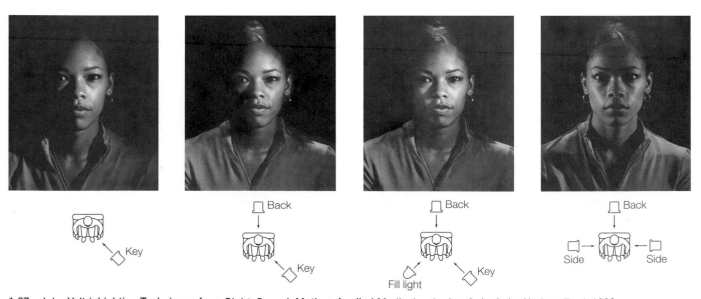

1.67 John Veltri, Lighting Techniques from *Sight, Sound, Motion: Applied Media Aesthetics,* 3rd ed., by Herbert Zettl, 1999.

All these aspects of lighting are used expressively in *Casablanca*, a classic film directed by Michael Curtiz. The lighting is fairly dark when we first enter Rick's Café Americain, the saloon where most of the action occurs. In this dark and mysterious place, a man will be shot, a seduction will be thwarted, and a romance will be rekindled. In the same shot, the piano player, Sam, and the audience members closest to the stage are brightly lit as Sam sings an optimistic song (1.68A). A strong sidelight is often used on the two villains in the film, Major Strasser and Captain Renault, to make them more formidable and enhance the texture in their faces (1.68B). By contrast, much softer light is used for the faces of Victor and especially the heroine, Ilsa, who is emotionally and politically vulnerable (1.68C).

Indeed, light is used to accentuate Ilsa's emotions throughout the film. When she tries to explain to Rick the reason that she had left him in Paris two years earlier, she wears a pure white dress and enters the darkened saloon like a virginal beam of light (1.68D). Later, when she visits Rick in his apartment, shadows cover her face, accentuating her conflicting emotions as she tries to decide whether to remain with Victor, whom she idealizes or return to Rick, whom she loves. In the final scene at the airport, diffused lighting again emphasizes Ilsa's vulnerability (1.68E). She and Victor disappear into the foggy night, escaping from Casablanca, while Rick and a reformed Renault stroll away together to join the foreign legion.

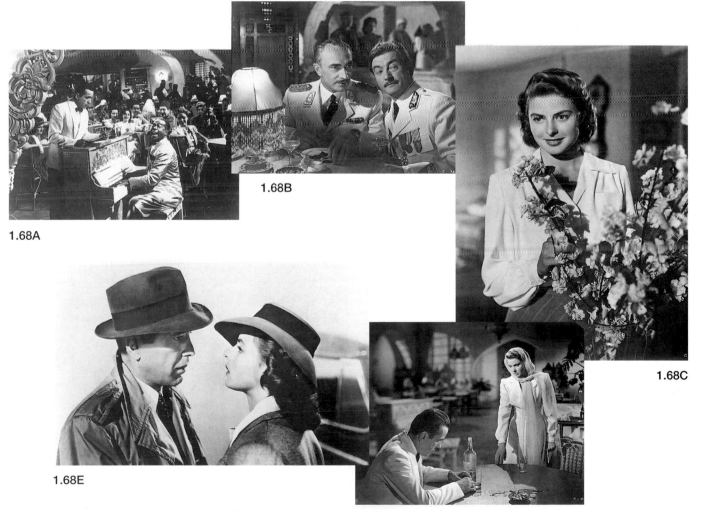

1.68A

1.68B

1.68C

1.68E

1.68D

Profile:
Phillia Yi, Printmaker

Energy and Expression Using
Woodcut on a Large Scale

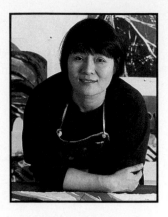

Phillia Changhi Yi has revitalized the ancient process of woodcut through her large-scale prints. Drawing directly on luan plywood, Yi cuts away the negative shapes and inks the raised positive shapes to create abstract images that vigorously combine color, texture, and movement. Yi has exhibited widely, with over fifteen solo shows and numerous international group shows to her credit. She lectures widely and has taught workshops at Manhattan Graphics Center, Women's Studio Workshop, and the Southern Graphics Council Conference. She is currently the chair of the Art Department at Hobart and William Smith Colleges.

MS: The energy in your images immediately attracts attention. What is its source?

PY: Conflict is my primary source, conceptually and compositionally. As a woman from Korea living in the United States, I find myself caught between cultures. This isolates me in an interesting way and gives me a unique persepective. My work reflects the day-to-day dilemmas and tension of my multicultural experience.

Crisis moments often trigger ideas, but historical events are never treated literally. I combine abstract imagery with representational elements in my prints. Both flat and illusory space is created, suggesting an altered sense of time and scale. "Tight" movement is juxtaposed with fluid shapes, and warm and cool colors are used in opaque and translucent layers. This activates the psychological space and creates a complex, highly charged composition.

MS: Your family is dominated by doctors and business-people. How did you become an artist?

PY: Getting the right encouragement at the right time gave me the confidence to pursue art. All of my five siblings are talented, I think, but for them, choosing an art career seemed too risky. My father encouraged me to study graphic design, but I found that printmaking was my real passion. My mentor, Professor Romas Viesulas at Tyler School of Art, said that I had the commitment and ability for a career in art. His confidence gave me confidence.

MS: How do you develop your images?

PY: I begin with a month of drawing, usually in charcoal, on 29 × 41 in. sheets of printmaking paper. In the draw-

ings, I work out my images and ideas. Social and political themes dominate. The beating of Rodney King by members of the Los Angeles Police Department and the subsequent burning of Koreatown inspired *Dance*. The historical lack of funding for medical research for women inspired *Silence*.

The Other Side deals with the power of women, who must prevail in a world dominated by men. The whole composition is based on the intersection between these two forces, near the center of the print. In a sense, the large black shape represents the unconscious, while the curving red shape suggests that which is conscious, palpable, and real. I am interested in the uneasy alliance, or balance, between complex life forces, rather than a simple battle between adversaries. Each corner is treated differently, adding more variety and energy to the print.

MS: The size of *The Other Side* piece is extraordinary. Using eight panels, you have created a print that is 12 feet long!

PY: When I was studying printmaking at the State University of New York, New Paltz, I was surrounded by printmakers. The size of the printing press, acid trays, rollers, and other equipment seemed to limit the size of the artwork. When I went to Tyler in Philadelphia, my roommate, who was a painter, introduced me to her friends. Some were completing a 5 × 7 ft painting a day! I realized that the small size and slow process of printmaking had historically given it a "second-class" status. I was determined to overcome this perception, so I developed a working method that is forceful, spontaneous, and direct. There is still a great deal of deliberation, but the cutting and printing processes are relatively fast.

MS: Some artists work very methodically over a long period of time while others work in short, intensive bursts. What is your approach?

PY: I have adapted my method to my situation. I have obligations as a teacher, a mother, and an administrator, so summer is my only solid block of work time. A regular schedule is best for me. At the beginning of the summer, I go to the studio for a few hours each day. I soon increase this to about 6 hours a day for drawing. When I am cutting the blocks and printing, I often work for 8 to 10 hours a day. I am very consistent.

MS: What is the best work method for your students?

PY: Success is primarily based on commitment. I would say that art-making is about 5 percent talent and inspiration and 95 percent tenacity and hard work. A profes-sional or a serious student continues to work despite obstacles. It is important for students to explore ideas and make mistakes; that is the best way to learn.

MS: What is the purpose of your artwork?

PY: Art is expression, not explanation. Artists must be attentive, noticing every detail of experience. Art both reflects and influences society and culture. In that sense, I feel that artists have a responsibility to their generation, not just to create objects of beauty, but to create objects of truth—whether they are beautiful or not.

My ideas come from my daily life and my personal experience, both good and bad. The most important characteristic is my belief that art should be expressed in terms of human experience. My work is essentially optimistic: I embrace all that the world has to offer.

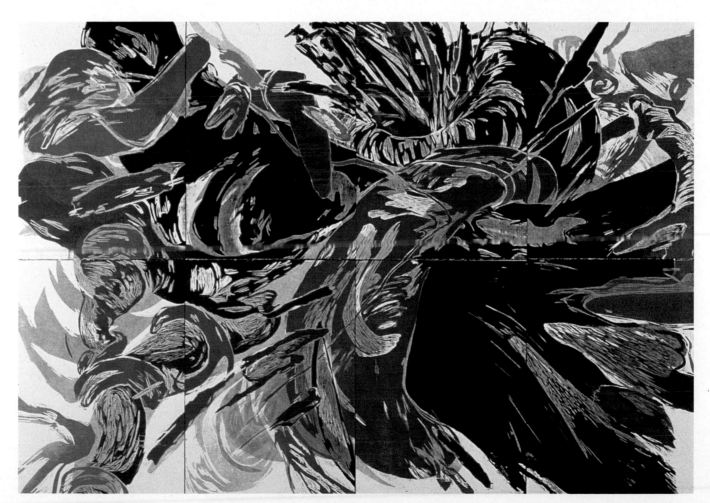

Phillia Changhi Yi, *The Other Side*, 1993. Color woodcut, 84 × 120 in. (213 × 305 cm).

Summary

- The basic elements of two-dimensional design are line, shape, texture, value, and color.

- Lines can contain, define, dissect, and connect. When multipled to create cross contours and cross-hatching, lines can create both value and volume.

- A shape is created whenever an area is enclosed. The figure, or positive shape, is most prominent, while the ground, or negative shape, provides the surrounding context. When the figure and ground shapes are equally strong, figure/ground reversal can occur, adding energy to the design.

- There are many types of shapes, including rectilinear, curvilinear, geometric, organic, representational, nonobjective, and abstract. When gradated, shapes can appear volumetric.

- Texture refers to the visual or tactile surface of a shape. Visual texture can be created through multiple marks, while physical variations in the surface create tactile textures.

- Lightness or darkness in an artwork is called value. Value can be used to create the illusion of space, to shift compositional balance, or to heighten emotion.

Keywords

abstract shape
actual line
attached
   shadow
backlight
calligraphic
   line
cast shadow
closure
collage
contour line
cross contour
cross-hatching
curvilinear
   shape
definition
density

descriptive
   shape
figure
figure/ground
   reversal
fill light
floodlight
format
geometric
   shape
gesture
   drawing
gradation
grisaille
ground
hatching
high definition

illusory texture
implied line
key light
line
low definition
negative shape
nonobjective
   shape
organic shape
orientation
positive shape
pure form
rectilinear
   shape
representational
   shape
shading

shape
sidelight
spotlight
tactile texture
texture
trompe l'oeil
value
value scale
visual texture
volume
volume
   summary

1. Experiment with the widest range of lines your pencil, brush, or marker can create. How can a line become more dynamic? How can lines be used to create the illusion of space?

2. What is the relationship between the visual elements and the format in which they are placed? The edge of the format is like an electric wire: carefully used, it can generate great energy.

3. Experiment with a wide variety of shapes: rectilinear, curvilinear, geometric, organic, positive, negative. Which type of shape is most appropriate for the idea you want to communicate?

4. Is every square inch of the composition fully engaged? Note especially the role of negative space in creating a balance with positive elements.

5. What happens when some or all of the shapes in your design are gradated? How do variations in the direction of the gradation affect the illusion of space?

6. How many different textures can be created with the medium you are using? Which texture is most appropriate for your particular image? Can textural contradiction add to the meaning of your art work?

7. Experiment with the range of values used in your composition. What happens when a full range of values is used? What happens when a narrow range of values is used? How can attached or cast shadows affect meaning?

Roy R. Behrens, *Design in the Visual Arts.* Englewood Cliffs, NJ, Prentice-Hall, Inc. 1984.

Frank Cheathan, Jane Hart Cheathan, Sheryl A. Haler, *Design Concepts and Applications.* Englewood Cliffs, NJ, Prentice-Hall, Inc., 1983.

David A. Lauer and Stephen Pentak, *Design Basics,* 5th edition. Orlando, FL, Harcourt, Brace & Company, 2000.

Donis Dondis, *A Primer of Visual Literacy.* Cambridge, MA, MIT Press, 1973.

Edward Hill, *The Language of Drawing.* Englewood Cliffs, NJ, Prentice-Hall, Inc., 1966.

Jack Fredrick Myers, *The Language of Visual Art: Perception as a Basis for Design.* Orlando, FL, Holt Rinehart and Winston, Inc. 1989.

Herbert Zettl. *Sight, Sound, Motion: Applied Media Aesthetics.* 3rd edition. Belmont, CA, Wadsworth Publishing Company, 1999.

chapter two

Color and Composition

Initial design planning is often done in black and white. Working within these limitations, we can focus on developing our ideas and creating basic compositions. Relationships among visual elements can be seen most clearly when the design is distilled down to the bare essentials. By expanding the palette to include all aspects of color, we begin to work with a much more complex set of variables, including harmony, contrast, and symbolic meaning. Because of its complexity, color requires a chapter of its own.

Color immediately attracts attention. The small red lines in Gerrit Rietveld's *Model of the Schröder House* (2.1) are more powerful than the surrounding black, white, and gray walls. An interior designer may use rose-red walls in a restaurant to increase emotional warmth while using light blue walls in a day care center to encourage calm. In Caravaggio's *The Deposition* (2.2), the blood-red robe behind the dead man adds a critical compositional shape as well as symbolic meaning. Even very small children, presented with a collection of bottles filled with liquid in various colors, will group the bottles by color rather than by size or shape. The visual and emotional force generated by color is extraordinary. By harnessing its power, we can add conceptual complexity and compositional strength to any design.

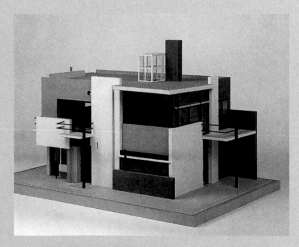

2.1 Gerrit Rietveld, Model for the Rietveld–Schröder House, 1923–24. Glass and wood, 7⅜ × 28⅜ × 19¼ in. (44.1 × 72.1 × 48.9 cm).

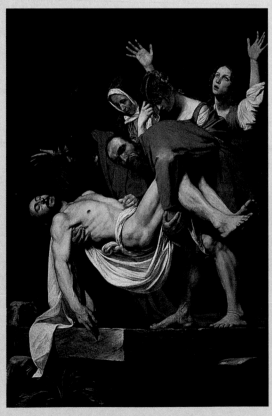

2.2 Caravaggio, *The Deposition*, 1604. Oil on canvas, 9 ft 10⅛ in. × 6 ft 7⅞ in. (3 × 2.03 m).

Studying Color

Color theory is a science as well as an art. Indeed, it was mathematician Sir Isaac Newton who developed the first scientific experiments relating color and light. In *The Art of Color*,[1] Johannes Itten lists the following approaches to color theory:

- The physicist studies electromagnetic wavelengths in order to measure and classify color.

- The chemist, working with the molecular structure of dyes and pigments, seeks to produce highly permanent colors and excellent paint consistency.

- The physiologist investigates the effects of color and light on our eyes and brain.

- The psychologist studies the expressive effects of color on our mind and spirit.

An artist combines all these areas of knowledge. Like the physicist, the artist can create new wavelengths through color mixing. Like the chemist, the artist must be aware of the safety and permanence of dyes and pigments. When using color to create the illusion of space or to shift visual balance, the artist puts into practice theories developed by physiologists. Finally, the psychological effects of color strongly influence both communication and expression.

Seeing Color

Color and light are inseparable. Without light, there can be no color. When white light passes through a prism, a spectrum of colors from violet to red becomes visible (2.3). When white light hits an apple (2.4), the red wavelengths are reflected while the other colors are absorbed. When there is limited light, as at night, we see a world of light and dark values, rather than a world of full color.

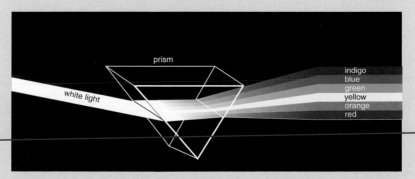

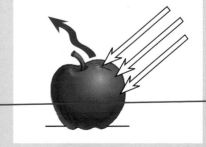

2.3 When white light passes through a prism, the spectrum becomes visible.

2.4 Reflected light defines this red apple.

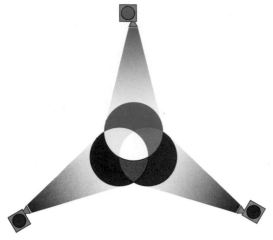

2.5 Light itself creates additive color.

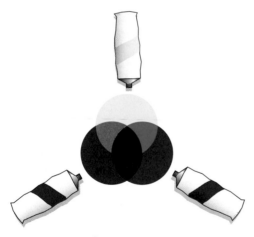

2.6 Subtractive color is created when light is reflected off a surface.

Two primary systems are created through this interplay of color and light. Light in itself creates **additive color.** Video artists, theatrical set designers, and Website artists primarily work with additive color. Red, green, and blue are the primary colors in this system. When these colors are combined as beams of light, white light results (2.5).

Subtractive color is created when light is reflected off a surface. Pigment colors are created through such reflected light. As with the actual red apple, a painted red apple appears when the red wavelengths of light are reflected while the other colors are absorbed. The subtractive primaries are cyan blue, magenta red, and yellow (2.6). When mixed, they produce a type of black. Painters, printmakers, and illustrators use subtractive color in various forms, including acrylics, pastels, and inks. A printed computer image is also created through reflected light. Since most foundation color projects require the use of reflected light, the remainder of this chapter focuses on subtractive color.

Colors are never seen in isolation. The blue sheet of paper we examine in an art supply store reminds us of the blue of the sky, the ocean, or the fabrics in a clothing store. Lighting also affects our perceptions. Incandescent light creates a warm orange glow, while standard fluorescent lights produce a bluish ambiance. When our blue paper is added to a design, it is further affected by the other colors chosen. This effect, called **simultaneous contrast,** is demonstrated in Figure 2.7. When we place a square of blue on a yellow square, the blue appears darker and cooler. The same blue square appears much lighter when it is placed on a black ground.

 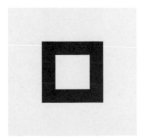 

2.7 When we place a square of blue on a yellow square, the blue appears darker and cooler. The same blue appears much lighter when it is placed on a black background.

This effect is especially dramatic when the blue square is placed on a scarlet square. The orange-red and cyan blue are **complementary colors:** they are opposites on a color wheel. Two types of cells, known as rods and cones, are arranged in layers on the retina of the eye and serve as photoreceptors. The rods record lightness and darkness, while the cones are used to distinguish the red from the blue. According to **opponent theory,** the cones can register only one color in a complementary pair at a time. Constant shifting between the opposing colors creates a visual overload at the edges of the shapes, resulting in an electric glow.

The same characteristic of human vision can be used to create an **afterimage.** If we stare at a cyan-blue dot for a minute, then stare at a white sheet of paper, an orange-red shape will seem to appear. Jasper Johns used this effect to create *Flag* (2.8). Part of a series of paintings based on the American flag, this print presents a reversal of the usual colors at the top. If we stare at this flag, then shift our attention to a white sheet of paper, we will once again see the familiar red, white, and blue.

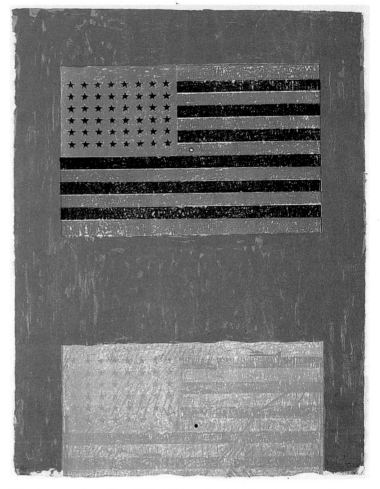

2.8 **Jasper Johns, *Flag*, 1968.** Lithograph, printed in color, composition: 34⅝ × 25⅞ in. (87.9 × 65.7 cm).

Defining Color

Hue

The **hue** of a color is determined by its wavelength. For example while blue has a wavelength of 480 to 460 millimicrons, red has a wavelength of 800 to 650 millimicrons.[2] Red, blue, green, yellow, and so forth are all hues, or names, of colors.

Physicists, painters, and philosophers have devised numerous systems to organize hues. Johannes Itten's 12-step color wheel and the Albert Munsell color system are the familiar examples. The Itten model (2.9) has the advantage of simplicity and clarity. Red, blue, and yellow **primary colors** are in the center. These colors can be mixed to produce virtually all other colors. The **secondary colors** of green, orange, and violet follow. These colors are mixed from adjacent primaries. A circular spectrum of **tertiary colors** completes the wheel. The 10-step

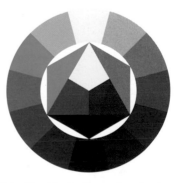

2.9 The 12-step Itten color wheel.

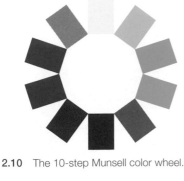

2.10 The 10-step Munsell color wheel.

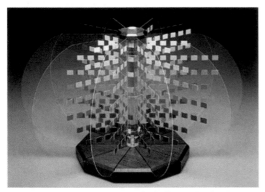

2.11 Munsell color tree, 1972. Clear plastic chart, 10½ × 12 in. (26.7 × 30.5 cm); base size 12 in. (30.5 cm) diameter; center pole size 12⅝ in. (32.1 cm) high; chip size ¾ × 1⅜ in. (1.9 × 3.5 cm).

Munsell color wheel (2.10) more accurately identifies cyan blue, magenta red, and yellow as the primaries, while the three-dimensional Munsell color system (2.11) provides examples of changes in color value and intensity as well as hue.

Artists use a wide range of hues to capture the richness of reality. In *Wheel of Fortune* (2.12), Audrey Flack used a full spectrum of hues to define various objects in relentless detail. However, a limited number of hues can be equally effective. By limiting his palette, Robert Lazuka created an image with hypnotic power in *Thoughts of Summer* (2.13).

Value

In color theory, **value** refers to the relative lightness or darkness of a color. By removing hue from the equation, we can create a simple value scale (2.14A) that shifts from white to black through a series of grays. As shown in Figure 2.14B, hues such as violet, blue, and green are inherently darker in value than pure yellow or orange. When white is added to a hue, the resulting **tint** will be lighter in value. The addition of black produces a darker **shade**. The addition of both white and black creates a **tone**. Tints and shades of red are shown in Figure 2.14C.

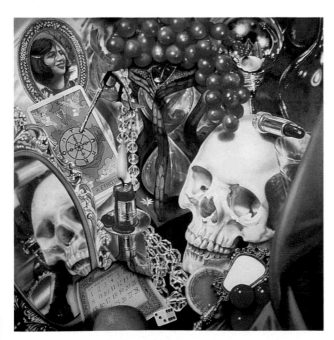

2.12 Audrey Flack, *Wheel of Fortune*, 1977–78. Oil over acrylic on canvas, 8 × 8 ft.

2.13 Robert Lazuka, *Thoughts of Summer*, 1999. 21 × 21 in. (53 × 53 cm).

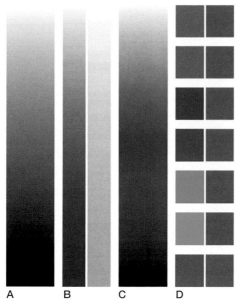

A　　　B　　　C　　　D

2.14 Value scales.

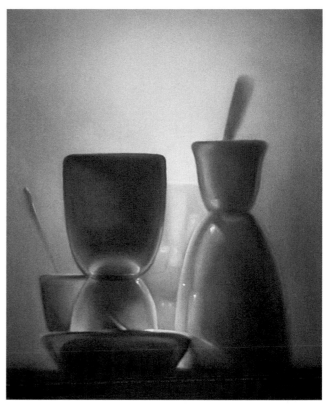

2.15 Nicora Gangi, *Vision*, 1994. Pastel, 10 × 14 in. (25 × 36 cm).

Translation of color into value is shown in 2.14D. Despite the wide variety of hues, all these colors have essentially the same value.

Initial design work is often done in the basic values of black, white, and gray. This simple palette provides dramatic contrast while eliminating the other color variables of hue, intensity, and temperature. Through this limitation we can focus our attention on line, shape, and texture. Furthermore, value in itself can be highly expressive. As shown in Figure 1.39 on page 1-12, Ansel Adams used black and white photography to enhance the grandeur of the Sierra mountains. Color would diminish the impact of *Man Waiting* (1.44) by Sidney Goodman. And film lovers have adamantly argued against the colorization of classic American films such as *Casablanca* and *Citizen Kane*.

As with hue, a narrow range of values can be as effective as a wide range. In *Vision* by Nicora Gangi (2.15), light and dark values transform a simple still life into a theatrical drama. The limited range of values in David Hockney's *Mist* (2.16) is equally effective. The gray-green palm trees dissolve into the peach-colored fog as quietly as a whisper.

Likewise, color is a dominant force in some paintings, while value is the dominant force in others. Henri Matisse's *Green Stripe* (2.17) is defined by

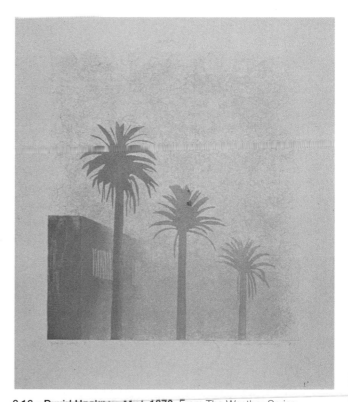

2.16 David Hockney, *Mist*, 1973. From The Weather Series. Lithograph in 5 colors, edition 98, 37 × 32 in. (93.9 × 81.2 cm).

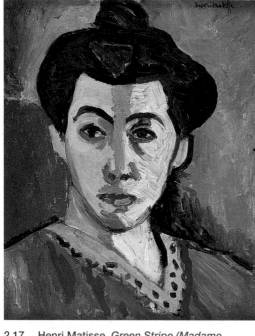

2.17 Henri Matisse, *Green Stripe (Madame Matisse)*, **1905.** Oil on canvas, 16 × 12 ¾ in. (40.6 × 32.4 cm).

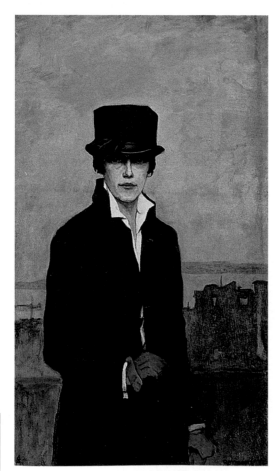

2.18 Romaine Brooks, *Self-Portrait*, **1923.** Oil on canvas. 46¼ × 26⅞ in. (117.5 × 68.3 cm).

color, whereas value defines Romaine Brooks' *Self-Portrait* (2.18).

Intensity

Intensity, saturation, and **chroma** are all words used to describe the purity of a color. Taken directly from the tube, primary colors such as phthalocyanide blue, quindacradone magenta, and hansa yellow, and secondary colors such as phthalocyanide green, cadmium orange, and acra violet, or dioxazine purple, provide the greatest intensity. The intensity diminishes when the colors are mixed, especially when cheap paint is used.

Figure 2.19 offers three intensity scales. Column A shows the most intense primary and secondary colors. Column B demonstrates the loss of intensity when black is added. In column C, two complementary colors are mixed, producing a range of elegant, low-intensity colors.

High-intensity colors are often used to maximize impact. Grace Hartigan's *City Life* (2.20) explodes with energy, as the rich blues, reds, and yellows dance across the canvas. Using too many intense colors, however, can reduce rather than increase impact. In Figure 2.21, Arshile Gorky used a combination of brilliant primary colors and low-intensity earth tones to create a magical image.

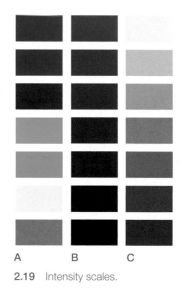

2.19 Intensity scales.

A similar comparison can be made between the Japanese robes in Figures 2.22 and 2.23. The first offers an evocation of spring. Delicate plum tree blossoms spread across the gradated purple background, which dissolves into open space. The composition and colors of this robe, like the season it depicts, suggest potential growth rather than full fruition. The second robe depicts summer. Crowded with intensely colored patterns, the composition is bursting with energy. The potential suggested in the first robe has been fulfilled.

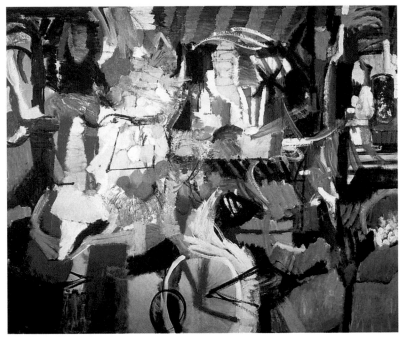

2.20 Grace Hartigan, *City Life,* 1956. Oil on canvas, 81 × 98½ in. (205.7 × 250.2 cm).

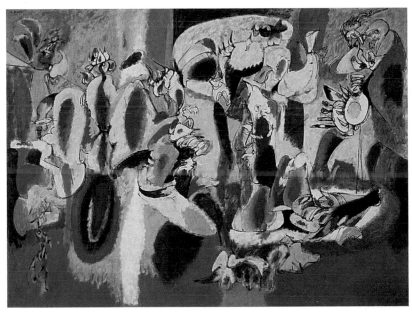

2.21 Arshile Gorky, *The Liver Is the Cock's Comb,* 1944. Oil on canvas, 6 ft 1¼ in. × 8 ft 2 in. (1.86 × 2.49 cm).

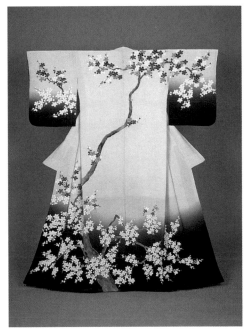

2.22 **Woman's Kimono, 20th century.** Silk crepe, painted design of plum tree in blossom, 58 × 48 in. (147.3 × 121.9 cm).

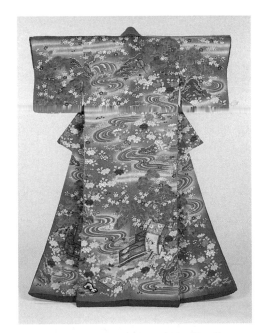

2.23 **Kosode with Flowing Water, Pine Trees, Bridge, and Scroll, Japan, Edo period (1615–1867).** Silk plain weave with yuzen dyeing, stenciled imitation tie-dyeing, and silk and gilt thread, back length 67 in. (170.2 cm).

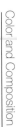

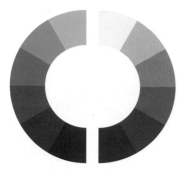

2.24 Separation of the color wheel by temperature.

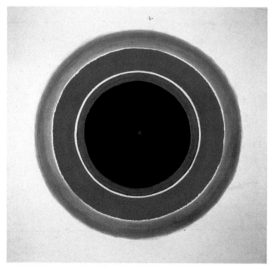

2.25 Kenneth Noland, *A Warm Sound in a Gray Field*, **1961.** 6 ft 10½ in. × 6 ft 9 in. (2.1 × 2.06 m).

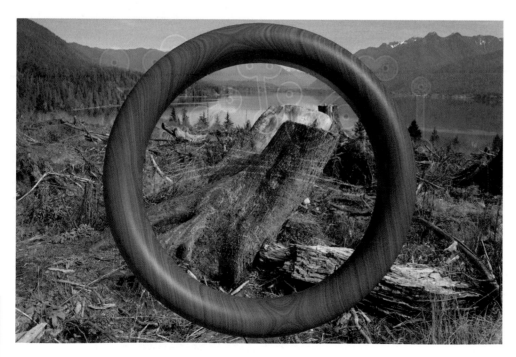

2.26 MANUAL (Suzanne Bloom and Ed Hill), *Quinault,* **from** *A Constructed Forest*, **1993.** Chromogenic print, 24 × 36 in. (61 × 91.4 cm).

Temperature

Temperature refers to the heat a color generates, both physically and psychologically. Try laying six colored squares on fresh snow on a sunny day. By the end of the day, the warm-colored squares of red, yellow, and orange will sink into the melting snow, while the blue, green, and violet squares will remain closer to the surface. Figure 2.24 shows a simple division of the color wheel by temperature.

Color temperature plays a critical role in creating the illusion of space. Under most circumstances, warm colors advance while cool colors recede. This effect is demonstrated very clearly in Kenneth Noland's *A Warm Sound in a Gray Field* (2.25). The scarlet ring with its yellow halo pushes toward us, while the blue-black circle pulls us inward. The small red dot in the center of the composition further activates the void by creating another advancing shape.

In *Quinault* (2.26), Suzanne Bloom and Ed Hill used a similar combination of warm and cool colors to create a very different illusion of space. A volumetric wooden ring dominates the image, targeting the tree stump in the center. A lake and blue mountains recede into the background. Combining traditional photography with computer graphics, these collaborators have created an image based on natural and artificial sources.

By combining warm and cool colors, we can cause various areas in a painting to expand or contract. In Wolf Kahn's *The Yellow Square* (2.27), the green and violet pastels defining the exterior of the barn gently pull the viewer into the painting, while the blazing yellow window inside the barn pushes out as forcefully as the beacon in a lighthouse. This effect, described by painter Hans Hofmann as "push/pull" can play an even more important role in nonobjective paintings since they rely so heavily on basic visual forces for their impact. In Hofmann's *Magnum Opus* (2.28), this push/pull effect is heightened by variations in definition, from the loosely painted reds to the sharply defined yellow rectangle.

Because our perception of warm and cool color is based on psychological as well as physical experience, color temperature offers a wide range of expressive possibilities. Warm and cool colors evoke a physical response in Kiera Cunningham's textbook cover design (2.29). The bright yellow flame and the scarlet, yellow, and brown stripes energize the design and forcefully launch the balloon.

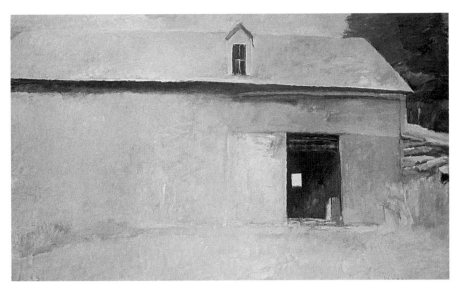

2.27 Wolf Kahn, *The Yellow Square*, 1981. Oil on canvas, 44 × 72 in. (112 × 183 cm).

2.28 Hans Hofmann, *Magnum Opus*, 1962. Oil on canvas, 84⅛ × 78⅛ in. 213 × 198 cm).

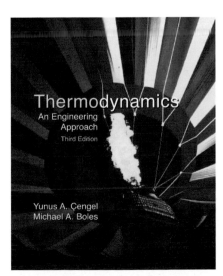

2.29 Kiera Cunningham, Cover of *Thermodynamics*, by Çengel and Boles.

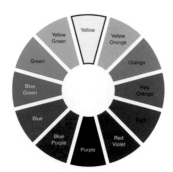

2.30 Monochromatic color system.

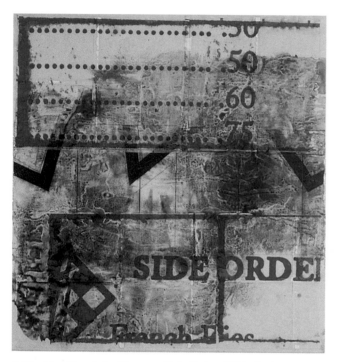

2.31 Guy Goodwin, *Tracers–Side Order,* **1999.** Resin, polyurethane, ink on polycarbonate, 51 × 54 × 4 in. (130 × 137 × 10 cm).

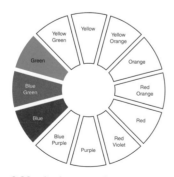

2.32 Analogous color system.

2.33 Paul Cézanne, *Houses in Provence (Vicinity of L'Estaque),* **1880.** Oil on canvas, 25⅝ × 32 in. (65 × 81 cm).

Composing in Color
Color Systems

Variations in hue, value intensity, and temperature can result in millions of colors. Because relationships among colors are so critical to the success or failure of a design, many theories of **color harmony** have been developed to help artists, architects, and designers make good choices. The simple Itten color wheel can help illustrate the five traditional systems.

Monochromatic

Variations on a single hue are used in a **monochromatic** system (2.30). A range of values is often used to help increase the illusion of space. The advantage of this system is a high level of unity: all the colors are strongly related. Boredom, due to the lack of variety, is a potential disadvantage. In *Tracers–Side Order* (2.31), Guy Goodwin used a variety of textures, patterns, and words to add interest to a fairly monochromatic painting.

Analogous

Adjacent colors in the spectrum are used in an **analogous color** scheme (2.32). As with monochromatic harmony, a high degree of unity is ensured, but the wider range of hues offers greater variety and interest. In *Houses in Provence* (2.33), Paul Cézanne used analogous colors to create a highly unified landscape.

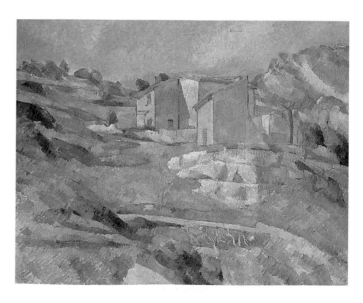

Complementary

The palette dramatically expands in a complementary system (2.34). Complementary colors are opposites. When mixed, they produce a neutral brownish or grayish black. When used in a composition, however, they become ideal partners: each increases the power of the other. In Henri Toulouse-Lautrec's *A Corner of the Moulin de la Galette* (2.35), the adjacent reds and greens are highly animated, while the browns they created when mixed add coloristic unity.

Any two complements will generate extreme simultaneous contrast. The red and green in Victor Vasarely's *Vega Per* (2.36A) add another level of energy to an optical circus. When we replace the green with the cyan blue from the Munsell color system (2.36B), the design becomes even more agitated. The cones in our eyes shift back and forth between the two complements, electrifying the image.

Each complementary pair has its own distinctive strengths. Violet and yellow provide the widest value range, while orange and blue provide the widest range of temperature. Red and cyan or red and green are similar in value and create the most extreme agitation when juxtaposed. In all cases, by using two complements plus black and white, we are able to create a range of colors that can suggest the full spectrum.

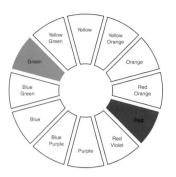

2.34   Complementary color system.

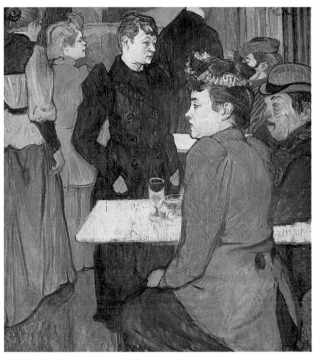

2.35   Henri Toulouse-Lautrec, *A Corner of the Moulin de la Galette*, 1892, Paris. Oil on cardboard, 39⅜ × 35⅛ in. (100 × 89.2 cm).

2.36A   Victor Vasarely, *Vega Per*, 1969. Oil on canvas, 64 × 64 in. (162.6 × 162.6 cm).

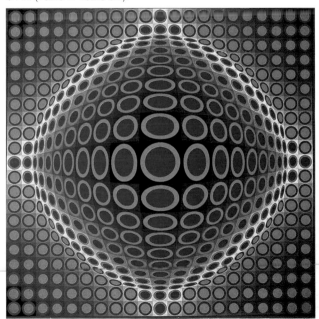

2.36B   In this variation on 2.36A, cyan blue has been used to create even more electricity.

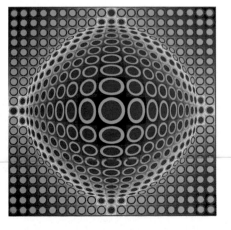

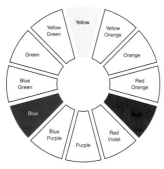

2.37 Split complementary system.

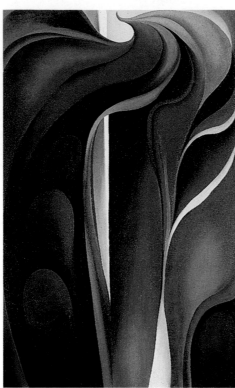

2.38 Georgia O'Keeffe, *Jack in the Pulpit No. V*, 1930. Oil on canvas, 48 × 30 in. (122 × 76 cm).

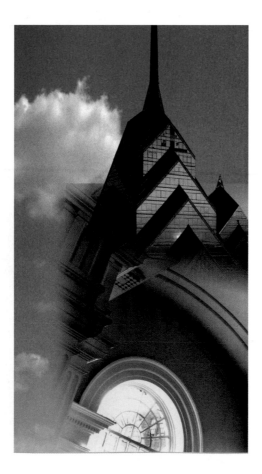

2.39 Triadic system.

2.40 Joel Katz Design Associates, Cover of *Philadelphia Architecture: A Guide to the City*, 2nd ed., 1984.

Split Complementary

An even wider range of possibilities is offered by the **split complementary** system (2.37). Rather than pair colors that are in opposite positions on the color wheel, the artist completes the scheme using the two colors on either side of one of the complements. Georgia O'Keeffe's *Jack in the Pulpit No. V* (2.38) is dominated by rich green and violets, with accents of yellow at the top of and a line of scarlet down the center of the composition.

Triadic

The triadic system pushes the choices even farther apart so that they are now located in a triangular position, equally spaced around the wheel (2.39). This scheme is often used when variety and a strong impact are essential, as in Figure 2.40.

Chromatic Grays and Earth Colors

While the Itten color wheel can help us identify many kinds of relationships, two important types of colors are not included: chromatic grays and earth colors. A **chromatic gray** is made from a mixture of color, rather than a simple blend of black and white. The result is both subtle and vibrant. In *The Magpie* (2.41), the grays vary widely, from the purples and blue-grays in the shadows to the golden-gray light in the foreground and the silvery grays for the snow-covered trees. This is not a dark, sullen winter day; through the use of chromatic grays, Claude Monet makes the warm light and transparent shadows sparkle in the crisp air.

Earth colors, including raw sienna and burnt sienna, raw and burnt umber and yellow ochre, are made literally from pigments found in soil. Generally warm in temperature, when used together they create a type of analogous harmony. Browns, oranges, and tans accentuate the gestural energy and organic shapes in *Bush Cabbage Dreaming at Ngarlu* (2.42), by Australian artists Cookie Stewart Japaljarri, Alma Nungarrayi Granites, and Robin Japanangka Granites. When used alone or in combination with higher-intensity colors, earth colors can bring welcome variety to design.

Color Combinations

Disharmony

Selecting harmonious colors can make the difference between a visual atrocity and a visual delight. As a result, color harmony is the subject of endless books offering advice to artists, architects, and surface pattern designers. Nonetheless, cultural definitions of harmony are as changeable as popular music. In a search for fresh and eye-catching images, designers in all fields invent new color combinations each year. The pink, gray, and black prized by designers in one year may seem passé in the next year. Furthermore, when the subject matter in a painting is disturbing, conventional harmony is inappropriate. In *Triptych* (2.43), Francis Bacon used an unusual combination of pinks, grays, blues, and black to produce a painting that is as disturbing as it is beautiful.

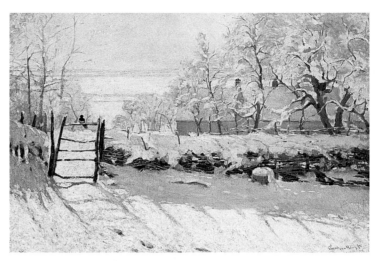

2.41   Claude Monet, *The Magpie*, 1869. Oil on canvas, 35 × 51 in. (89 × 130 cm).

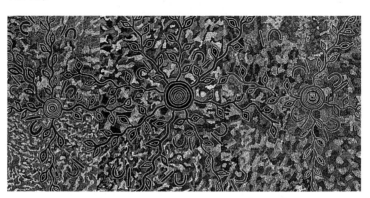

2.42   Cookie Stewart Japaljarri, Alma Nungarrayi Granites, and Robin Japanangka Granites; *Bush Cabbage Dreaming at Ngarlu;* Yuendumn, Central Australia, 1986. Acrylic on canvas, 47½ × 93½ in. (120.5 × 237.5 cm).

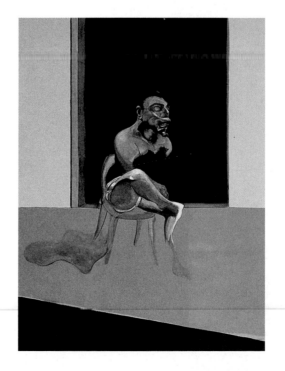

2.43   Francis Bacon, *Triptych,* 1972. Oil on canvas, one of 3 panels, each 78 × 58 in. (198.1 × 147.3 cm).

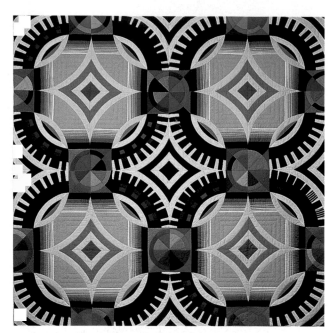

2.44 Nancy Crow, *Double Mexican Wedding Rings 1*, 1988. Hand quilted by Marie Moore. 72 × 72 in. (183 × 183 cm).

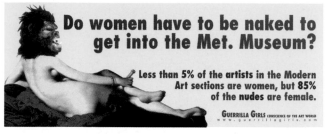

2.45 Guerrilla Girls, "Do women have to be naked to get into the Met. Museum? Less than 5% of the artists in the Modern Art sections are women, but 85% of the nudes are female," 1989. Poster, 11 × 28 in. (27.9 × 71.1 cm).

Color Distribution

Through careful distribution, even the most disharmonious colors can work beautifully. In Nancy Crow's *Double Mexican Wedding Rings 1* (2.44), radial symmetry, combined with a strong use of pattern, helps harmonize colors we would expect to clash. Creating such harmony between opposing visual forces adds vitality and gives the composition a distinctive look.

In Figure 2.45, the Guerrilla Girls used an intense yellow and glowing violet to heighten the impact of a black and white layout. Designed to call attention to the disparity in visibility between male and female artists, the poster had to be as powerful as possible. The violet words in the text offer a direct indictment of the exhibition policies of a major museum.

Weight and Balance

The effect of color on visual weight and balance is equally dramatic. In *Icarus* (2.46), by Henri Matisse,

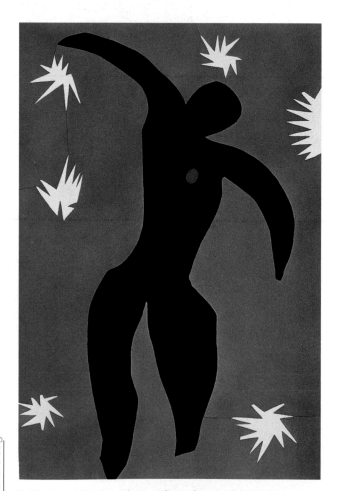

2.46 Henri Matisse, *Icarus,* from *Jazz* series, 1947. Gouache on paper, cut and pasted, 17⅛ × 13⅜ in. (43.6 × 34 cm).

2.47 Wolf Kahn, *Evening Meadow,* 1987. Oil on linen, 18 × 29 in. (46 × 74 cm).

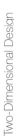

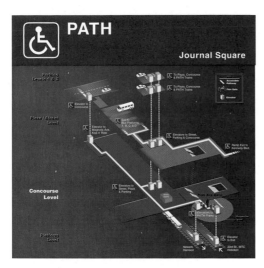

2.48 PATH Station Maps, Louis Nelson Associates, Inc., NY. Graphic designer: Jennifer Stoller.

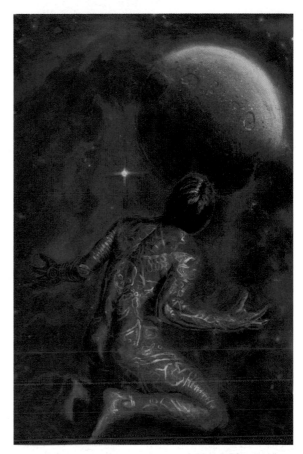

2.49 Joseph Spadaford, *Illustrated Man*, 1998. Acrylic and airbrush on illustration board.

the black shape of the body "falls" into the surrounding blue sea, while the scarlet heart continues to pull the figure upward, away from death. Through an astute use of color, Matisse eloquently retells the Greek myth of the boy who flew too close to the sun, melting his wax wings and plunging into the ocean. Likewise, in Wolf Kahn's *Evening Meadow* (2.47), the yellow-orange meadow burns with afternoon light, while the band of dark green trees and the cobalt sky suggest the weight of an impending night.

Emphasis/Focal Point

Color can also be used to highlight essential areas in a composition. The subway map in Figure 2.48 provides a good example. Cooler areas of gray, green, and blue, placed on a black background, provide basic structural information. The bright yellow lines show the path through the subway. Red, which is used at only one point in the diagram, clearly locates the viewer on the map.

Color Keys

A **color key,** or dominant color, can heighten psychological as well as compositional impact. The blues that dominate Joe Spadaford's *Illustrated Man* (2.49) suggest both the magic and mystery of the night. At the other extreme, in Egon Schiele's *Portrait of Paris von Gütersloh* (2.50), the flaming orange around and within the figure places the anxious man in an emotional electric chair.

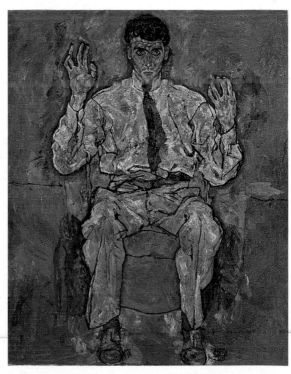

2.50 Egon Schiele, *Portrait of Paris von Gütersloh*, 1918. Oil on canvas, 55¼ × 43¼ in. (140.3 × 109.8 cm).

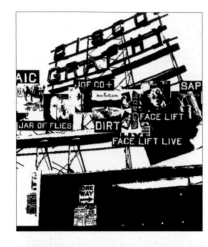

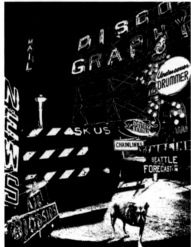

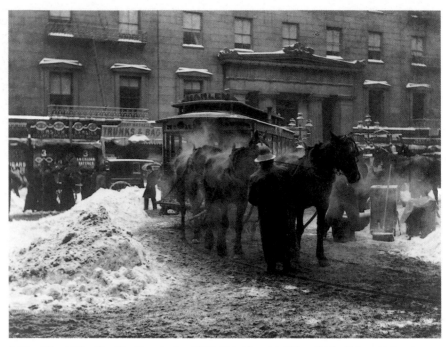

2.52 Alfred Stieglitz, *The Terminal,* **c.1892.** Chloride print, 3½ × 4½ in. (8.8 × 11.3 cm).

2.53 Keisei Eisen, *Oiran Parading in a Blue Dress,* **c. 1830.** Woodblock print, 29 × 9¾ in. (73.7 × 24.8 cm).

2.51 Alice in Chains, "Dog's Breath" Website. Sony Music Creative Services, Santa Monica, CA. Graphic Interface Designer: Mary Maurer.

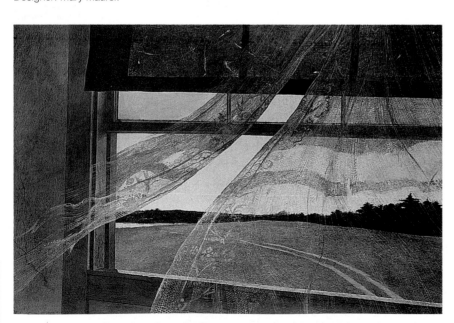

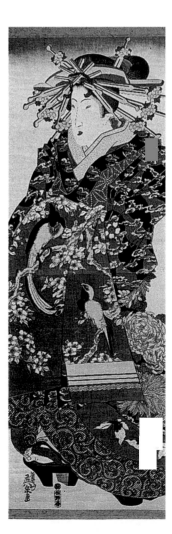

2.54 Andrew Wyeth, *Wind from the Sea,* **1947.** Tempera on masonite, 18½ × 27½ in. (47 × 69.9 cm).

Color and Communication

Contrast

Contrast, an inherent aspect of value, can heighten impact and shift meaning. A gritty, high-contrast photograph such as Figure 2.51 creates a very different world than does a delicate, low-contrast photograph such as Alfred Stieglitz's *The Terminal* (2.52). Japanese woodblock prints, such as Keisei Eisen's *Oiran Parading in a Blue Dress* (2.53), often combine the elegance of subtle color with the impact of contrast. Crisp shapes provide clarity, while color gradation adds grace.

Emotional Effects

Colors are never emotionally neutral. The subtle browns and greens in Andrew Wyeth's *Wind from the Sea* (2.54) suggest the sepia color of a nineteenth-century photograph and evoke the slow pace and serenity of a countryside at rest. Richard Diebenkorn's *Interior with Book* (2.55), painted only 12 years later, provides a very different interpretation of a similar interior/exterior scene. The yellows and oranges in the background push toward us, while the solid blocks of blue pull inward, flattening the image. The tension and power thus generated create a California landscape that is a world apart from Wyeth's New England. The color in Sandy Skoglund's *Radioactive Cats* (2.56) creates yet another interpretation of an interior space. The gray humans seem lifeless, while the lime-green cats glow with an inquisitive energy that may be toxic!

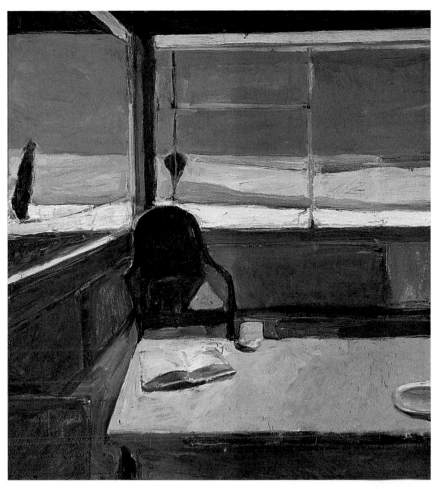

2.55   Richard Diebenkorn, *Interior with Book*, 1959. Oil on canvas, 70 × 64 in. (178 × 163 cm).

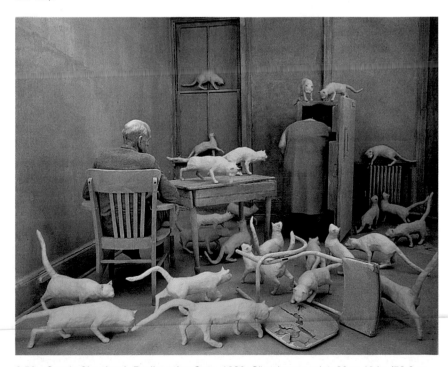

2.56   Sandy Skoglund, *Radioactive Cats*, 1980. Cibachrome print, 30 × 40 in. (76.2 × 101.6 cm).

Symbolic Color

Colors are often assigned symbolic meaning. These meanings may vary widely from culture to culture. In *The Primary Colors*, Alexander Theroux writes:

> [Blue] is the symbol of baby boys in America, mourning in Borneo, tribulation to the American Indian and the direction South in Tibet. Blue indicates mercy in the Kabbalah and carbon monoxide in gas canisters. Chinese emperors wore blue to worship the sky. To Egyptians it represented virtue, faith, and truth. The color was worn by slaves in Gaul. It was the color of the sixth level of the Temple of Nebuchadnezzar II, devoted to the planet Mercury. In Jerusalem a blue hand painted on a door gives protection . . . and in East Africa, blue beads represent fertility."[3]

In Hopi culture, colors symbolize spatial location and geographic direction. Butterfly Maiden, a benevolent spirit, is represented by the Kachina doll in Figure 2.57. Red represents a southerly direction, white the east or northeast, and blue or green the west. The polished black granite used for the Vietnam Veterans Memorial (2.58) is equally symbolic. The Vietnam War, with its 50,000 dead, was a black period in the life of America. From a distance, the memorial is a dark gash in the earth. Upon entering the site, the viewer confronts himself or herself through the mirrored effect of the polished wall. And, at sunrise, the wall can become golden as it reflects the morning light.

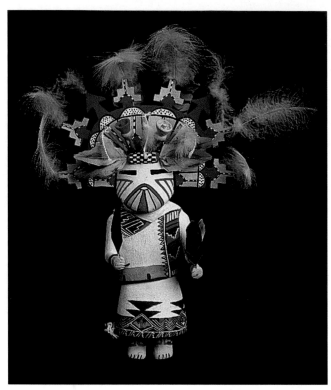

2.57 Butterfly Maiden, Hopi Kachina. Carved cottonwood, 13½ in. (35 cm).

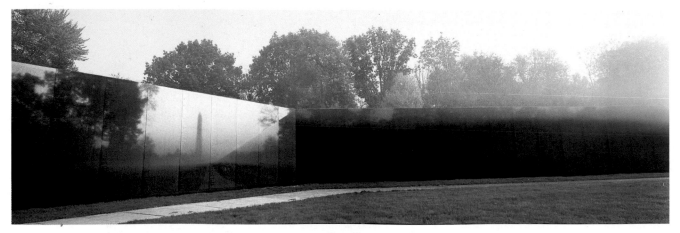

2.58 Maya Ying Lin, Vietnam Veterans Memorial, The Mall, Washington, D.C., 1981–83. Polished black granite.

Four self-portraits by Käthe Kollwitz demonstrate the unique power of each approach to color. A monochromatic drawing on a cream-colored paper (2.59) has a simple eloquence, while a more developed value drawing (2.60) provides solidarity and creates the illusion of space. Higher contrast (2.61) adds drama and dimensionality, while a full palette (2.62) creates a sense of immediacy and life.

Color, well used, is one of the most expressive elements of art and design.

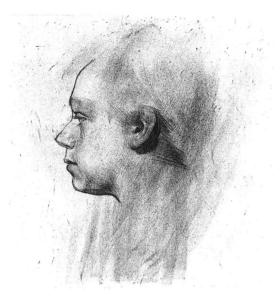

2.59 Käthe Kollwitz, *Self-Portrait in Profile, Facing Left, I*, 1889. Lithograph, 5⅞ × 5⅞ in. (15 × 15 cm).

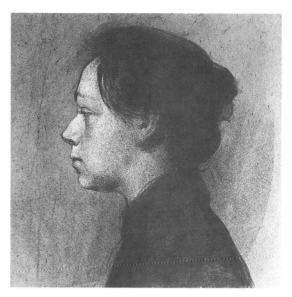

2.60 Käthe Kollwitz, Self-Portrait in Profile, Facing Left, II, 1889. Lithograph in two colors, 5⅞ × 5⅞ in. (15 × 15 cm).

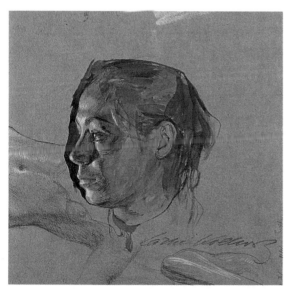

2.61 Käthe Kollwitz, *Selbstbildnis und Aktstudien (Self-portrait and Nude Studies)*, 1900. Pencil, dark gray ink wash, with white and yellowish highlights, on heavy brown paper, 11 × 17½ in. (27.8 × 44.5 cm).

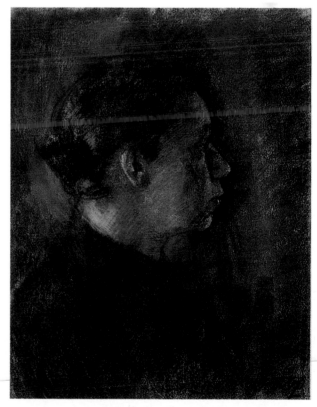

2.62 Käthe Kollwitz, *Selbstbildnis im Profil Nach Rechts*, c. 1900. Pastel on laid paper, 19 × 14⅜ in. (46.8 × 36.5 cm).

Profile:
Ann Baddeley Keister, Weaver

Color, Construction, and
Communication: Designing a Tapestry

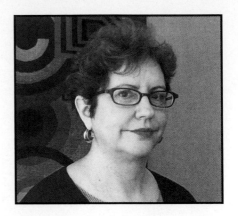

Ann Baddeley Keister is a nationally renowned fiber artist. She has a BFA and an MFA from the University of Kansas and received further training in Aubusson tapestry techniques from Jean Pierre Larochette at the San Francisco Tapestry Workshop. Her work has been exhibited both nationally and internationally and is in many private and corporate collections, including The Vanguard Group, The Discovery Channel, and the Indianapolis Museum of Art.

Keister is a professor of Foundations at Grand Valley State University. She maintains an active schedule of lectures and has taught many workshops both in tapestry and in the use of Adobe Illustrator as a design tool, including a session at the National Surface Design Conference in 1997 and for the Kentucky Crafts Foundation in 1998. Keister has received an Indiana Individual Artist Fellowship and an NEA Arts Midwest Fellowship. She has recently finished a large-scale tapestry, now installed in the new downtown campus for Grand Valley State University in Michigan.

MS: When I look at your work, I am impressed by the very deliberate use of design in your complex, narrative tapestries. These images could be painted or done on a computer so much more quickly. What is the advantage of weaving? What attracted you to fiber arts?

AK: My undergraduate degree actually was a general degree in design, which allowed me to explore a number of different craft and fine art media, including textiles. The University of Kansas has a great fiber facility, and since I had learned how to knit and sew at the age of seven, the materials of textile art just felt natural and familiar to me. I love making the structure through the repetitive action of weaving. And, I'm attracted to the pliability of the material. For me, metals are too unforgiving, clay is too messy—fiber, as a material, just feels "right" to me. I feel that there is a strong symbiosis between the images that I am interested in making and the material from which those images are constructed. One seems to feed off the other.

MS: Designer Paul Rand said, "Art is an idea that has found its perfect form. Design is the means by which this is realized." And, it is often said that art is about expression, while design is about communication. Is your work both art and design?

AK: Yes, and it is also craft and decoration. Contemporary fiber arts is such a diverse field. I love pure pattern

and I love storytelling. I love looking at beautiful colors and want to offer the viewer a visual feast through my work!

MS: What is your usual work process?

AK: Many of my projects begin with a commission. I determine the client's requirements, then puzzle over possible solutions. With *Memory,* during a walk along the Grand River, I saw an historical marker describing a late-nineteenth-century flood. I began to think about this terrible storm that washed away bridges and created piles of logs careening through the city. I immediately realized that this event could provide my image.

Next, I made a number of pencil sketches, which were developed further on the computer. I have an extensive knowledge of color theory, and this actually gives me the freedom to choose my colors very intuitively. I am using a lot of blue in this piece, since it is one of the school's colors, and I have a lot of discordant colors, which seem appropriate for such a devastating event.

A full-size, 6 × 10 ft computer print comes next. I match colors from my collection of approximately 200 colors of wool yarns. One strand on the loom is made up of six strands of yarn. I use a lot of optical mixing to create very subtle gradations. Finally, I weave the piece. The most useful thing I learned from my teachers is this: DO YOUR WORK! There is no substitute for action. Weaving is slow and simply has to be done consistently. During my summer work time, I am in the studio from about 9 in the morning to 6 in the evening, an average of five or six days a week. Since weaving is an activity that makes demands on the body and the concentration, I do take breaks in my daily work with forays into the garden or other household chores. This is one reason that I find working at home so satisfying. My domestic interests in cooking, the garden, and my home often find their way into my imagery as well.

MS: What are your criteria for excellence?
AK: I seek unity between concept and composition. Each of the formal elements—line, shape, texture, and color—

is essential. There is almost always a dynamic sense of space in my work, which makes the tapestry read well in an architectural setting. I seek an inseparable connection between imagery, technique, and material.

MS: Do you have any advice for my students?
AK: Take the time to be inventive. Try out many possibilities. If you don't like an image, don't do it! Invent another way to solve the problem. The joy you bring to the creative process will be apparent in the final design.

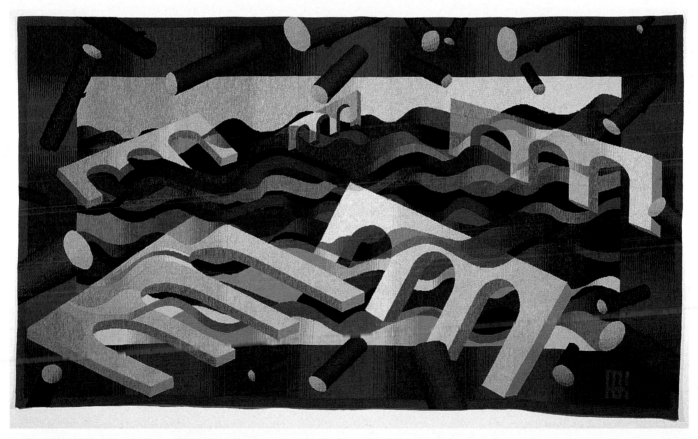

Ann Baddeley Keister, *Memory*, 2000. Wool tapestry, 6 × 10 ft (1.83 × 3.1 m).

Summary

- Color immediately attracts attention. Its emotional and physiological impact can heighten communication.

- Red, green, and blue are the additive color primaries. Cyan blue, magenta red, and yellow are the subtractive color primaries.

- The four basic qualities of color are hue (the name of the color), value (its lightness or darkness), intensity (its purity), and temperature (warmth).

- Major color systems include monochromatic, analogous, complementary, split complementary, and triadic.

- The level of color harmony must match the expressive intent. Disharmony is often more expressive than harmony.

- Color can expand a shape, shift compositional weight, create a focal point, or heighten emotion.

Keywords

accent color	hue	split complementary
additive color	intensity	subtractive color
afterimage	monochromatic	symbolic color
analogous color	opponent theory	temperature
chroma	primary color	tertiary color
chromatic gray	saturation	tint
color harmony	secondary color	tone
color key	shade	triadic
complementary	simultaneous	value
color	contrast	
contrast		

1. What is the advantage of a limited color palette? What is the advantage of a broad color palette? Which will better serve your needs in a specific design?

2. When a limited palette is used, how can a few colors create the greatest impact? When a broad palette is chosen, what strategies can be used to create unity?

3. What is the advantage of transparent colors? What is the advantage of opaque colors?

4. What can gradation contribute to your design?

5. To what extent should traditional harmony be used? When is disharmony more appropriate?

6. Try exaggerating your distribution of colors; unconventional proportions can result in distinctive design.

Josef Albers, *Interaction of Color*. New Haven, CT, Yale University Press, 1963.

Frans Gerritsen, *Theory and Practice of Color*. New York, Van Nostrand Reinhold, 1975.

Johannes Itten, *The Art of Color*. New York, Van Nostrand Reinhold, 1974.

Harald Kuppers, *Color: Origin, Systems, Uses*. New York, Van Nostrand Reinhold, 1972.

Harold Linton, *Color Model Environments*. New York, Van Nostrand Reinhold, 1985.

Albert Munsell, *A Color Notation*. Munsell Color, 1981.

Richard B. Norman, *Electronic Color*. New York, Van Nostrand Reinhold, 1990.

John F. Pile, *Interior Design*. New York, Harry N. Abrams, 1988.

chapter three

Two-Dimensional Design: Organization

Imagine yourself practicing jumpshots on a deserted basketball court. By focusing all your attention on the basket, you can master the sequence of moves needed to score. Next, imagine yourself playing in a high-paced game, surrounded by skillful and cooperative teammates. The skills you practiced alone become heightened as you take passes and make shots in an actual game. The complexities increase and the stakes rise when players fill the court.

Developing a complex design can be equally exhilarating. Just as a boundary line defines the basketball court, so the outer edge of a composition defines the design, creating the playing field for a visual game. When the parts of the puzzle are multiplied, we can create more complex forms of balance, increase the illusion of space, and explore the implications of movement. Opposing forces generate energy. When one element becomes dominant, other elements must become subordinate. The opportunities for visual invention are endless.

Pay attention. This chapter completes the first stage of the rocket we are using to launch the imagination. As a result, there is a *lot* of information here. Four fundamental principles of composition are presented in the first section, followed by an extended discussion of the illusion of space and the illusion of movement. Finally, profiles of graphic designer Ken Botnick and painter Ken Stout demonstrate uses of composition for very different purposes.

Basic Composition

Composition may be defined as "the combination of multiple parts into a harmonious whole." Two-dimensional compositions are constructed using line, shape, texture, color, and value. Even the most elusive idea can be expressed eloquently when the visual components fit together just right. Teamwork is essential. As with a basketball team, the individual parts of any compositional puzzle are less important than the composition as a whole.

Unity and Variety

Unity and variety are the cornerstones of visual communication. **Unity** may be defined as oneness, togetherness, or cohesion. The main purpose of composition is to create unity. In a well-composed design, lines, shapes, textures, value, and color are combined to express an idea or emotion. **Variety** may be defined as difference. Even the slightest difference can add both visual and conceptual interest to a design. For example, the single red umbrella in Figure 3.1 breaks the pattern set by the 18 surrounding white umbrellas. The resulting focal point attracts the viewer's attention and adds individuality to the composition.

Finding the right balance between unity and variety is always a challenge. Excessive unity can be monotonous while excessive variety can be chaotic. Furthermore, the right solution to one compositional problem may be the wrong solution to another. In Vija Celmins' *Untitled (Ocean)* (3.2), an extremely unified drawing of waves creates a quiet, contemplative image. On the other hand, Hannah Höch's *Cut with a Kitchen Knife* (3.3) is crowded with conflicting images and fragmentary words. Created shortly after the end

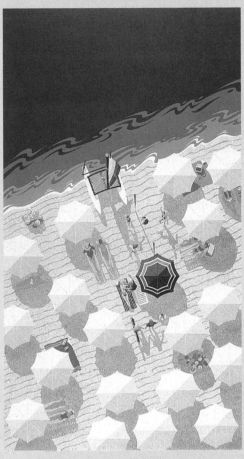

3.1 Mark Riedy, *Day at the Beach*, 1988. Acrylic airbrush.

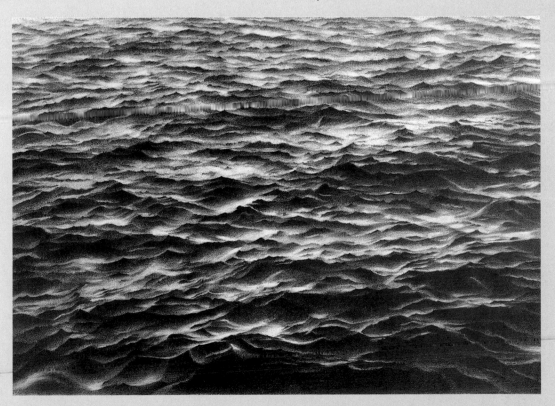

3.2 Vija Celmins, *Untitled (Ocean)*, **1969.** Graphite on acrylic ground on paper, 14 × 18 in. (35.6 × 45.7 cm).

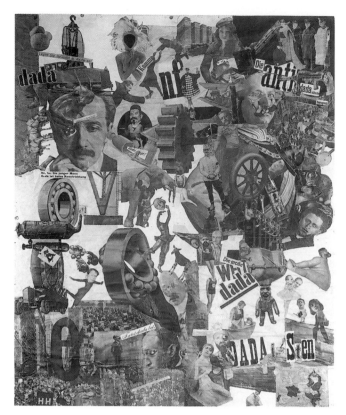

3.3 Hannah Höch, *Cut with a Kitchen Knife,* **1919.** Collage, 44⅞ × 35½ in. (114 × 90 cm).

of World War I, this collage reflects the tumultuous economic and political conditions in postwar Germany. Military leaders are juxtaposed with images of exotic dancers. Albert Einstein appears in the upper left corner, and fragments of machinery suggest the increasing importance of technology. Here, the artist used a variety of images to express impending chaos.

Creating Unity: An Introduction to Gestalt

Gestalt psychology emphasizes the importance of unity, connection, and completion. Indeed, "whole" is an appropriate English translation of this German word. According to this theory, visual information is understood holistically before it is examined separately. Furthermore, the mind can absorb only a limited number of disparate units within an image. An image composed of units that are unrelated in size, style, orientation, and color will appear incomplete and unresolved.

To achieve unity, the designer creates deliberate relationships among disparate visual elements. Six aspects of unity are discussed in the sections that follow.

Containment

Relationships automatically occur when visual elements share a common container. The outer edge of the design provides this container and helps to define the negative space around each positive shape. As shown in Figure 3.4, just by adding a boundary we can create a series of simple compositions from a random collection of shapes. Any shift in the location of this boundary creates a new set of relationships. A vertical rectangle is often used when a rising or sinking movement is needed, while a horizontal format can provide a panoramic space.

Proximity

Let's begin by placing three shapes and one line inside a rectangular format. The distance between visual elements is called **proximity.** As shown in Figure 3.5, shapes or volumes placed close together are easily unified, while more distant shapes or volumes read as separate units. **Fusion**

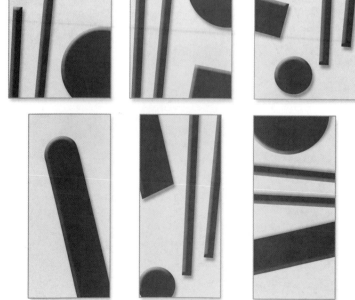

3.4

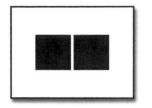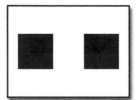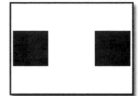

3.5 Variations in proximity.

occurs when shapes or volumes are placed so close together that they share common edges (3.6A). When shapes of similar color and texture fuse, new shapes can be created as the ground area or negative space becomes clearly defined (3.6B). Through gradation or transparency, these same figure/ground boundaries can be dissolved, fusing positive and negative shapes (3.6C, 3.6D).

Proximity dramatically influences every aspect of design. Through proximity, diverse visual elements can become connected. A large yellow square connects eight small rectangles in Nancy Graves' *Rheo* (3.7A). When this visual anchor is removed, the smaller shapes float aimlessly (3.7B).

Collagists often use proximity to create conceptual as well as compositional connections. Close proximity can increase compositional energy. In

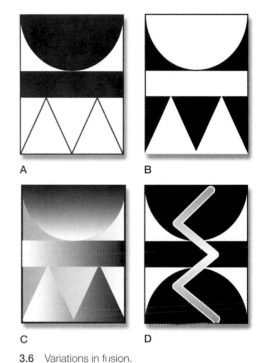

A   B

C   D

3.6 Variations in fusion.

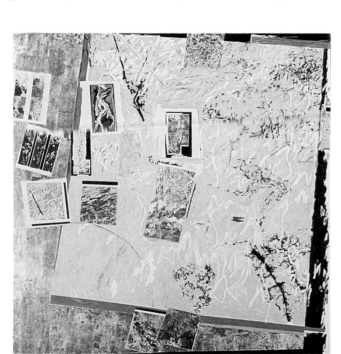

3.7A Nancy Graves, *Rheo*, 1975. Acrylic, oil, gold leaf on Masonite, 64 × 64 in. (102.5 × 162.5 cm).

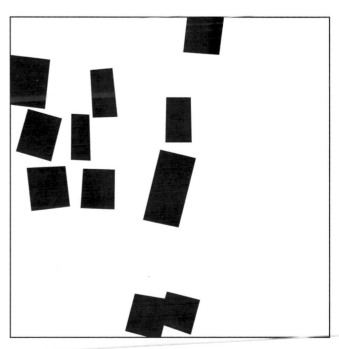

3.7B Removal of the yellow shape decreases compositional unity.

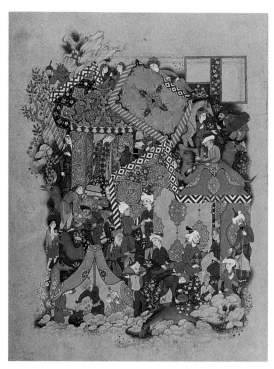

3.8 Miniature attributed to Shaykh Muhammad, *Majnun Eaves-drops on Layla's Camp,* from *Jami Haft Aurang,* Mashhad, Iran?

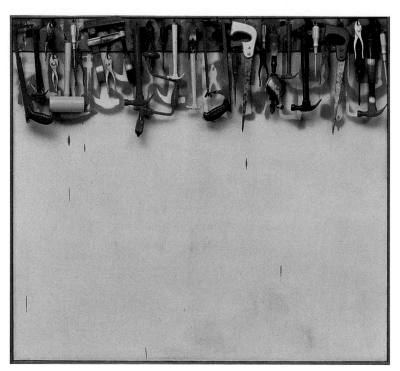

3.9 Jim Dine, *Five Feet of Colorful Tools,* 1962. Oil on unprimed canvas surmounted by a board on which thirty-two painted tools hang from hooks; overall 55⅝ × 60¼ × 4⅜ in. (141.2 × 152.9 × 11 cm).

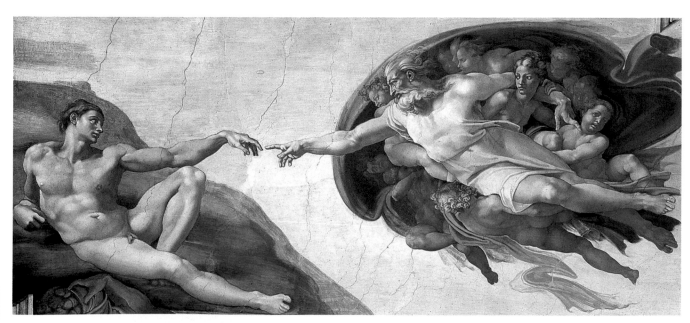

3.10 Michelangelo, *Creation of Adam* (after cleaning, 1989), c. 1510. Sistine Chapel, Rome.

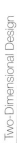

Figure 3.8, by Shaykh Muhammad, 28 humans, five animals, three tents, and four carpets fill a single book page. The painting just bustles with activity. At the other extreme, the large open space in Jim Dine's sculptural painting (3.9) adds a dangerous quality to a collection of ordinary tools. Suspended above this void, the sharp tools seems ready to fall at any moment.

Michelangelo's *Creation of Adam* (3.10) clearly demonstrates the expressive power of proximity. Jehovah's hand, on the right, nearly touches Adam's hand, on the left. Less than four inches of space separate the two. In this cosmology, all of human history begins when the spark of life jumps this gap. If the hands had been placed too far apart or too close together, the spark that animates both the man and the painting would have been lost.

Continuity

Continuity creates a fluid connection among compositional parts. In Frank Stella's *Lac Laronge IV* (3.11), the curving lines and shapes flow from one circle to the next, creating a sense of movement. Continuation by eye direction is shown in Figure 3.12. The woman on the left looks right; the woman on the right looks left. Both faces are cut off, or **cropped,** by the border. Our eyes move between the women, keeping our attention focused on the advertisement and on the jewelry being sold.

Similarity

Any similarity in a design tends to increase unity. In Aaron Macsai's *Panels of Movement* (3.13), similar lines, shapes, textures, and colors, were used in each of the 10 panels from which the bracelet was constructed.

Visual Systems

An underlying pattern or grid can be used to create connections among even the most

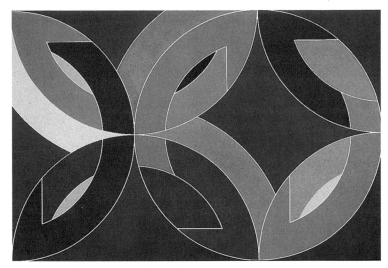

3.11 Frank Stella, *Lac Laronge IV,* 1969. Acrylic polymer on canvas, 9 ft ⅛ in. × 13 ft 6 in. (2.75 × 3.11 m).

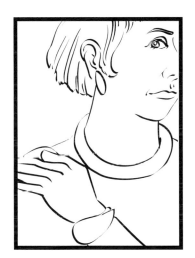

3.12 Example of cropping and continuity.

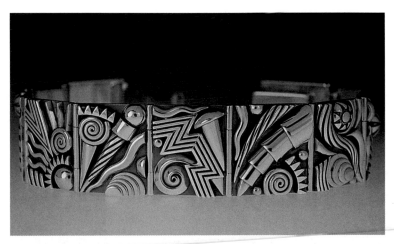

3.13 Aaron Macsai, *Panels of Movement.* Bracelet, 18K gold, sterling, copper, ⅞ × 7 in. (2 × 18 cm).

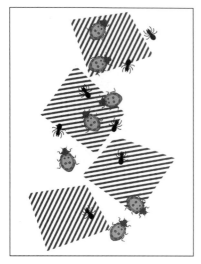

3.14 Example of unifying pattern. Four patterned shapes give structure to a random collection of shapes.

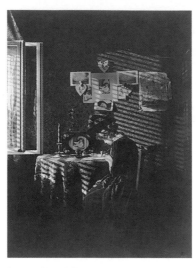

3.15 Alfred Stieglitz, *Paula*, Berlin, **1889.** Contact print on azo, dry plate, 8⅞ × 6½ in. (22.5 × 16.5 cm).

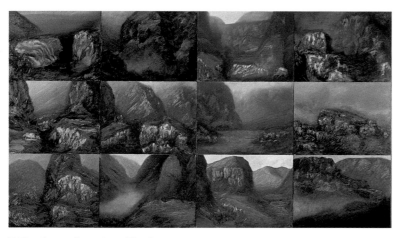

3.16 James Lavadour, *The Seven Valleys and the Five Valleys*, **1988.** Oil on canvas, 54 × 96 in. (137 × 244 cm).

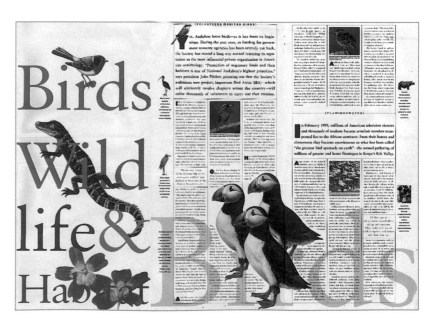

3.17 Pentagram Design, NYC, **National Audubon Society 1995 Annual Report.** Page showing three puffins and the words: Birds, Wild life & Habitat.

disparate visual elements. In Figure 3.14, a crisp pattern of diagonal lines has been used to unify a variety of separate shapes. If this pattern were removed, the composition would become unstable. By using the unifying pattern, the designer was able to create a lively, informal layout while retaining a feeling of unity. In *Paula* (3.15), Alfred Stieglitz used a dominant light source to produce a similar effect. The woman writing a letter is surrounded by various objects on the table and pictures on the wall. The pattern of diagonal lines unifies the various parts of the image and contributes to the contemplative mood.

A grid can provide both proximity and pattern. For example, the three horizontal lines and four vertical lines in Lavadour's *The Seven Valleys and the Five Valleys* (3.16) create a clear structure with each of the 12 landscapes in perfect proximity. Even when the grid is fairly loosely constructed, as with the 1995 Audubon Society Annual Report (3.17), the recurrent vertical and horizontal divisions help increase unity.

Closure

Given enough clues, the human mind will automatically connect visual fragments.

Closure, as this action is called, is an especially powerful force in visual communication. We can mentally connect four lines to create a square (3.18). Thousands of letters can be connected to form a face (3.19). Skillfully chosen, a few clues can be used to convey a complex message. In Figure 3.20, closure helps us read the disordered words at the top of the design and then helps us connect these words to the doll's face in the image below. The text provides us with the title of the play; the image provides us with the emotion.

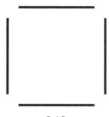

3.18

Closure makes it possible to communicate using implication. Freed of the necessity to provide every detail, the artist can convey an idea by using suggestion, rather than description. When the viewer completes the image in his or her mind, it is often more memorable than a more explicit image. Experienced filmmakers use implication with particular care. By suggesting rather than showing the witch, directors Eduardo Sanchez and Daniel Myrick substantially heightened the feeling of terror in *The Blair Witch Project.*

Weight and Gravity

Visual weight refers to the inclination of shapes to float or sink based on their solidity and compositional location. Solid shapes generally weigh more than open shapes. Shapes that appear to extend beyond the upper edge of the format tend to rise, while shapes that appear to extend below the format tend to sink.

The vertical, horizontal, or diagonal orientation of a line or shape also affects visual weight. Try this simple experiment. Which is the most dynamic and which is the most static position for the box in Figure 3.21? Most viewers find positions A and B the most **static,** or stable. The box stands still, with the vertical and horizontal edges reconfirming the stability we experience when objects are at rest in the real world. In contrast, position C and especially position D place the box in a **dynamic** position, caught halfway between standing and falling.

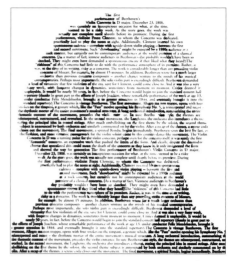

3.19   Because of closure, hundreds of separate shapes can be combined to create a face.

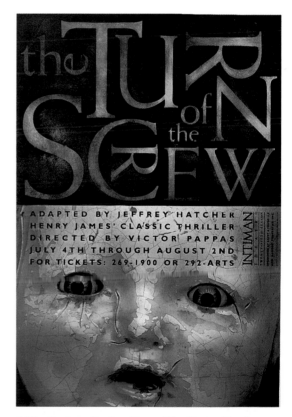

3.20   Cyclone Design, *Turn of the Screw.* Theater poster.

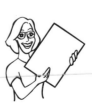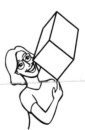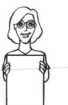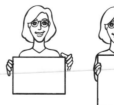

3.21   Which box is the most static? Which is the most dynamic?

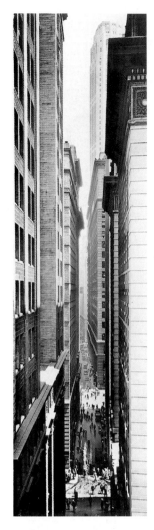

3.22 Bernice Abbott, *Exchange Place*, New York, 1934. Photograph.

3.23 Tetsurō Sawada, *Brilliant Scape (Blue)*,1985. Silkscreen, 22⅞ × 15¾ in. (58 × 40 cm).

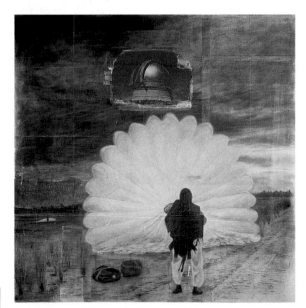

3.24 Vernon Fisher, *Objects in a Field*, 1986. Acrylic on canvas, 8 × 8 ft (2.4 × 2.4 m).

Bernice Abbott's photograph of New York skyscrapers (3.22) demonstrates the power of orientation. Using dramatic vertical shapes within a tall vertical format, she captured the soaring energy of Wall Street within a small image.

Even the most abstract design is governed by gravity. In Figure 3.23, a rectangle filled with horizontal lines suggests the stability and tranquility of a landscape. Image stability would increase even more if the format were positioned horizontally. Instead, by using a vertical orientation and devoting the upper half to a gradated blue shape, Tetsurō Sawada has combined the serenity of a landscape with the expansive feel of the soaring sky.

Visual weight can also refer to the relative importance of a visual element within a design. In Vernon Fisher's *Objects in a Field* (3.24), the image of the astronomical observatory has great visual weight despite its small size. Centrally located in the upper half of the painting, it commands our attention while creating a connection to the parachutist in the foreground.

In *Moonrise, Hernandez, New Mexico, 1941* (3.25) Ansel Adams combined balance, gravity, and movement to create an image that is both tranquil and dramatic. The squarish format, dominated by horizontal lines, provides stability. The quiet village sinks to the bottom of the photograph. The moon, positioned just to the right of compositional center, pulls us into the velvety black sky at the top half of the composition. An equilibrium in visual forces creates a magical image.

Balance

A variety of visual elements can work cooperatively within a balanced design. As with physical balance, visual **balance** requires equilibrium, or equality in size, weight, or force among design elements. Unlike physical balance, however, visual balance can be created through absence as well as presence. For example, in *Moonrise, Hernandez, New Mexico, 1941,* the crowded village filling the bottom half of the composition is easily balanced by the open sky above.

Symmetrical Balance

Designers generally use various forms of symmetry and asymmetry to create balance. Let's start by dividing the format down the center. In strict **symmetrical balance,** shapes or volumes are mirrored on either side of this vertical axis (3.26A). A shift in this axis (3.26B) creates symmetry between the top and bottom of the design. Symmetrically balanced images can be harmonious, evocative, or confrontational, depending on the subject matter and compositional context. In Figure 3.27, symmetrical balance brings grace and serenity to the Taj Mahal, while in Figure 3.28, symmetrical balance creates a confrontation.

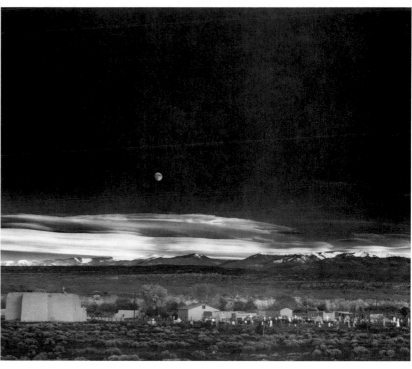

3.25 Ansel Adams, *Moonrise, Hernandez, New Mexico, 1941.* Photograph.

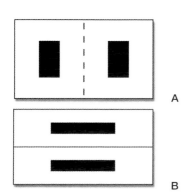

3.26 Examples of symmetrical balance.

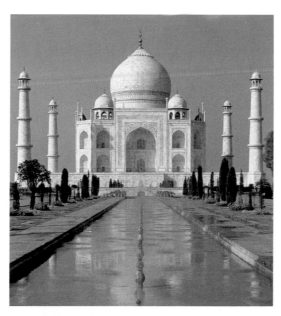

3.27 Taj Mahal, Agra, India.

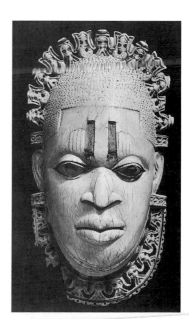

3.28 Nigerian Belt Mask, 16th century. Ivory, 9⅜ in. (23.8 cm).

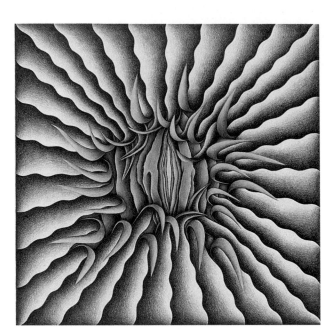

3.30 Judy Chicago, *Rejection Quintet: Female Rejection Drawing*, **1974.** Prismacolor and graphite on rag / board, 39⅝ × 29⅝ in. (101 × 75 cm).

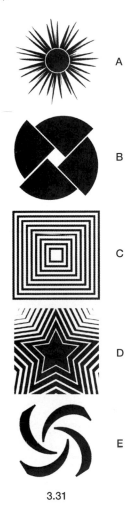

3.31

Radial Symmetry

Now divide the format horizontally as well as vertically. With **radial symmetry,** lines and shapes are mirrored both vertically and horizontally, with the center of the composition acting as a focal point (3.29). An

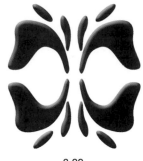

3.29

expanded approach to radial symmetry is shown in Judy Chicago's *Rejection Quintet: Female Rejection Drawing* (3.30). Because the format is now divided diagonally as well as vertically and horizontally, the entire design radiates from the center.

Within a square or circular format, radial symmetry is often used to generate four types of dynamic balance:

- **Centrifugal balance** occurs when the visual forces expand outward (3.31A).

- **Centripetal balance** occurs when the visual forces move inward, suggesting a compression of space. Figure 3.31B whirls inward, propelled by four spiraling extensions to the circle, while Figure 3.31C pulls inward on a more direct path.

- **Concentric balance** occurs when the boundary is repeated in diminishing size to create a bull's-eye effect (3.31D). Used skillfully, concentric balance can harness both the expanding energy of centrifugal balance and the compressive energy of centripetal balance. This star pulls us inward while simultaneously pushing outward.

A final variant on radial balance is the spiral (3.31E). A spiral can heighten energy in a circular format or generate movement within a rectilinear format. In Rubens' *Tiger Hunt* (3.32 A), the compositional spiral twists inward and breaks apart, creating a painting that swirls with energy. The compositional drawing in Figure 3.32B demonstrate this effect.

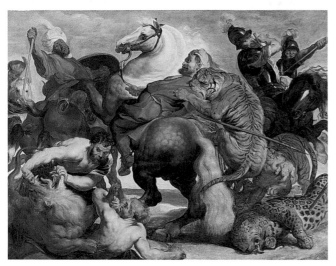

3.32A Workshop of Peter Paul Rubens, *Tiger Hunt,* c. 1616. Oil on canvas, 38⅞ × 49¼ in. (98.8 × 125 cm).

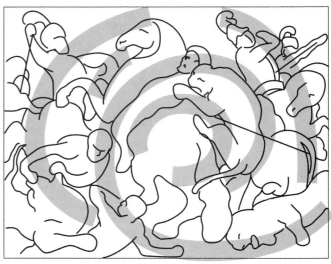

3.32B Diagram of compositional forces.

Asymmetrical Balance

Asymmetrical balance creates equilibrium between visual elements that differ in size, number, weight, color, or texture. Depending on the degree of difference and the overall organization, the resulting design may be stable, dynamic, or nearly chaotic. Asymmetrical balance generates a lot of energy and is often used for eye-catching posters that must aggressively compete for viewer attention.

Many strategies can be used to create asymmetrical balance.

- A large shape is placed close to the fulcrum, while a small shape is placed further away. Just as a child at the end of a seesaw can balance an adult near the center, so large and small shapes can be balanced in a design (3.33A).

- Multiple small squares, acting together, can balance a large square (3.33B).

- A small, solid square can balance a large, open circle. The solidity and stability of the square give it additional weight (3.33C).

- A textured shape placed near the fulcrum can be balanced by a distant open shape (3.33D).

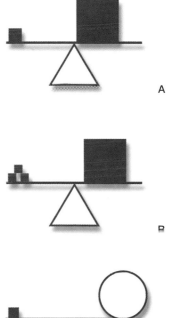

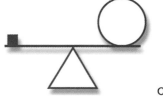

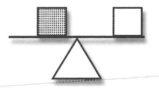

3.33

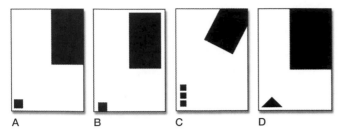

3.34 Examples of asymmetrical balance.

Asymmetrical balance becomes even more interesting when the format is added. Because the negative space (or ground) is just as important as each positive shape, more complex compositions can now be created.

- A small shape placed near the bottom of the format balances a large shape placed along the top. Especially within a tall rectangle, shapes placed near the top tend to rise while shapes placed near the bottom tend to sink (3.34A).

- When the small square intersects the bottom edge and the large square moves away from the edge, the differences in weight become even more pronounced (3.34B).

- Here the top shape gains energy through its diagonal orientation. Three bottom shapes are now needed to create balance (3.34C).

- Finally, a small, aggressive shape can balance a large, passive shape (3.34D).

Balance in a composition shifts each time a visual element is added or subtracted. A complex network of negative and positive lines and shapes creates the balance in Mondrian's *Composition with Blue and Yellow* (3.35). The large yellow square positioned along the top edge is easily balanced by the small blue rectangle that sinks to the bottom. In Frank Miller's digital design (3.36), a horizontal line extends from left to right in descending steps.

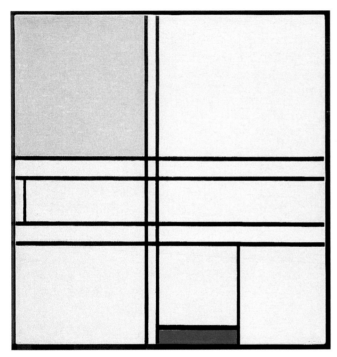

3.35 Piet Mondrian, *Composition with Blue and Yellow*, 1935. Oil on canvas, 28¾ × 27¼ in. (73 × 69.2 cm).

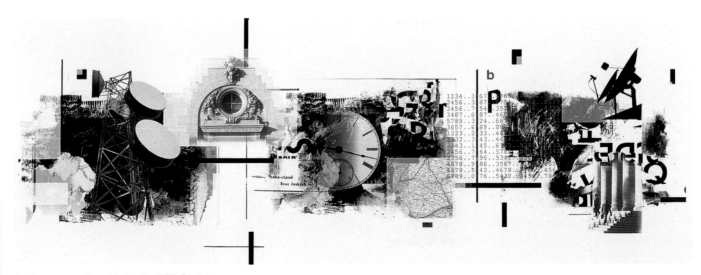

3.36 Frank Miller, *Untitled*, 1997. Digital image.

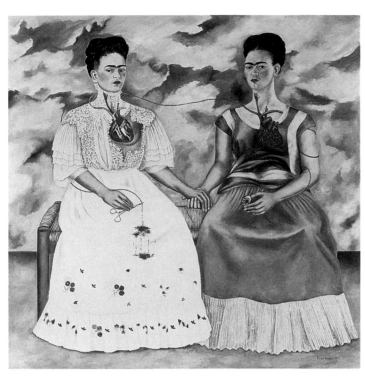

3.37 Frida Kahlo, *Las Dos Fridas*, 1939. Oil on canvas, 69⅕ × 69⅕ in. (176 × 176 cm).

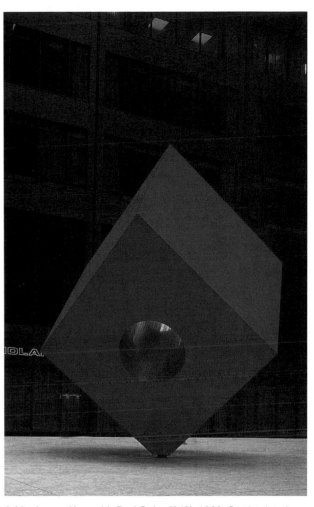

3.38 Isamu Noguchi, *Red Cube (648)*, 1969. Steel painted red, height 28 ft (8.53 m).

Four broken vertical lines divide the design into three major sections. Within these sections, the curving satellite dishes, clock, and letters add both unity and variety.

Each type of balance has its advantages. The symmetrical balance Frida Kahlo used for her double self-portrait (3.37) is symbolically appropriate and compositionally stable. Painted in response to her divorce from painter Diego Rivera, it presents the beloved Frida in a native costume on the right and the rejected Frida in European dress on the left. A linear vein connects the women's hearts. On the other hand, in Figure 3.38 asymmetrical balance is used to accentuate the dynamic orientation of Isamu Noguchi's *Red Cube*. This photographic composition is as dynamic as the cube itself. When the type of balance used is appropriate to the content of the artwork, both expression and communication increase.

Scale and Proportion

Proportion refers to the relative size of visual elements *within* an image. When we compare the width of the head to its height, we are establishing a proportional relationship (3.39). **Scale** refers to

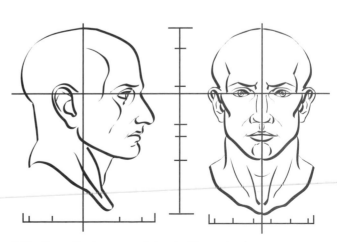

3.39 Proportion is an essential part of figure drawing.

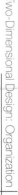

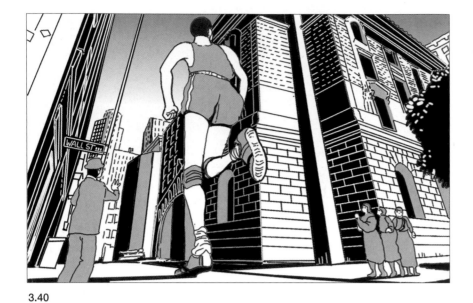

3.40

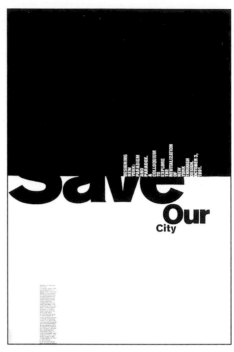

3.41 Michael Bierut, *Save Our City.* Design Firm: Pentagram, NYC.

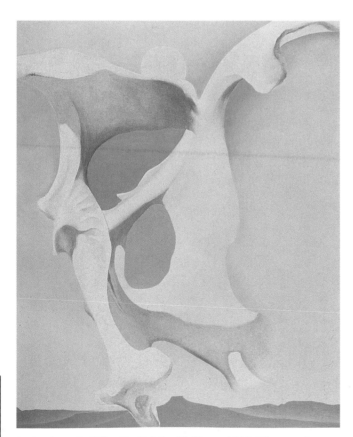

3.42 Georgia O'Keeffe, *Pelvis with Moon,* 1943. Oil on canvas, 30 × 24 in. (76.2 × 61 cm).

the size of an image or object when compared to our own human size. Compared to the awestruck pedestrians, the large-scale athletes running through the city in Figure 3.40 seem to possess superhuman strength.

Most designs distribute information quite evenly within the format, with only modest size variation among the parts. Exaggerating these proportions can be eye-catching because the image immediately stands out from the norm. When this visual impact is matched to the message conveyed, the results can be memorable. In *Save Our City* by Michael Bierut (3.41), the large black rectangle at the top presses down on the white shape below, covering the top part of the word "Save." Meanwhile, the vertical white text suggests a city skyline and helps pull the white half of the poster upward. This tension between the upper and lower sections of the design perfectly matches the urgency of the message.

When the scale of images and objects is exaggerated, a number of expressive possibilities occurs. In *Pelvis with Moon* (3.42), Georgia O'Keeffe held a bone up to the sky, trapping patches of blue within the voids while expanding the bone to a cosmic scale. *Intermission* (3.43), a 50-foot-long painting for the Walton Arts Center, presented various challenges to painter Ken Stout. The physical size of

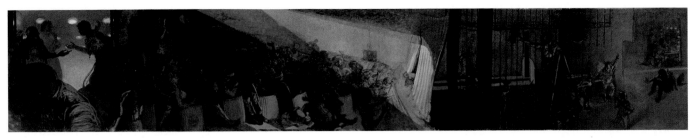

3.43 Ken Stout, *Intermission*, 1994. Oil on canvas, 9 × 50 ft (2.74 × 15.24 m). Also see enlargement, page 3-39.

the painting had to become an asset, rather than a liability. To this end, Stout created a swirling panorama of figures engaged in a wide variety of activities, onstage, backstage, and in the audience. Two men in the balcony further contribute to the action, as one aims a peashooter and another launches a paper airplane. This large-scale painting creates a panorama of action both on and off the stage.

Emphasis

Emphasis is used to give part of a design particular prominence. Emphasis is often used to attract attention. Because the viewer must first stop and *look* at the painting, poster, or photograph if communication is to occur, emphasizing the most important aspect of a design is crucial. A tour of three Websites provides examples of compositional clarity, compositional confusion, and compositional complexity, all due to emphasis.

The GTS Companies Website (3.44) is a model of simplicity, clarity and restraint. Information is sized and organized according to its significance. The company name is prominently displayed, followed by a description of services provided. By clicking on three simple boxes, viewers can get detailed information on major divisions in the company and additional links are provided in a column on the left. An update on company activities appears in an open box when the visitor enters the site. The blues that dominate the design provide unity, while a single red header is used for emphasis.

By contrast, the Website shown in Figure 3.45 is overloaded with competing information, beginning with the banner ads at the top of the screen. Multiple typestyles, colors, buttons, and layers of information all compete for attention. There are no supporting actors in this play; each visual element is accorded star status, regardless of importance.

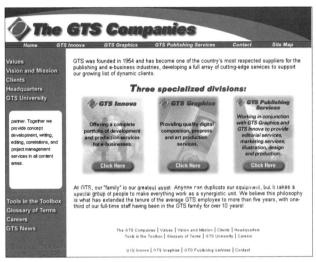

3.44 GTS Companies Website.

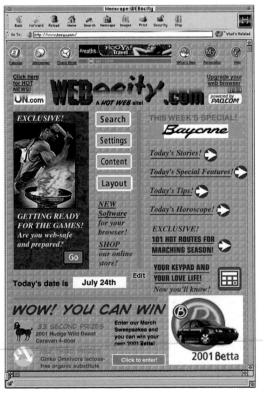

3.45 An example of bad Website design.

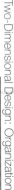

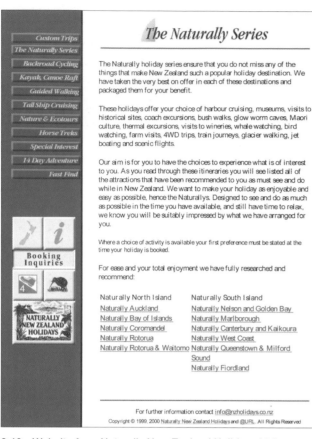

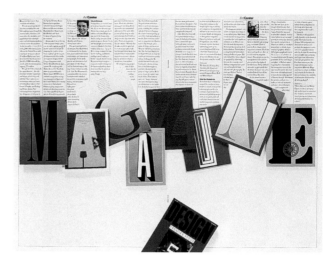

3.47 **Pentagram Design, Magazine.** Publisher: Art Center College of Design, Pasadena, CA.

3.46 Website from Naturally New Zealand Holidays Ltd.

The 1998 Naturally New Zealand Website (3.46) is an example of compositional complexity. All the colors, images, and typestyles used reflect the upscale adventure touring promoted by the company. The green band on the left provides a menu of links, so that the visitor can easily proceed to any interesting section. Graphic buttons provide immediate links to a map of New Zealand, general information, and booking inquiries. Further specific topics of interest are listed by location. Using simple animation, the boot button moves from a horizontal position to a diagonal position to indicate trip difficulty as the climb becomes steeper. The entire site provides easy access to information, even for a novice Web surfer.

Separation and Connection

Any **anomaly,** or break from the norm, tends to stand out. Because we seek to connect and unify any verbal or visual information we are given, a mismatched shape immediately attracts attention. In Figure 3.47, the word "design" is emphasized through its separation from the word "magazine." By breaking the bottom edge, this shape gains even more power. Jennifer Bartlett's *Yellow and Black Boats* (3.48) creates an even stronger separation between various parts in a composition. Two boats have completely escaped the painting and entered the physical world.

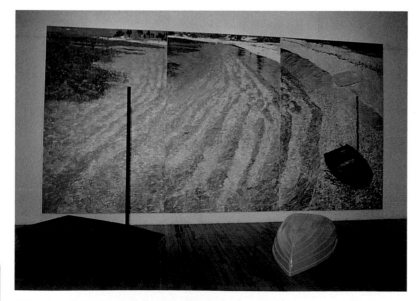

3.48 Jennifer Bartlett, *Yellow and Black Boats,* **1985.** Oil on three canvases, each 10 ft × 6 ft 6 in (3 × 2 m). Yellow boat: Wood and enamel paint, 14 × 60½ × 31 in. (35.6 × 153.7 × 78.7 cm). Black boat: Wood and flat oil-base paint, 6 ft 6 in. × 5 ft 8 in. × 3 ft 2 in. (2 × 1.73 × .097 m).

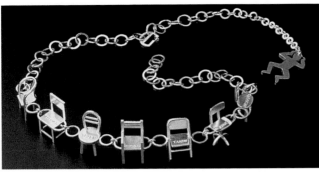

3.49 Joana Kao, *I Never Liked Musical Chairs.* Bracelet, sterling, 24K, 2¾ × 1¾ in. (7 × 4 cm).

Creating a clear pattern can increase connection among visual elements. Conversely, any break in the pattern accentuates separation. In Figure 3.1, 18 white umbrellas establish the pattern that is so beautifully broken by the single red umbrella. In *I Never Liked Musical Chairs* (3.49), metalsmith Joana Kao created a pattern using seven tiny chairs connected by a silver chain. The figure at the end of the chain breaks the pattern. Here, compositional separation conveys the sense of isolation felt by a child ejected from the game.

Location

The very location of a line or shape within the format can attract attention. The compositional center is particularly powerful. In *Flash Point*, (3.50) Sam Francis placed a white square in the middle of his painting. Surrounded by explosive energy, this shape becomes a focal point through its central location and distinctive stability.

The focal point in Gericault's *Raft of the Medusa* (3.51) was created using a pattern of compositional lines. The arms and legs of the sailors, the floorboards of the raft, and even the angle of the sail all direct our attention toward the rescue ship in the upper right corner. This dramatic use of eye direction greatly increases the painting's emotional power. One-hundred-and-forty-nine survivors from a sinking ship began a desperate journey on the raft; when rescued two weeks later, only 15 survived. The pattern of bodies and extended arms pulls us irresistibly toward the sailor at the front of

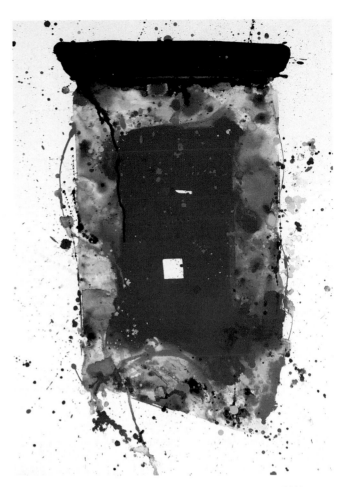

3.50 Sam Francis, *Flash Point*, 1975. Acrylic on paper, 32¼ × 22⅞ in. (82 × 59 cm).

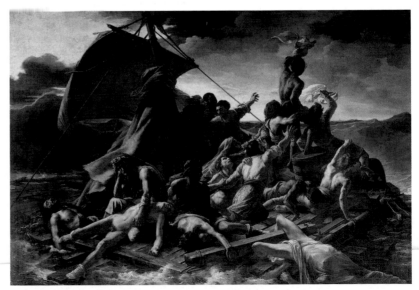

3.51 Théodore Gericault, *Raft of the Medusa,* 1818–19. Oil on canvas, 16 ft 1 in. × 23 ft 6 in. (4.9 × 7.2 m).

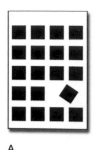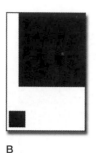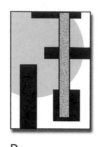

A B C D

3.52 Examples of contrast.

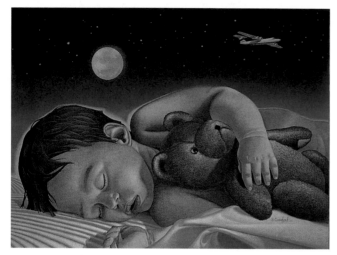

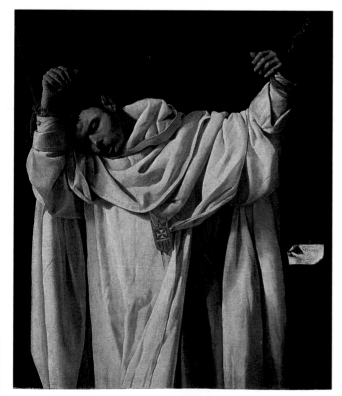

3.53 Robert Crawford, *Jamie Sleeping,* 1988. Acrylic on canvas, 20 × 14 in. (50.8 × 35.5 cm).

3.54 Francisco de Zurbarán, *Saint Serapion,* 1628. Oil on canvas, 47½ × 41 in. (120.7 × 103.5).

the raft, whose very life depends on the attention he can attract.

Contrast

Contrast is created when two or more forces operate in opposition. By reviewing the elements and principles of design discussed in the preceding chapters, we can quickly create a long list of potential adversaries, including: **static/dynamic, small/large, solid/textured,** and **curvilinear/rectilinear** (3.52 A-D).

When the balance is just right, powerful compositions can be created from any of these combinations. Devoting about 80 percent of the compositional space to one force and about 20 percent to the other is especially effective. The larger force sets the standard, while the smaller force creates the exception. Just as a single basketball player wearing a red uniform will stand out if the other four players wear green, so a smaller force can dominate a design. Consider these examples:

Contrast in size. In Figure 3.53 the small airplane and the moon become charged with meaning when combined with the image of the sleeping child. Dreams take flight.

Contrast in shape. Zurbarán's *Saint Serapion* (3.54) provides a brilliant example of contrast by shape and an effective example of emphasis by separation. The small note pinned at the right edge of the canvas gains so much power

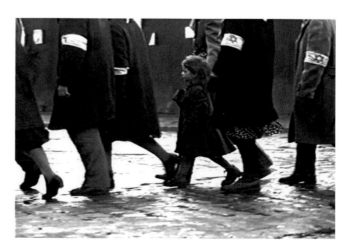

3.55 Still from *Schindler's List,* by Steven Spielberg.

that it easily balances the large figure filling the rest of the frame.

Contrast in color. One of the most compelling uses of emphasis by color occurs in *Schindler's List,* by Steven Spielberg (3.55). Midway through the black-and-white film, a small girl in a red coat is shown walking toward her death. She breaks away from the line and runs back to hide under a bed in a nearby house. This is the only use of color in the main body of the film. When her red coat appears again, her body is being transported to a bonfire. This simple use of color creates one of the most memorable moments in a remarkable film.

Expanded Composition

When the size, variety, or number of design elements increases, opportunities for both compositional complexity and compositional chaos expand. The illusion of space and the illusion of movement, discussed in the sections that follow, are two particularly rich areas to explore.

Illusion of Space

Returning to the basketball game for a moment, first place yourself in the audience, watching the game. As a spectator, you can easily observe the overall distribution of players across the court and follow the flow of the game. Now place yourself in the middle of the game, passing the ball and making shots. As a player, you are physically engaged in a complex and ever-changing event. The game swirls with activity as players advance and recede in space.

Just as symmetrical balance is appropriate for some images while asymmetrical balance is appropriate for others, so each type of space offers distinct advantages. The lines, shapes, textures, and colors in Figure 3.56 are wonderfully intricate. Here, the flat surface of the vellum page is perfect for the patterned image. At the other extreme, the illusion of space in Altdorfer's *Battle of Alexander* (3.57) is so convincing that we almost feel we can enter this battle between Alexander the Great and Darius II of Persia. The two-dimensional canvas has been transformed through the illusion of space.

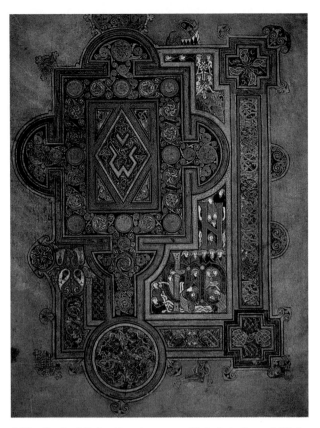

3.56 Book of Kells: Opening page, St. Luke's Gospel. Trinity College, Dublin. 9½ × 13 in. (24 × 33 cm).

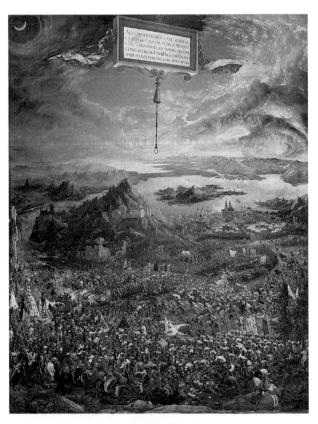

3.57 Albrecht Altdorfer, *Battle of Alexander*, 1529. Limewood, 47¼ × 62¼ in. (120 × 158 cm).

Profile:
Ken Botnick,
Graphic Designer

Landscape of the Page:
Conceiving and Composing Books

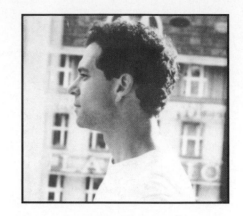

Ken Botnick has been making books for over 20 years. From 1979 to 1988, he was co-proprietor with Steve Miller of Red Ozier Press in New York City, producing over 50 limited-edition titles of contemporary poetry and fiction. Red Ozier books are in collections of The Bodleian Library, Brown University, Washington University in St Louis, the University of Virginia, Yale University, and the New York Public Library. From 1988 to 1993, Botnick was production and design manager of the art books at Yale University Press, with three of his book designs winning medals from the American Association of University Presses. Botnick has also designed books for Princeton Architectural Press, Harry N. Abrams, Princeton School of Architecture, and the University of Alabama Press. Professor Botnick was Executive Director of the Penland School of Crafts in North Carolina for four years, has taught typography at Yale University School of Design, and is currently an associate professor of art at Washington University in St. Louis.

MS: Some artists pursue a very linear career path. Other artists, who are equally or even more interesting, come to art and design through a more circuitous route. Please describe your path.
KB: My origin is in landscape design. I trained in this field and worked on a whole range of projects, from community gardens to artist-designed parks. I was fascinated by the relationship of the parts to the whole and love physical materials, such as plants, soil, and stone.

MS: How, and why, did you shift to book design?
KB: For me, landscape design became more and more about proposals and paperwork and less and less about the actual designs and the doing. I kept wanting to do smaller projects, and I loved making everything myself.

Since I had been involved with books since my undergraduate years at the University of Wisconsin, joining my friend Steve Miller at Red Ozier Press seemed like the right move. I loved the essential materials. I think of the words as the soil and the paper, the type and ink as the plants that grow from it. So the fine press work gave me the opportunity to combine my design skills, my love of craft, and my great affection for writing. In quick order, Steve and I were partners and publishers running a very active press in New York City, working with the most amazing writers and artists. We took our role of publisher very seriously and made careful choices as to whom we would publish. When you are setting type or printing 150 copies of a book, you see the text differently. You get to read in a way that you would never do ordinarily.

MS: "Landscape" is an unusual word to associate with book design. What is the meaning of this title?
KB: Like a landscape, a well-designed book is full of nuances and complex relationships. The page size, the weight and texture of the paper, the size and style of the type, and the amount and layout of information on the page all contribute to the reading experience. For me, the page is a construct that you move through, literally and figuratively. Like the window on a train, the frame remains constant, while the landscape continually changes.

MS: Please talk us through your design process for *The Bicycle Rider,* a novel in 100 sections by Guy Davenport. which was produced as a limited edition at Red Ozier Press.
KB: In designing typography for a text, I first ask "What are my emotional responses to the content of the story?" Throughout *The Bicycle Rider,* Davenport refers to Dutch painter Piet Mondrian and the primary colors he used in his mature work. Like the bicycle rider, Mondrian was a master of proportion, balance, and daring. Reds and blues pop up throughout the text. So, instead of using illustration, I used various typographic embellishments and created a title page inspired by Mondrian's paintings. The book was bound in a subtle brown handmade paper, with simple typography and color in order to play off the idea of the plain wrappers of not-so-plain books. This brown text paper is filled with red and blue fibers that echo the color of the ink.

Next, I assess my current visual surroundings, including other design books, painting, sculpture, and so on. I assume that I am looking at certain things for a reason and employ these impulses and ideas in my own designs. When working on *The Bicycle Rider,* I was looking at a pamphlet of poems by Kenneth Patchen that had been printed during World War II, with big red numbers in the margins of each poem. This book seems to do everything "wrong" typographically, yet because of its great energy, it is one of my favorite books. To emulate Patchen, I selected a clear and classic-looking typeface, then adapted his bold red numbers for the section numbers. Combined with the classic typeface, these numbers added a syncopated beat to the pages.

MS: It seems that a lot of planning is required and that everything in your design is intentional.
KB: The planning has to be there to support the spontaneity. I especially enjoy working with students who are planning their projects. Making the dummies of a book, exploring alternatives, and giving shape to the ideas are the most enjoyable part of the process. Most people are surprised at how much planning happens before production, yet that is where the magic really happens.

The beauty of craft is that there are all these repetitive functions one must go through in the studio: cutting paper, setting type, cleaning the presses, printing. These hours are vital to the creative process because they place you into direct contact with the materials, physically and sensually. That is the fertile time when many of the best ideas are formed. Creativity is not segmented out into "big-idea time" versus "boring production time"—it is all part of a fluid process. Ideas are elusive. The more you try to trap them, the more they tend to escape. I try to be alert and open at all times.

MS: From whom did you learn the most?
KB: Even though I never took a book course, I worked closely with book artist Walter Hamady during my last year at the University of Wisconsin. I went to his house to plant trees, then stayed on to cook a meal and talk. It was really about building a life. I learned that a personal investment in life and a willingness to pour all of your energy into an activity is crucial.

My collaboration with Steve Miller was also pivotal. We learned a lot about ourselves and each other during that time. When it is working well, a partnership can be a wonderful mirror, reflecting what you do especially well and what your partner does especially well. It also taught me a great deal about transforming a vision into reality.

MS: What advice do you have for my students?
KB: First, keep your eyes open: don't limit yourself through rigid self-definitions. If I had limited myself to architecture, I would never have become a graphic designer. Mindless careerism can be the path to ruin. Be willing to take side trips: they may change your life. Second, read, read, and read some more! The opportunities for learning are endless and through books, you can access the wisdom of the masters in all fields.

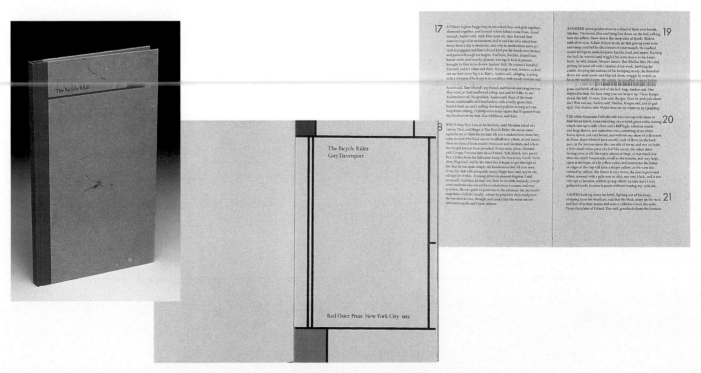

Ken Botnick, *The Bicycle Rider*, 1985. Guy Davenport, author. Letterpress printing, 5½ × 9½ in. (14 × 24 cm).

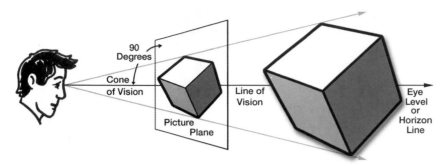

3.58 The fundamental concepts of perspective are shown in this diagram. From a fixed position, the man sees the box projected onto the picture plane. The horizon line is level with his eyes. His peripheral vision limits the area visible from his fixed position.

Linear Perspective

Linear perspective is a mathematical system for projecting the apparent dimensions of a sculptural object onto a flat surface. This surface, called the **picture plane,** is comparable to a window overlooking a city street. By tracing the outlines of the buildings on the pane of glass, you can make a simple perspective drawing.

Developed during the Renaissance, perspective offered a methodical approach to depicting the rational reality perceived by artists in the fifteenth century. It soon gained wide acceptance as a means of systematically diminishing the size of objects as they recede in space. Even though many recent philosophical and aesthetic theories challenge this conception of reality, perspective remains the most persuasive Western system for suggesting three-dimensionality on the two-dimensional surface.

Perspective is based on five fundamental concepts (3.58):

1. Objects appear to diminish in size as they recede into the distance. This diminishing effect persists until all objects disappear. Perspective is possible because the objects diminish in size with mathematical regularity.

2. The point at which objects disappear entirely is called a **vanishing point.** Sets of parallel lines such as train tracks converge at a vanishing point as they go into the distance, creating deep, illusionistic space.

3. In basic one- and two-point perspective, all vanishing points are positioned on the **eye level** or **horizon line,** which is level with the viewer's eyes.

4. Because all proportional relationships shift with each change in your position, a fixed viewing position is essential.

5. Only a limited area is clearly visible from a fixed position. To accommodate a larger viewing area, you must step further away from the object to be drawn. This expands the **cone of vision** and increases the area being viewed.

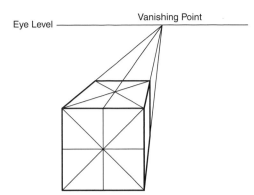

3.59 One-point perspective.

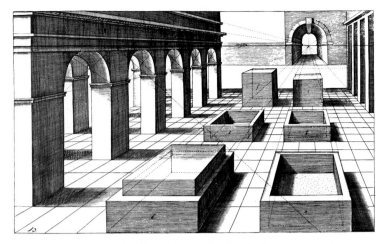

3.60 Jan Vredeman de Vries, *Perspective Study,* from *Perspective,* Leiden, 1604.

Now let's try putting this theory into practice, using a simple cube.

One-point perspective occurs when the lines receding into space appear to converge at a single point on the eye level. This occurs when the viewer is confronted with the flat front of the cube, and it results in a drawing in which vertical lines and horizontal lines parallel the edges of your sheet of paper (3.59). One-point perspective is relatively simple and can be very dramatic (3.60). However, as the viewer moves to the right or left of the cube being drawn, increasing amounts of distortion begin to occur. To correct this distortion, a second vanishing point is introduced.

Two-point perspective is used when the lines receding into space appear to converge at two vanishing points on the eye level. This occurs when the viewer is confronted with the edge of the cube, rather than the flat front (3.61). Now, only the vertical lines remain parallel to each other and the edge of the paper. All other lines recede back to the two vanishing points on the eye level. Because it clearly shows two sides of an object, two-point perspective is especially useful for diagrams and architectural renderings, such as the drawing of Frank Lloyd Wright's *Fallingwater* in Figure 3.62. However, as the viewer moves above or below the cube, exposing more of its top or bottom, distortion again begins to occur. To correct this distortion, a third point is added.

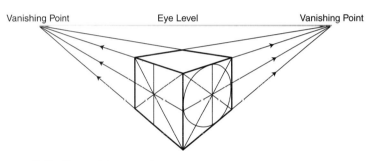

3.61 Two-point perspective.

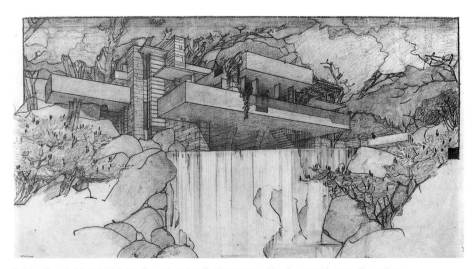

3.62 Frank Lloyd Wright, Drawing for *Fallingwater,* Kaufmann House, Bear Run, Pennsylvania, 1936. 15⅜ × 27¼ in. (39 × 69 cm).

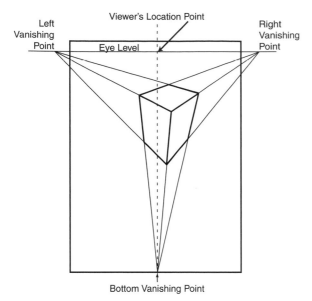

Left Vanishing Point

Viewer's Location Point

Eye Level

Right Vanishing Point

Bottom Vanishing Point

3.63 Three-point perspective.

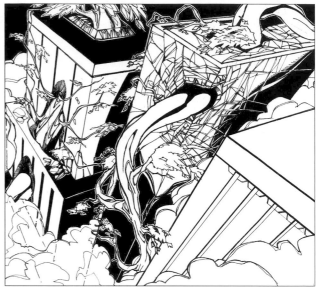

3.64 **Ely Itara, Jr.** Pen and ink, 9 × 10 in. (22.8 × 25.4 cm).

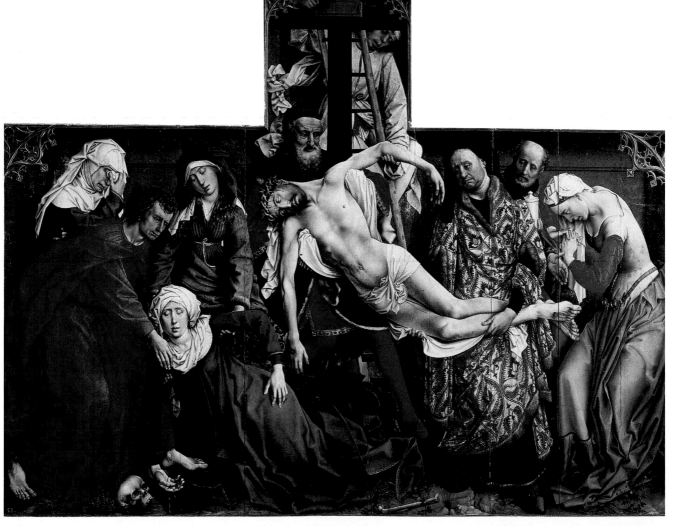

3.65 **Rogier van der Weyden,** *Deposition,* **from an altarpiece commissioned by the Crossbowman's Guild, Louvain, Brabant, Belgium, c. 1435.** Oil on panel, 7 ft 2⅝ in. × 8 ft 7⅛ in. (2.2 × 2.6 m).

Three-point perspective is used when the lines receding into space appear to converge at two vanishing points on the eye level, plus a third point placed above or below the eye level. This occurs when the viewer is facing a *corner* of the cube, rather than the front or a simple edge (3.63). Now, all the lines converge at the various vanishing points: none of the lines parallel the edge of the paper. As shown in Figure 3.64, three-point perspective is often used by comic book artists to create menacing architecture or to provide an aerial view.

Other Spatial Systems

Overlap. This is a the simplest way to suggest space, and it can be especially effective when combined with size variation. In *Deposition* (3.65), Rogier van der Weyden used overlap combined with value to create convincing human figures within a crowded compositional space.

Size variation. Because the diminishing size of distant objects is a basic characteristic of human vision, any systematic variation in size will increase the illusion of space. This effect is demonstrated most clearly when the distance is great. In Adams' *Yosemite Valley from Inspiration Point* (3.66), the large size of the cliffs in the foreground creates the illusion of space.

Definition. Sharply focused shapes also tend to advance, while blurred shapes tend to recede. In a landscape, water droplets in the air blur outlines and add a bluish color to distant shapes, creating an effect known as **atmospheric perspective.** Atmospheric perspective dissolves the most distant mountains in *Yosemite Valley from Inspiration Point*, extending the space even further.

Location. Visual elements placed near the top of the page tend to recede, while shapes placed at the bottom tend to advance. In *A Thousand Peaks and Myriad Ravines* (3.67), the mountains at the top of the scroll appear more distant despite their large size.

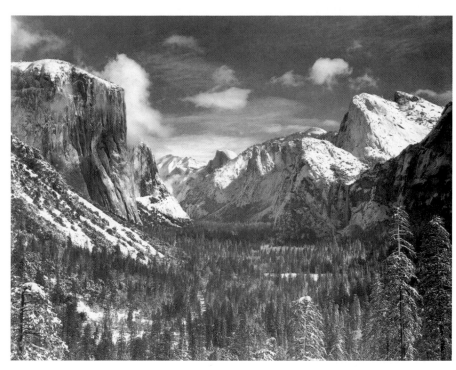

3.66 Ansel Adams, *Yosemite Valley from Inspiration Point*, c. 1936. Photograph.

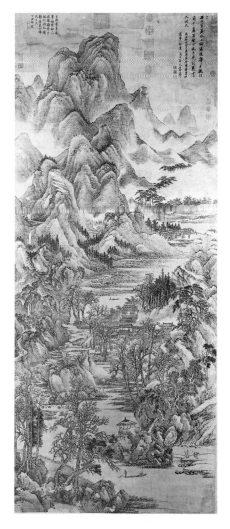

3.67 Wang Hui, *A Thousand Peaks and Myriad Ravines*, Qing dynasty, 1693. Hanging scroll, ink on paper, 8 ft 2½ in. × 3 ft 4½ in. (2.54 × 1.03 m).

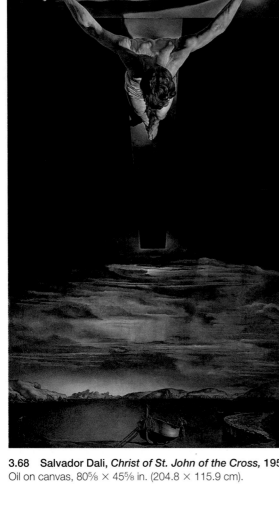

3.68 Salvador Dali, *Christ of St. John of the Cross,* 1951. Oil on canvas, 80⅝ × 45⅝ in. (204.8 × 115.9 cm).

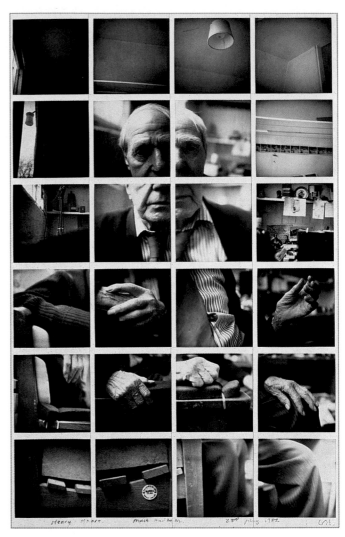

3.69 David Hockney, *Henry Moore Much Hadham 23rd July 1982,* **1982.** Composite Polaroid, 21 × 14 in. (53 × 36 cm).

Expressive Uses of Space

Through the illusion of space, artists invite viewers to enter an imaginary world. Expression can be heightened when the world created is particularly intriguing or when the spatial illusion is especially dramatic.

Amplified Perspective. This technique changes our interpretation of the crucifixion of Christ in Dali's *Christ of St. John of the Cross* (3.68). Dramatic three-point perspective emphasizes the importance of the note pinned at the top of the cross. As we look down, the vulnerability of Jesus emphasizes his humanity while the hovering position of the figure suggests his divinity.

Constructed Space. In his portrait of sculptor *Henry Moore* (3.69), David Hockney used multiple photographs to expand space and suggest the passage of time. The repeated hands gesture to us as we visually converse with the old master.

Layers of Space. Separating compositional space into foreground, middle ground, and background presents many expressive possibilities while increasing compositional complexity. Layers of space are used extensively in the film *Citizen Kane*. In Figure 3.70, young Charlie Kane plays in the background while his mother in the foreground signs over his care to a lawyer. His father, who is opposed to this action, occupies the middle ground, caught between the mother and the child. The tensions in the family, the determination of the mother, and the innocence of the child are heightened when Charlie shouts "the Union forever!" as part of his game. When the lawyer takes charge of him, the family will be split apart forever. These three layers of space communicate complex emotions while simultaneously telling a story.

Spatial Complexity. When you have mastered the skills needed to create the illusion of space, the creative and expressive possibilities expand. The swirling space in Thomas Hart Benton's *City Building* (3.71) has been constructed using a combination of conflicting spatial systems. The size variation between the figures in the foreground and the ship in the background creates a strong sense of space, which is extended even further by the faint skyscrapers in the distance. The dark cranes and pulleys, however, tend to push forward in space, creating a conflict between the background and the foreground. The curving white line extending from the center of the painting to the upper edge complicates matters even further. Part of the wall itself, this bit of molding disrupts the illusion of space by drawing our attention to the flat surface. In this mural, Thomas Hart Benton orchestrated contrasting compositional forces to create an explosive image.

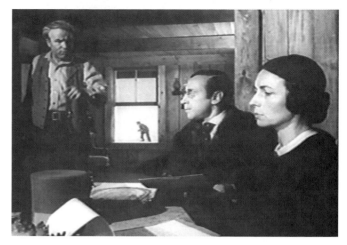

3.70 Scene from *Citizen Kane*. Three layers of space divide this shot from *Citizen Kane:* the mother in the foreground, the father in the middleground, and the child in the background.

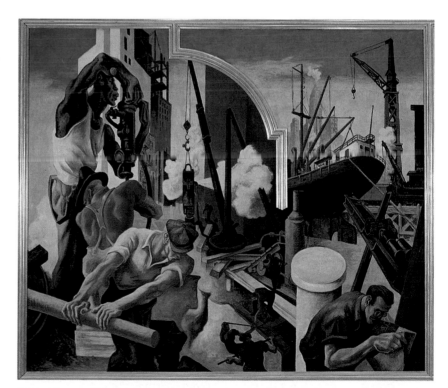

3.71 Thomas Hart Benton, *City Building*, from the mural series *America Today*, 1930. Distemper and egg tempera on gessoed linen with oil glaze. 7 ft 8 in. × 9 ft 9 in. (2.3 × 3 m).

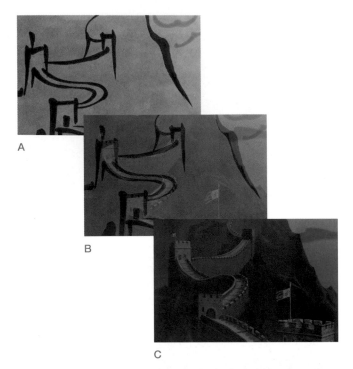

A

B

C

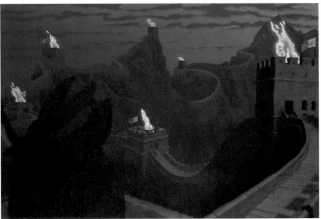

D

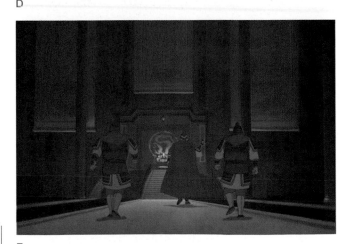

E

3.72A–E

The Dynamics of Space: Bringing *Mulan* to Life

Animators use the illusion of space with great inventiveness. Freed from the restrictions of reality, they invent and explore space with abandon. Indeed, every type of space is used beautifully in Disney's *Mulan*. From the opening shots to the grand finale, the illusion of space is of critical importance to the visual and conceptual power of the film.

- *From Line to Space.* At the end of the opening credits, a linear ink drawing is gradually transformed into an image of the Great Wall of China (3.72A-C). Cast shadows and variations in light create an illusion of space, providing a stage for the action to follow.

- *Overlap.* After a brief battle with Shan-Yu and his men, a Chinese soldier lights a signal fire to warn of the invasion. With Shan-Yu filling the foreground, we see six different towers, with signal fires gradually blazing forth from each (3.72D). Here, overlap and size variation enhance the illusion of space.

- *Linear perspective* is used in the next sequence when General Li enters the imperial palace to inform the emperor of the invasion. One-point perspective is used to create the large, majestic hall (3.72E). As the general approaches the throne, the angle of vision shifts to an aerial view. Three-point perspective is now used to emphasize the insignificance of the figures within this great hall (3.72F).

- *Atmospheric perspective* is often used as the troops travel through the mountains. After learning of the death of his father in battle, Captain Shang walks to the edge of a cliff. Like the massive mountains in the background, his seemingly invincible father has dissolved in the mist. A small figure within a large landscape, Captain Shang remains sharply focused, dignified, and powerful even as he grieves (3.72G).

- *Camera Angles.* **Camera angles** determine the amount and type of space to be included in each shot. An aerial view can provide the sweeping panorama needed to convey the enormity of a battle, while a low camera angle can provide an expansive view of the sky. The major battle scene in *Mulan* beautifully demonstrates the critical role a camera angle can play in a film. The enormity of the enemy forces is first shown in Figure 3.72H. A low camera angle positions the vast enemy army along a ridge, above the small company of Chinese soldiers. As the Mongols pour over the ridge and gallop toward Mulan, the camera angle shifts to a slanted, oblique view (3.72I), then to a complete aerial view (3.72J). The shifting perspectives give us a more comprehensive view of the extent of the battle and emphasize the hopelessness of the emperor's warriors, who are confronted with an apparently invincible enemy. When Mulan grabs the one remaining cannon and races forward to create an avalanche, an aerial view is again used to show her vulnerability against the advancing Huns. Throughout the battle, shifts in camera angle provide the emotional and compositional power needed to create a dramatic battle sequence using the fewest number of shots.

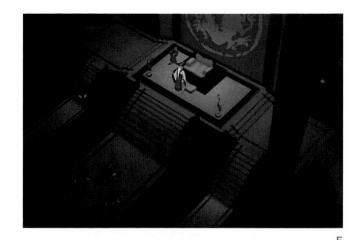

F

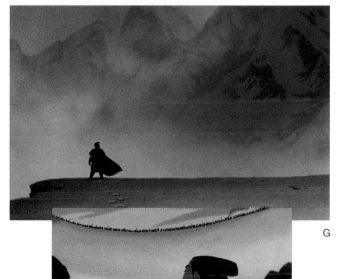

G

H

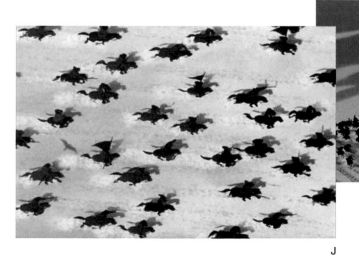

J

I

3.72F–J

Two-Dimensional Design: Organization

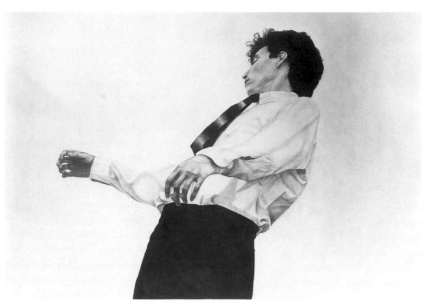

3.73 Robert Longo, *Untitled*, 1980. From the *Men in Cities* series. Crayon & graphite on paper, 40½ × 28 in. (102.9 × 71.1 cm).

Illusion of Movement

Mulan is constructed from thousands of tiny frames. When run through a film projector, they create the fluid movement that is the hallmark of Disney animation. Animation is possible because we have the perceptual ability to integrate the sequential images into a continuous flow. Substantial audience involvement is also required to create the illusion of movement. Presented with multiple images on a single surface, we must feel the movement, complete the action, or anticipate the next event. Based on our day-to-day experience in an ever-changing world, we use our imagination to connect static images to create the illusion of movement.

The Kinesthetic Response

Kinesthetics is the science of movement. Through the very process of walking, we consistently engage in a complex balancing act as we fall forward, then catch ourselves with the next step. When confronted by a life-sized figure such as this man from Robert Longo's *Men in Cities* series (3.73), the lunging movement of the model resonates on a physical level. Based on our personal experience, we feel as well as see the gesture. Capturing the gesture at the right moment is critical. In Myron's *Discus Thrower* (3.74), the athlete is caught at the moment *before* the whirling vortex of energy explodes, releasing the disc. By capturing this moment rather than the moment of release, the sculptor has trapped within the marble the energy of the throw.

The Decisive Moment

Photographer Henri Cartier-Bresson used his understanding of impending change to formulate a theory of photography he called "the decisive moment." A pioneer in the use of the 35-mm camera, he, too, caught images at the moment of greatest impact, creating photographs that are charged

3.74 Myron, *Discus Thrower (Diskobolos).* Roman copy after the original bronze of c. 450 B.C. Marble, height 5 ft 1 in. (1.54 m).

with possibilities. Indeed, all photographers bring a special awareness of time and movement to their work. In Figure 3.75, W. Eugene Smith photographed a girl in a glowing white dress as she exited a flower shop. Combined with the police car in the foreground, the child is caught between worlds of magic and menace.

Before and After

The kinesthetic response and the decisive moment both rely on our past experience. Based on our physical experience, we can feel the awkward position of the Longo figure; through our emotional experience we realize that the Smith photograph is just one moment in a more extensive story. Likewise, to create a story through a single image, many illustrators deliberately plan the moment *before* and *after* the actual drawing. For example, anticipation plays a major role in Chris Van Allsburg's *The Mysteries of Harris Burdick* (3.76). Each drawing is accompanied by a title and an abbreviated text. Based on the clues, we can invent all sorts of marvelous stories.

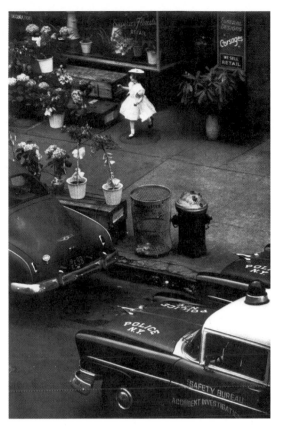

3.75 W. Eugene Smith, New York, 1958. Gelatin silver photograph.

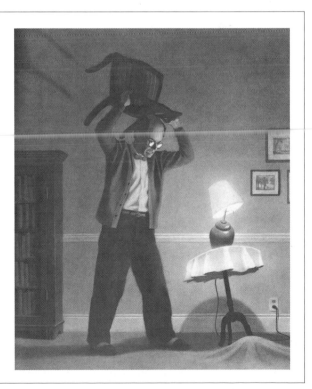

UNDER THE RUG

Two weeks passed and it happened again.

3.76 Chris Van Allsburg, "Under the Rug" from *The Mysteries of Harris Burdick*, Houghton-Mifflin, 1984.

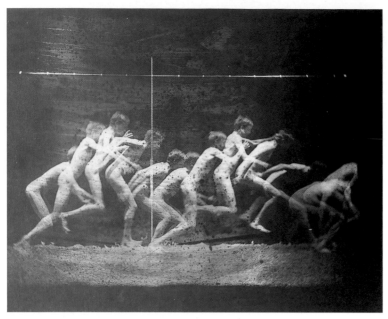

3.77 Thomas Eakins, *Double Jump,* 1885. Modern print from a dry-plate negative.

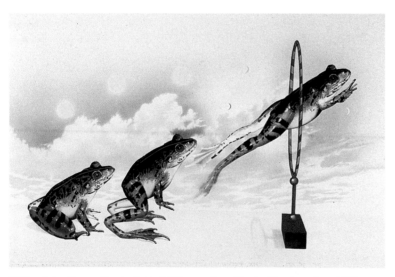

3.78 John Rowe, Illustration of 3 Frogs, from Seated to Jumping, 1991. Acrylic, 26 × 18 in. (66 × 45.7 cm).

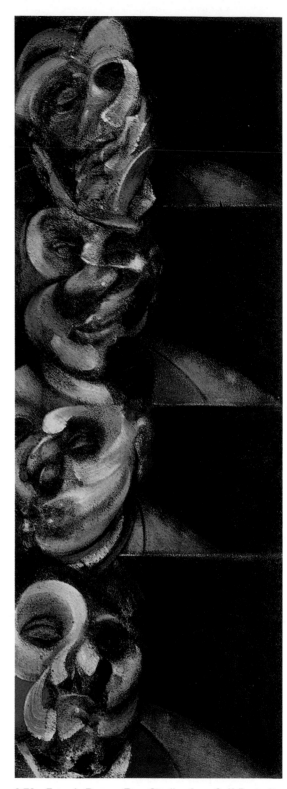

3.79 Francis Bacon, *Four Studies for a Self-Portrait,* 1967. Oil on canvas, 36 × 13 in. (91.5 × 33 cm).

Multiplication

As an object moves, it sequentially occupies multiple spaces. Visual multiplication helps capture such movement. The superimposed figures in Thomas Eakins' *Double Jump* (3.77) record the multiple spaces the man occupies during this athletic event. Even when figures are simply repeated, as in John Rowe's illustration of frogs (3.78), movement is strongly suggested.

As soon as shapes begin to lose definition, they tend to lose stability. Shifts can occur in both time and space. A self-portrait by Francis Bacon (3.79) provides a strong sense of three-dimensional volume while simultaneously dissolving any conventional sense of anatomy.

Multiplication can also play a role in visual storytelling. In this page from *Inhumans* (3.80), by Paul Jenkins and Jae Lee, a dialog between an alien child and a human politician unfolds over five panels. Multiplication creates a very different effect in George Tooker's *Government Bureau* (3.81). Repeated images of the central male figure combined with endless bureaucratic faces creates a scene from a nightmare. No matter where the man goes in this hall of mirrors, he always returns to the beginning.

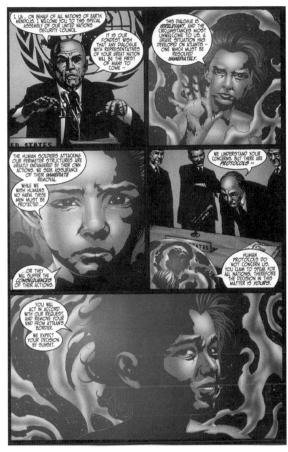

3.80 Paul Jenkins and Jae Lee, from *Inhumans:* "First Contact." Volume 2, Issue 5, March 1999. Comic book.

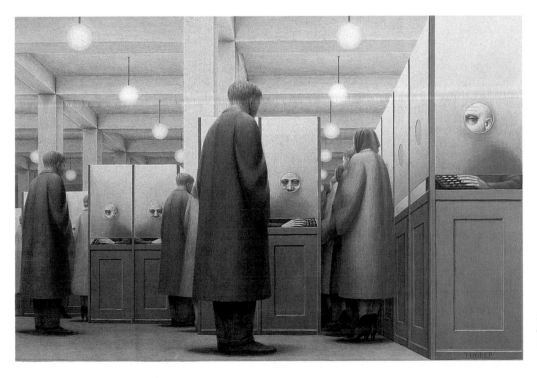

3.81 George Tooker, *Government Bureau*, 1956. Egg tempera on gesso panel, 19⅝ × 29⅝ in. (50 × 75 cm).

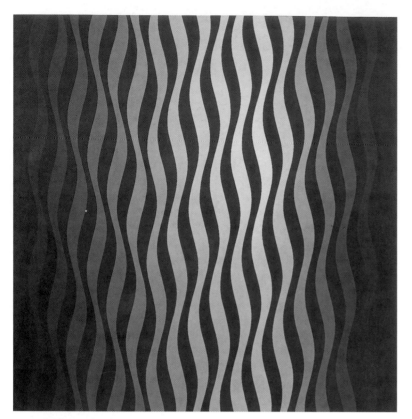

3.82 Bridget Riley, *Drift No. 2*, 1966. Acrylic on canvas, 7 ft 7½ in. × 7 ft 5½ in. 2.32 × 2.27 m).

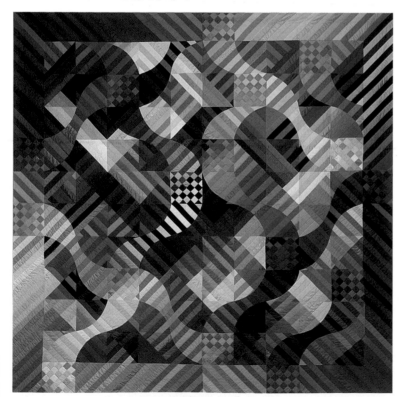

3.83 Michael James, *Rhythm/Color: Improvisation*, 1985. Machine-pieced and -quilted cotton and silk, 99½ × 99½ in. (253 × 253 cm).

Rhythm

Rhythm can be created when multiple parts are presented in a deliberate pattern. In many ways, visual rhythm is similar to musical rhythm. In music, rhythm is created through the organization of sound in time. **Meter** (the basic pattern of sound and silence), **accents** (which emphasize specific notes), and **tempo** (the speed with which the music is played) can be combined to create a dazzling array of compositional possibilities.

As with music, visual compositions can be constructed using very simple means. In Bridget Riley's *Drift No. 2* (3.82), a simple line has been repeated to create a hypnotic rhythm. A more complex composition is shown in *Rhythm/Color: Improvisation* (3.83). Here, Michael James used a series of square blocks to create the basic grid on which the quilt was based. Diagonal lines within each block and the curving shapes between blocks add another layer of movement. Fifteen blocks covered with diamond shapes provide accents, while a pattern of radiating diagonals energizes the border. Using a combination of forces, James created a fascinating composition from hundreds of strips of fabric.

Visual rhythm can be as regular as a metronome or as syncopated as jazz. Multiplication, fragmentation, and superimposition propel the nude descending Duchamp's staircase (3.84). The jerking rhythm demonstrates the alternating stability and instability of human locomotion, rather than physical grace. By contrast, the rhythm in Figure 3.85 is as fluid as water. In this portrait of poet Carl Sandburg, Edward Steichen used six head shots to convey the energy and the animation of both the man and his words. Arranged in an ascending diagonal pattern, the repeated portraits begin with a contem-

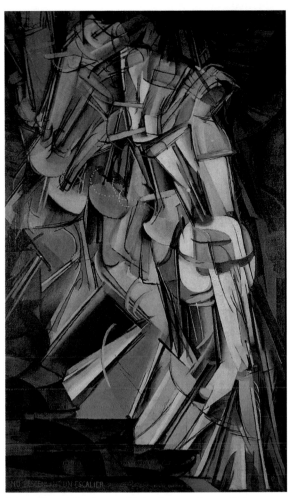

3.84 Marcel Duchamp, *Nude Descending a Staircase, No. 2,* **1912.** Oil on canvas, 58 × 35 in. (147.3 × 88.9 cm).

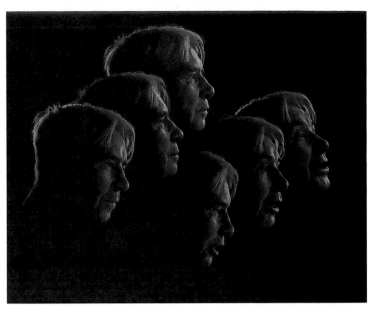

3.85 Edward Steichen, *Carl Sandburg,* **Connecticut, 1936.** Montage, gelatin-silver print, 13¹¹⁄₁₆ × 16⅞ in. (34.8 × 42.9 cm).

plative pose in the lower left corner and culminate in an exuberantly expressive pose at the right edge.

Pattern

A **pattern** is created when shapes repeat over an extended area. As shown in James's quilt, a pattern can be used to unify many small bits of visual information. Pattern can also be used to add an undercurrent of order to an energetic design. In *White Squares* (3.86), Lee Krasner combined the expressive power of a calligraphic line with the stability of a grid. The underlying pattern of vertical and horizontal lines contrasts beautifully with the looser marks inside the squares. Even a very informal

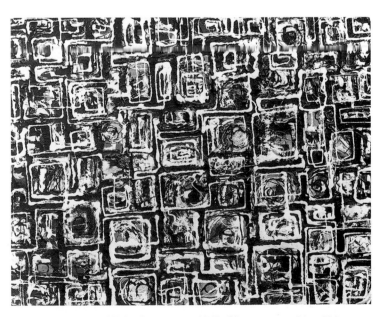

3.86 Lee Krasner, *White Squares,* **c. 1948.** Oil on canvas, 24 × 30 in. (61 × 76.2 cm).

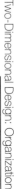

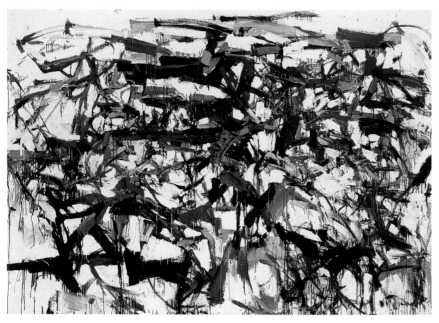

3.87 Joan Mitchell, *Ladybug,* 1957. Oil on canvas, 6 ft 5⅞ in. × 9 ft (197.9 × 274 cm).

pattern can help to unify a design. The matrix of horizontal lines and repeated white shapes in Joan Mitchell's *Ladybug* (3.87) create an exuberant dance.

Inherently unified, patterns are often used to decorate or embellish walls, books, or fabrics. In his *Canterbury Tales* (3.88), William Morris used complex floral patterns to create multiple borders and backgrounds for each page.

Pattern can also add emotional and conceptual power to films. In Alfred Hitchcock's *Vertigo,* actor James Stewart descends a seemingly endless flight of stairs (3.89). His character is terrified of heights and becomes disoriented on even

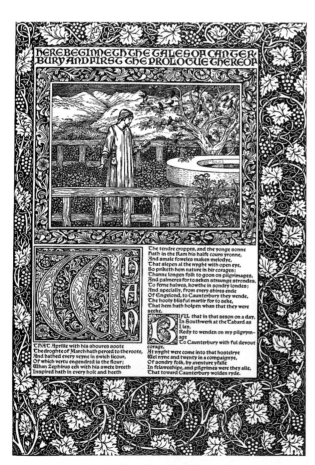

3.88 William Morris, Illustrated Page from *The Canterbury Tales*, 1896.

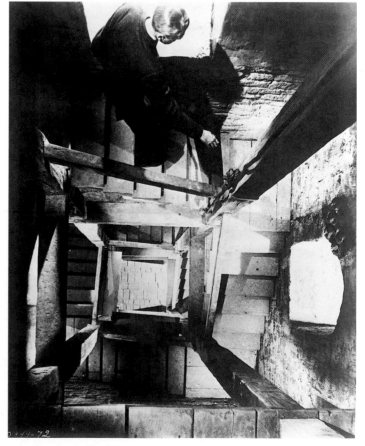

3.89 Still from *Vertigo*, by Alfred Hitchcock.

ordinary stairs; in the context of the film, this spiraling descent becomes especially nightmarish. Another famous example occurs in *Citizen Kane*, a film that is often described as the best American movie of all time. The millionaire Kane has been deserted by his wife. Despite his wealth and power, he is now completely alone, isolated in a world of his own megalomania. As he slowly walks down the corridors of his castle (3.90), his silent figure is repeated again and again and again. No matter how many figures fill the room, Kane has only himself for company.

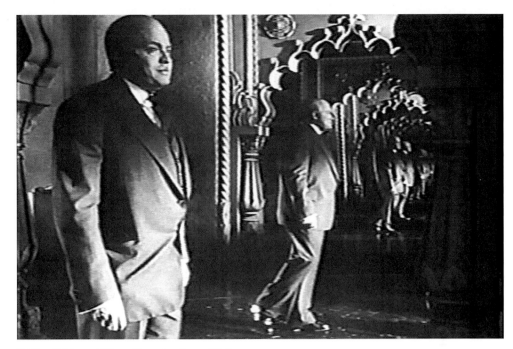

3.90   Still from *Citizen Kane*, by Orson Welles.

Maximizing Visual Impact

Complexity can be a virtue in design. It is like killing two birds with one stone: you are getting as much as possible from every visual element. On the other hand, complication in an artwork can be an obstacle. Complication is like throwing 20 stones at one bird—and missing. By focusing on compositional relationships and creating an ideal balance among visual elements, clarity of communication and powerful emotion can emerge.

Profile:
Ken Stout, Painter
Immediacy and Energy in Large Scale

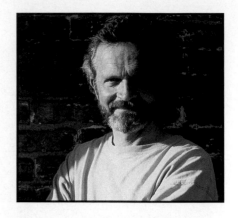

Ken Stout is an internationally renowned figurative painter. He has shown his work widely, including group shows at the Nelson-Atkins Museum of Art in Kansas City and the Butler Museum of American Art, as well as solo shows at the Goldstrom Gallery in New York City, the Arkansas Art Center, and the Cité Internationale des Arts in Paris. Stout has received numerous awards including a National Endowment for the Arts Painting Award in 1990 and the Arkansas Arts Council painting award 1999 as well as residencies at the MacDowell Colony in Vermont, and the Cité Internationale de Arts in Paris.

Intermission was commissioned by the Walton Arts Center in Fayetteville, Arkansas, funded by Saatchi and Saatchi in 1992 and permanently installed in 1994.

MS: How did *Intermission* begin?
KS: I actually began work on the mural in 1989. During visits to Paris and Madrid, I was bowled over by a Toulouse-Latrec mural I saw at the Orsay Museum, and by a mural by Delacroix at St. Sulpice. Both were vibrant with energy, and the strident reds and greens in the Delacroix sent the viewer's eyes hurtling around and through the composition. I also loved Velasquez' *Las Meninas* and Goya's frescos for their immediacy and fearlessness. I was interested in the mural project because it gave me an opportunity to combine the immediacy of drawing with the richness of painting.

MS: Why show the intermission, not the play?
KS: It is a moment in time that is highly charged. The mural depicts a cross section of the theater, from backstage to stage and from audience to lobby. The performer on stage is like a toggle switch, connecting the audience to the action backstage. As he bows through the closing curtain, the audience begins to break apart, dissolving into its own private plays. Applause fills the theater, children begin to awaken and neighbors discuss the performance. I wanted to pull the viewer in to a scene bursting with energy, as if all things were in orbit, pushing and pulling, as in dance. The whole painting is a gesture, an embodiment of bodies in motion, with both the volumes and voids ignited with energy.

MS: I know that you love art history and that your preliminary research on this project was extensive. What did you learn from the masters?
KS: Mostly I learned ways to increase compositional complexity without sacrificing gestural energy. These compositional lessons helped me sustain a vigorous visual pace for all 50 feet of the painting.

Technically, though, my work method was more exploratory and direct than is the usual practice.

First, the 300 premiliary drawings and paintings I did stand as autonomous images in themselves. I learned from all of them—but didn't copy any of them when I painted the mural. I confronted the painting directly, rather than replicating ideas I had worked out beforehand.

Second, I didn't graph out, slide project, or otherwise draw the outlines on the canvas. I just drew blue lines to divide the canvas into halves, quarters, and eighths, then drew freehand, using a brush attached to a three-foot-long bamboo pole, starting with light washes in earth colors, then building up more layers as necessary.

Finally, every figure was painted from life, using over 50 community members as models. They were amazingly generous and patient, considering it wasn't putting a penny in their pockets. This process increased the connection between the audience and the artwork, and we had a great party for everyone when the painting was installed. I continue to meet these townspeople on the street, and as participants in the project, they have a continuing relationship with the painting.

MS: So, it sounds like you didn't really know what would happen when you began to paint each day.
KS: Each model, each pose, and each prop provided variations and surprises. I actually used at least two models for each figure in the painting, which basically means that there is another 50-foot-long painting underneath the one that you see!

MS: What advice do you have for my students?
KS: Take risks. Without daring, indeed, without great daring, there is no beauty. We must go beyond ourselves if we are ever to fulfill our real potential.

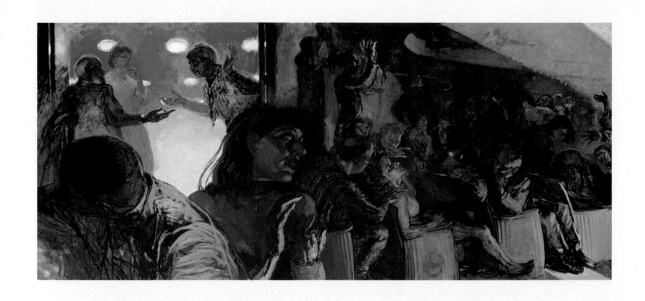

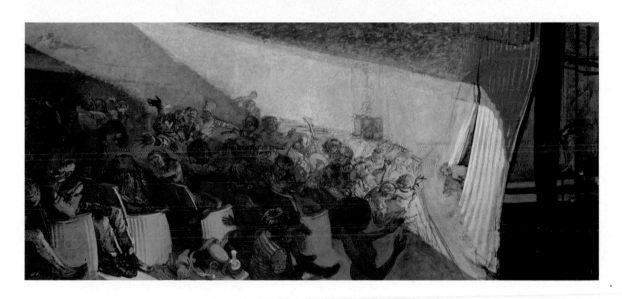

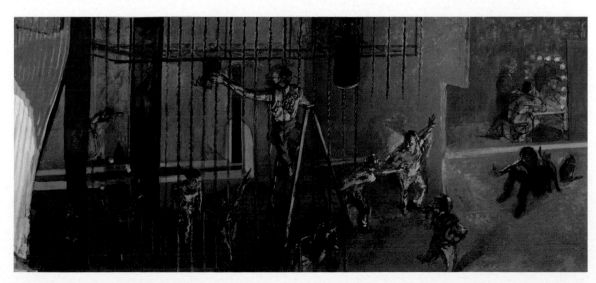

Ken Stout, *Intermission,* 1994. Oil on canvas, 9 × 50 ft (2.74 × 15.24 m).

Summary

- Effective design requires a balance between unity and variety. Too much unity can lead to boredom, while too much variety can lead to chaos. Any similarity between visual elements tends to increase unity; any difference between visual elements tends to increase variety.

- Visual weight refers to the inclination of shapes to float or sink based on their solidity and compositional location. Solid shapes generally weigh more than open shapes, and shapes that extend beyond the upper edge of the format tend to rise while shapes that extend below the format tend to sink.

- Symmetry, radial symmetry, and asymmetry can be used to create three forms of balance. Complex forms of balance, the illusion of space, and the illusion of movement can be created when multiple elements are organized within a format.

- Scale and proportion are two types of size relationships. Proportion refers to the size relationships within an image, while scale involves a size comparison to our physical reality.

- By determining compositional priorities, we can emphasize the most important aspects of a design. Knowing what to leave out is as important as knowing what to include in a design. Every visual element must be used fully.

- The illusion of space can be created through linear perspective, overlap, size variation, location, definition, and atmospheric perspective.

- The illusion of movement can be created by selecting the most telling moment or through various types of multiplication.

Keywords

accent
amplified
  perspective
anomaly
asymmetrical
  balance
atmospheric
  perspective
balance
camera angle
centrifugal
  balance
centripetal
  balance

closure
concentric
  balance
cone of vision
continuity
contrast
cropped
dynamic
emphasis
eye level
fusion
gestalt
horizon line
kinesthetics

linear
  perspective
meter
one-point
  perspective
overlap
pattern
proportion
proximity
radial symmetry
rhythm
scale
spiral
static

symmetrical
  balance
tempo
three-point
  perspective
two-point
  perspective
unity
vanishing point
variety
visual weight

1. What is the relationship between the visual elements and the format? The edge of the format is like an electric wire; carefully used, it can generate great tension. Experiment with the position of each visual element relative to this edge.

2. Is every square inch of the composition fully engaged? Note especially the role of negative space in creating a balance with positive elements.

3. Which lines, shapes, or textures are doing the most work? How?

4. Are there any superfluous elements? Just as a textbook loses power when it overexplains information, so a design loses impact when extraneous elements are included. Economy is a virtue.

5. Does the idea you want to communicate require the stability of symmetrical balance or the energy of asymmetrical balance? Experiment with extremes of each.

6. How much spatial depth is there in your composition? If more depth is needed, how can it be created?

Roy R. Behrens, *Design in the Visual Arts*. Englewood Cliffs, NJ, Prentice-Hall, Inc., 1984.

Arthur Asa Berger, *Seeing Is Believing: An Introduction to Visual Communication*, 2nd edition. Mountain View, CA, Mayfield Publishing Company, 1998.

John Berger, *Ways of Seeing*. London, British Broadcasting Corporation, 1987.

Frank Cheathan, Jane Hart Cheathan, and Sheryl A. Haler, *Design Concepts and Applications*. Englewood Cliffs, NJ, Prentice-Hall, Inc., 1983

Donis Dondis, *A Primer of Visual Literacy*. Cambridge, MA, MIT Press, 1973.

Jack Fredrick Myers, *The Language of Visual Art: Perception as a Basis for Design*. Orlando, FL, Holt Rinehart and Winston, Inc., 1989.

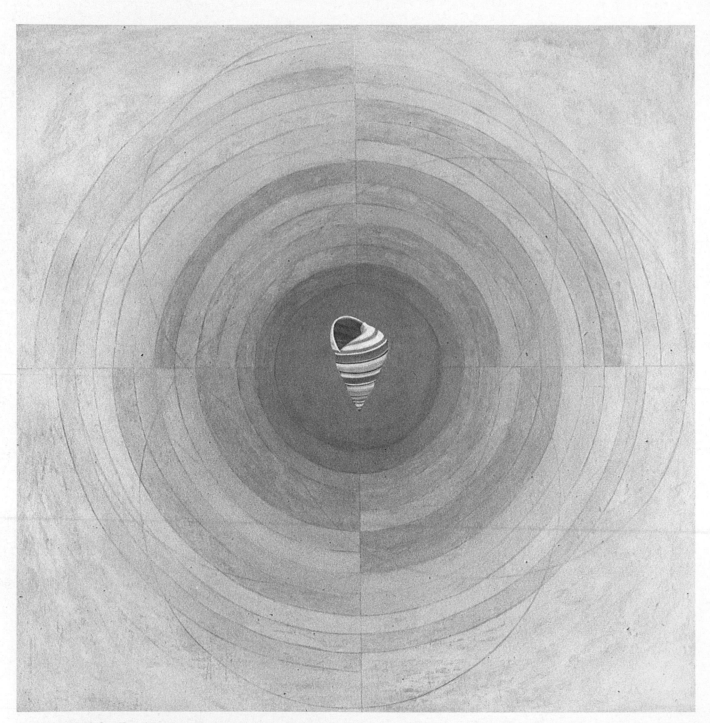

Georgiana Nehl, *Sun/Star* **(detail), 1996.** Oil paint on gessoed wood, 25¾ in. w. × 13¼ in. h. × 1 in. d. (65 × 34 × 3 cm)

Concepts and Critical Thinking

In *A Kick in the Seat of the Pants,* Roger Von Oech identifies four distinct roles in the creative process. An *explorer* learns as much as possible about a problem. Research is crucial. Ignorance of a topic may result in a superficial solution, while finalizing the first solution envisioned often results in a cliché. An *artist* experiments with a wide variety of solutions, using all sort of combinations, proportions, and materials. By creating 10 answers to each question, the artist can select the best solution rather than accepting the only solution. Next, the *judge* assesses the work in progress and determines what revisions are required. Innovative ideas are never fully developed when first presented; most need extensive revision and expansion. Being able to recognize the potential in a raw design is invaluable. Rather than discard an underdeveloped idea, you can identify its potential and determine ways to increase its strength. Finally, the *warrior* implements the idea. When the project is large and complex, implementing the plan requires great tenacity. When obstacles appear, the warrior assesses the situation, determines the best course of action, and then completes the project.

We will explore each of these roles in this section. Playing the right role at the right time is essential. Judging a design prematurely or galloping onto the visual battlefield before exploring the terrain can crush creativity. Strategies for cultivating creativity and improving time management are discussed in Chapter Four. Chapter Five deals with concept development and visual problem solving. Chapter Six is devoted to critical thinking and provides specific ways to improve any design.

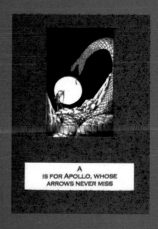

A
IS FOR APOLLO, WHOSE
ARROWS NEVER MISS

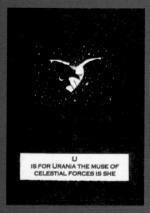

U
IS FOR URANIA THE MUSE OF
CELESTIAL FORCES IS SHE

Cultivating Creativity

"The heart of all new ideas lies in the borrowing, adding, combining or modifying of old ones. Do it by accident and people call you lucky. Do it by design and they'll call you creative."

Michael LeBoeuf, in *Imagineering*

Design and Creativity

Design and creativity are natural partners. The quality of a design is determined by the integration of its parts into a cohesive whole. The design will work when the parts fit together well. Many compositional possibilities are invented and discarded during the design process. Likewise, creative thinking requires extensive exploration and innovative combinations. By looking at familiar elements in a new way and by combining ideas that have traditionally been separate, we can invent fresh ideas and create new images.

Once viewed as peripheral, creativity and innovation have become highly valued in the current business climate. In the Information Age, intellectual property can be the most important asset in a business. Innovation in art and design, always highly valued in Western culture, has accelerated. New technologies have expanded the range of approaches available, and new ideas drawn from literature, science, philosophy, and history inspire contemporary artists and designers. The sky is the limit. An effective artist or designer cannot simply follow instructions. Cultivating creative thinking is as important as mastering any technical skill.

Seven Characteristics of Creative Thinking

Creativity is inherently unpredictable. Through creative thinking, old habits are broken and familiar patterns of thought are transformed. Anything can happen. Predicting the future based on past experience becomes inadequate when a creative breakthrough occurs. Like a shimmering drop of mercury, creativity eludes capture.

Creative thinking can, however, be cultivated. Rather than passively wait for inspiration, we can set up the conditions favorable to creativity and pursue actions that encourage insight. Creativity takes many forms. Based on observation and on interviews, various researchers have noted the following characteristics in many creative people.

Receptivity

Creative people are open to new ideas and welcome new experiences. Never complacent, they question the status quo and embrace alternative solutions to existing problems. Rather than dismiss new ideas, they enthusiastically seek alternative solutions to existing problems.

Curiosity

A good designer brings an insatiable curiosity to his or her work. Researching unfamiliar topics and analyzing unusual systems is a source of delight rather than a cause for concern. Like a child, the designer is eager to learn new things and explore new places. "How does it work?" and "How can it work better?" are frequently asked questions.

Wide Range of Interests

With a broad knowledge base, a creative person can make innumerable connections. Consider the number of words you can create from the letters in the word *image*:

age, game, gem, am, aim

Try the same game with the word *imagination:*

gin, nation, gnat, ton, not, man, again, gain, aim, ant, no, on, tin, gamin, inn, ingot

With more components, the number of combinations increases. Likewise, an artist who has a background in literature, geology, archery, music, and history can make more connections than the single-minded art specialist.

Attentiveness

Realizing that every experience is potentially valuable, creative people pay attention to seemingly minor details. Scientists often develop major theories by observing small events which they then organize into complex patterns. Artists can often see past superficial visual chaos to discern an underlying order. Playwrights develop drama by looking past the surface of human behavior to explore the substance of the human condition. By looking carefully, creative people see possibilities that others miss.

Seeking Connections

Seeing the similarity among seemingly disparate parts has often sparked a creative breakthrough. For example, Egyptian hieroglyphs became readable when a young French scholar realized that they carried the same message as an adjacent Greek inscription on a slab of stone. By comparing the two and cracking the code, Jean-François Champollion opened the door for all subsequent students of ancient Egyptian culture.

Conviction

Creative people value existing knowledge. Since new ideas are often derived from old ideas, it is foolish to ignore or dismiss the past. However, creative people also love change. Never satisfied with routine answers to familiar questions, they constantly consider new possibilities and often challenge the authorities. Convinced of the value of their ideas, they tenaciously pursue an independent path.

Complexity

In lecture classes, we must accurately take notes during lectures, memorize facts, and collect and analyze data. We are encouraged to think rationally, write clearly, and present our ideas in a linear progression. In studio classes, exploration, experimentation, and intuition are encouraged, especially during brainstorming sessions. Synthesis, emotion, visualization, spatial perception, and nonlinear thinking are highly valued.

To be fully effective, a creative person needs to combine the rational with the intuitive. While intuition may be used to generate a new idea, logic and analysis are often needed for its realization. As a result, the actions of creative people are often complex or even contradictory. As noted by psychologist Mihaly Csikszentmihalyi,[1] creative people often combine:

- Physical energy with a respect for rest. They work long hours with great concentration, then rest and relax, fully recharging their batteries. They view balance between work and play as essential.

- Savvy with innocence. They use common sense as well as intellect in completing their work, yet remain naive, open to experience. Creative people tend to view the world and themselves with a sense of wonder, rather than cling to preconceptions.

- Responsibility with playfulness. When the situation requires serious attention, creative people are remarkably diligent and determined. They realize that there is no substitute for hard work and drive themselves relentlessly when nearing completion of a major project. On the other hand, when the situation permits, a playful, devil-may-care attitude may prevail, providing a release from the previous period of work.

- Risk-taking with safe-keeping. Creativity expert George Prince has noted two behavioral extremes in people.[2] Safe-keepers always look before they leap, avoid surprises, punish mistakes, follow the rules, and watch the clock. A safe-keeper is most comfortable when there is only one right answer to memorize or one solution to produce. Risk-takers are just the opposite. They break the rules, leap before they look, like surprises, are impetuous, and may lose track of time. A risk-taker enjoys inventing multiple answers to every question.

An imbalance in either direction inhibits creativity. The safe-keeper lives in fear, while the extreme risk-taker lives brilliantly—but briefly. Creative thinking requires a mix of risk-taking and safe-keeping. When brainstorming new ideas, open-ended exploration is used: anything is possible. But when implementing new ideas, deadlines, budgets, and feasibility become major concerns. The risk-taker gets the job started; the safe-keeper gets the job done.

- Extroversion with introversion. When starting a new project, creative people are often talkative and gregarious, eager to share insights and explore ideas. When a clear sense of direction develops, however, they often withdraw, seeking solitude and quiet work time. This capacity for solitude is crucial. Several studies have shown that talented teenagers who cannot stand solitude rarely develop their creative skills.

- Passion with objectivity. Mature artists tend to plunge into new projects, convinced of the significance of the work and confident of their skills. Any attempt to distract or dissuade them at this point is futile. However, when the model or rough study is done, most artists will pause to assess progress to date. This period of analysis and judgment may occur in a group setting or may be done by the artist alone. In either case, the emotional attachment required while creating is now replaced by a dispassionate objectivity. Work that does not pass this review is redone or discarded, regardless of the hours spent in its development. In major projects, this alternating process of creation and analysis may be repeated many times.

- Disregard for time with attention to deadlines. Time often dissolves when studio work begins. An artist or designer can become engrossed in a project: when the work is going well, six hours can feel like 20 minutes. On the other hand, an acute attention to deadlines is necessary when preparing an exhibition or working for a client.

- Modesty with pride. As they mature, creative people often become increasingly aware of the contributions to their success made by teachers, family, and colleagues. Rather than brag about past accomplishments, creative people tend to focus on current projects. On the other hand, as creative people become aware of their significance within a field, they gain a powerful sense of purpose.

Distractions are deleted from the schedule, and increasingly ambitious goals are set. When the balance is right, all these complex characteristics fuel even greater achievement.

Goal Setting

The "Imagineer" has one of the most prized jobs within the Disney corporation. Combining imagination with engineering, Imagineers create new ideas that can be effectively *realized*. This combination is crucial. Creativity without result accomplishes nothing.

Goal setting is especially important for the most highly creative people. A wide range of interests and a disregard for time constraints can make them scatterbrained. As humans, our behavior is goal-directed. Every action occurs for a reason. When we focus our attention on a specific task, we can accomplish just about anything. Goals help us channel our energy and manage our time. When we reach our goals, our self-esteem increases, which then helps us overcome obstacles. And, with each goal met, our knowledge increases. Michael LeBoeuf has diagrammed this effect clearly (4.1).

A Goal-Setting Strategy

Self-knowledge is essential. To be effective, goals must be authentic. No matter how hard you try, you will never really fulfill your potential by pur-

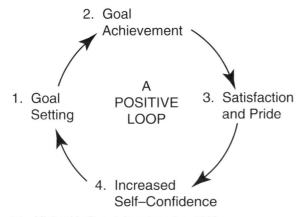

4.1 Michael LeBoeuf, *Imagineering*, 1980.

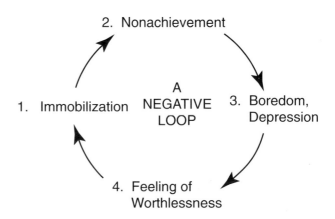

suing goals set by others. Identifying your real interests, strengths, and objectives can be liberating. The following exercise can help clarify your interests.

1. Get a package of small Post-it notes. Working spontaneously, write one of your characteristics on each note, such as "I am creative," "I love music," "I write well." Identify as many attributes as possible.

2. When you finish, lay out the notes on a table and look at them for a while. Consider the type of person they describe. What are this person's strengths? What additional interests might this person need to develop?

3. On a fresh stack of notes, write a new set of responses, this time dealing with the question "Why not?" as an expansion of these interests. Why not travel to Tibet? Why not learn Spanish? Why not master canoeing? Add these to the grid.

4. Then, leave the room. Go for a walk, have dinner, or head to class. Let your subconscious mind play with the possibilities suggested by your notes.

5. Next, organize the notes into four general categories: intellectual goals, personal-relationship goals, spiritual or emotional goals, physical fitness goals. If you are an extreme safe-keeper, add a category called "Adventure." If you are an extreme risk-taker, add a category called "Organization." Since a mix of activities helps feed the psyche, working with each of these categories is important. Even though spiritual, emotional, or social development is fluid and continuous, recognition of these categories can contribute to effective time management.

6. Prioritize the notes within each category. On the top note, write "This is first because _____." One the second, write "This is second because _____." Continue until you complete the grid. Discard notes that you now realize are unnecessary.

7. Choose one goal from each of the four categories. It is tempting to choose the top goal in each case, but this is unrealistic. Even the most experienced businessperson can rarely manage more than three major goals at a time. Choosing one primary goal and two secondary goals is more realistic.

8. Now, specify your goals. "I want to become a better artist" is too vague. Consider specific actions you can take to improve your artwork. "I need to improve my drawing" is more specific. "I want to learn anatomy" is better still. To learn anatomy, you can take a class, study an anatomy book, or draw from a skeleton. These are tangible actions: you now know what to do.

9. Determine how to achieve your goals and develop a rough timetable, listing weekly goals, semester goals, and one-year goals. It is not necessary to list career goals just yet. Most of us explore many ideas during our first year of college, and formalizing career goals prematurely is counterproductive. After you are clearly committed to a major field of study, you can add a page of long-term goals, projecting your priorities for the next three to five years.

10. At least once a month, review your chart and add or delete information as necessary, If you realize that you are overextended this term, shift one of your minor goals to next semester or delete it altogether. This system is intended to provide you with a target, not to create a straitjacket. Make adjustments as necessary, so that your primary goals are met.

11. If you achieve all your goals, congratulate yourself—then set more ambitious goals next term. If you achieve half of your goals, congratulate yourself—then prioritize more carefully next term. You may have taken on too many tasks and thus dissipated your energy. Because there is always a gap between intention and outcome, a 70 to 80 percent completion rate is fine.

Characteristics of Good Goals

Challenging but Attainable

Too modest a goal will provide no sense of accomplishment. Too ambitious a goal will reduce, rather than increase, motivation. No one wants to fight a losing battle! Knowing your strengths and weaknesses will help you set realistic goals.

Compatible

Training for the Boston Marathon while simultaneously trying to gain 20 pounds is unwise, since you will burn off every calorie you consume. Trying to save a thousand dollars while touring Europe is unrealistic, since travel always costs more than you expect. On the other hand, by taking a dance class or joining a hiking club, you may be able to combine a fitness goal with a social goal.

Self-Directed

Avoid goals that are primarily dependent on someone else's actions or options. "I want to earn an A in drawing" is a common example. Since your grade is determined by a teacher, your control in this area is limited. Instead, focus on improving your drawing as much as possible. This will increase your receptivity to learning and will focus your attention on actions you can control. When you do your best work, good grades generally follow.

Temporary

Set clear target dates, get the job done, and move on to the next project. Each completed task increases your self-confidence and adds momentum. Unfinished work, on the other hand, can drain energy and decrease momentum. If you are overloaded, delete secondary goals so that you can complete primary goals.

Time Management

Time management can help you achieve your goals. Working smarter is usually more effective than simply working harder. In a world bursting with opportunity, using your work time well can increase the time available for travel, volunteer work, or socializing. The following time-management strategies have been used by many artists and designers.

Setting the Stage

Choosing when and where to work can significantly increase your output. If you are a lark, bursting with energy and enthusiasm in the morning, tackle major projects before noon. If you are an owl, equipped with night vision and able to hunt after dark, work on major projects after dinner. If you are distracted by clutter, clean your desk before beginning your workday, and tidy up your desk before you leave. These seemingly minor actions can substantially increase your productivity.

First Things First

Use your goal list to help determine your priorities. Note which tasks are most *urgent* and which tasks are most *important*. Timing can be crucial. When you pay your phone bill on time, you easily complete an urgent but unimportant task. When your phone bill is overdue and the service is cut off, this unimportant task becomes a major headache. Dispense with urgent tasks quickly. Distribute important tasks over several weeks if necessary.

Step One, Step Two, Step Three

Many activities are best done in a specific sequence. If you are writing a 20-page paper, it is best to start with research, make an outline, complete a rough draft, make corrections, then write the final draft. If you are designing a poster, it is best to start with research, make thumbnail sketches, assess the results, make a full-size rough layout, consult the client, and *then* complete the poster. It is tempting to try to cut out the intermediate steps and move directly to the final draft, but this is rarely effective. With most large projects, you learn more, save time, and do better work by following the right sequence of events.

Use Parts to Create the Whole

Seen as a whole, a major project can become overwhelming. In an extreme case, creative paralysis sets in, resulting in a condition similar to writer's block. Breaking down big jobs into smaller parts helps enormously. In *Bird by Bird,* Anne Lamott gives a wonderful description of this process:

> Thirty years ago my other brother, who was ten years old at the time, was trying to get a report on birds written that he'd had three months to write. [It] was due the next day . . . he was at the kitchen table close to tears, surrounded by binder paper and pencils and unopened books on birds, immobilized by the hugeness of the task ahead. Then my father sat down beside him, put his arm around my brother's shoulder, and said, "Bird by bird, buddy. Just take it bird by bird.[3]

By doing the job incrementally, you are likely to learn more and procrastinate less.

Making the Most of Class Time

Psychologists tell us that beginnings and endings of events are especially memorable. An experienced teacher knows that the first 10 minutes of class sets the tone for the rest of the session, and that a summary at the end can help students remember the lesson. A choreographer knows that the first ten minutes of a performance can set the stage for the next two hours and that the end of a dance determines the overall impact. Similarly, the wise student arrives five minutes early for class, and maintains attention to the end of class.

Be an active learner. You can use that five minutes before class to review your notes from the previous session. This helps to create a bridge between what you know and the new information to be presented. Try to end the class on a high note, either by completing a project or by clearly determining the strengths and weaknesses of the work in progress. By writing down your assessment, you can organize your thinking and provide a solid beginning point for the next work session.

Start Early

Momentum is extremely powerful. It is much easier to climb a hill when you are already moving forward, rather than reclining. When you receive a long-term assignment such as a 20-page paper, start it right away. Even one hour of research will help focus your attention on the problem and get you going. A slow start is better than no start!

When in Doubt, Crank It Out

Fear is one of the greatest obstacles to creative thinking. When we are afraid, we tend to avoid action and consequently miss opportunities. It is difficult to act decisively or pursue the unknown potential of a new idea. Both habit and perfectionism feed fear. If you consistently repeat the same activities and limit yourself to the most familiar friendships, you will become more and more fearful of new experiences. If you insist on doing each job perfectly, you can waste time on minor defects and avoid exploring new ideas. Perfectionism is especially destructive during brainstorming, which requires a loose, open approach.

Creativity takes courage. As IBM founder, Thomas Watson, noted, "If you are not satisfied with your rate of success, try failing more." Baseball player Reggie Jackson is renowned for his 563 home runs—but he also struck out 2,597 times. Thomas Edison's research team tried over 6,000 materials before finding the carbon-fiber filament used in lightbulbs.

"When in doubt, don't!" is the safe-keeper's motto. "When in doubt, do!" is the risk-taker's motto. Creativity requires risk-taking. By starting each project with a sense of adventure, you increase your level of both learning and creativity.

Work Collaboratively

Many areas of art and design, including filmmaking, industrial design, and ad design are often done

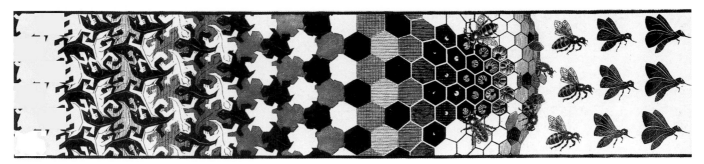

4.2   M. C. Escher, Part of *Metamorphosis II*, 1939-40. Woodcut in black, green, and brown, printed from 20 blocks on three combined sheets, 7¹/₂ × 153³/₈ in. (19 × 390 cm).

in collaboration. Working together, artists and designers can complete projects that are too complex or time-consuming to be done alone. Through collaborative thinking, we can pursue unfamiliar lines of inquiry, try out our ideas on colleagues, and consider many different approaches to creative thinking. Collaborative thinking helps us break familiar patterns and teaches us to listen to alternative or opposing ideas.

Here is one example. Gather 20 people. Start with a copied fragment from an existing image, such as *Metamophosis II*, an 8 × 160 in. banner by M. C. Escher (4.2). In this case, students in a design class were provided with a one-inch strip of the banner to create a beginning point and another one-inch strip of the banner to create the ending point (4.3A). Each person invented an 8½ × 11 in. connection between the two strips. Participants drew buildings, plants, abstract shapes, chess pieces, and other images to bridge the gap between the strips at the beginning and the end. The images were then connected end to end, like cars in a train. When combined, they created a collaborative banner, 20 feet long (4.3B). Students had to negotiate with the person ahead of them in the line,

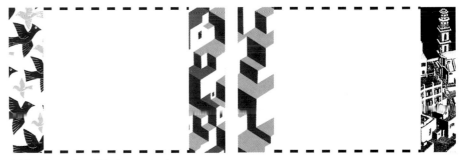

4.3A   Examples of Escher starter images.

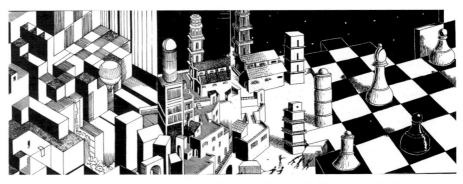

4.3B   Mary Stewart and Jesse Wummer, Expanded Escher Collaboration. Student work.

and with the person behind them, in order to make a continuous image with graceful transitions. In effect, all 20 participants become members of a creative team. Finally, each 8½ × 11 in. section was photocopied and traded, providing each person with the completed artwork. In a collaboration of this kind, everyone gains, both in the learning process and in the sharing of the product.

Reduce Stress

Finally, good time management can help you avoid excessive stress. When you are pushing beyond familiar limits, some stress is inevitable. Excessive stress, however, leads to illness, anger, insomnia, mental paralysis, exhaustion, and depression. Here are some strategies that can help.

No Blame

No matter what happens, blaming yourself or others is never useful. Work on the solution rather than remaining stuck in the problem.

Keep Your Balance

A mix of emotional, spiritual, physical, and intellectual activities will help feed all areas of your psyche. No matter how significant a particular assignment may appear to be, remember that it is only one aspect of your life. Taking a break can often give you the fresh perspective you need to solve a difficult problem. Value rest. When the balance is right, your time off can actually increase your productivity.

Positives Attract

A creative person seeks change. Any change tends to present a combination of obstacles and opportunities. Focusing on the opportunities rather than on the obstacles increases confidence. Furthermore, an upbeat, positive attitude attracts other creative thinkers, while a negative, excessively critical attitude drives creative thinkers away. By assuming that you *can* do the job well, you start the spiral of accomplishment needed to fully realize your creative potential. Accentuate the positive!

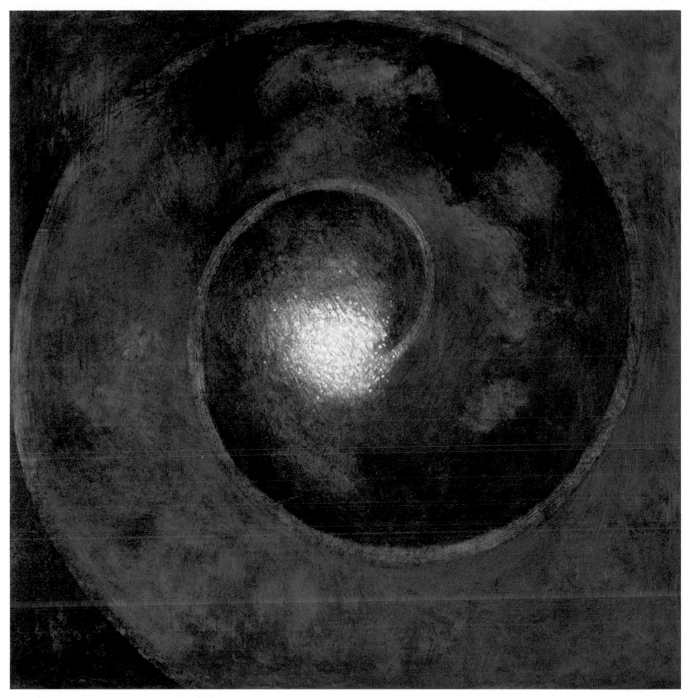

Georgiana Nehl, *Sun/Star* (detail), 1996. Oil paint on gessoed wood, 25¾ in. w. × 13¼ in. h. × 1 in. d. (65 × 34 × 3 cm).

Profile:
Nancy Callahan, Artist, and Diane Gallo, Writer

Storefront Stories: Creating a Collaborative Community

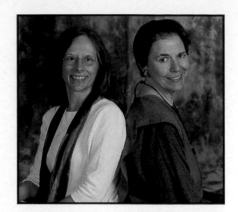

Nancy Callahan (left in photo) is a leader in the field of artists' books and is known for her creative work in screen printing. She has exhibited her work widely, and in 1994, she was one of four artists chosen to represent the United States at the International Book and Paper Exhibition in Belgium. In 1999 she participated in the International Artists' Book Workshop and Symposium in Mor, Hungary. In addition to her full-time teaching at the State University of New York at Oneonta, Callahan has taught workshops at major book centers around the country, including the Center for Book Arts in New York City and The Women's Studio Workshop.

Diane Gallo (right in photo) is an award-winning writer, performance poet, and a master teacher. Her film work has received awards from the American Women in Radio & Television and nominations from the American Film Institute. Gallo teaches creative writing and life-story workshops at universities and cultural institutes throughout the country and is a visiting poet with the Dodge Foundation Poetry Program, a humanist scholar with the National Endowment for the Humanities Poets in Person program, and co-founder of the newly formed Association of Teaching Artists.

Callahan and Gallo began working together in 1984 as a photographer/writer team for the Binghamton Press. As a result of many years of collaborative teaching, they became the first teaching artist team working with the Empire State Partnership project, jointly sponsored by the New York State Education Department and the New York State Council of the Arts. In 1996 they received fellowships to the Virginia Center for the Creative Arts where they began working on a major project that led to their selection by the Mid-Atlantic Foundation for their millennium project. Funded by the National Endowment for the Arts, the project—Artists & Communities: America Creates for the Millennium— named Callahan and Gallo as two of America's 250 most creative community artists.

MS: You've gained a lot of recognition for your recent text-based installations. Please describe Storefront Stories.

NC: Over the past two years we've had an extraordinary collaborative experience. As an extension of our writing, we developed a new type of text-based installation. One day as we worked on a story about ironing, we playfully hung a single wrinkled white shirt in the front window of our studio in Gilbertsville, New York. Below the shirt, we placed a small sign that said, "No one irons anymore." As the lone shirt turned, it attracted attention, causing people on the sidewalk to stop, read the window, and react. Storefront Stories was born.

DG: Objects became words, words transformed objects. Week by week, using storefront windows as a public stage, we wrote and presented installments of autobiographical stories. In one town, a single window was changed every ten days, creating an ongoing narrative. In another, we used five windows in a row, like pages in a book. Bits of text and symbolic objects were used to tell stories about personal change. Stories and objects—combined with the unexpected street location—sparked curiosity and started a community dialog.

MS: How did members of the community become participants?

NC: They just began telling us their stories. An elderly woman on her way to the post office stopped to tell us the story of how she had learned to type on an old Smith typewriter, just like the one in the window. Eleven-year-old boys on bicycles stopped by. A mother brought her children to the windows each week to read the story aloud. Couples strolling by in the evening asked, "What's coming next?"

DG: People talked to us easily, asking questions and encouraging us. Many times, we'd return to find handwritten stories, comments, and suggestions. We watched passersby examine the windows and heard them laughing and talking to each other as they pieced together the story. When a viewer made a good suggestion, we incorporated the idea into the next window. When community members saw their ideas so quickly incorporated, they realized they were more than passive viewers. They were now active participants, with a vital involvement in the artistic process. The collaboration which began between two artists quickly expanded, engaging the entire town.

MS: In your household installations you create complete environments to frame your stories. To create these environments, you spend many hours scouting thrift shops and garage sales searching for just the right objects to evoke an exact time and place. Why are these objects so important?

NC: Household objects are the vocabulary of the everyday world. Everyone feels comfortable with them. The objects are a bridge—they allow the viewer to cross easily from everyday life into the world of our installations.

DG: After the object is safely in the viewer's mind, it becomes a psychic spark which triggers associations and amplifies memories. For example, while we were doing the ironing installation, a delivery man who stopped for a moment to watch us work said, "I don't know anything about art," and began talking deeply and at length about how when he was a boy, his mother took in ironing to make extra money so that he could have a bicycle.

NC: His narrative then created another layer of collaboration.

MS: When you began creating the installations, did you expect this kind of public reaction?

NC: No. It was a shock. From the moment we hung that first wrinkled shirt in the studio window, people on the street were responsive. The immediate feedback was exhilarating.

MS: What are the characteristics of a good collaboration?

DG: Quiet attention is crucial. We both have to really listen, not only to words but also to the implications.

NC: Always tell the truth. There can be no censoring. If something's bothering you, it's important to talk about it right away. Honesty and careful listening build trust. When you trust your partner, you can reveal more.

MS: When people first see your installations, many are almost overwhelmed. Why?

DG: We're balancing on a fine line between life and art, between the personal and the universal, the public and the private, the conscious and the unconscious. We're working on the edge of consciousness, looking for things you might only be half aware of under ordinary circumstances. It's like watching a horizon line in your mind, waiting for a thought or answer to rise.

Diane Gallo and Nancy Callahan, *Storefront Stories*, 1999. Mixed medium installation, 6 × 6 × 6 ft (1.83 × 1.83 × 1.83 m).

Summary

- Creativity and design both require new combinations of old ideas.

- Creative people are receptive to new ideas, are curious, have a wide range of interests, are attentive, seek connections, and work with great conviction.

- Creative people combine rational and intuitive thinking. While intuition may be used to generate a new idea, logic and analysis are often needed for its completion. As a result, the actions of creative people are often complex or even contradictory.

- Goals you set are goals you get. Establishing priorities and setting appropriate goals will help you achieve your potential. Good goals are challenging but attainable, compatible, and self-directed. Deadlines encourage completion of complex projects.

- Creating a good work area, completing tasks in an appropriate sequence, making the most of each work period, maintaining momentum, and reducing stress are major aspects of time management.

- Collaborative work can help us expand our ideas, explore new fields, and pursue projects that are too complex or time-consuming to do alone.

1. What qualities have you noticed in unusually creative people? Reading a biography of your favorite artist or designer may provide further insight into the creative process.

2. What are your primary goals? How can a general goal be translated into a specific action?

3. Under what conditions do you work best? How can you cultivate the conditions most favorable to your own creative thinking?

Anne Lamott, *Bird by Bird: Some Instructions on Writing and Life*. New York, Anchor Books,1998.

Mihaly Csikszentmihalyi, *Creativity: Flow and the Psychology of Discovery and Invention*. New York, HarperCollins, 1996.

John Briggs, Fire in the Crucible: *Understanding the Process of Creative Genius*. Grand Rapids, MI, Phanes Press, 2000.

David Bohm, *On Creativity*. New York, Routledge, 2000.

Michael LeBoeuf, *Imagineering: How to Profit from Your Creative Powers*. New York, McGraw-Hill, 1980.

Howard Gardner, *Art, Mind and Brain: A Cognitive Approach to Creativity*. New York, Basic Books, Inc., 1982.

Howard Gardner, *Frames of Mind: The Theory of Multiple Intelligences*, New York, Basic Books, Inc., 1985.

Denise Shekerjian, *Uncommon Genius: How Great Ideas Are Born*. Penguin Books, New York, 1991.

Doris B. Wallace and Howard E. Gruber, editors, *Creative People at Work*. New York, Oxford University Press, 1989.

chapter five

Problem Seeking and Problem Solving

Artworks are generally experienced visually. By learning the basic elements of design and exploring many approaches to composition, you can increase the visual power of your work. Composition, however, is only part of the puzzle. With the continuing emphasis on visual communication throughout our culture, the ideas being expressed by artists and designers have become more varied and complex. As a result, conceptual invention is now as important as compositional strength. New ideas invite development of new images. When the concept is fresh and the composition is compelling, expression and communication expand.

Problem Seeking

The Design Process

In its most basic form, the creative process can be distilled down to four basic steps. When beginning a project, the designer asks:

1. What is required?

2. What existing designs are similar to the required design?

3. What is the difference between these designs and the required design?

4. How can we transform, combine, or expand these existing designs?

By studying the classic Eames chair, we can see this process clearly. Charles and Ray Eames were two of the most innovative and influential designers of the postwar era. Trained as an architect, Charles was a master of engineering and had a gift for design integration. Trained as a painter, Ray brought a love of visual structure, a sense of adventure, and an understanding of marketing to their work. Combining their strengths, this husband-and-wife team designed furniture, toys, exhibitions, and architecture, and directed over 80 experimental films.

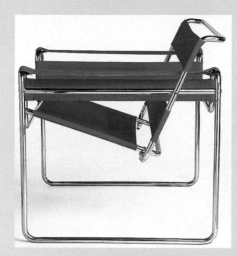

5.1 Marcel Breuer, Armchair, Dessau, Germany, 1925. Tubular steel, canvas. 28¹¹⁄₁₆ in. h. × 30⁵⁄₁₆ in. w. × 26¾ in. d. (72.8 × 77 × 68 cm).

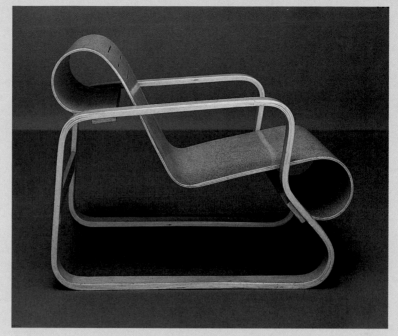

5.2 Alvar Aalto, Paimio Lounge Chair, 1931–33. Laminated birch, molded plywood, lacquered, 26 × 23¾ × 34⅞ in. (66 × 60.5 × 88.5 cm).

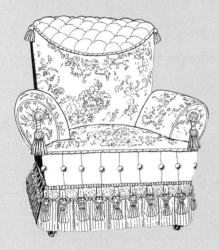

5.3 Overstuffed Chair.

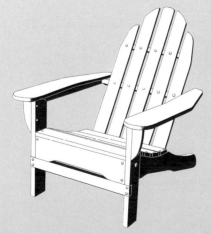

5.4 Adirondack Chair.

Their first breakthrough in furniture design began in 1940, when they entered a competition sponsored by the Museum of Modern Art. Many architects had designed furniture, and the Eameses were eager to explore this field. Many similar products existed. The most common was the overstuffed chair, which continues to dominate many American living rooms. Extensive padding on a boxy framework supported the sitter. Another popular design was the Adirondack chair, made from a series of flat wooden planes. Of greatest interest, however, were designs by architects such as Marcel Breuer (5.1) and Alvar Aalto (5.2). These designs used modern materials and clearly displayed their structure.

By comparing existing chairs with the chair required, Charles and Ray could identify some qualities they wanted to retain and some qualities that needed change. The familiar overstuffed chair (5.3) was bulky and awkward, but it was comfortable. The Adirondack chair (5.4) was easy to mass-produce, but too large for interior use. The modern chairs were elegant and inventive but were expensive and often uncomfortable. The Eameses wanted to produce a modern chair that was comfortable, elegant, and inexpensive.

During World War II, the Eames team had designed and manufactured molded plywood splints that were used by doctors in the U.S. Navy. After extensive research and

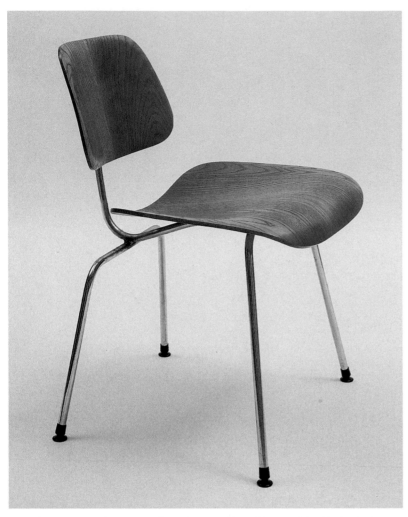

5.5   Charles and Ray Eames, Side Chair, Model DCM, 1946. Molded ash plywood, steel rod, and rubber shockmounts, 28¾ in. h. × 19½ in. d. × 20 in. w. (73 × 49.5 × 50.8 cm).

experimentation, they had mastered the process of steaming and reshaping the sheets of plywood into complex curves. In developing their competition entry, they combined their knowledge of splints, love of modern chairs, understanding of painting, and mastery of architecture. The first plywood chair, designed in collaboration with architect Eero Saarinen, was awarded the first prize.

A series of Eames designs followed, including a metal and plywood version in 1946 (5.5) and several cast plastic versions. One popular chair was mass produced by the hundreds of thousands.

By addressing a need, visualizing existing designs, making comparisons, and combining the best characteristics of existing chairs, the Eames team produced a new kind of chair and thus firmly established themselves as leaders in the design field.

The Art Process

For a designer, the problem-solving process begins when a client requests help or the designer identifies a specific need. With the Eames chair, the museum competition provided the impetus for an experiment that reshaped an industry. Design is generally utilitarian, and the problem is usually determined by a client.

Contemporary sculptors, printmakers, filmmakers, and other artists generally invent their own aesthetic problems. Ideas often arise from personal experience and from the cultural context. Combining self-awareness with empathy for others, many artists have transformed a specific event into a universal statement. For example, Picasso's *Guernica* (see Figure 5.21, page 5-21) painted in response to the 1937 bombing of a specific Spanish village, is now revered as a universal statement about the horrors of war. Working independently and without firm deadlines, artists can explore ideas and issues of personal interest.

Sources of Ideas

Regardless of the initial motivation for their work, both artists and designers constantly scan their surroundings in an omnivorous search for images and ideas. As demonstrated by the profiles that appear throughout this book, the most improbable object or idea may provide inspiration. Memories of growing up in small-town America provide the stimulus for *Storefront Stories*, by Nancy Callahan and Diane Gallo. Biological systems inspire sculptor Heidi Lasher-Oakes. Ordinary vegetables and African vessels influence ceramicist David MacDonald, while sculptor Rodger Mack derives many of his ideas from mythology. If you are at a loss for an idea, take a fresh look at what you can do with your surroundings.

Transform a Common Object

Architect Frank Gehry based this exuberant armchair (5.6) on the wood-strip bushel basket used by farmers (5.7). If you consider all the ideas that can be generated by a set of car keys, a pair of scissors, a baseball glove, or a compass, you will have more than enough to get a project started.

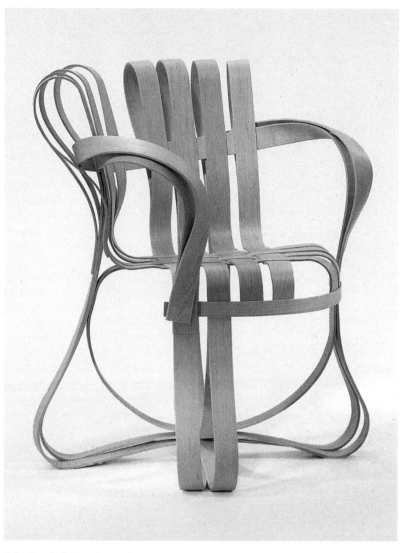

5.6 **Frank Gehry, Cross Check Armchair, 1992.** Maple, 33⅝ in. h. × 28½ in. d. × 28½ in. w. (85.3 × 72.4 × 72.4 cm).

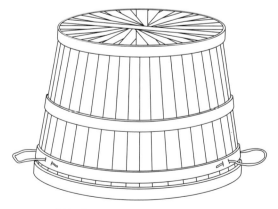

5.7 A wood-strip bushel basket.

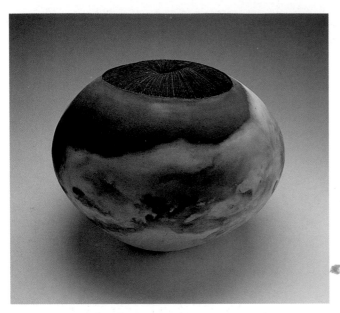

5.8 **Ray Rogers, Vessel, New Zealand, 1984.** Large, pit-fired (porous and nonfunctional) with "fungoid" decorative treatment in relief. Diameter approximately 21⅔ in. (55 cm).

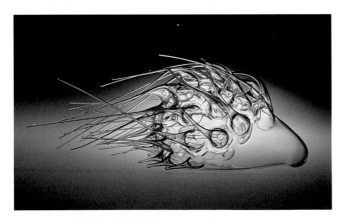

5.9 **Vera Lisková, _Porcupine_, 1972–80.** Flame-worked glass, 4¼ × 11 in. (10.8 × 28.2 cm).

Study Nature

Ceramicist Ray Rogers is inspired by many natural forms, including mushrooms, stones, and aquatic life. His spherical pots (5.8) often suggest the colors, textures, and economy of nature. In Figure 5.9, Vera Lisková used the fluidity and transparency of glass to create a humorous version of a prosaic porcupine. Through an inventive use of materials, both artists have reinterpreted nature.

Visit a Museum

Artists and designers frequently visit all kinds of museums. Carefully observed, the history and physical objects produced by any culture can be both instructive and inspirational. Looking at non-Western artwork is especially valuable. Unfamiliar concepts and compositions can suggest new ideas and fresh approaches. Beau Dick's _Mugamtl Mask_ (5.10) is one example. First developed by a man who had revived from a deadly illness, it depicts the supernatural abilities (including flight) that he gained during his experience. His descendants now have the right to construct and wear this special mask. By understanding the story and studying the mask structure, you can more readily generate your own mask based on your own experiences.

Characteristics of a Good Problem

Regardless of its source, the problem at hand must fully engage either the artist and the designer. By courageously confronting obstacles and seeking solutions, the artist/designer can develop increasingly ambitious work. Whether it is assigned or invented, a good problem includes many of the following characteristics.

Significant

When substantial amounts of time, effort, and money are being spent, it is wise to prioritize problems and focus on those of greatest consequence. Whether the project is the construction of the pyramids at Giza or completion of your bachelor's degree, assessing the importance of the project within a larger framework is important. Identifying and prioritizing major goals can help you determine the significance of a job. Balancing this analysis with a sense of adventure can help you combine the best qualities of a risk-taker and a safe-keeper.

Socially Responsible

With the human population above six billion, it is unwise to pursue a project that squanders natural resources. In the past 20 years, designers have become increasingly aware of the environmental and social consequences of their actions. What natural resources will be required for a major project, and how will you dispose of resulting waste? Increasingly, designers consider the environmental as well as the economic implications of each project.

Comprehensible

It is almost impossible to solve a problem you don't understand. When working on a class assignment, ask questions if the assignment is unclear to you.

Leaves Room for Experimentation

It is important to distinguish between clear definition and restrictive limitations. Consider these two assignment descriptions:

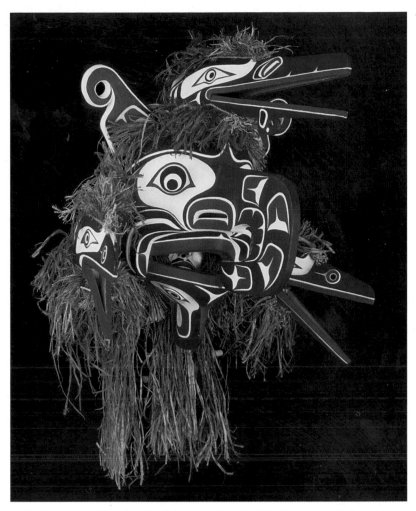

5.10 Beau Dick, *Mugamtl Mask (Crooked Beak),* **1993.** Red cedar, cedar bark, paint, 24 × 26 × 16 in. (61 × 66 × 40.6 cm).

1. **Organize at least 10 photocopies in such a way that they convey an idea or emotion.**

2. **Organize 10 photographs by American Civil War photographer Mathew Brady in order to tell a story about the life of Abraham Lincoln.**

In the first case, the requirements of the project are clearly stated, but the solution remains open to invention. In the second case, the *solution* as well as the *problem* is described. For the inventive artist or designer, there are no "bad" problems, only bad solutions. Nonetheless, when limited to a narrow range of possible solutions, even the most inventive person will become ineffective. If you find yourself in a straitjacket, rethink the problem and try a fresh approach.

Ambitious, Yet Achievable

When the problem is too easy or the solution is too familiar, little is learned and nothing is gained. When the problem is too difficult or the solution is too time-consuming, completion is delayed and costs increase. Continued indefinitely, even the most exciting project can become a trap!

Authentic

Regardless of the source, every person approaches each problem on his or her own terms. Each of us has a unique perspective, and the connections, which are so important in design, will vary. Likewise, as a design student, you will learn more when you really embrace each assignment and make it your own. Ask questions, so that you can understand the substance as well as the surface of each assignment. When you reframe the assignment in your own terms and plunge into the work wholeheartedly, the creative possibilities will expand and the imagination will ignite.

Problem-Solving Strategies

To see how it all works, let's work our way through an actual assignment.

Problem: Organize up to 20 photocopies from the library so that they tell a story. Use any size and type of format as appropriate. Any image can be enlarged, reduced, or repeated.

Solution #1: Using Convergent Thinking

Convergent thinking involves the pursuit of a predetermined goal, usually in a linear progression and using a highly focused problem-solving technique. The word "prose" can help you remember the basic steps:

1. Define the *problem*

2. Do *research*

3. Determine your *objective*

4. Devise a *strategy*

5. *Execute* the strategy

6. *Evaluate* the results

In convergent thinking, the end determines the means. You know what you are seeking before you begin. For this reason, clear definition of the problem is essential: even the most brilliant idea is useless if it doesn't solve the problem.

Convergent thinking is familiar to most of us through the scientific method, which follows the same basic procedure. It is orderly, logical, and empirical; there are clear boundaries and specific guidelines. Clearly focused on the final result, convergent thinking is a good way to achieve a goal and meet a deadline. Let's analyze each step.

Define the Problem

Determine the exact requirements of the assignment. Ask lots of questions so that you understand the purpose of the project and the objectives of the teacher. Determine the physical and technical requirements, and ask whether there are any stylistic limitations. Be sure that you understand the preliminary steps in the assignment as well as the final due date.

Next, assess your strengths and weaknesses relative to the problem assigned, and determine your best work strategy. Let's consider the approaches taken by two hypothetical students, Jeremy and Angela.

Jeremy decides to take a methodical approach to the assignment. He begins by defining "story," "images," and "library." From the dictionary, he finds that a *story* is shorter than a novel, that it may be true or fictitious, that a series of connected events is needed, and that it may take many forms, including a memoir, a play, or a newspaper article. Thus, he determines that the project is limited in length, and that the photocopies used should present a variety of characters or events in a cohesive way.

Next, he finds that an *image* is a representation of a person or thing, a visual impression produced by reflection in a mirror, or a mental picture of something: an idea or impression. This means that photographs from books or magazines, or reproductions of paintings, are fair game. Jeremy realizes that he can even include a mirror in the project, to reflect the viewer's own image.

Finally, by exploring the computer system in the *library*, he finds that Internet resources as well as books are available. He spends the first hour of the class on brainstorming, then decides on a story about Irish immigration to America at the turn of the century.

Do Research

Creativity is highly dependent on seeking connections and making new combinations. The more information you have, the more connections you can make. Through research, you can collect and assess technical, visual, and conceptual information. For this assignment, Jeremy develops a plausible story based on immigrant diaries. He begins to collect images of ships, cities, and people.

Determine Your Objective

Jeremy now has the raw material needed to solve the problem. However, many questions remain unanswered, including:

- What happens in this story? Is it fiction or non-fiction?

- Who is the storyteller? A 12-year-old boy will tell a very different story than a 20-year-old woman.

- What is the best format to use? A dozen letters, sent between fictitious brothers in Dublin and Boston? A Website, describing actual families? A photo album?

At this point, Jeremy pauses to determine his objective, both as an artist and as a student. What does he really want to communicate? He considers:

- *Does it solve the problem?* He reviews the assignment parameters.

- *Is the solution conceptually inventive?* Is it really intriguing, or is it something we've all seen before, a cliché? (Clichés have the virtue of being familiar, but to have real impact, you need a new idea or a fresh approach to an old idea.)

- *How visually inventive is the solution?* Through his work on previous assignments, Jeremy has learned that a familiar subject can have great impact when visualized well.

- *Can this solution be completed by the due date?* To meet the due date, it may be necessary to distill a complex problem down to an essential statement. In this case, Jeremy decides to simplify his project by focusing on one main character.

Devise a Strategy

While some assignments can be done in an afternoon, three-dimensional projects and multiple-image works tend to take longer. Jeremy determines the supplies he needs and considers the best time and place to work on the project.

Execute the Strategy

Now, Jeremy just digs in and works. He has found it best to work with great concentration and determination at this point, rather than second-guessing himself.

Evaluate the Results

At the end of each work session, Jeremy considers the strengths and weaknesses of the work in progress. What areas in each composition seem timid or confusing? How can those areas be strengthened? He finally presents the project for a class critique.

Convergent thinking is most effective when

- The problem can be defined clearly.

- The problem can be solved rationally.

- The problem must be solved sequentially.

- Firm deadlines must be met.

Because many problems in science and industry fit these criteria, convergent thinking is widely used by scientists, businesspeople, and graphic designers.

Solution #2: Using Divergent Thinking

The advantages of convergent thinking are clarity, control, focus, and a strong sense of direction. For many tasks, convergent thinking is ideal. In some cases, however, convergent thinking can offer *too* much clarity and not enough chaos. Inspiration is elusive. Over-the-edge creativity is messy and rarely occurs in an orderly progression. If you want to find something new, you will have to leave the beaten path.

In **divergent thinking,** the means determines the end. The process is more open-ended; specific results are hard to predict. Divergent thinking is a great way to generate ideas and move beyond preconceptions: any number of lines of inquiry can develop.

There are two major differences between convergent and divergent thinking. In divergent thinking, the problem is defined much more broadly, with less attention to "what the client wants." Research is more expansive and less tightly focused. Experimentation is open-ended: anything can happen.

With divergent thinking, the process may be as highly valued as the product. It is necessary to make many mistakes, and deadlines are harder to meet. Because the convergent thinker discards weak ideas in the thumbnail stage, the final image is preplanned and, thus, predictable. The divergent thinker, on the other hand, generates many variables, is less methodical, and may have to produce multiple drafts of a composition in order to get the desired result.

While convergent thinking is usually more efficient, divergent thinking is often more inventive. It opens up unfamiliar lines of inquiry and can lead to a creative breakthrough. Divergent thinking is a high-risk/high-gain approach. By breaking traditional rules, the artist can explore unexpected connections and create new possibilities. Let's try the same assignment again, now using Angela's divergent thinking.

Problem: Organize up to 20 photocopies from the library so that they tell a story. Use any size and type of format as appropriate. Any image can be enlarged, reduced, or repeated.

Realizing that the strength of the source images is critical, Angela immediately heads for the section of the library devoted to photography. By leafing though a dozen books, she finds 30 great photographs, ranging from images of train stations to trapeze artists. She photocopies the photographs, enlarging and reducing pictures to provide more options. Laying them out on a table, she begins to move the images around, considering the stories that might be generated. Twenty of the images are soon discarded; they are unrelated to the story she begins to develop. She then finds five more images to flesh out her idea.

At this point, her process becomes similar to the final steps described above. Like Jeremy, she must clarify her objective, develop characters, decide on a format, and construct the final piece. However, because she started with such a disparate collection of images, her final story may be nonlinear in nature. Like a dream, her images suggest ideas rather than describe specific actions.

Divergent thinking is most effective when

- The problem definition is elusive or evolving.

- A rational solution is not required.

- A sequential work method is unnecessary.

- Deadlines are flexible.

Many creative people have used divergent thinking to explore the subconscious and reveal unexpected new patterns of thought. Surrealism, an art movement that flourished in Europe between the world wars, provides many notable examples of divergent thinking in art and literature. More interested in the essential substance of ideas and objects

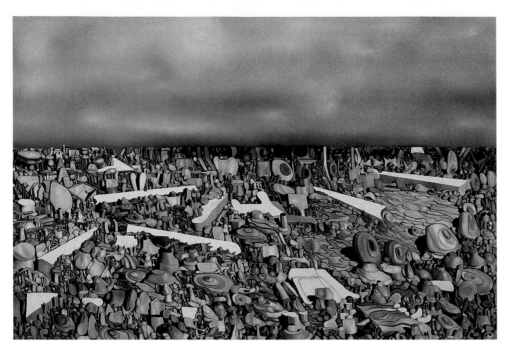

5.11 Yves Tanguy, *Multiplication of the Arcs*, **1954.** Oil on canvas, 40 × 60 in. (101.6 × 152.4 cm).

than in surface appearances, painter Yves Tanguy constructed *Multiplication of the Arcs* (5.11) from evocative abstract shapes. In *The Mystery and Melancholy of a Street* (5.12), Giorgio de Chirico used distorted perspective, relentless repetition, and threatening cast shadows to create a feeling of anxiety. More interested in stimulating the viewer's own response than in imposing a specific vision, the surrealists rejected rational thought.

Which is better—convergent or divergent thinking? A good problem-solving strategy is one that works. If five people are working on a Website design, a clear sense of direction, agreement on style, understanding of individual responsibilities, and adherence to deadlines are essential. Such a design team will usually use convergent thinking. On the other hand, when an artist is working independently, the open-ended divergent approach can lead to a real breakthrough. By understanding both approaches, you can select the work method that is best for you.

Brainstorming

Brainstorming plays an important role in both convergent and divergent thinking. It is a great way to expand ideas, see connections, and explore implications. Here are four common strategies.

Make a List

Let's say that the assignment involves visualizing an emotion. Start by listing every emotion you can, regardless of your interest in any specific area. Getting into the practice of opening up and actively exploring possibilities is crucial: just pour out ideas!

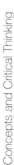

joy   sorrow   anger   passion   jealousy
sympathy   horror   exaltation

From the list of emotions, circle one that looks promising. To move from the intangible name of the emotion to a visual solution, develop a list of the *kinds, causes,* and *effects* of the emotion. Here's one example, using "Anger" as a starting point.

KINDS	CAUSES	EFFECTS
annoyance	wrong-number phone call at 5 A.M.	slammed down phone
smoldering rage	friend gets award you want	argument with friend
desperate anger	fired from job	shouted at your child
anger at self	poor performance on test	major studying

By investigating specific kinds of anger and determining the causes and the effects, you now have some specific images to develop, rather than struggling with a vague, intangible emotion.

Use a Thesaurus

Another way to explore the potential of an idea is to use a thesaurus. Be sure to get a thesaurus that lists words conceptually rather than alphabetically. Use the index in the back to look up the specific word you need. For example, *The Concise Roget's International Thesaurus* has a whole section titled "Feelings," including everything from *acrimony* to *zeal*. Here is a listing of synonyms from the section on *Resentment and Anger:* anger, wrath, ire, indignation, heat, more heat than light, dudgeon, fit of anger, tantrum, outburst, explosion, storm, scene, passion, fury, burn, vehemence, violence, vent one's anger, seethe, simmer, and sizzle! Thinking about a wide range of implications and connections to other emotions can give you a new approach to a familiar word.

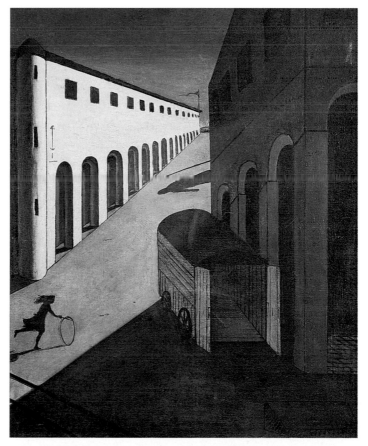

5.12 Giorgio de Chirico, *The Mystery and Melancholy of a Street,* **1914.** Oil on canvas, 24¼ × 28½ in. (62 × 72 cm).

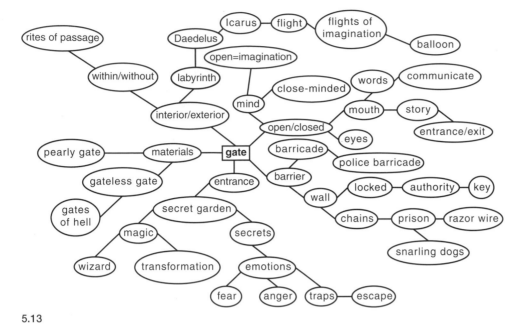

5.13

By creating a verbal diagram, you can create your own thesaurus. Start with a central word. Then, branch out in all directions, pursuing connections and word associations as widely as possible. In a sense, this approach lets you visualize your thinking, as the branches show the patterns and connections that occurred as you explored the idea (5.13).

Explore Connections

In *Structure of the Visual Book,* Keith Smith demonstrates the value of the mapping approach. Smith seeks immersion in his subject. He wants to know it so well that when he begins to work, he can pursue his images intuitively, with all the power and grace of a skillful cyclist. Try to follow all of the steps as he explores the word "bicycle."

If I am going to make drawings or photographs which include a bicycle, I might go for a bike ride, but more importantly I would fantasize about a bike. I would picture a bike in my mind. The most obvious depiction is the side view because this is the *significant profile.* I would then imagine a standing bicycle with no rider, looking from above, directly down on the bike, or from behind or in front of the standing bike with my eye-level midway between the ground and the handlebars. In these three positions the bicycle is seen from the least significant profile. It is a thin vertical line with horizontal protrusions of the pedals, seat and handlebars. The area viewed is so minimal that the bicycle almost disappears.

Before long in examining a bike I would become involved with circles. Looking at the tires, I think about the suspension of the rim and the tire, indeed, the entire vehicle and rider, by the thin spokes. It amazes me that everything is floating in space, connected only by thin lines. I imagine riding the bike through puddles and the trace of the linear journey from the congruent and diverging water marks left by the tread on the pavement. I might think about two friends together and separated. Symbolism.

I think about cycles of being with friends and apart. And again I would think literally of cycles, circles and tires.

I would think of the full moon as a circle and how in its cycle it turns into a line. I would see the tires from the significant profile and in my mind I would turn it in space and it would become an ellipse.

If I turned it further, until it was on an axis 90 degrees from the significant profile, it would no longer be a circle or an ellipse, but it would be a line. So again, line comes into my thoughts.

A circle is a line.

A circle is a straight line.[1]

Research

Library and Internet Research

Most libraries have computer systems that allow searches by subject, author, title, and keyword. Most offer searches on the Internet, including access to a variety of art-related databases. Some of the hits are very directly related to your basic idea, while others can be used to help expand an idea. A keyword search is especially broad: all sorts of books and Websites emerge. Websites are useful for getting an overview of possibilities and getting current information. Reading a book is preferable when more traditional, substantial, or extensive information is needed.

As practitioners of art and design, we can underestimate the value of research. Primarily concerned with technical and compositional problems, we may view research as extraneous. Professional artists and designers, however, value research highly. From experience, they learn that knowledge expands the imagination.

Visual Research

Thumbnail Sketches

While it is useful to generate many ideas verbally, it is in the visualization stage that the work really takes off. Return to your original list of emotions. Circle the most promising words or phrases you have generated, and look for connections between them. Start working on thumbnail sketches, about 1.5 × 2 in. in size (5.14). Be sure to draw a clear boundary for the sketches. The edge of the frame is like an electric fence; by using the edge wisely, you can generate a lot of power! As with the verbal brainstorming, move fast and stay loose at this point. It is better to generate 10 to 20 possibilities than to refine any single idea. You may find yourself producing very different solutions, or

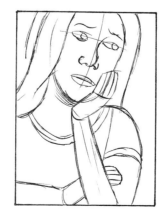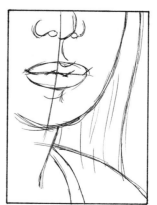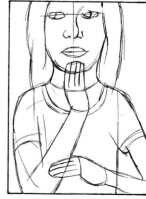

5.14 Examples of thumbnail sketches.

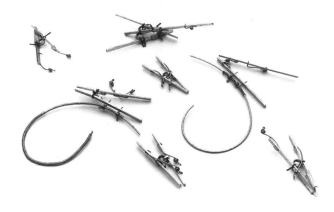

5.15A   Susan Cohn, *Cosmetic Manipulations*, 1992. Silver, binding wire, masking tape.

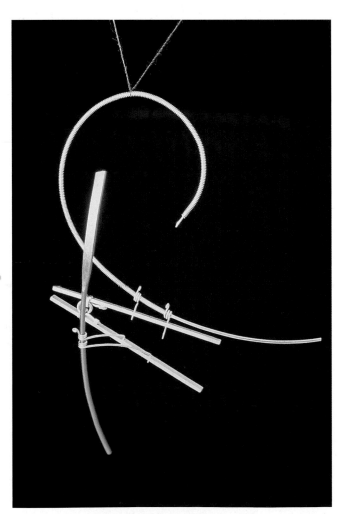

5.15B   Susan Cohn, *Cosmetic Manipulations*, 1992. Earring. 750 yellow gold, 375 pink gold, anodized aluminum; earring piece: 2½ × 3½ in. (6.5 × 9 cm); earring line: 4 in. (10 cm).

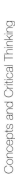
you may make a series of different solutions to the same idea: either approach is fine. Just keep moving. An open, nonjudgmental attitude is essential.

Thinking with Your Fingers

It is useful to make physical sketches as well as visual sketches when planning a three-dimensional object. Most physical objects are seen from many angles. While it is possible to draw multiple views, compositions can often be constructed more quickly from inexpensive materials such as paper, cardboard, wire, or plasticine. As shown in Figures 5.15A and 5.15B, a sketched structure can often be refined and used to create a much more polished final piece. Jeweler Susan Cohn developed a whole series of earrings and brooches from these *Cosmetic Manipulations*.

Model-Making

When working two dimensionally, it is often necessary to make one or more full-sized rough drafts to see how the design looks when enlarged. Refinements made at this stage can make all the difference between an adequate solution and an inspired solution.

Prototypes, models, and maquettes serve a similar purpose when you are working three dimensionally. A **maquette** is a well developed three-dimensional sketch. Figure 5.16A shows Peter Forbes's maquette for *Shelter/Surveillance Sculpture*. In this chipboard "sketch" Forbes determined the size of the sculpture relative to the viewer and developed a construction strategy. As a result, when he constructed the final eleven-foot-tall sculpture, Forbes was able to proceed with confidence. A **model** is a technical experiment. A **prototype** can be quite refined, as with the fully functional test cars developed by automobile companies. In addition to the aesthetic benefit of these preliminary studies, it is often necessary to solve technical problems at this stage. Is the cardboard you are using heavy enough to stand vertically, or does it bow? Is your adhesive effective? If there are moving parts, is the action fluid and easy, or does the structure consistently get stuck?

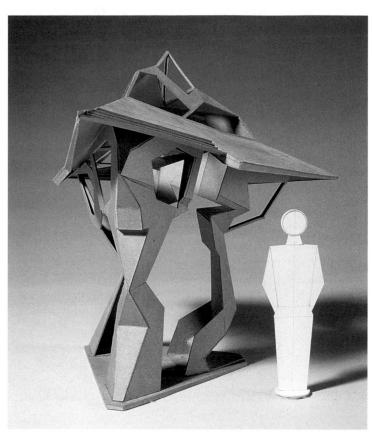

5.16A Peter Forbes, Models for *Shelter/Surveillance Sculpture*, 1994.
Mixed media, 10½ × 9½ × 9 in. (27 × 24 × 23 cm).

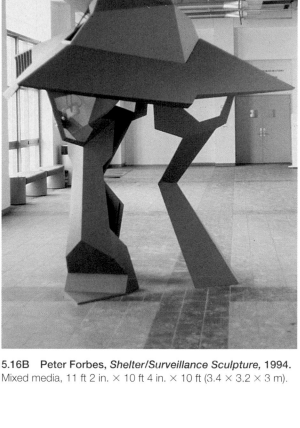

5.16B Peter Forbes, *Shelter/Surveillance Sculpture*, 1994.
Mixed media, 11 ft 2 in. × 10 ft 4 in. × 10 ft (3.4 × 3.2 × 3 m).

By completing these preliminary studies, the artist or designer can refine the idea, strengthen the composition, and improve the craft of the final piece. As with a well-rehearsed performance, the work you bring to the critique is now really ready for discussion.

Conceptual Expansion

When we work creatively, the idea develops right along with the image. As the project evolves, we see other implications that go beyond our initial intention. By courageously pursuing these implications, we can exceed our original expectations. Just as the landscape appears to expand when we climb a mountain, so an image can expand when our conceptual understanding increases. Concepts can be expanded using variations on a theme, metaphorical thinking, and interdisciplinary thinking.

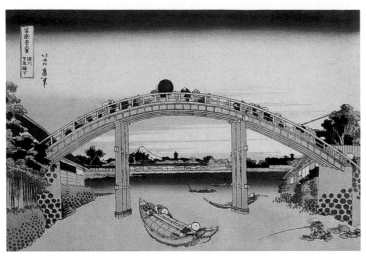

5.17A Katsushika Hokusai, *Thirty-six Views of Mount Fuji: Under the Mannen Bridge at Fukagawa,* Edo period, c. 1830. Color woodblock print, 10¹/₁₆ × 14¹¹/₁₆ in. (25.7 × 37.5 cm).

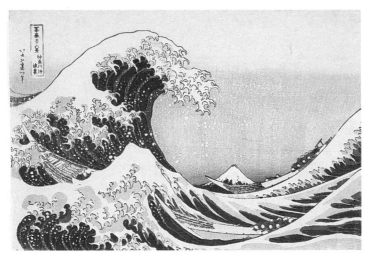

5.17B Katsushika Hokusai, *Thirty-six Views of Mount Fuji: The Great Wave off Kanagawa,* Edo period, c. 1830. Color woodblock print, 10³/₁₆ × 14¹⁵/₁₆ in. (25.9 × 37.5 cm).

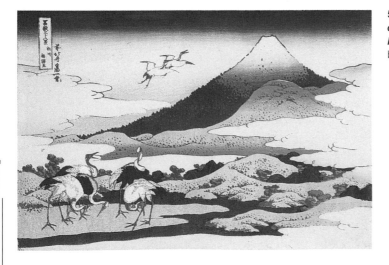

Variations on a Theme

A great deal of energy and commitment is needed to fully realize your vision, especially with complex sculptural or time-based assignments. One way to get a lot of mileage out of an idea is through variations on a theme. Professional artists rarely do just one painting or sculpture of a given idea—most do 30 or more variants before moving to a new subject.

Thirty-six Views of Mount Fuji is one example of the power of variations on a theme. Printmaker Katsushika Hokusai was 70 years old when he began this series. The revered and beautiful Mount Fuji appeared in each of the designs in some way. Variations in the time of year and size of the mountain helped Hokusai produce very different images while retaining the same basic theme (5.17 A–C).

A very different series of variations is presented in Figures 5.18 and 5.19. Here, the two artists offer very individual interpretations of the basic bracelet. Leslie Leupp's three bracelets present a playful dialog between form and space. Lines, planes, and simple volumes dance around the wearer's wrist. In contrast, Lisa Gralnick's three bracelets are dark, massive, and threatening. The crisp angles, simple forms, and black acrylic are more suggestive of armor than of jewelry.

5.17C Katsushika Hokusai, *Thirty-six Views of Mount Fuji: Near Umezawa in Sagami Province,* Edo period, c. 1830. Color woodblock print, 10¹/₁₆ × 14⁷/₈ in. (25.6 × 37.8 cm).

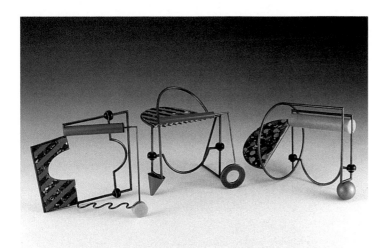

5.18 Leslie Leupp, Three Bracelets: Solidified Reality, Frivolous Vitality, Compound Simplicity, 1984. Steel, plastic, linoleum, laminate, aluminum. Constructed, each 3 × 4 × 3 in. (8 × 10 × 8 cm).

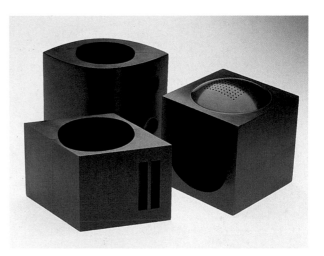

5.19 Lisa Gralnick, Three Bracelets, 1988. Black acrylic, gold, hollow construction, left to right: 3 × 3½ × 3½ in; 4½ × 3½ × 3 in; 3½ × 3½ × 3½ in; (7.6 × 8.9 × 8.9 cm; 11.4 × 8.9 × 7.6 cm; 8.9 × 8.9 × 8.9 cm).

Metaphorical Thinking

Metaphors, similes, or **analogies** are figures of speech that link one thing to another. Through this connection, the original word is given the qualities of the linked word. For example, when Robert Burns wrote the simile "My love is like a red red rose," he gave the abstract concept of "love" the attributes of a glorious, colorful, fragrant, thorny, and transient rose.

Metaphorical thinking creates a bridge between an image and an idea. Take the phrase, "I have butterflies in my stomach." This phrase is widely used to describe nervousness, often before a performance. Substitute other insects for "butterflies," such as bees or wasps. How does this change the meaning? To push it even further, start with the phrase, "My mind was full of clouds." What happens when "clouds" is replaced by mice on treadmills, rats in mazes, shadowy staircases, beating drums, screaming children—or even butterflies? When my mind is full of butterflies, I am happy, but butterflies in my stomach indicate fear. In addition to expanding your ideas, metaphors can help provide specific images for elusive ideas.

Metaphorical thinking and symbolism have always been used by artists and designers to heighten an idea or an emotion. Exaggerated metaphors are often used in advertising design.

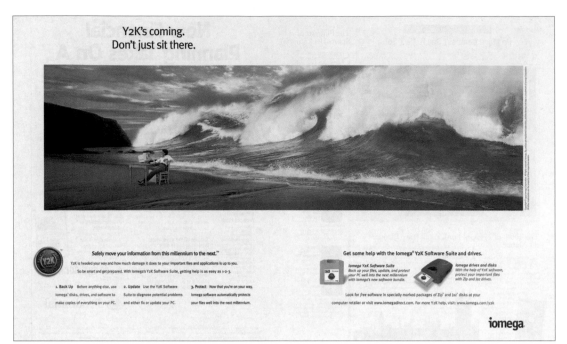

5.20 "Y2K's coming.
Don't just sit there."
Iomega Corporation.

The massive wave that threatens the computer user in Figure 5.20 is a metaphor for the destructive power of the Y2K computer bug that once seemed likely to create massive computer failures on January 1, 2000.

Picasso's *Guernica* (5.21) is also full of metaphors. In *A World of Art*, Henry Sayre offers the following description:

> The horse, at the center left, speared and dying in anguish, represents the fate of the dreamer's creativity. The entire scene is surveyed by a bull, which represents at once Spain itself, the simultaneous heroism and tragedy of the bullfight, and the Minotaur, the bull-man who for the surrealists stood for the irrational forces of the human psyche. The significance of the electric light bulb at the top center of the painting, and the oil lamp, held by the woman reaching out the window, has been much debated, but they represent, at least, old and new ways of seeing.[2]

Rather than showing exploding bombs or collapsing buildings, Picasso filled his painting with abstracted animals, screaming humans, and various light sources. In so doing, he focused on the meaning and emotion of the event, rather than the appearance.

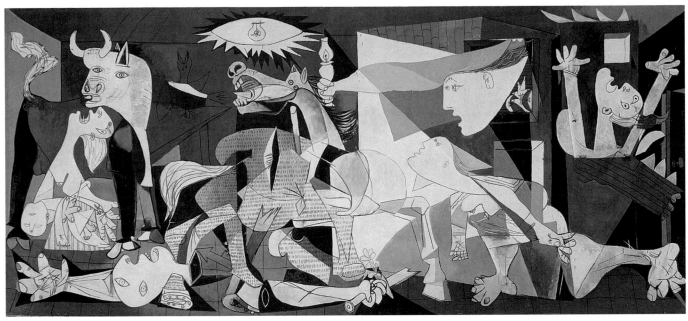

5.21 Pablo Picasso, *Guernica*, 1937. Oil on canvas, 11 ft 5½ in. × 25 ft 5¼ in. (3.5 × 7.8 m).

Interdisciplinary Thinking

As noted in Chapter 4, most creative people have a wide range of interests. The very best artists and designers are often accomplished in more than one field. For example, Michelangelo was acclaimed as a painter, sculptor, and poet, while da Vinci was a master of art, biology, and engineering. The study of philosophy has had a major impact on videographer Bill Viola and installation artist Robert Irwin. Performer Laurie Anderson is equally an artist and a musician and derives many of her ideas from literature. Whenever the base of knowledge expands, the range of potential connections increases. When the islands of knowledge are widely scattered, as with interdisciplinary work, the imaginative leap is especially great.

The message is clear. The more you know, the more you can say. Read a book. Attend a lecture. Take a course in astronomy, archaeology, psychology, or poetry. Art and design require conceptual development as well as perceptual and technical skill. By engaging your heart, your eye, your hand, and your mind, you can fully use your emotional perceptual, technical, and conceptual resources to create your very best work.

Profile:
Heidi Lasher-Oakes, Sculptor

The Infinite Journey: Exploring Ideas in
Art and Science

Heidi Lasher-Oakes is best known for her Biological Abstractions
Series. Her exhibitions include "Seductive Matter, Sensual Form,"
which was installed in the Corcoran Art Gallery, and "In Three
Dimensions: Women Sculptors of the 90's," which was held at the
Snug Harbor Cultural Center. Educated at Reed College, the Pacific
Northwest College of Art, and Syracuse University, Lasher-Oakes was awarded a residency at the
Bemis Art Center in Omaha, Nebraska, and received a Pollock-Krasner Individual Artist Grant in 1997.

MS: What do art and science have in common?

HL: I have always believed that artistic and scientific
methods are closely linked. A scientific experiment is aesthetically pleasing when it is simply and elegantly designed and takes into consideration all possible variables.
On the other hand, the full exploration of an artistic idea
requires the same rigor of inquiry and careful documen-
tation as the exploration of a scientific hypothesis. In either discipline, if a process is aesthetically successful, it
will lead to a coherent result. An aesthetic process requires that all components be ruthlessly considered and
evaluated individually and as a unit. The aesthetic integrity of a process does not guarantee that the resulting
artwork or experiment will be successful, but it does
seem to guarantee that the subsequent work will not con-
stitute a waste of time, either for the investigator or for
the audience.

The Shakers have a philosophy of work that expresses
this viewpoint simply: if you are going to do something,
do it as well as you can.

MS: What is the connection between art and science in
your work?

HL: The sculptures in my current Biological Abstraction
Series are inspired by human anatomy and physiology,
by the forms of cell and tissue structures as seen through
an electron microscope, and by the relationships of these
forms to manmade structures and objects. They also in-
corporate plant, animal, and rock forms. Science really
provides the starting point for my artwork.

MS: Why are you a sculptor rather than a scientist?

HL: Art gives me a way to express my ideas and observations through the creation of physical objects. I am a hap-
tic person, which means that I am as influenced by touch
as I am by sight. I think this ties into a phrase common in
our culture, "Let me see that!" which really means, "Give
that to me: I want to hold it." To know a thing, I have to
hold it, turn it over in my hands, take it apart, then put it
back together.

MS: I'm intrigued by your strong emphasis on research,
both in your own work and in the classes you teach.
What is the value of research?

HL: Research is valuable for two reasons. It provides information for existing ideas and is a way of generating
new ideas. Personally, I never know where research will
take me. To my mind, the act of researching a subject is
very much like exploring a hypertext site on the Internet—once you start clicking, you soon find that you have
wandered far from your original reference point. While I
understand the value of staying focused, it is the digres-
sions and distractions that give me the best ideas, months
or even years later.

Research is insurance. It provides context and fertilizes
ideas. The more pieces of information you have, the more
connections or associations you will be able to make. And
associations are essential. Associative thinking is the ability to make original or unexpected connections. It is an
essential part of creativity. Some people start out thinking
this way, while for others it is a learned trait.

A wide range of interests seems to encourage associative thinking, so I keep my mind open. For example, I am
currently reading a book on grasshoppers, two histories
of military battle dress, a mystery novel by Antonia
Fraser, three collections of American English proverbs, an

introduction to chemistry, and a book by Jorge Luis Borges—and several others waiting in the wings!

MS: How do you get your ideas?
HL: Just about anything in my environment and experience can generate an idea—a book I read, a conversation, a walk in the woods . . .

MS: Your ideas are pretty complex. How do you communicate this information?
HL: Using association, I try to put as many ideas as possible into the forms I construct. For example, Biological Abstraction III, which depicts an ovary and associated seed structures, also embodies references to dandelion seeds, diving bells, and bomb casings. Each reference contains another piece of information which expands on a physical quality of the object and adds another layer of meaning. I'm not interested in making copies of the structures I study. Instead, I try to understand and express their essential forces and overriding themes.

MS: Please describe your working process.
HL: First, I identify a system for study. Since I am especially interested in human anatomy and physiology, I think of a system as an organ or group of organs in the human body. In this series, I have studied the female reproductive tract, the skin, the respiratory tract , and the inner ear.

Once I have chosen a system, I study it at microscopic and macroscopic levels to try to learn something about the relationship between its structure and function. Scale is really important: the microscopic view reveals an astonishing level of complexity in the simplest of structures! During this phase, I also look for materials that share the structural and functional properties of my system's cellular building blocks. I experiment by combining these materials to see how they might work together. At the same time, I begin to make plans and drawings for different aspects of the piece. When I have gathered enough information to give me a solid foundation, I begin construction.

MS: It sounds so orderly! My creative process is much more chaotic.
HL: Actually, my process is definitely *not* as linear as it sounds! The research, while extensive, is never complete: all art-making requires a balance between analysis and intuition. The materials always have something new to teach me if I am willing to learn. This element of unpredictability can be frustrating and uncomfortable, but it is absolutely essential. If I play it safe, if I'm inflexible, too insistent on sticking to a set plan, the resulting piece will be dull and lifeless. For me, learning comes from experimenting and making mistakes. It is the desire to learn about my materials, myself, and the world around me that keeps me actively engaged during many hours of physical work.

MS: I think we can appreciate the function of science in our culture. What is the function of art?
HL: For me, art helps to stimulate thought, encourage contemplation, increase understanding, and express emotion. Like science, it gives us a way to see beyond everyday experience and embrace the complexity and beauty of our world.

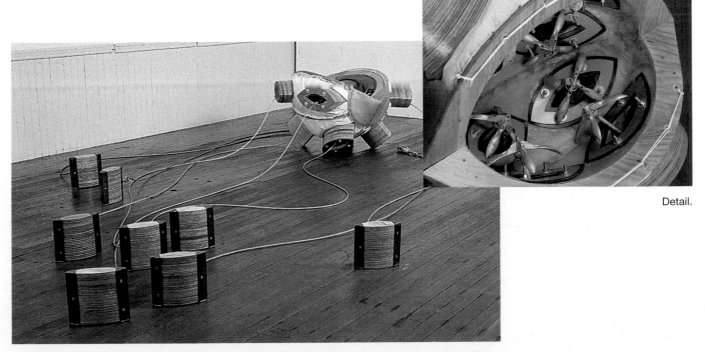

Detail.

Heidi Lasher-Oakes, *Biological Abstraction III*, 1996. Wood, fiberglass, foam rubber, canvas, steel, dinghy anchors, rubber gasket material, fabricated and purchased hardware. Primary structure: 4 ft l. × 4 ft w. × 3½ ft h. (1.21 × 1.21 × 1.07 m), entire assembly approx. 15 ft l. (4.5 m).

Summary

- Concept and composition are equally important aspects of art and design.

- Designers usually solve problems presented by clients. Artists usually invent aesthetic problems for themselves. Both explore many alternatives before achieving the desired result.

- Ideas come from many sources, including common objects, nature, mythology, or history.

- Good problems are significant, socially responsible, comprehensible, achievable, and authentic. They provide basic parameters without inhibiting exploration.

- Convergent thinking is highly linear. The word "prose" can help you remember the steps.

- Divergent thinking is nonlinear and more open-ended. It is less predictable and may lead to a creative breakthrough.

- Any idea can be expanded or enriched using brainstorming. List-making, using a thesaurus, mapping, and creating connections are common strategies.

- Visual and verbal research can provide the background information needed to create a truly inventive solution.

- Pursuing an idea through variations on a theme, metaphorical thinking, or interdisciplinary connections can help you realize its full potential.

Keywords

analogy	interdisciplinary	model
brainstorming	thinking	prototype
convergent thinking	maquette	simile
divergent thinking	metaphor	

1. How many meanings can be derived from individual words, such as "water," "hidden," or "parallel"? Use a dictionary, a thesaurus and an encyclopedia to investigate each word thoroughly.

2. How many meanings can be derived from everyday objects, such as keys, rulers, or eyeglasses? Consider every possible association and implication.

3. How many ways can an idea be visualized? Try different forms of balance, variations in emphasis, use of contrast, etc. Most professional designers make dozens of thumbnail sketches or maquettes before starting work on a final piece.

4. How do materials affect meaning? What is the difference between a marker drawing of a given subject, a charcoal drawing of the same subject, a photograph, and a wooden sculpture?

5. How many variations can be invented from a single theme? Any aspect of an image can be changed, including size, color, complexity, style, materials used, and so forth.

James L. Adams, *Conceptual Blockbusting*. Reading, MA, Addison-Wesley, 1986.

Edward de Bono, *Lateral Thinking*. London, England, Ward Educational Limited, 1970.

Malcolm Grear. *Inside/Outside: From the Basics to the Practice of Design.* New York, Van Nostrand Reinhold, 1993.

Mary Frisbee Johnson. *Visual Workouts: A Collection of Art-Making Problems.* Englewood Cliffs, NJ, Prentice-Hall, 1983.

George Lakoff and Mark Johnson. *Metaphors We Live By.* Chicago, University of Chicago Press, 1981.

Ben Shahn. *The Shape of Content.* Cambridge MA, Havard University Press, 1957.

Judith and Richard Wilde. *Visual Literacy: A Conceptual Approach to Graphic Problem Solving.* New York, Watson-Guptill, 1991.

Developing Critical Thinking

chapter six

Critical thinking combines

- Careful evaluation of all available information.
- The analysis of visual relationships.
- The exploration of alternative solutions.

   Critical thinking is motivated by the desire to pursue an idea to the limit. Never complacent, the best artists and designers continually seek to improve each image and expand each idea. Critical thinking is used to determine compositional strengths, expand concepts, and improve visual communication. Knowing what to keep and what to change is essential. By expanding the best aspects of a design and deleting weak areas, we can dramatically strengthen both communication and expression.

Establishing Criteria

Establishing the criteria on which judgments will be made is the first step. For example, if technical skills are being emphasized in an assignment, craftsmanship will be highly valued. Likewise, if the assignment must be done in analogous colors, a black-and-white painting will not meet the criteria, no matter how carefully it is composed. By determining the major questions being raised in each problem, we can understand the basis on which judgments will be reached. Consider:

- What is the purpose of the assignment? Does your teacher want you to learn any specific skills? What compositional and conceptual variables will you need to explore?

- What are the assignment parameters? Are there limitations in the size, style, or materials?

- When is the assignment due and in what form must it be presented?

   It is important to distinguish between understanding assignment criteria and seeking the "right answer." In the first case, by determining the boundaries, you can fully focus your energy when you begin to work. Just as a magnifying glass can be used to focus sunlight into a powerful beam, so assignment parameters can help you focus creative energy. On the other hand, students who try to determine the "right answer" to a problem often simply want to know the teacher's solution. Such knowledge is rarely helpful. Any problem presented by a teacher simply sets a learning process in motion: you learn through your work. Since learning requires a personal process of investigation, finding your own answer is essential.

Form, Subject, and Content

The most effective compositions present a unified visualization of an idea or emotion. As a result, it is often difficult to dissect and analyze a design. Identifying three major aspects of an artwork can provide a beginning point for discussion.

Form may be defined as the physical manifestation of an idea or emotion. Two-dimensional forms are created using line, shape, texture, value, and color. The building blocks of three-dimensional forms are line, plane, volume, mass, space, texture, and color. Duration, tempo, intensity, scope, setting, and chronology are combined to create time-based art forms. For example, film is the form in which *Star Wars* was first presented.

The **subject,** or topic, of an artwork is most apparent when a person, object, event, or setting is clearly represented. For example, the conflict between the rebels and the Empire provides the subject for *Star Wars*.

The emotional or intellectual message of an artwork provides its **content,** or underlying theme. The theme of the *Star Wars* trilogy is the journey into the self. Luke Skywalker's gradual understanding of himself and acceptance of Darth Vader as his father adds an emotional undercurrent to all the events in the the entire *Star War* series.

Critique Basics:
Stop, Look, Listen, Learn

Any of these aspects of design can be discussed critically. A **critique** is the most common structure used. During the critique, the entire class analyzes the work completed at the end of an assignment. Many solutions are presented, demonstrating a wide range of possibilities. The strengths and weaknesses in each design are determined, and areas needing revision are revealed. These insights can be used to improve the current design or to generate possibilities for the next assignment.

Critiques can be extremely helpful, extremely destructive, or just plain boring, largely depending on the amount and type of student involvement. The main purpose of the critique is to determine which designs are most effective, and why. Specific recommendations are most helpful: be sure to substantiate each judgment so that your rationale is clear. Whether you are giving or receiving advice, come with your mind open, rather than your fists closed. A critique is not a combat zone! Listen carefully to any explanations offered, and generously offer your insights to others. Likewise, receive their suggestions gracefully rather than defensively. You will make the final decision on any further actions needed to strengthen your design; if someone gives you bad advice, quietly discard it. An open, substantial, and supportive critique is the best way to determine the effect your design has on an audience, so speak thoughtfully, listen carefully, and weigh seriously every suggestion you receive.

When beginning a critique, it is useful to distinguish between objective and subjective criticism. **Objective criticism** is used to assess how well a work of art or design utilizes the elements and principles of design. Discussion generally focuses on formal concerns, such as

- The type of balance used in the composition and how it was created.

- The spatial depth of a design and its compositional effect.

- The degree of unity in a design and how it was achieved.

Objective criticism is based on direct observation and a shared understanding of assignment parameters. Discussion is usually clear and straightforward. Alternative solutions to a problem may be discussed in depth.

Subjective criticism is used to describe the personal impact of an image, the narrative implications of an idea, or the cultural ramifications of an action. Discussion generally focuses on the subject and content of the design, including

- The meaning of the artwork.

- The feelings it evokes.

- Its relationships to other cultural events.

- The artist's intent.

Because subjective criticism is not based on simple observation, it is more difficult for most groups to remain focused on the artwork itself or to reach any clear conclusions regarding possible improvements. The discussion may become more general and wide-ranging, as political or social questions raised by the works of art and design are analyzed. While these are important topics, because of the potential lack of clarity, subjective criticism may be used sparingly during the foundation year.

Types of Critiques
Description

The first step is to look carefully and report clearly. Without evaluating, telling stories, drawing conclusions, or making recommendations, simply describe the visual organization of the work presented. A **descriptive critique** can help you see details and heighten your understanding of the design. The student whose work you describe learns which aspects of the design are most eye-catching and readable and which areas are muddled and need work.

This is a particularly useful exercise when analyzing a complex piece, such as Figure 6.1. In an art history class you might write:

> *Place de l'Europe on a Rainy Day* is a rectangular painting depicting a street in Paris. A vertical lamppost and its shadow extend from the top edge to the bottom edge, neatly dividing the painting in half. A horizon line, extending from the left side and three-quarters of the way to the right, further divides the painting, creating four major quadrants. Because this horizon line is positioned above center, the bottom half of the composition is larger than the top half.
>
> A dozen pedestrians with umbrellas occupy the bottom half of the painting. At the right edge, a man strides into the painting, while next to him a couple moves out of the painting, toward the viewer. To the left of the lamppost, most of the movement is horizontal, as people cross the cobblestone streets.

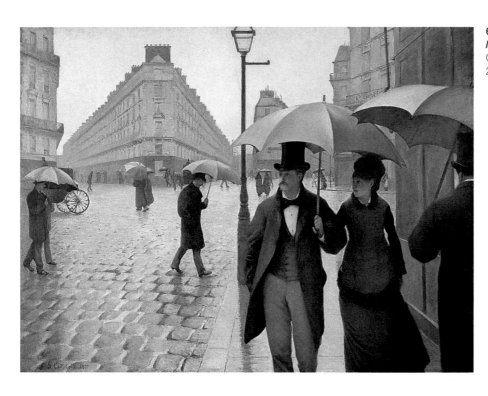

When using description in a spoken critique, it is useful to consider the following compositional characteristics:

- What is the format or boundary for the design? A circle or sphere presents a very different compositional playing field than a cube or a square.

- What range of colors has been used? A black-and-white design is very different from a design in full color.

- What is the size of the project? Extremes are especially notable. A sculpture that is 10 feet tall or a painting that is one-inch square will immediately attract attention.

- Is the visual information tightly packed, creating a very dense design, or is the design more spacious, with a lot of space between shapes or volumes?

Cause and Effect

A descriptive critique helps us analyze the compositional choices made by the artist. A **cause-and-effect critique** builds on this description. In a simple description, you might say that the design is primarily composed of diagonals. Using cause and effect, you might conclude that *because* of the many diagonals, the design is very dynamic. In a cause-and-effect critique, you discuss consequences as well as choices. Analyzing the same painting, you might write:

> *Place de l'Europe on a Rainy Day* depicts a city street in Paris near the end of the nineteenth century. A vertical lamppost, positioned near the center, compositionally dissects the painting in half. A dozen pedestrians in dark clothing cross the cobblestone streets from left to right, creating a flowing movement. To the right of the post, the pedestrians move in and out of the painting, from background to foreground. Two men and one woman are the most prominent figures. The man at the far right edge pulls us into the painting, while the couple to his immediate left moves toward us, pushing out of their world and into our world. The movement that dominates each side of the painting is arrested by the lamppost. It is almost like we are getting two paintings on one canvas.

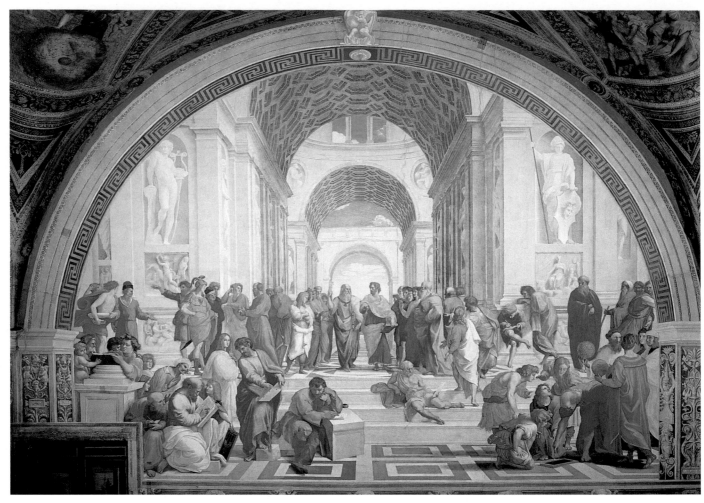

6.2 Raphael, *The School of Athens*, 1509–11. Fresco, 26 × 18 ft (7.92 × 5.49 m). Stanza della Segnatura, Vatican, Rome.

Compare and Contrast

In a **compare/contrast critique,** similarities and differences between two images are noted. We will use the Caillebotte painting one more time, now comparing the perspective used with the perspective in Raphael's *The School of Athens* (6.2).

   The city streets depicted in *The School of Athens* and *Place de l'Europe* demonstrate many differences between Renaissance and Impressionist perspective.

   The one-point perspective used in Raphael's painting leads our eyes to Plato and Aristotle, positioned just below the center of the composition. The other figures in the painting are massed in a horizontal band from the far right to the far left side and in two lower groups, to the right and left of the central figures. Our eyes are led back to the philosophers by a man sprawled on the steps to the right and by the scribes' tables on the left. Like a proscenium arch in a theater, a broad arch in the foreground frames the scene. Overlapping arches add to the depth of the painting. This composition combines the stability of one-point perspective with a powerful illusion of space.

   In the Caillebotte painting, a lamppost occupies center stage, rather than a philosopher. The one-point perspective in the cobblestone street and in the buildings on the right is complicated by the two-point perspective used for a large background building on the left. This unusual illusion of space, combined with the movement of the pedestrians, creates a feeling of instability.

All these approaches are often used in art history classes. The same strategies, however, may be used in the studio, for either spoken or written critiques. Here is an example, written by two students in a basic design class. The assignment was to complete an 18 × 24 in. design, transforming the music building (Crouse College) into a labyrinth.

Looking at Cally's design (6.3), Trish wrote:

Cally's piece uses strong black-and-white contrast, with both negative and positive space clearly developed. On the other hand, my design is brightly colored, representing a kaleidoscope based on the stained glass windows in the building.

We both use the staircase as a major element. Cally's stair leads you in and around the building, creating a way to explore the space. My stair becomes part of the overall pattern.

I thought of the labyrinth as an abstract puzzle, a design you could draw your pencil through to find the ending. I wanted my design to be playful. Cally's design focuses on the psychological, creating an entry into the human mind. Cally's design is mysterious. Her staircases seem to lead nowhere.

We both use lines very deliberately. Where one line ends, another begins. Without lines in a labyrinth, it wouldn't be as puzzling or mysterious. It would just be another design, rather than a puzzle to solve or a fun house to explore.

Looking at Trish's design (6.4), Cally wrote:

The first difference I notice is that my labyrinth uses black and white to form a high-contrast composition whereas Trish uses color to transform the building into a complex pattern. My vertical format helps suggest the height of the building, which is dominated by two amazing staircases. Trish's horizontal format contains a design that is as abstract as a computer circuit board.

Next, I notice conceptual differences between our solutions. My drawing is representational, depicting a psychological labyrinth, whereas Trish's turns this labyrinth into a puzzle. She took several architectural elements of Crouse College and juxtaposed them as motifs within the drawing. The pipework, in particular, was abstracted and expanded

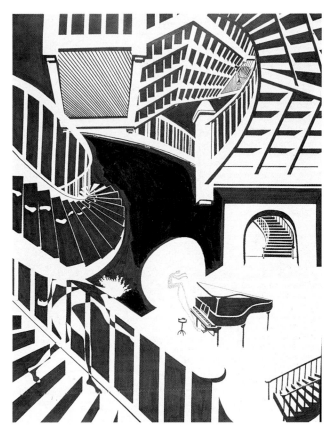

6.3 Cally Iden, *Transforming Crouse College into a Labyrinth.* Student work. 18 × 24 in.

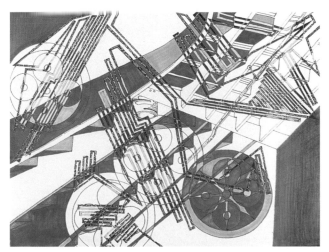

6.4 Tricia Tripp, *Transforming Crouse College into a Labyrinth.* Student work. 24 × 18 in.

into an elaborate maze. It creates a definite boundary between the background and the foreground. The space is essentially flat in Trish's design: color is used to create a balanced composition rather than being used to create any illusion of space. On the other hand, because my design is representational, I used the illusion of space to create a convincing interior space.

One similarity between our drawings is in the inclusion of the staircase. Trish used the stairs as a *background* shape that adds dynamism to the composition. I used the stair as a primary motif, a means by which people using the building can explore their own minds.

For me, Trish's design creates a sense of alienation. There is no evidence of human experience here—it is a purely visual world, made up of complex shapes. It produces no strong emotion for me, no sense of mystery. It is purely visual.

On the other hand, there are hints of "the human" in my composition, but it is lost within the maze of repetitive stairs: only traces remain. This stark contrast helps communicate the confusion and mystery of my psychological labyrinth. I want to convey the feeling of being caught in a labyrinth, solving mysteries, and finding one's self.

Both critiques are honest without being abusive and offer a discussion of both concept and composition. While they are very different, each of the students clearly respects the approach taken by the other.

Greatest Strength/Greatest Potential

Many projects have one notable strength and one glaring weakness. To create a positive atmosphere, start by pointing out the strength in the work. Begin by looking for:

• The level of unity in the design and how was it achieved.

• The amount of variety in the design, and how much energy it generates.

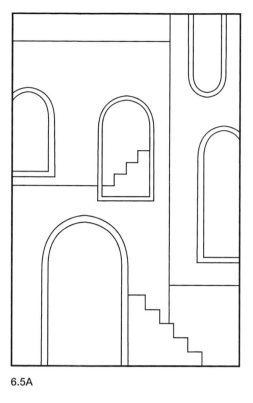

6.5A

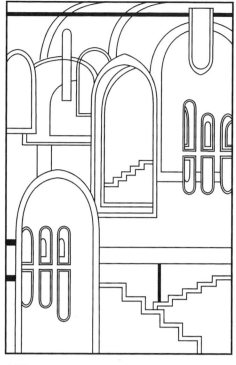

6.5B

- The visual rhythms used and their emotional effect.

- The attention to detail. This could include craftsmanship, conceptual nuance, or compositional economy.

- A conceptual spark. We all love to see an unexpected solution that re-defines the imaginative potential of a project.

Using Figure 6.5A as an example, you could say:

> The primary strength of this project is unity. Use of black marker throughout gives the design a simple, clean, and consistent look. The repetition of the arches helps tie it all together. Vertical and horizontal lines dominate, creating a type of grid.

Next, consider ways to improve the project. Mentally arm yourself with a magic wand. If you could instantly transform the design, what single aspect would you change? How can the potential of the project be more fully realized? Some basic questions follow.

- Is it big enough? Is it small enough?

- Is it bold enough? Is it subtle enough?

- How rich is the concept? Can it be expanded?

- How can the concept be communicated more clearly? How can the concept be communicated more fully?

The assignment was to create a labyrinth. Figure 6.5A is spatially shallow. To create 6.5B you might suggest:

> When I think about a labyrinth, I think of it as a mysterious place that I can enter and explore. As it now stands, this design is spatially flat: it gives me no place to go. For further work, you might try increasing the illusion of space. Greater size variation in the arches, with larger ones in the front and smaller ones in the back could help. Overlapping some of the arches could increase the space and add a rhythmic quality to the work. And, have you considered using gray marker for the background shapes? This would reduce the contrast and push them back in space.

Developing a Long-Term Project

Critical thinking is useful at many points in a project, not just at the end. When working on a project for 10 hours or more, it is useful to assess progress at the beginning or the end of each work period. This may be done in a large-group critique, in small teams, in discussion with your teacher, or on your own. Several effective strategies follow.

Week One Assessment

Determine Essential Concept

As a project begins to evolve from brainstorming, to thumbnails, to rough drafts, the concept may also evolve. Your initial idea may expand or shift during the translation from the mind to the hand to the page. Stopping to reconsider your central concept and refine your image can bring great clarity and purpose to the work. What is the design really about? You can speak more forcefully when you know what you want to say.

Explore Polarities

Sometimes, the best way to strengthen an idea is to present the exact opposite. For example, if you want to show the *joy* a political prisoner feels on being released from jail, you may need to show the *despair* she felt before release. To increase the *dynamism* in a design, add some emphatically *static* elements. The contrast created by polarities can heighten communication.

Move from General to Specific

"Be specific!" demands your writing teacher. Just as vague generalities weaken your writing, so vague generalities can weaken your designs. Details are important. "A bird watched people walk down the street" is far less compelling than "Two vultures hovered over University Avenue, hungrily watching the two hapless freshmen stagger from bar to bar." Specifying the kind of bird, type of people, and exact location makes the image come alive.

Move from Personal to Universal

Autobiography is a particularly rich source for images and ideas. The authenticity of personal experience is extremely powerful. However, if you focus too tightly on your own family, friends, and experience, the viewer must know you personally in order to appreciate your design. Try expanding your field of vision. Use a story about your high school graduation to say something about *all* rites of passage from childhood to adulthood.

Week Two Assessment

A well-developed rough or a full-scale model may be presented at this stage. The purpose of this critique is to help the artist or designer determine ways to increase the visual and conceptual impact of an existing idea. Here are three major strategies.

Develop Alternatives

By helping someone else solve a problem, we can often solve our own problem. Organize a team of four or five classmates. Working individually, design 5 to 10 possible solutions to a visual problem using 3 × 4 in. thumbnail sketches. Then, have one person present his or her ideas verbally and visually. Each team member must then propose an alternative way to solve the problem. This can be done verbally; however, once you get going, it is more effective and stimulating if everyone (including the artist) draws alternative solutions. This process helps the artist see the unrealized potential in his or her idea. And, because of the number of alternatives presented, the artist rarely adopts any single suggestion. Instead, the exercise simply becomes a means of demonstrating ways to clarify, expand, and strengthen intentions already formed. Continue until everyone has made a presentation.

Edit Out Nonessentials

Have you ever found it difficult to determine the real point of a lengthy lecture and thus lost interest? In our zeal to communicate, teachers sometimes provide so many examples and side issues that students get lost. Likewise, if your design is overloaded with peripheral detail or if a secondary visual element is given the starring role, the result will be cluttered and impact will be lost. Look carefully at your design, focusing on visual relationships. Are there any extra shapes or volumes that can be deleted?

Amplify Essentials

Just as it is necessary to delete extraneous information, it is equally important to strengthen the essential information. Review the section on emphasis in Chapter 3 and consider ways to increase your compositional power. Try "going too far," wildly exaggerating the size, color, or texture of an important visual element. The only way to get an extraordinary image is to make extraordinary choices.

Student Response: Developing a Self-Assignment

In the following two pages, Jason Chin describes the development of a month-long self-assignment he completed near the end of his freshman year. The original project proposal is given at the top of the first page. The rest of the text is devoted to Jason's analysis of his actual work process. This type of personal assessment can bring an extended project to a deliberate conclusion.

Self-Assignment:
Jason Chin

The Mythological Alphabet

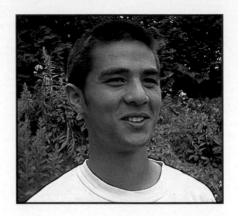

Original Proposal:

Description: I plan to make an illustrated alphabet book with 32 pages and a cover. The theme of the book will be myths and heroes. I am interested in illustrating the essence of each hero's story. Specifically, how can I visually communicate the story of a tragic hero versus a triumphant one? Further concerns with the book will be making it work as a whole. That means keeping it balanced and making it flow: I don't want the images to become disjointed.

Primary Concerns:

1. How do I communicate the individual nature of the characters?
2. How do I connect each hero to all the others?
3. How will the book affect the reader? I want to get the reader fully involved in the book.
4. How can I best use the unique characteristics of the book format?

Time Management:

Week 1: Research myths and heroes. Identify possible characters for the book.

Week 2: Bring at least 20 thumbnail sketches to the first team meeting.

Week 3: Bring finalized design/layout for book. Each page must have a final design in the form of thumbnails.

Week 4: Complete half of the pages.

Week 5: Finish remaining pages and present at the critique.

Commentary:

The independent project was both a blessing and a curse. Given the freedom to do what I chose was liberating, but the burden of what to do with that freedom was great. Ultimately, it became one of the best learning experiences of my freshman year.

I had decided to pursue illustration as my major, because of my interest in storytelling. This interest in stories led me to choose to make a book for my self-assignment project. The next step was to find a story to tell. To limit my workload, I looked for a story that had already been told, one that I could reinterpret, as opposed to writing my own story. At this point, I came across two books, one of Greek myths, and an alphabet book illustrated by Norman Rockwell, and my initial concept was born.

Once the idea was initiated, I set to work researching Greek myths. The idea was to find one character for each letter of the alphabet. It proved more difficult than I had

first thought. I found about 20 names with no problem, but I soon realized that several letters in our alphabet did not exist in the Greek alphabet. To overcome this hurdle, I took some liberties on the original problem and did not limit myself strictly to characters from myths (for example, I included the White Island for the letter *W*). Once the subject of each illustration was chosen, I set about the task of doing the images and designing the format of the book.

Doing the illustrations and designing the format of the book all came together at about the same time. As I was working out the drawings I made several key decisions that heavily influenced the outcome of the project. First, I decided that each picture would have to be black and white if I was going to pull this whole thing off. Second, I knew that they would have to be relatively small. Through my art history class, I gained a strong interest in Japanese woodblock prints and was especially attracted to their strong compositional sensibility. This became the focus of my attention while working out the illustrations. Finally, the decision to make the illustrations small helped determine the way I used text in the book, because it all but eliminated the possibility of overlaying text on image.

I designed each image in my sketchbook, doing thumbnails and comp sketches of all sizes and shapes, until I found the image that I felt best represented the character. For example, Zeus has the biggest and busiest frame in the book because he is the king of the gods, while the image of the White Island is quite serene because it is a burial ground. When I had each individual image worked out, I redrew them in order in the pages of my sketch book as if they were in the real book. I could now see how each image would work as a double-page spread, as well as how well the book could flow visually. With this mockup of the book in front of me it was very easy to see obvious mistakes and correct them before going to final art.

I did the final illustrations in pen and ink, on illustration board, and when they were finished, it was time to drop in the text. My first concept for the text was to be very minimal; each page would read, "A is for," "B is for," and so on. The more I thought about it, however, the more I realized that making each page rhyme would drastically increase the reader's interest in the book. So I wrote a more extensive text and put the rhyming parts on opposite pages in order to give the reader one more incentive to turn the page.

The final touch for the book was putting the colored paper down. The decision to do this came when I went to place the type. The only means I had to get good type was to print it out on the computer, but I had no way to print it on the illustration board. So I had to put it on printer paper and cut and paste it. No matter how carefully I cut the paper and pasted it on, it just didn't look right. I came up with two solutions: one, print the words on colored paper and paste it on, or two, cut frames of colored paper to cover over the entire page except for the image and the text. I chose the latter and was pleased to discover that the local art store had a vast selection of handmade and colored papers.

Today I look back on this project as a pivotal experience in my art education, because I had free range to pursue storytelling, something that has since become an essential aspect of my art. In the professional world, bookmaking is rarely an individual process. It is a collaborative process, involving editors, artists, and writers, so for me to be able to pursue it on my own was in fact a blessing. I got to make a book the way that I thought it should be done, and pursue my own personal vision of what a Mythological Alphabet should be. By making this book, I discovered something that I love to do, and want to make a career of doing, and to me the vision that I have gained from this experience is invaluable.

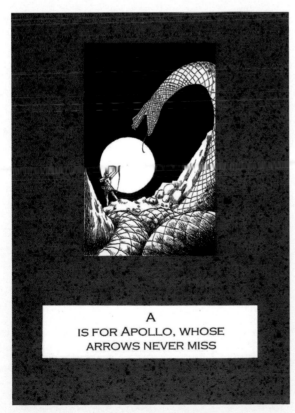

Jason Chin, *A Is for Apollo*. Student work.

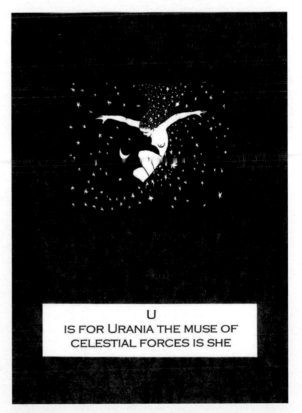

Jason Chin, *U Is for Urania*. Student work.

Turn Up the Heat: Pushing Your Project's Potential

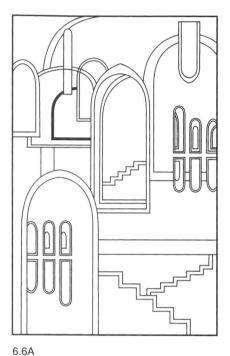

6.6A

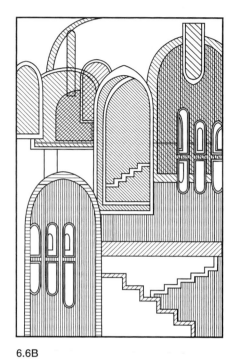

6.6B

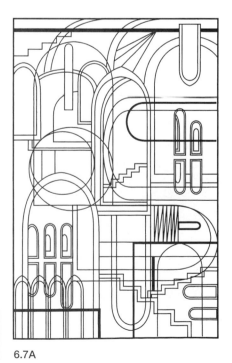

6.7A

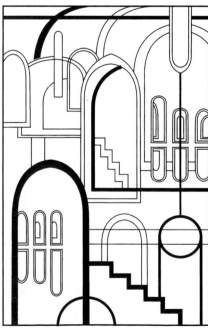

6.7B

Some compositions are so bold that they seem to explode off the page. Other compositions have all the right ingredients, but never really take off. By asking the following questions, you can more fully realize the potential of any assignment.

Basic Arithmetic

1. Should anything be *added* to the design? If your composition lacks energy, consider adding another layer of information. Notice how texture changes the energy level in Figures 6.6A and 6.6B.

2. Should anything be *subtracted*? If the composition is cluttered, try discarding 25 percent of the visual information. Then, use the remaining shapes more deliberately (6.7 A–B). Get as much as possible from every visual element.

3. What happens when any component is *multiplied*? As shown in Figures 6.8A and 6.8B, repetition can unify a design, add rhythm, and increase the illusion of space.

4. Can this design be *divided* into two or more separate compositions? When a design is too complicated, it may become impossible to resolve.

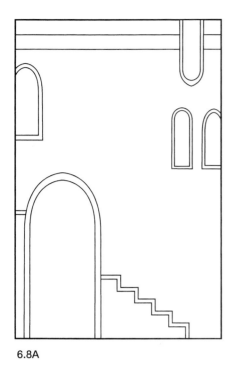

6.8A

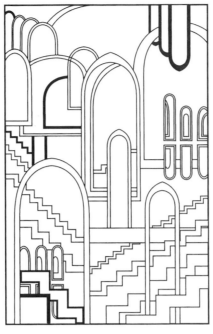

6.8B

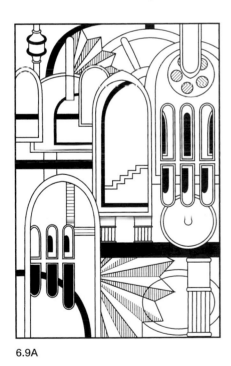

6.9A

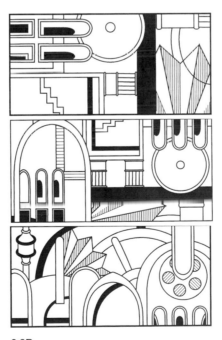

6.9B

Packing 20 ideas into a single design can
become a cure for sanity. In Figure 6.9A and
6.9B, a complicated source image has been separated into several different designs, creating a
whole series of excellent images.

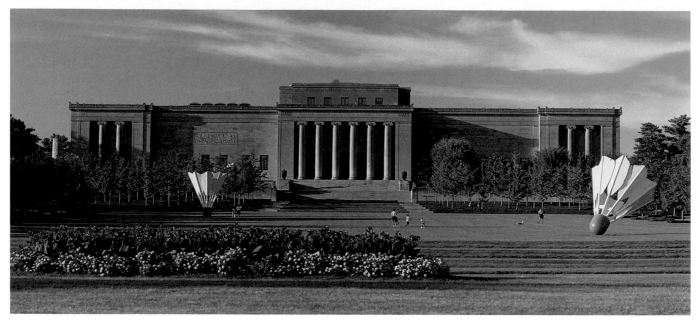

6.10 Claes Oldenburg and Coosje van Bruggen, *Shuttlecocks,*
1994. South facade of the Nelson-Atkins Museum of Art and the
Kansas City Sculpture Park. Aluminum, fiberglass-reinforced plastic,
urethane paint, approx. 19 ft 2⅜ in. h. × 16 ft diameter (5.9 × 4.9 m).

Transformation

Works of art and design present ideas in physical
form. Each composition is strongly influenced by
the materials used, the relationships created, and
the viewing context chosen. Consider these
alternatives:

1. What happens when the medium is changed?
    Even when the shapes stay the same, a silver
    teapot is very different from a glass, steel, or
    ceramic teapot. Sculptor Claes Oldenburg has
    used transformations in material extensively,
    often changing hard, reflective materials into
    soft vinyl. This form of transformation is espe-
    cially effective when the new material brings
    structural qualities and conceptual connota-
    tions that challenge our expectations.

2. What is the relationship of the piece to the
    viewer? What is the relationship between the
    artwork and its surroundings? What happens
    when a chair is reduced to the size of a salt
    shaker? Or when a 20-foot-tall badminton shut-
    tlecock (6.10) is placed in front of a museum?
    How does any image change, both visually and
    conceptually, when size is dramatically reduced
    or increased?

3. Can a change in proportion increase impact?
    Working with the same basic information, a

seemingly endless number of solutions can be produced through variations in proportion (6.11).

4. Is a physical object compelling from all points of view? Does the composition of the piece encourage the viewer to view it from other angles?

5. Can a change in viewing context increase meaning? The context in which a composition is seen can dramatically alter its meaning. For example, a side of beef has a very different meaning when it is hung in a gallery rather than staying in a slaughterhouse. Likewise, pop artists such as Andy Warhol and Roy Lichtenstein brought new meaning to soup cans and comic books by using them as subject matter in their paintings.

Reorganization

Time-based work, such as visual books, comic books, film, and video, is generally constructed from multiple images. Changing the organization of the parts of the puzzle can completely alter the meaning of the piece. For example, Angela contemplates entering the building in the sequence shown in Figure 6.12. Using a different organization of the same three images, Angela now wonders what will happen when she opens the door at the top of the stairs (6.13). By repeating the image of Angela, we can present a dilemma: she is now in a labyrinth—which route should she take (6.14)?

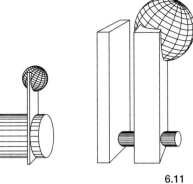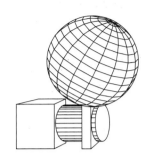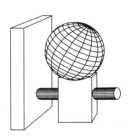

6.11

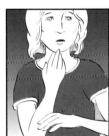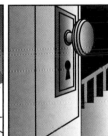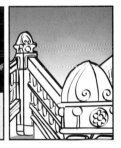

6.12

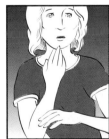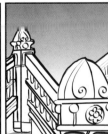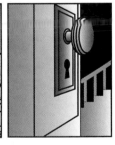

6.13

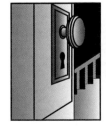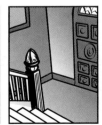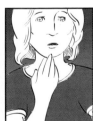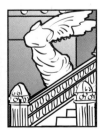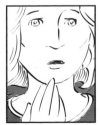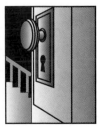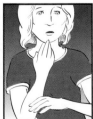

6.14

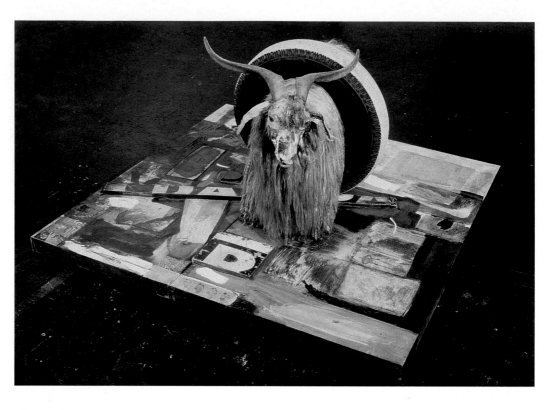

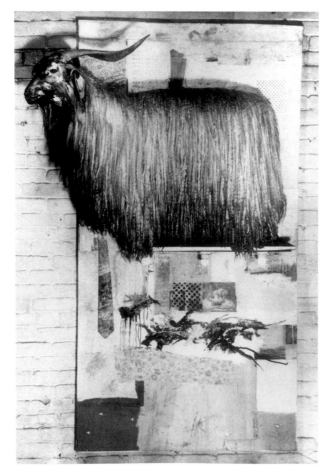

Concept and Composition

Any compositional change affects the conceptual impact of an artwork. Henry M. Sayre provides a striking example in *A World of Art.*[1] A distilled version of his ideas follows.

Robert Rauschenberg's *Monogram* (6.15) is constructed from a stuffed goat, an automobile tire, and a painted plywood base. Seeking to combine painting and sculpture, Rauschenberg created three different versions of this piece. In the first version (6.16), he placed the goat on a shelf that extended from the center of a six-foot-tall painting. This created a connection between the painting and the goat, but diminished its sculptural impact. In the second version, Rauschenberg placed a tire around the goat's midsection and moved the animal in front of the painting (6.17). This enhanced its three-dimensionality but created too much of a

6.16 **Robert Rauschenberg,** *Monogram, 1st State,* **c. 1955.** Combine painting: oil, paper, fabric, wood on canvas, plus stuffed Angora goat and three electric light fixtures, approximately 75 × 46 × 12 in. (190.5 × 114.3 × 30.5 cm). No longer in existence.

separation between the animal and the painting. He finally hit on the right combination when he placed the painting on the floor and positioned the goat in the center. The painting retained its integrity as a two-dimensional surface, the goat retained its physical presence, and a highly unified combination of the two elements was achieved. The addition of the tire enhanced the goat's sculptural form and gave the artwork a humorous twist.

Accepting Responsibility

We have explored only a few of the many approaches to critical thinking in this chapter. Every assignment presents new possibilities for critiques, and each teacher continually invents new approaches to address the needs of a specific class.

Regardless of the specifics, however, two facts are inescapable. First, you will learn only what you want to learn. If you reject out-of-hand the alternatives suggested, or if you avoid responsibility for your conceptual and compositional choices, you will gain nothing from the critique, no matter what strategy is used. Second, there are no free rides. Everyone in the class is responsible for the success of the session. It is often difficult to sustain your attention or honestly assess your work or the work of others. When you get a superficial response to a project, insisting on further clarification is not easy. Every critique demands sincere and sustained attention from each participant. And when the responses are supportive and substantial, remarkable improvements in works of art and design can be made.

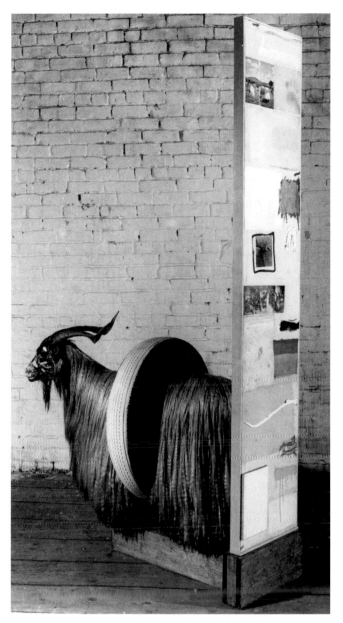

6.17 Robert Rauschenberg, *Monogram, 2nd State*, c. 1956. Combine: oil, paper, fabric, wood, plus rubber tire and stuffed Angora goat on wood, 115 × 32 × 44 in. (292 × 81.3 × 111.8 cm).

Profile:
Bob Dacey, Illustrator

Tell Me a Story: Illustrating *Miriam's Cup*

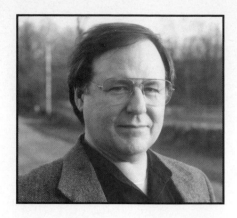

Bob Dacey is an internationally renowned artist whose drawings and paintings have been published as limited- and multiple-edition prints as well as in a wide range of books and periodicals, including *McCall's,* Ballantine Books, Book-of-the-Month Club, *Playboy,* and Scholastic Publications. His commercial clients include The White House, ABC, CBS, NBC, PBS, Mobil Oil, Sony, the U.S. Post Office, Air Japan, and many others.

Dacey has recently received a Silver Medal from the Society of Illustrators in New York for 1 of the 16 paintings he produced for Scholastic Publications illustrating a 32-page book, *Miriam's Cup,* which is themed on the Exodus of the Israelites from Egypt. The book tells the story of Miriam, the older sister of the prophet Moses. Dacey collected an extensive library of books on Egypt and spent almost a year on research. From costumes to musical instruments, Dacey insisted on getting all the details just right.

MS: Give me a bit of background on *Miriam's Cup.* What was the significance of this project, and what aspects of the story did you want to emphasize in the illustrations?
BD: *Miriam's Cup* gave me a chance to expand on my single-image work. I've always approached each illustration as a moment in time, as if it had a "before" and an "after." This book gave me a chance to push that much further. I started every painting by focusing on the emotion in the moment being depicted. I always ask myself: "What is the essence of this moment?" The composition follows. Shapes and values serve the emotional content, while movement is used to unify the composition.

MS: You have said that 75 percent of your work on this project was devoted to research. Can you describe your research, and tell me why it was so important?
BD: For *Miriam's Cup* I had to understand the culture of Egypt and the Jewish culture of the time. Fortunately, I've always had an extensive interest in both. My personal library contains more books on Egypt than the local library system. Research helped open new ideas, leading in some unexpected directions. Those bullrushes are one example. I looked up the word in three dictionaries and two encyclopedias. One of these sources mentioned that the bullrushes of ancient Egypt are papyrus, those beautiful fan-shaped reeds that can be fashioned into a kind of paper. Without that knowledge, the image I arrived at would have been impossible.

MS: I understand that you have a seven-step process by which you refine and expand your ideas. Can you describe this process as it applies to the cover image for *Miriam's Cup?*
BD: I first consider the intent of each painting: what must this piece communicate? In this painting I focused on Miriam's exuberance as she celebrates her escape from Egypt. Second, the composition must support my intent. The circular movement of the tambourine and flowers dominates this painting. The movement from the raised hand holding the tambourine, to Miriam's hair, to her face, and on to her cupped hand provides a secondary pattern. And, that cupped hand repeats the curve of the flowers. Third, the shapes depend on both the intent and the composition. If I am painting a very stoic character, I use a lot of verticals. Diagonals are used when the character or event is very dynamic. Value is fourth on my checklist. I assign value according to the mood of the painting. Lighter values are used for celebratory images, like this one; darker values dominate when the mood is somber. A mix of light and dark value is best. I base my compositions on the Golden Section [a classic use of proportion], and I often use a 60/40 proportion between light and dark values. Texture, step five, often results from the placement of shape and value—but it really deserves a place of its own, due to its importance as a constructive or destructive factor. When everything else works but the image

still suffers, textural discord is usually the culprit! Color comes next. I really have to have the other questions resolved first. Color without composition, value, or intent just doesn't cut it. This painting is dominated by rich pastel colors, which help convey the exuberant emotion.

All of this contributes to the overall image, the final step. If all of the preceding factors serve my intent, the image can emerge naturally and effectively.

MS: In addition to the extensive research you did for *Miriam's Cup*, it seems that you have a very wide range of interests in general.
BD: Well, everything feeds into my work—and I've always been interested in everything! My undergraduate majors included theater and anthropology before I settled on ad design as the field in which I finally got my degree. Now, my readings range from archaeology to philosophy to psychology to paleontology, and more. I'm also developing my interest in writing and plan to pursue a Masters in writing in order to increase my understanding of narrative.

MS: One of the questions my students often have is this: How do I get from where I am as a student to where you are as a professional?
BD: Focus on your goals, and research the field. Talk to professionals you admire. Set high standards for yourself, and be realistic about the level of professionalism and quality required.

MS: Any final bits of advice?
DB: Don't limit yourself. We all have great potential that serves the higher purpose of society. Pursue your goals with the knowledge that you can succeed. And, remain flexible and open-minded, so that you can redirect your efforts as opportunities present themselves. Read everything! Draw everything!

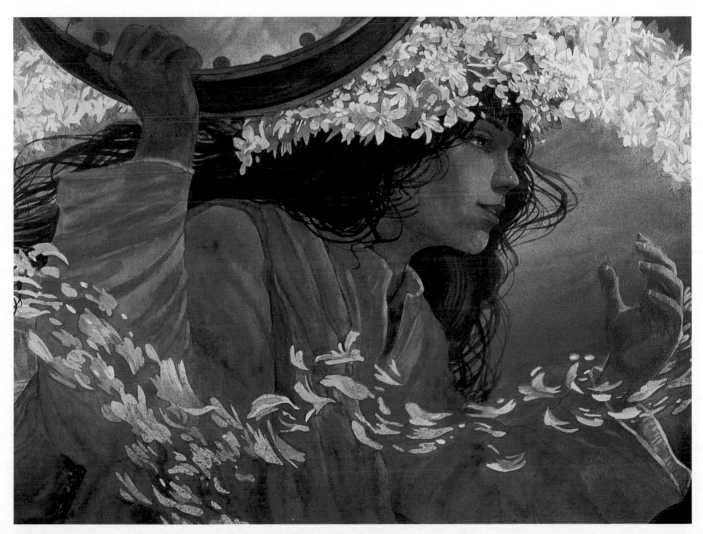

Bob Dacey, Cover of *Miriam's Cup* by Fran Manushkin, 1988. Scholastic Press.

Summary

- Through the use of critical thinking, an artist or designer can identify strengths and weaknesses in a project and determine the improvements that need to be made.

- Understanding the criteria on which a project will be judged helps focus critical thinking.

- Many artworks can be analyzed in terms of three basic aspects: form, subject, and content.

- Objective critiques focus on observable facts. Subjective critiques focus on feelings, intentions, and implications.

- Four common critique methods are description, cause and effect, compare and contrast, and greatest strength/greatest potential.

- Many critique methods may be used when you are working on a long-term project. In every case, there are three primary objectives: explore alternatives, delete nonessentials, and strengthen essentials.

- It is only by pushing a project to the limit that its potential will be fulfilled. Basic arithmetic, transformation, and reorganization can be used to increase compositional power.

- Responsibility for the success of a critique rests with each participant. Come with your mind open rather than your fists closed.

Keywords

cause-and-effect
    critique
compare/contrast
    critique
content
critique

descriptive
    critique
form
objective
    criticism
subject

subjective
    criticism

1. What is the subject matter of the artwork? What is the artist trying to say about the subject?

2. To what extent and by what means have the compositional choices supported this intent?

3. Is the artwork contained or does it seem to expand into the viewer's space?

4. What is the spatial depth of the artwork? How does space contribute to the meaning of the work?

5. How have each of the principles of design been used in this artwork?

6. By what means is the artwork unified? What adds variety?

7. What will you remember about this artwork two weeks from now?

8. If you were to make a second version of this project, what changes would you make? Why?

Sylvia Barnet, *A Short Guide to Writing about Art*, 3rd edition. Scott, Foresman, 1989.

Terry Barrett, *Criticizing Photographs: An Introduction to Understanding Images*, 2nd edition. Mountain View, CA, Mayfield, 1996.

Otto G. Ocvirk, Robert E. Stinson, Philip R. Wigg, Robert O. Bone, and David L. Cayton, *Art Fundamentals: Theory and Practice*, 9th edition. Burr Ridge, IL, McGraw-Hill, 2002.

Henry M. Sayre, *A World of Art*, 3rd edition. Upper Saddle River, NJ, Prentice-Hall, Inc., 2000.

Henry M. Sayre, *Writing about Art*, 3rd edition. Upper Saddle River, NJ, Prentice-Hall, Inc., 1999.

Amy Tucker, *Visual Literacy: Writing about Art*. Burr Ridge, IL, McGraw-Hill, 2002.

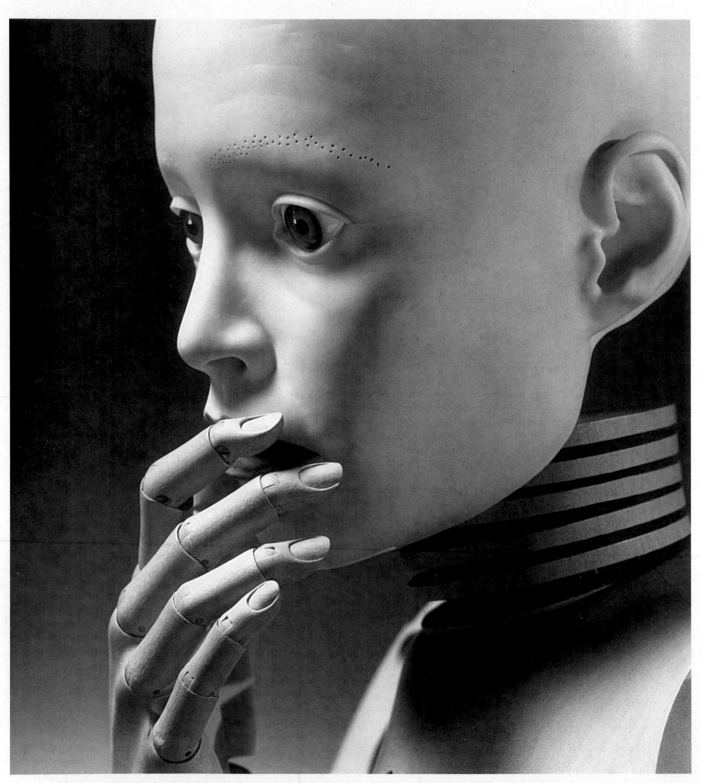

Katherine Wetzel (photograph), Elizabeth King (sculpture), *Pupil* from *Attention's Loop* **(detail), 1987–90.** Installation at the Bunting Institute, Radcliffe College, 1997. Porcelain, glass eyes, carved wood, brass. One-half life size.

Three-Dimensional Design

As we begin our investigation of three-dimensional design, it is useful to consider both the similarities and differences between flat compositions and physical constructions. In both cases, basic design elements are organized to communicate ideas, express emotions, and create functional objects. The basic principles of design are used to create images and objects that offer an effective balance between unity and variety. And, in both two- and three-dimensional design, concept development and critical thinking are essential aspects of the creative process.

However, in two-dimensional design, we use our technical, perceptual, and conceptual skills to create flat visual patterns and convincing illusions. It is the viewer's *mental* response that gives the artwork meaning. By contrast, our experience in the three-dimensional world is physical and direct. As we traverse an architectural space, we alter our perception with each step we take. When we circle a sculpture, we encounter new information on each side. The materials used in the construction of a three-dimensional object determine its structural strength as well as its aesthetic appeal.

This physical connection gives three-dimensional design an inherent power. When we shift from an illusory world to a tangible world, a substantial shift in communication occurs. Confronted by the physical presence of a three-dimensional object, the viewer responds viscerally as well as visually.

This section is devoted to the elements, organization, and implications of three-dimensional design. The basic building blocks of three-dimensional design are discussed in Chapter Seven. In Chapter Eight, the principles of three-dimensional design are described, and the unique characteristics of various materials are considered. Chapter Nine is devoted to the ways in which artists have transformed their ideas into physical objects and to a discussion of differences between traditional and contemporary sculpture.

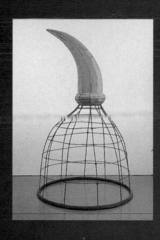

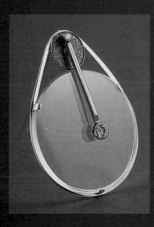

chapter seven

Three-Dimensional Design:
Aspects and Elements

Thinking in Three Dimensions

When we paint a realistic seascape, we use our technical, perceptual, and conceptual skills to create a convincing illusion. Like the letters in an alphabet, the lines, shapes, colors, and textures in the painting are combined to represent a three-dimensional world. Based on these clues, each viewer mentally reconstructs the setting. Those who have walked on a beach can create a detailed mental image of sea, sand, and sky. Others, who have never seen the ocean, may create a more fanciful world. For both viewers, however, it is the imagination that constructs the cosmos.

Our experience in the three-dimensional world is more direct. As we traverse an architectural space, we alter our perception with each step we take. When we circle a sculpture, we encounter new information on each side. Tangible evidence of three-dimensional design surrounds us. We can judge the strength of materials and the quality of construction by simply sitting in a chair. This physical connection gives three-dimensional design an inherent power.

Form and Function

To harness this power, we must first determine the purpose of a given design.

Sculpture is primarily designed to express ideas and evoke emotions. The sculptor explores an idea, chooses materials, and develops a composition based on his or her aesthetic intention. Public art projects, such as Maya Ying Lin's *Vietnam Memorial* (7.1), and ritual objects, such as Beau Dick's *Mugamtl Mask* (7.2), often commemorate historical events or express social values.

A designer uses the same mastery of composition and materials to create an object that is functional as well as beautiful. For example, when designing the aquatic gear shown in Figure 7.3, Oceanic had to create a product that was strong, flexible, durable, and relatively inexpensive to produce. For the designer, the **form,** or physical manifestation of the design, must fulfill its specific **function,** or purpose.

However, the basic elements and principles of design are the same for the artist and the designer. Both must organize line, plane, volume, mass, and

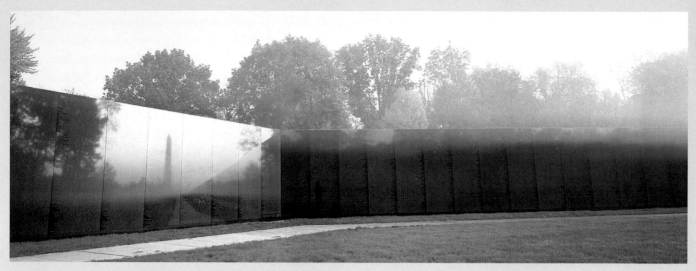

7.1   Maya Ying Lin, Vietnam Veterans Memorial, The Mall, Washington, DC, 1981–83. Polished black granite.

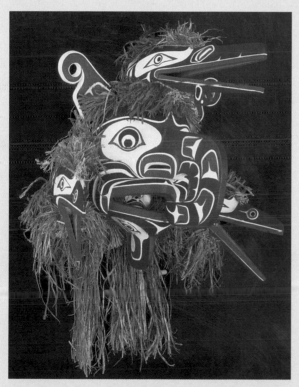

7.2   Beau Dick, Mugamtl Mask (Crooked Beak), 1993. Red cedar, cedar bark, paint, 24 × 26 × 16 in. (61 × 66 × 40.6 cm).

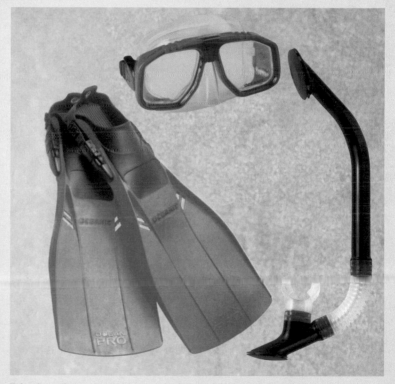

7.3   Aquatic gear used for snorkeling and scuba diving. Oceanic USA, San Leandro, CA.

space into coherent form. The structural integrity of a sculpture is just as important as the structural integrity of a wheelchair, and a teapot that is both beautiful and functional is ideal. By thoroughly exploring the elements of three-dimensional design and understanding their uses, both the artist and designer can create compelling work.

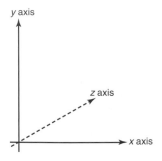

7.4 The three dimensions are defined through height, width, and depth.

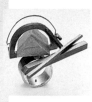

A

B

C

7.5 Variations on a cube.

The Three Dimensions

Height, width, and depth are the three dimensions in three-dimensional design. In computer-aided design, these three dimensions are defined using the x, y, and z axes used in geometry (7.4). Using the cube as a basic building block, we can create many variations, working from the outside in or the inside out (7.5 A–C).

Drafting for Designers

As demonstrated by these five views of Jens-Rüdiger Lorenzen's *Ring* (7.6), a physical object looks quite different from the top, bottom, and side. **Orthographic projection** can be used to describe these views accurately. The word "orthographic" means "true picture." Lines are used to provide an indication of height, width, and depth. Unlike perspective drawing, which is designed to create the illusion of space, orthographic projection accurately delineates structural details.

An orthographic projection represents six views of a three-dimensional form. Imagine that your project is enclosed in a glass box (7.7A). As you look through the top, bottom, front, back and right and left sides, you can see six distinctive views. In effect, an orthographic drawing is created when you unfold and flatten this imaginary box (7.7B).

Orthographic projection is widely used in manufacturing because it offers a specific vocabulary and is based on shared conventions. Architects use orthographic projection to plan three-dimensional forms in large scale. The basic layouts shown in

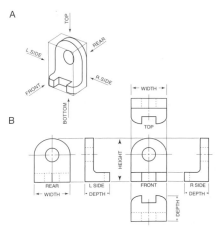

7.6 Jens-Rüdiger Lorenzen, *Ring*, 1992. Steel, argentan, 2⅕ × 2 in. (5.5 × 5 cm).

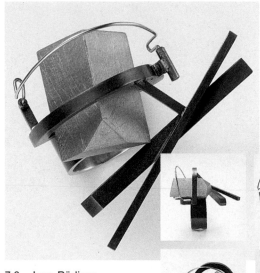

7.7 Orthographic projection.

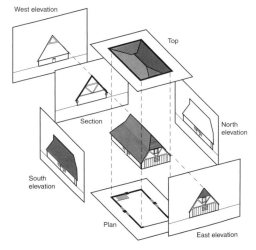

7.8 Simple architectural drawing.

Three-Dimensional Design

7-2

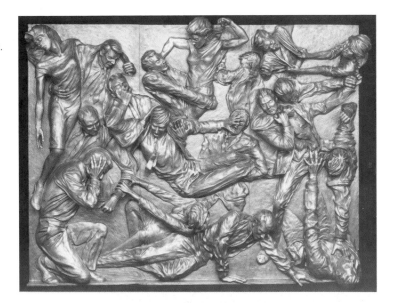

7.9 Robert Longo, *Corporate Wars* (detail), 1982. Cast aluminum, lacquer on wood relief, 7 × 9 × 3 ft (2.1 × 2.7 × .9 m).

Figure 7.8 are standard. In architecture, the top view is called the **top** view, the bottom view is called the **plan** view, and the sides are designated as **elevations.** A **section** is used when a slice of the object must be shown. Dashed lines are used to indicate the outlines of shapes that are invisible from a given viewpoint.

Degrees of Dimensionality

The degree of dimensionality in sculpture and design varies widely. When developing a three-dimensional object, it is wise to consider at least four approaches to the third dimension.

Relief

When working in **relief,** the artist uses a flat backing (such as a wall or ceiling) as a base for three-dimensional forms. For example, Robert Longo's *Corporate Wars* (7.9) is like a sculptural painting. Using the boundaries created by the supporting wall and the four outer edges, it presents a group of white-collar warriors engaged in hand-to-hand combat. The figures are trapped, bound both to the backing and by their struggle for money.

Three-Quarter Works

A **three-quarter work** is designed to be viewed from the front and sides only. The Tairona pendant in Figure 7.10 is one example. Designed to be worn on the chief's chest during festive occasions, it is vigorously defined on the front and relatively plain on the back.

Freestanding Works

Freestanding works, or works **in the round,** are designed to be seen from all sides. When we circle August Rodin's *The Kiss* (7.11), we capture every nuance in the movement of the two figures. Details, such as the man's stroking hand and the woman's raised foot, give life to the inanimate stone.

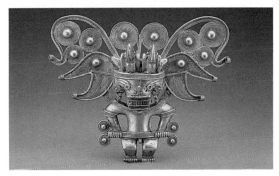

7.10 **Bat-Man Pendant, Columbia, Tairona, 1200–1600.** Gold.

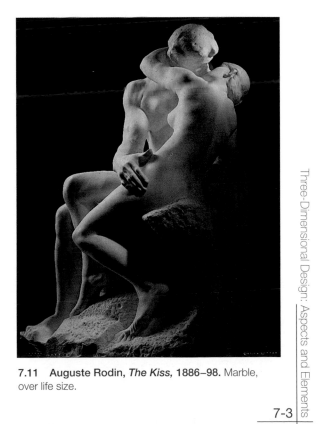

7.11 **Auguste Rodin, *The Kiss*, 1886–98.** Marble, over life size.

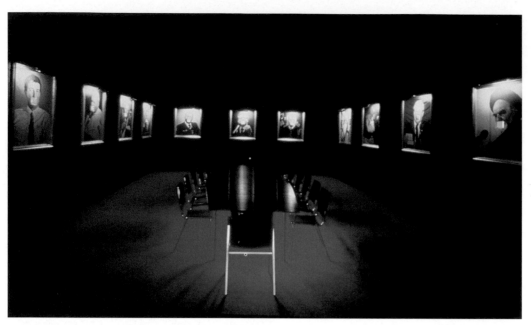

Installations

An **installation,** or **walk-through** work, may expand to fill an entire room. On entering Antoni Muntadas' *The Board Room* (7.12), the viewer confronts 13 chairs facing a long table. In a reference to the Last Supper described in the Bible, these chairs are accompanied by photographs of contemporary religious leaders, from the Ayatollah Khomeini to Billy Graham. A small video monitor, inserted in the mouth of each man, plays a film clip showing him in action. In an installation of this kind, the viewer must enter the work physically as well as mentally.

The viewer plays an even more active role in Christian Marclay's *Amplification* (7.13). This installation consists of six photographic enlargements plus six additional images that were printed on translucent cotton scrim. Installed in the Swiss Pavilion at the 1995 Venice Bienniale, the images shift, merge, and divide, depending on the viewer's position.

7.12 Antoni Muntadas, *The Board Room*, 1987. Installation at North Hall Gallery at Massachusetts College of Art, Boston. Thirteen chairs placed around a boardroom table. Behind each chair is a photo of a religious leader, in whose mouth a small video monitor shows the leader speaking. Subjects include Ayatolla Khomeini, Billy Graham, Sun Myung Moon, and Pope John Paul II.

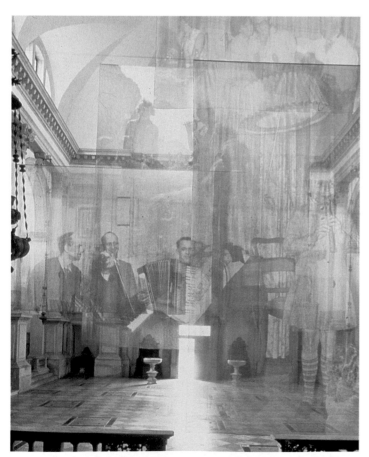

7.13 Christian Marclay, *Amplification*, 1995. Mixed media with six found prints and six photographic enlargements on cotton scrim. Dimensions variable. Installation at the Chiesa di San Stae, Venice, Italy.

Design Elements

Line

In three-dimensional design, **line** can be created through

- *A connection between points.* Two kinds of line are used in *Free Ride Home*, by Kenneth Snelson (7.14). The aluminum tubes provide a skeleton that becomes elevated when the connecting cables are attached. The resulting sculpture is dominated by diagonal lines that

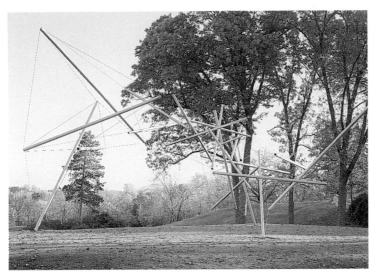

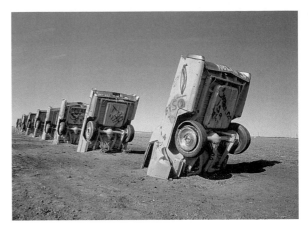

7.14 **Kenneth Snelson,** *Free Ride Home,* **1974.** Aluminum and stainless steel, 30 × 30 × 60 ft. (9.1 × 9.1 × 18.2 m). Storm King Art Center, Mountainville, NY.

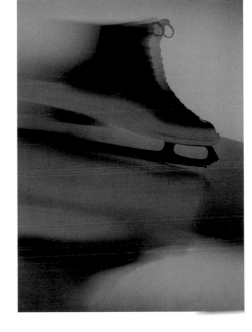

7.16 **Moira North and Rudi Stern,** *Neon Skates,* **1986.** Battery-operated neon skates for performance by The Ice Theater of New York, Moira North, director.

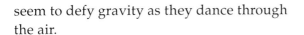

seem to defy gravity as they dance through the air.

- *A series of adjacent points.* The cars that make up Ant Farm's *Cadillac Ranch* (7.15) are distinct objects in themselves as well as the points that create a line of cars. Commissioned by a rancher in Texas, this sculpture has been described as a requiem for the gas-guzzling American automobile.[1]

- *A point in motion.* When a skater wears the *Neon Skates* by Moira North and Rudi Stern, she can literally create lines from a moving point of light (7.16). To create *A Line in the Himalayas* (7.17), Richard Long became the point in motion. As he walked, he paused to rearrange the stones on the trail to create a line. Because few of us will ever visit this remote site, the journey and the sculpture now exist as a line in a photograph.

Types of Line

Straight lines can slice through space with the speed and energy of an arrow in flight. Vertical lines tend to exaggerate height and add elegance to a design. Horizontal lines tend to increase visual and physical stability. Diagonal lines can add dynamism.

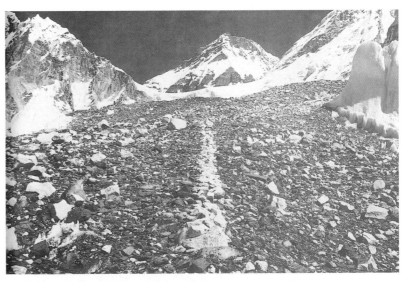

7.17 **Richard Long,** *A Line in the Himalayas.* Black-and-white photograph.

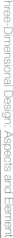

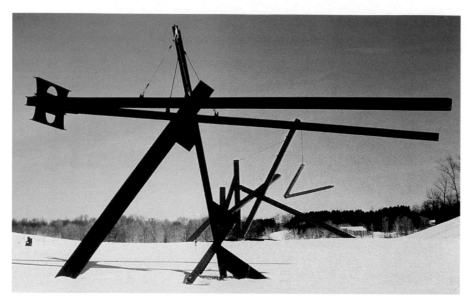

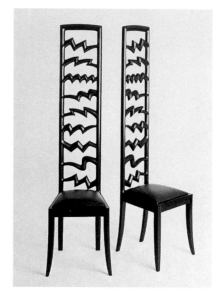

7.18 Mark di Suvero, *Ik Ook Eindhoven*, **1971–72** . Painted steel, 24 × 24 × 33 ft (7.3 × 7.3 × 10 m). In the background: *Are Years What?* **(For Marianne Moore), 1967.** Painted steel, 40 × 40 ft × 30 ft (12.2 × 12.2 × 9.1 m).

7.19 Peter Pierobon, *Ladderback Chair.* Firm & Manufacturer: Snyderman Gallery.

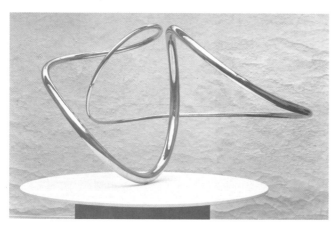

7.20 José de Riviera, *Brussels Construction,* **1958.** Stainless steel, 46¹/₂ × 79 in. (118.1 × 200.6 cm).

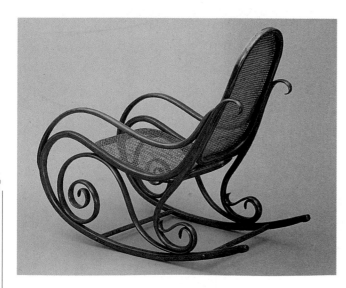

All three types of line are used in Mark di Suvero's *Ik Ook Eindhoven* (7.18) and Peter Pierobon's *Ladderback Chair* (7.19). The di Suvero sculpture is dominated by two horizontal I beams suspended from a vertical support. The diagonal lines that are connected to this primary structure emphasize the gravity of the artwork and add energy. On the other hand, it is the tall vertical back that transforms Pierobon's chair into a whimsical sculpture. Its exaggerated height pulls our eyes upward and provides a support for the jagged lines that create the rungs of the ladder.

Curved lines tend to flow though space more slowly, often encompassing all sides of an object to create a harmonious whole. In José de Riviera's *Brussels Construction* (7.20), a single line of steel activates a sculptural space. As the sculpture slowly rotates on its motorized base, the movement suggested by the line is accentuated by its physical rotation.

Curved lines can also suggest natural forms and forces. Gebrüder Thonet's *Rocking Chair* (7.21) was especially popular near the end of the nineteenth century, as interest in nature and natural forces blossomed both in Europe and America.

7.21 Gebrüder Thonet, Rocking Chair, c. 1860. Beech wood, cane, 37⁵/₈ in. h. × 22³/₄ in. w. × 42¹/₂ in. d. (95.6 × 57.8 × 107.9 cm). Manufacturer: Gebrüder Thonet, Vienna, Austria.

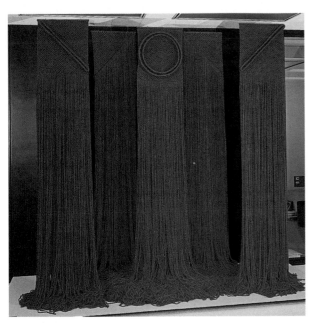

7.22 Claire Zeisler, *Red Forest*, 1968. Dyed jute, 8 ft 2 in. h. × 7 ft 4 in. w. × 2 ft d. (249 × 224 × 61 cm).

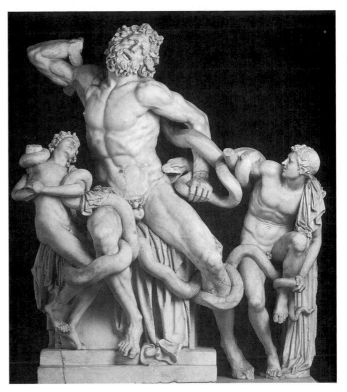

7.23 Laocoön and His Two Sons. Marble, 7 ft (2.13 cm).

Single lines, such as the steel rod in *Brussels Construction*, can bring a simple eloquence to an artwork. On the other hand, multiple lines can be used to create new sculptural forms. As shown in Claire Zeisler's *Red Forest* (7.22), many fiber works are created through the organization of multiple lines of thread, yarn, or other materials.

Uses of Line

Through their physical presence, **actual lines** can connect, define, or divide a design. The ancient Greek sculpture *Laocoön and His Two Sons* (7.23) depicts a scene from the Trojan War. When the Greeks offer a large, hollow, wooden horse to the Trojans, Laocoön warns against accepting the gift. The Greek goddess Athena then sends two serpents to attack and kill the seer, thus gaining entry into Troy for the Greeks hidden in the horse. In this sculpture, the writhing serpent compositionally connects the three terrified men while adding emotional power to this tale of Athena's wrath.

In Figure 7.24, dancers from the Nikolais Dance Theatre push against the elastic lines that define their space. It is the interaction between these boundaries and the dancers that gives this performance power.

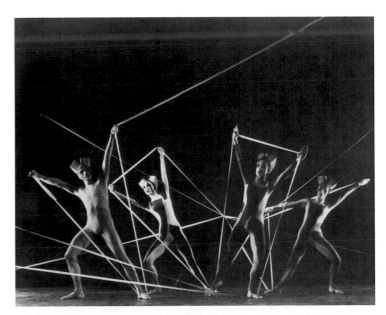

7.24 **The Nikolais Dance Theatre Performing *Sanctum*.** With Amy Broussard, Phyllis Lambat, and Murray Louis.

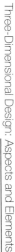

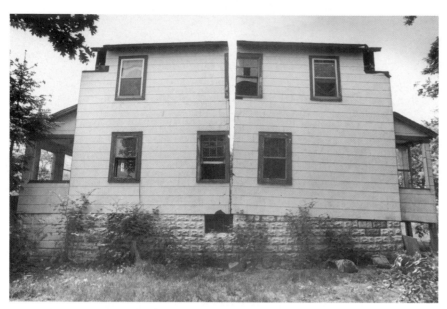

7.25 Gordon Matta–Clark, *Splitting: Exterior,* 1974. Black-and-white photograph.

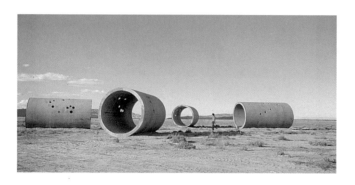

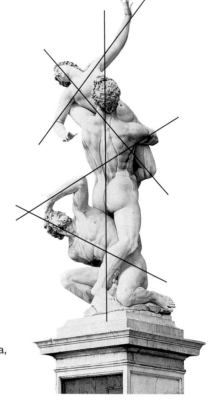

7.26 Giovanni da Bologna, *The Rape of the Sabine Women,* completed 1583. Marble. 13 ft 6 in. (4.1 m).

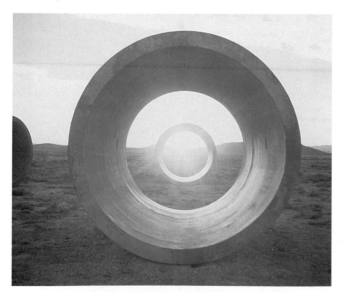

7.27 Nancy Holt, *Sun Tunnels,* 1973–76. Great Basin Desert, Utah. Four tunnels, each 18 ft long × 9 ft 4 in. diameter (5.5 × 2.8 m), each axis 86 ft long (26.2 m). Aligned with sunrises and sunsets on the solstices.

The line dividing Gordon Matta-Clark's *Splitting: Exterior* (7.25) changes an abandoned house into an evocative sculpture. Combining his background in architecture with a propensity for anarchy, Matta-Clark often seeks to "undo" a building and the social conditions that led to its construction.[2]

Implied lines can play an equally important role in a design. Such lines are created through mental rather than physical connections. *The Rape of the Sabine Women,* by Giovanni da Bologna (7.26), relies on a series of implied lines for its impact. Starting at the bottom and exploding upward, the repeated diagonals in the sculpture create a vortex as powerful as a whirlpool. At the bottom is the husband of the captured woman. In the center, a standing Roman soldier is intent on securing a wife for himself. The agitated movement culminates at the top with the extended arm of the embattled woman.

A **sight line** gives Nancy Holt's *Sun Tunnels* (7.27) its power. At first glance, the four 22-ton concrete tunnels seem static. Upon entering each tunnel, the viewer discovers a series of holes that duplicate the size and position of the stars in four major constellations. The light pouring in through these holes shifts as the sun rises, travels across the sky, then sets. During the winter and summer solstices, the sculpture is further transformed as light from the rising and setting sun is framed by an alignment in the repeated circular shapes. Like a telescope, the massive cylinders are more important for the visions they create than as objects in themselves.

Shapes and Planes

A two-dimensional **shape** is created when any area is clearly separated from its surroundings (7.28). A shape can be created when a line connects to enclose or outline an area; when an area of color or texture is defined by a clear boundary; or when an area is surrounded by contrasting values, colors, or textures. For example, Jonathan Borofsky's *Man with Briefcase* (7.29) was created when a shape was removed from a steel plate. Raised to frame the sky, the static panel is constantly activated by the surrounding sky. Such a cutout is often called a **negative shape.**

Shapes that have been combined to create three-dimensional structures are called **planes.** For example, the linear skeleton of Gerrit Rietveld's *Red and Blue Chair* (7.30) clearly defines three-dimensional space. To support a human body, a structure with height, width, and depth had to be created. As intersecting elements in a cohesive structure, the plywood panels that form the seat and back are called planes, rather than shapes.

In his famous mobiles (7.31), Alexander Calder put simple planes in motion. Inspired by the delicate weights and balances he saw in the paintings of Piet Mondrian (see 3.35, page 3-12), Calder used these structures to represent the movement of heavenly bodies within the universe. The flat shapes and curving lines continually move, creating a variety of configurations.

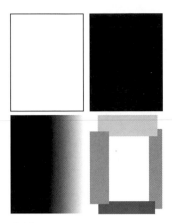

7.28

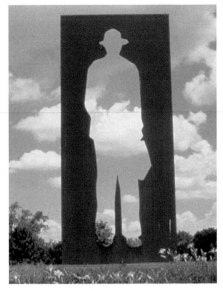

7.29 Jonathan Borofsky, *Man with Briefcase*, 1987. Corten steel, 30 ft × 13 ft 6 in. × 2 in. (9.1 m × 4.1 m × 5 cm).

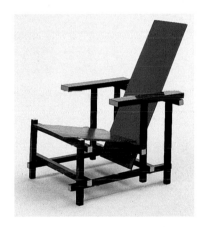

7.30 Gerrit Rietveld, *Red and Blue Chair*, c. 1918. Painted wood, 34⅛ in. h. × 26 in. w. × 33 in. d. Seat 13 in. h. (86.7 × 66 × 83.8 cm).

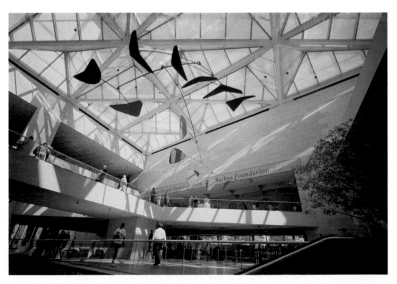

7.31 Alexander Calder, *Untitled*, 1976. Painted aluminum and tempered steel, 29 ft 10½ in. × 76 ft (9.1 × 23.2 m). National Gallery of Art, Washington, DC.

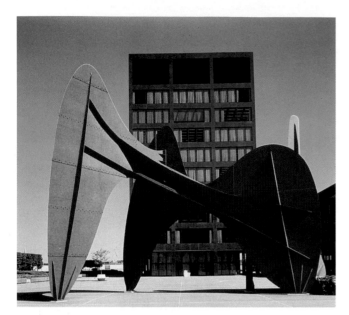

7.32 Alexander Calder, *La Grande Vitesse*, 1969. Painted steel plate, 43 × 55 ft (13.1 × 16.8 m). Calder Plaza, Vandenberg Center, Grand Rapids, MI.

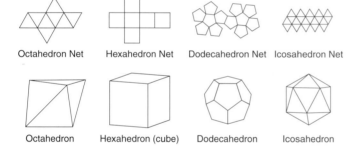

Octahedron Net   Hexahedron Net   Dodecahedron Net   Icosahedron Net

Octahedron   Hexahedron (cube)   Dodecahedron   Icosahedron

7.33 A variety of polyhedra

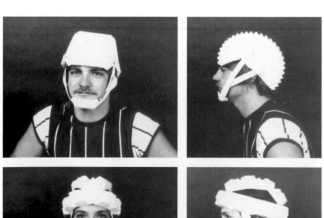

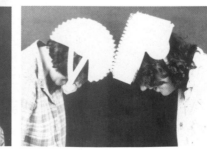

When slotted together, planes can create large-scale structures that are remarkably strong. With outdoor sculptures, such as Alexander Calder's *La Grande Vitesse* (7.32), structural integrity is essential. Located in a public plaza, the sculpture must withstand wind, rain, and snow while presenting minimal risk to pedestrians. Intersecting planes, combined with a ribbed reinforcement at stress points, have been used to create a durable structure.

Volume

A **volume** is an enclosed area of three-dimensional space. Cubes, cones, cylinders, and spheres are the most familiar volumes. Industrial designers often use a variety of **polyhedra,** or multifaceted volumes (7.33). Such volumes can be surprisingly strong. In an assignment at Ohio State University (7.34), students used polyhedra to construct their bristol board helmets.

While the size and shape of an interior volume is important in all three-dimensional work, the specific amount of enclosed space is essential to all containers, from architecture to glassware. *The Ginevra Carafe*, by Ettore Sottsass (7.35), easily holds a liter of wine. This narrow cylinder requires little table space and an extra disk of glass at the base provides weight and stability. An additional glass cylinder at the top ensures that the lid will remain firmly in place. For an industrial designer, a simple cylinder is rarely simple. The most elegant design will fail unless it fulfills its basic function.

The sphere Bill Parker used for *Jewel of Enlightenment (Hashi-no Toma)* (7.36) combines the aesthetic requirements of sculpture with the functional requirements of industrial design. Measuring 40 inches in diameter, the transparent globe is both a container for electricity and a compelling volume

7.34 OSU students used a variety of polyhedra to construct bristol board helmets. Charles Wallschlaeger, Professor Emeritus, The Ohio State University, Department of Industrial, Interior, and Visual Communication Design.

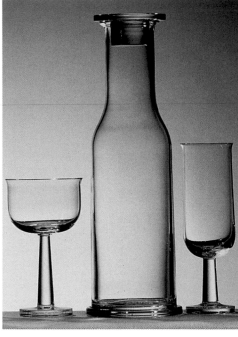

7.35 Ettore Sottsass, *Ginevra Carafe*, 1997. Manufactured by Alessi, Crusinallo, Italy.

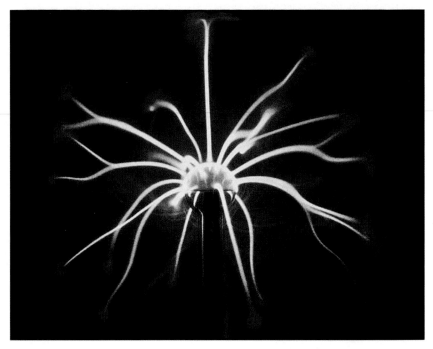

7.36 Bill Parker, *Jewel of Enlightenment (Hashi-no Toma)*, 1989. 40 in. (101.6 cm) diameter sphere standing 5 ft (1.5 m) from the floor, glass sphere, gas mixture, high voltage at high frequency.

in itself. Positioned five feet from the floor, the sphere is slightly above ordinary eye level, making it even more awe-inspiring.

Mass

A **mass** is an enclosed area of three-dimensional substance.

The most massive sculptures are usually carved from a solid block of plaster, wood, clay, or stone. Just as Alexander Calder took advantage of the buoyancy of a thin plane to create the mobile, so Henry Moore took advantage of the imposing power of mass when he created *Locking Piece* (7.37A). In such structures, the **primary contours** (or outer edges) are complemented by the **secondary contours** created by internal edges (7.37B). As the viewer circles the form, these contours visually alternate, as the primary contours become the secondary contours, and the secondary contours become the primary contours.

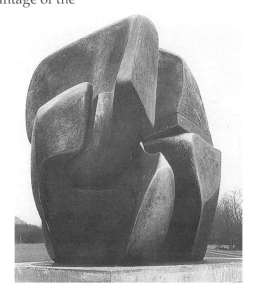

Secondary Contours   Primary Contour

7.37A and B   Henry Moore, *Locking Piece*, 1963–64. Bronze, 115 × 110¼ × 90½ in. (292 × 280 × 230 cm).

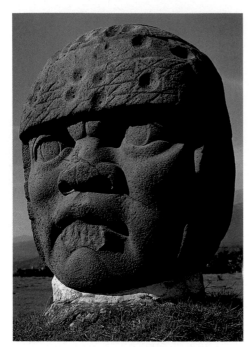

7.38   Colossal Head, 1300-800 B.C. Stone. Mexico, Olmec culture, Jalapa, Veracruz, Mexico.

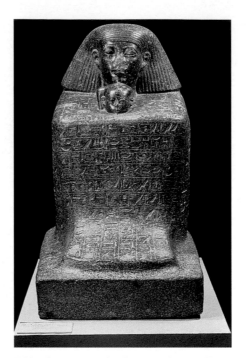

7.39   Senenmut with Princess Nefrua, The Deceased Moves on to the Other World, c. 1480 B.C. Thebes. Black granite, approximately 39½ in. (100.5 cm).

A massive form is often chosen when stability, permanence, and power are needed. A series of colossal heads produced by the Olmec people of ancient Mexico combines the abstract power of a sphere with the specific power of a portrait (7.38). The cubic block of stone that dominates *Senenmut with Princess Nefrua* (7.39) provides a surface for extensive hieroglyphic writing as well as an impressive support for the two heads. The pyramids at Giza offer a more extreme example. Built almost 5,000 years ago to memorialize and protect a deceased pharaoh, they remain solid and imposing.

Space

Space extends in all directions and has no boundary. A dialog between a structure and its surroundings is created as soon as an artist positions an object in space. An opening in a mass can increase our awareness of its solidity while the addition of a physical object can heighten our awareness of an architectural space. Space is the partner to substance. Without it, line, plane, volume, and mass lose both visual impact and conceptual purpose.

Presence and Absence

This interrelationship between space and substance is demonstrated in every area of three-dimensional design. David Smith's *Cubi XXVII* (7.40), constructed from nine solid cubic volumes and one cylinder, is dominated by a central void. The stainless steel construction activates and is activated by the empty space.

Space plays an equally important role in representational work. It is the open mouth in *Model of a Trophy Head* (7.41) that animates the mask. No facial

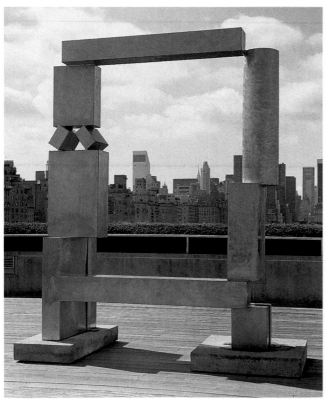

7.40   David Smith, *Cubi XXVII,* March 1965. Stainless steel, 111³/₈ × 87³/₄ × 34 in. (282.9 × 222.9 cm).

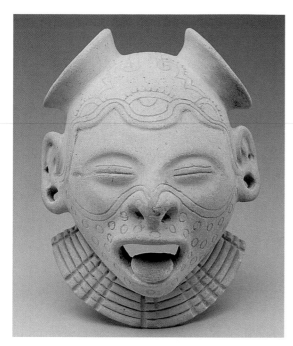

7.41 Model of a Trophy Head, Ecuador, La Tolita, 600 B.C.–400 A.D. Ceramic.

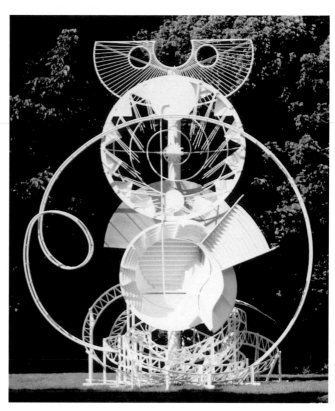

7.42 Alice Aycock, *Tree of Life Fantasy*, Synopsis of the Book of Questions concerning the world order and/or the order of worlds, 1990–92. Painted steel, fiberglass and wood, 20 × 15 × 8 ft (6.1 × 4.6 × 2.4 m).

expression, however extreme, would be as lively if the mouth were closed.

Open and Closed Space

Every three-dimensional object combines space, volume, and mass. The proportion of open space relative to solid substance is critical. The space in Alice Aycock's *Tree of Life Fantasy* (7.42) is defined by a filigree of delicate lines and planes. Inspired by the double-helix structure of DNA and by medieval illustrations showing people entering paradise through a spinning hole in the sky, sculptor Alice Aycock has combined a linear structure with a series of circular planes. The resulting sculpture is as open and playful as a roller coaster.

Karen Karnes's *Vessel* (7.43) is a closed structure, consisting of a cylindrical form capped by a simple lid. It is a functional pot, with the actual bottom of the container placed just above the vertical slit. Thus, the bottom third of the piece is like a pedestal for the functional container. In its own way, this pot is just as animated as the Aycock sculpture. The surprise and contrast created by the narrow channel of space completely redefine the familiar vessel form.

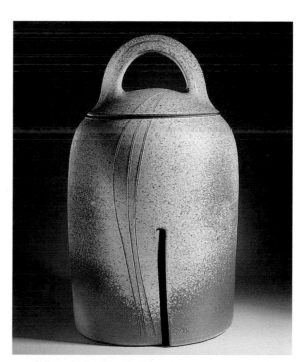

7.43 Karen Karnes, *Vessel*, 1987. Stoneware, wheel-thrown, glazed, and wood-fired, 16½ in. h. × 10½ in. d. (41.9 × 26.7 cm).

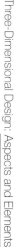

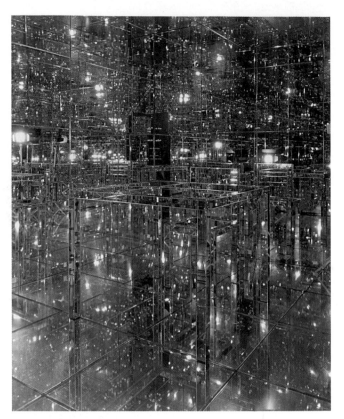

7.44 Lucas Samaras, *Mirrored Room,* **1966.** Mirrors on wooden frame, 8 × 8 × 10 ft (2.44 × 2.44 × 3 m).

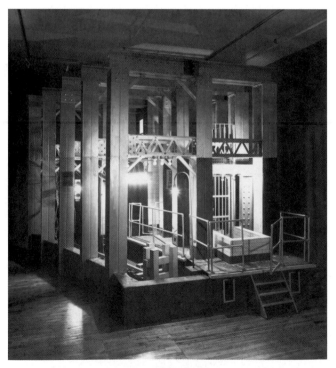

7.45 Donna Dennis, *Subway with Silver Girders,* **1981–82.** Wood, masonite, acrylic, enamel, cellulose compound, glass, electrical fixtures, and metal, 12 ft 2½ in. w. × 14 ft 3½ in. d. (31 × 36 cm).

Physical Entry, Conceptual Entry

Some sculptures are designed to be entered physically. Lucas Samaras's *Mirrored Room* (7.44) multiplies and divides the reflection of each visitor who enters. Other sculptures can only be entered mentally. *Subway with Silver Girders* (7.45), by Donna Dennis, recreates in great detail the architecture and lighting we find in a subway station. Constructed at two-thirds the scale of an actual station, the sculpture presents a magical entry into a prosaic place. This subway station provides transportation for the mind, rather than the body.

Kinetic Form

Early examples of **kinetic form** include puppets, fountains, and clocks. Medieval clockmakers delighted in creating moving figures to accentuate the passage of time. The jousting knights at the top of the Wells Cathedral clock (7.46) were designed to be seen in motion.

When time is combined with space, a sculpture can become as lively as a theatrical stage. Beautifully engineered, Calder's large mobiles continually rotate with ponderous grace. Placed beneath the skylights in the National Gallery, *Untitled* (see 7.31) is further activated by changes in light and shadow.

Another celestial force activates Walter De Maria's *The Lightning Field* (7.47). Arranged in a

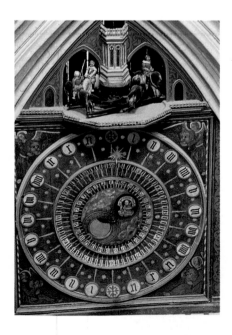

7.46 Wells Cathedral Clock, **1392–c. 1500.** Double-twelve astronomical clock dial, with jousting knights. Wells, UK.

grid over nearly one square mile of desert, 400 steel poles act as a collection of lightning rods. Impressive even in daylight, the site becomes awe-inspiring during a thunderstorm. Lightning jumps from pole to pole and from sky to earth, creating a remarkable display of pyrotechnics.

Texture

Texture refers to the visual or tactile quality of a form. The increased surface area of a volume, combined with the physical immediacy of sculpture, heightens the impact of texture in all types of three-dimensional design. The surface area shifts and turns, enclosing the physical volume.

Degrees of Texture

Variations in the surface of a volume may be subtle. In *Blackware Storage Jar*, by Maria Montoya Martinez and Julian Martinez (7.48), a polished, reflective surface is combined with a smooth, matte surface. The tactile and visual contrast between the two surfaces is minimal. Visible yet unobtrusive, the geometric and organic patterns enhance the jar but never compete with the purity of the graceful form.

Gertrud and Otto Natzler used a very different approach for *Pilgrim Bottle* (7.49). The volume as well as the textural surface is exaggerated. Between the narrow neck and compressed base, the jar bulges out in a circular shape, as magical and as pockmarked as the surface of the moon. The unusual union between volume and surface, combined with the intriguing title, invite intellectual speculation. Who is the pilgrim, and what might this bottle contain?

Uses of Texture

Texture can enhance or deny our understanding of a physical form. In Figure 7.50, the lines carved into the surface of the vessel increase its dimensionality. Concentric circles surrounding the knobs at the base of each handle create a series of visual targets that

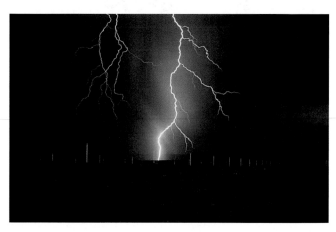

7.47 **Walter De Maria, *The Lightning Field*, 1977.** Near Quemado, NM. Stainless steel poles, average height 20 ft 7½ in. (6.1 m), overall 5,280 × 3,300 ft (1,609.34 × 1,005.84 m).

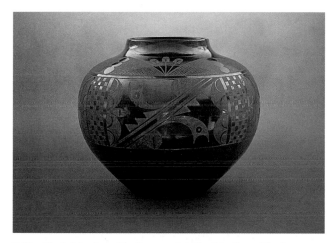

7.48 **Maria Montoya Martinez and Julian Martinez, *Blackware Storage Jar*, 1942.** Hopi, from San Ildefonso Pueblo, NM. Ceramic, 18¾ in. h. × 22½ in. d. (47.6 × 57.1 cm).

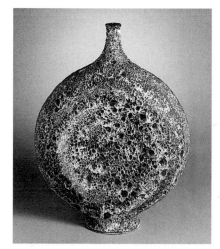

7.49 **Gertrud Natzler and Otto Natzler, *Pilgrim Bottle*, 1956.** Earthenware, wheel-thrown, and glazed, 17 × 13 × 5 in. (43.2 × 33 × 12.7 cm).

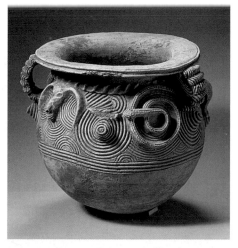

7.50 **Globular Vessel with Inverted Rim,** tenth century, Igbo, Nigeria. Terracotta, 16 in. (40.6 cm).

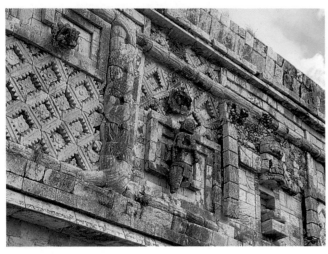

7.51 Detail of Maya Carvings on the "Nunnery," at Uxmal, **Mexico.** Stone.

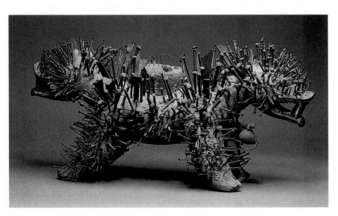

7.52 *Two-Headed Dog*, **Vili, Zaire.** Wood, resinous mass, metal, 13¾ in. (34.9 cm).

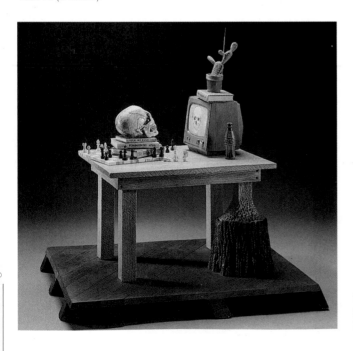

circle the globe, while additional grooves accentuate the surface of the sturdy handles.

By contrast, the patches of green and brown paint on the sides of a battleship are designed as camouflage. By mimicking visual information from the surrounding environment, the sailors seek to *minimize* the solidity of the ship. An invisible ship creates an elusive target.

Textural Animation

Many textures animate the surface of the "Nunnery," a Mayan building that adjoins the Pyramid of the Magician in Uxmal, Mexico (7.51). Human and animal figures in high relief are surrounded by bricks arranged in diagonal, vertical, and horizontal patterns. Curving lines have also been carved into the stone walls. The highly ornamented building seems alive with energy.

Two-Headed Dog (7.52), constructed by the Vili people in Zaire, generates even more energy. This simple wooden figure bristles with blades of iron and nails of various sizes. The embodiment of a powerful spirit, this guardian figure is provoked to attack wrongdoers through the use of verbal commands as well as the embedded nails.

Characteristic and Contradictory Textures

Every material has its own native textural properties. Fluid materials such as clay, glass, or metal can easily be formed into a wide variety of textures. Gold, which may occur in nature as dust, in nuggets, in veins, or in branching form, can be cast, hammered, or soldered. Despite the adaptability of most materials, however, we are accustomed to their use in specific ways. The gleaming reflective surface of a steel teapot, the transparent and reflective qualities of glass, and the earthy functionality of clay fulfill our expectations.

When a material is used in an uncharacteristic way, or when strange textures are added to familiar forms, we must reappraise both the material and the object it represents. Except for the wooden platform

7.53 Robert Notkin, *Vain Imaginings*, 1978. White earthenware, glaze, brass, redwood, white cedarwood, 16 × 13½ × 16½ in. (40.6 × 34.3 × 41.9 cm).

and brass screws, Robert Notkin's *Vain Imaginings* (7.53) is made of clay. The textures of wood, plastic, glass, and bone have been skillfully imitated. Clay is very unlike any of these materials, and a purist may argue that such mimicry violates its inherent nature. On closer examination, however, we can see a perfect match between the image and the idea. The table, which symbolizes the world, supports a chess set, suggesting risk, and a television set, which presents an illusion. The ceramic skull is placed on top of four books titled *The Shallow Life*, *Moth and Rust*, *Vain Imaginings*, and *By Bread Alone*. The image on the screen repeats the skull. The clay itself suggests impermanence (as in "he has feet of clay") and mortality (as in "earth to earth, dust to dust, " which is said during many funerals). In this masterwork of imitation, ceramicist Robert Notkin has created a "fake" sculpture for a false world.

Doormat by Mona Hatoum (7.54) offers an even more disorienting reinterpretation of a familiar object. Constructed from steel pins, this mat is part of a series of political art projects by Palestinian artist Mona Hatoum. Commenting on the realities of racism, Hatoum suggests that for African Americans, the opportunities offered by the Civil Rights movement may seem as illusory as a welcome mat made of pins.

Textural Elaboration

Given the versatility of materials, it is hardly surprising that artists rarely accept a surface at face value. Modifications in the surface can enhance the power of a sculpture or create very different effects from the same basic material. In *Rock Bible* (7.55), Takako Araki used three kinds of texture to animate an artwork and expand its meaning. The words on the pages of the *Bible* provide one texture, the rough surface of the disintegrating book provides a second, and the characteristic texture of the clay provides a third.

In Seiji Kunishima's *Suspended Pool '86–9* (7.56), a highly polished top surface becomes a pool of visual water while the pitted bottom surface reconfirms the solidity of the black granite. Through variations in the surface, the sculptor has created very different effects from a single block of stone.

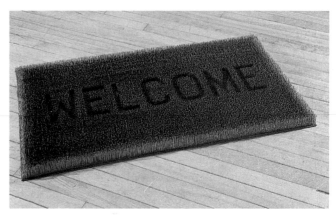

7.54 Mona Hatoum, *Doormat*, 1996. Stainless steel and nickel-plated pins, glue and canvas, 1 × 28 × 16 in. (2.5 × 71 × 40.6 cm).

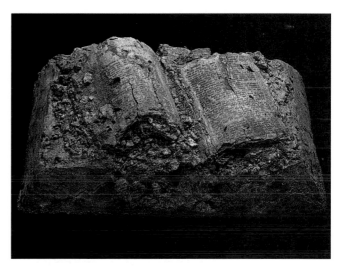

7.55 Takako Araki, *Rock Bible*, 1995. Ceramic, silkscreen, 8¼ × 23⅝ × 16½ in. (21 × 60 × 42 cm).

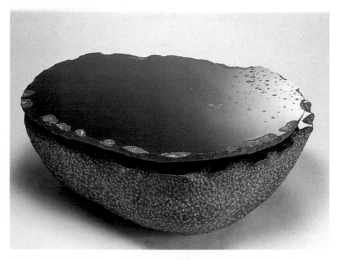

7.56 Seiji Kunishima, *Suspended Pool '86–9*, 1986. Black granite, 12⅝ × 34⅝ × 26⅜ in. (32 × 88 × 67 cm.)

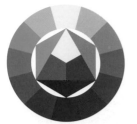

7.57A Hue

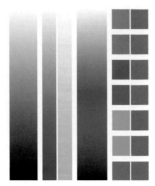

7.57B Value

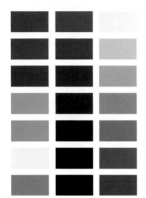

7.57C Intensity

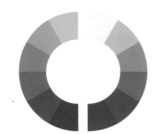

7.57D Temperature

Color and Light

Many color definitions and applications remain the same whether we are creating a three-dimensional or a two-dimensional form. Each color has a specific **hue** (7.57A), which is determined by its wavelength. **Value** (7.57B), the lightness or darkness of a color, helps determine legibility. **Intensity,** or **saturation** (7.57C), refers to the purity of a color. **Temperature** (7.57D) refers to the psychological heat attributed to a color.

Artists and designers use harmony and contrast to create unity and to evoke an appropriate emotion. These aspects of color and light are of particular importance to interior and exhibition designers. A restaurant that is beautifully designed and attractively lit will invite diners to enter. Color and light inform as well as invite visitors to an exhibition, encouraging the audience to follow a specific traffic pattern or to explore a hidden space. Color clues can also delineate the boundaries between various sections in an exhibition, thus dividing it into manageable parts.

Harmony and Discord

Selecting the right colors for a product and determining the degree of color **harmony** can make or break a design. The triadic harmony used in *Smartronics Learning System* by Fisher-Price (7.58) creates an attractive educational toy for young children. The large red and blue buttons are easy to push and invite even the most skeptical child to play. A very different type of harmony is offered in *Kita Collection*, by Toshiyuki Kita (7.59). These simple chairs with their removable seats can be color-customized to fit into any interior. By contrast, the green, blue, ochre, and black used by George Sowden in Figure 7.60 push this chair beyond any traditional system of color harmony. The combination of pastels and black is both distinctive and unconventional.

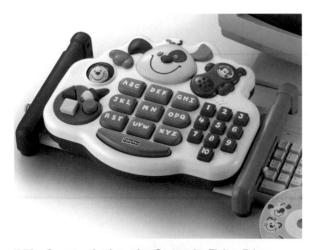

7.58 *Smartronics Learning System* by Fisher-Price.

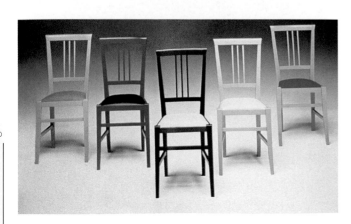

7.59 Toshiyuki Kita, *Kita Collection* of Chairs with Removable Seats for Stendig International Inc. Beech wood frame and upholstered seat.

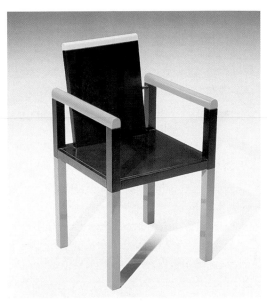

7.60 George J. Sowden, *Palace Chair,* 1983. Designed for Memphis. Lacquered beech wood and stained beech wood.

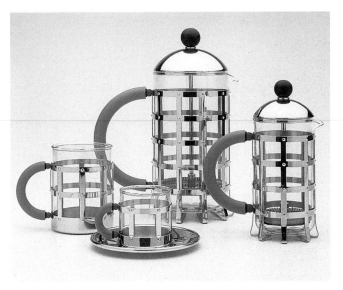

7.61 Michael Graves, Alessi Coffee Set. Glass, silver, mock ivory, and Bakelite.

Contrast

Designers often use **contrasting colors** to accentuate the function of a product or to create a distinctive image. Contrasting colors and materials distinguish Michael Graves' Alessi coffee set (7.61). The fragile, transparent glass is protected by metallic armor. These bands of metal accentuate the cylindrical forms, while the blue handles and bright red accents further animate the set. A similar **contrast** between opacity and transparency combined with a surprising use of color helped distinguish the iMac computer (7.62) from its monochromatic competitors. As with the Fisher-Price toy, color helped to personalize the iMac, inviting new users to play.

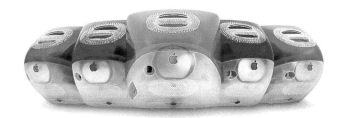

7.62 iMacs in 5 Colors. To illustrate the contrast between opacity and transparency, and to show how iMacs are distinguished from monochromatic competitors. Chiat/Day Advertising.

Color and Emotion

The emotional implications of color can be demonstrated by a visit to any car dealership. Bright red, black, or silver sports cars become oversized toys for single drivers, while more subdued colors are often used for the minivans and station wagons favored by families. In Figure 7.63, color is used to add a sporty look to quite a different vehicle. This manual wheelchair, designed by Adele Linarducci for children ages 6 to 11, gives the user a psychological boost while encouraging the development of physical strength and dexterity.

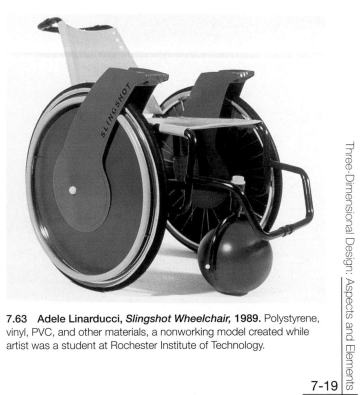

7.63 Adele Linarducci, *Slingshot Wheelchair,* 1989. Polystyrene, vinyl, PVC, and other materials, a nonworking model created while artist was a student at Rochester Institute of Technology.

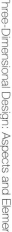

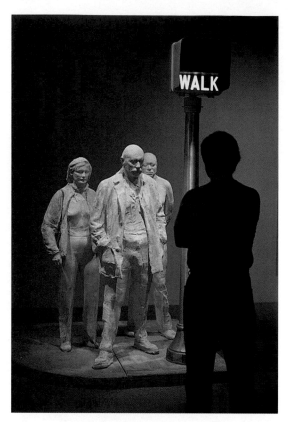

7.64 George Segal, *Walk, Don't Walk*, 1976. Museum Installation, with viewer. Plaster, cement, metal, painted wood, and electric light, 104 × 72 × 72 in. (264.2 × 182.9 × 182.9 cm).

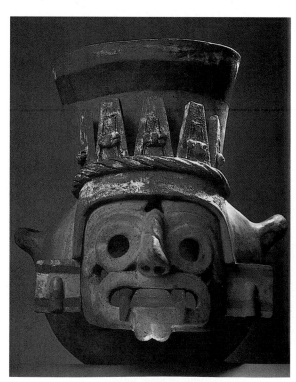

7.65 Ritual Vessel Depicting Mask of Tlaloc, Aztec, Mexico, Tenochtitlan, 1400–1521. Ceramic.

On the other hand, it is the absence of color that brings power to the life-sized figures in George Segal's installations. Despite their proximity to the viewer and their large scale, the white figures in *Walk, Don't Walk* (7.64) are drained of individuality and are emotionally distant. Here, an antiseptic white is used to suggest alienation.

Symbolic Color

All cultures use color symbolically. Ritual vessels, masks, banners, or regal costumes are rarely muted. On the contrary, the visual and psychological impact of color is used very deliberately, especially by political and religious leaders. The scarlet-and-gold feather cloak used by a Hawaiian king symbolized his power and was highly visible during ceremonies. In Europe, purple has long been associated with royalty, and scarlet red is a color associated with the British monarchy.

Symbolic color is culturally based and color associations vary. For example, the color yellow signifies the direction north in Tibet but the qualities of light, life, truth, and immortality to the Hindu.[3] Blue represents mourning in Borneo, while in New Mexico it is painted on window frames to block entrance by evil spirits. In ancient times, blue represented faith and truth to the Egyptians yet was the color worn by slaves in Gaul.[4]

The blue face that dominates the mask of the Aztec god Tlaloc in Figure 7.65 is both symbolically and visually appropriate. Symbolically, the blue represents sky and the rain that Tlaloc calls forth to nourish the crops. Visually, the contrast between the warm, reddish clay and the sky-blue paint increases the impact of the ferocious face.

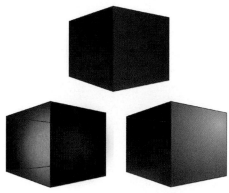

7.66

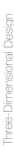

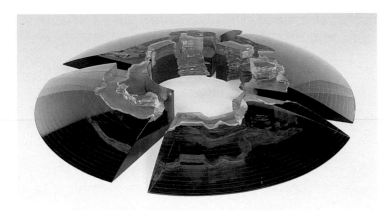

7.67 Maria Lugossy, *Amphitheatrum*, 1983. Laminated plate glass, cut, ground, and polished, 3½ in. h. × 30⅞ in. d. (8.7 × 78.5 cm).

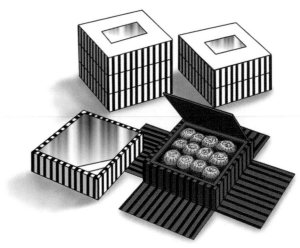

7.68

Color of, on, and within an Object

Color and light also have many unique qualities when used three-dimensionally. As shown in Figure 7.66, a designer can use the existing color *of* the object, apply color *on* the object, and use color *within* the object.

Depending on the material used, these simple variables can be used to compress or visually expand a design and to invite or deny entry into a piece. In Maria Lugossy's *Amphitheatrum* (7.67), clear and green glass has been laminated to create an elegant, stratified structure. A network of parallel lines radiates from the center, accentuating the circular form. As we walk around the sculpture, we can explore the structural and coloristic nuances of each layer as well as the overall form. In Figure 7.68, simple volumes and parallel lines create a series of containers for 12 pieces of chocolate. Starting with a simple black outer box, moving to the beautifully striped, pink-and-black inner box and ending with the individually wrapped treats, the user gradually reveals a hidden treasure. The packaging provides an aesthetic experience as well as a functional container. Hidden in this box, even mediocre chocolate would seem special.

A very different combination of parallel lines and surface color animates *Eagle Transforming into Human* by Terry Starr (7.69). The beautiful wood grain that flows through the image suggests a metamorphosis. Bold, black and red accents at the eyebrows, mouth, and eyes arrest this movement and suggest the piercing gaze of the fierce bird.

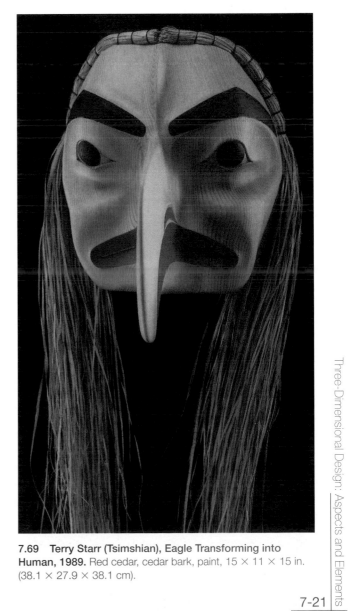

7.69 Terry Starr (Tsimshian), Eagle Transforming into Human, 1989. Red cedar, cedar bark, paint, 15 × 11 × 15 in. (38.1 × 27.9 × 38.1 cm).

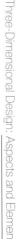

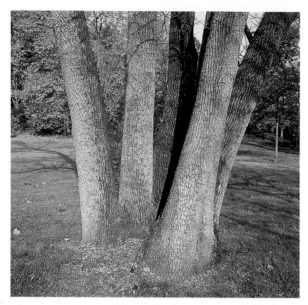

7.70 Andy Goldsworthy, *Maple Leaves Pinned with Thorns*, Plano, IL, 1992.

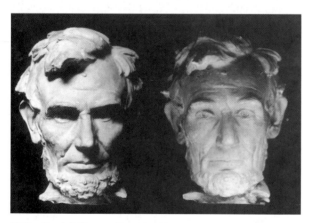

7.71 Daniel Chester French, Abraham Lincoln (Detail of Seated Figure), 1911–22. Full-size plaster model of head of marble statue, Lincoln Memorial, Washington, DC, 1917–18. Head 50½ in. h. (128.3 cm), total figure 19 ft h. (5.8 m).

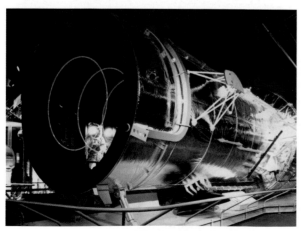

7.72 NASA Exhibit at the 1989 Paris Air Show. Designers: Bill Cannan, Tony Ortiz, H. Kurt Heinz. Design Firm: Bill Cannan & Co.

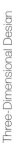

Finally, the shredded cedar-bark hair that frames the mask increases the human quality of the bird-like face.

Color is equally important in the work of Andy Goldsworthy. Using natural materials in natural settings, he often creates intense areas of red, green, or gold to alert the viewer to junctions, boundaries, or unusual configurations between objects in the landscape. These accents of color are especially powerful when the surrounding colors are subdued. The scarlet maple leaves in Figure 7.70 create a flaming arrow shape that activates the negative space between two tree trunks. If we are alert, after seeing this sculpture we will become more aware of the negative spaces throughout the landscape and begin to see all tree trunks differently.

Light of, on, and inside an Object

Light can heighten a sense of volume, define or obscure an interior, attract an audience, or create a mystery. A three-dimensional object can gain or lose power depending on the lighting used. Daniel Chester French's *Head of Abraham Lincoln* (7.71) loses dimensionality when lit from below but gains a quality of animation. When lit from above, the same figure seems more formidable and commanding. Theatrical set designers and installation artists are masters of light. To suggest the mystery of space travel and highlight individual displays, the designers of a 1989 NASA exhibition used bright pools of light within an otherwise dark display (7.72).

Indeed, light can create a composition. In Larry Bell's *The Iceberg and Its Shadow* (7.73), multiple plates of glass create reflections that continually shift, separate, and surround the viewer. This combination of volume, space, and light creates a world that is both physical and illusory. Like a house of mirrors, the sculpture is both tangible and transient.

The relationship between color and light is further demonstrated by Suzanne Harris's *Won for the One* (7.74). A plate glass cube has been suspended from the ceiling using piano wire. Lit by beams of red, yellow, and green light on three sides, the glass transmits a circle of radiant white light below the cube, illuminating the floor.

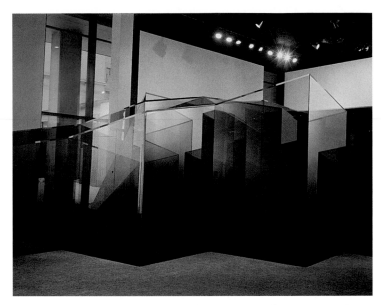

7.73 Larry Bell, *The Iceberg and Its Shadow,* **1977.** Clear and gray glass coated with inconel, 60 in. w. (152.4 cm), 57 in. to 100 in. h. (144.8 to 254 cm). Busch Lobby, MIT Permanent Collection.

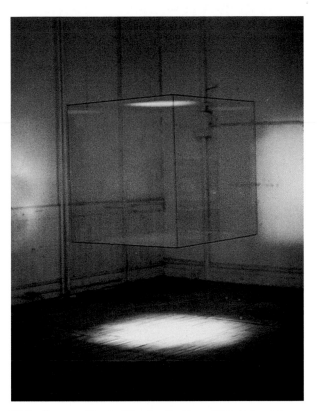

7.74 Suzanne Harris, *Won for the One,* **1974.** ¼ in. plate glass cube, 4 ft (1.22 m), 300 lb, piano wire, lit three sides, red, yellow, green, casting a white "shadow" floating effect.

Light can even become a sculpture. James Turrell's *Afrum-Proto* in Figure 7.75 was created when a powerful beam of light struck the corner of an empty room.

The Complexity of Three-Dimensional Design

Completing a new project every week or so is quite common in a basic two-dimensional-design class. On the other hand, a month of work may be devoted to a major project in a three-dimensional-design class. The materials may be less familiar, the construction methods are more time-consuming, and most important, the multiple surfaces of a physical object present a particular challenge. Used poorly, the various elements may clash, resulting in a disjointed composition. Used well, each element contributes to a complex and cohesive design. Awareness of the interrelationship of all design elements, attention to detail, and a willingness to experiment with many possibilities are essential qualities of a good designer.

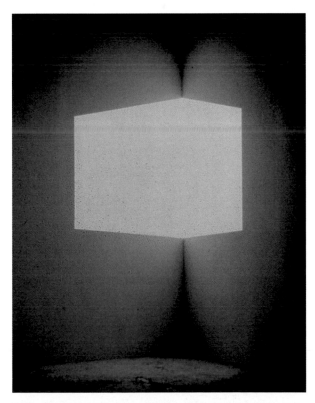

7.75 James Turrell, *Afrum-Proto,* **1966.** Quartz-halogen projection, as installed at the Whitney Museum of American Art, New York, 1980.

Profile:
Rodger Mack, Sculptor

The Oracle's Tears: Conception, Composition, and Construction

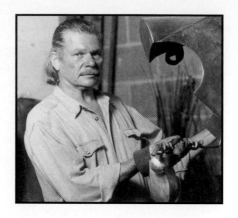

Rodger Mack is an internationally renowned sculptor best known for his work in bronze and steel. His work, which is equally divided between commissions and self-initiated projects, is included in the collections of the Museum of Modern Art in Barcelona, Spain, the Grand Hotel in Guayaquil, Ecuador, the Arkansas Arts Center Museum, Little Rock; the Albrecht-Kemper Museum of Art in St. Joseph, Missouri, the Munson-Williams-Proctor Institute in Utica, New York, and the Everson Museum in Syracuse, New York. Mack, who has always used travel as a major inspiration for his imagery, is the recipient of a Fulbright grant for study in Italy, grants from the National Endowment for the Arts and the New York State Council on the Arts; and workshop grants for projects in England, Barcelona, and South Africa.

My meeting with Mack was delayed for almost a year due to his many commissions and elaborate projects. Finally, with the departure date for his yearlong trip to Italy fast approaching, we got together over lunch. I had always admired Mack's abstract sculptures that so elegantly combine power and grace. Indeed, I expected our conversation to focus on the elements and principles of design. As you will see, the conversation that actually developed was equally devoted to concepts and composition.

MS: One of the biggest questions my students have is this: How do I get from where I am, as a beginner to where you are, as a professional? Could you describe that path briefly?

RM: I always knew that I wanted to study art, and I began my undergraduate work at the Cleveland Institute of Art, planning to become an automotive designer. In the fourth year of the five-year BFA program, I had the good fortune of being picked by General Motors to participate in an experimental summer internship. It was an exciting time: I was well paid, and directly involved in my intended career.

I realized, though, that automotive design limited my possibilities as an artist, and I turned instead to a major in sculpture, with a minor in ceramics. At Cleveland, ceramicist Toshiko Takaezu was a great influence. She taught me a level of professionalism and an understanding of a new level of quality, both in concept and in craft. I was further influenced by Toshiko's teacher, Maija Grotell, who had developed the ceramics program at Cranbrook, where I did my graduate work. At the age of 70, she was continuing to do pioneering work with ceramic glazes.

Finally, as an apprentice to William McBey, I learned about working on commissions and the realities of day-to-day work in the studio. With sculpture, cleaning up is important: if you don't control your work space, it will control you!

MS: How do you get started on a sculpture?

RM: I don't have to get started, because I never stop! I'm always watching, listening, and thinking. When I do stop the merry-go-round long enough, I record my ideas in a notebook. I always carry this notebook on the plane: while others read, I draw. I always have many more ideas than I can handle: I wish I could build them as fast as I can think them up.

Whenever I stop generating new material, I just visualize the inventory of sculptural parts I already have in the studio. Putting them together in new ways provides even more possibilities: an idea gets me working with the metal, which then generates more ideas. I always try to have something ready for casting each month, if only to add to this inventory of parts.

I only make maquettes when they are required for a commission. The small scale of a maquette is so different from the actual scale of the piece, especially for a major project. I remember one maquette I made for a commission in North Little Rock, Arkansas. It was made of bronze, and I charged them $200 for the maquette. Before the meeting to review the project, one of the city councilors put a box of multicolored sticks of plasticine in front of me and said, "Next time, make it out of this." He was annoyed that I had made the maquette in bronze. In fact, the city council was against the project—they just didn't want to spend the money—but a grassroots civic group saw the importance of the work, and the commission was approved.

MS: How do you choose which of the drawings to make into sculptures?
RM: I might choose a drawing because I can't see the other side. I get curious. There is something in the drawn side that compels me to spend the time and money on the sculpture, so that I can see the other side. Drawings that I really finish are the sculptures that I never make.

MS: It seems that you actually "draw" with the metal; that is, you approach it with the same openness with which I approach a sheet of paper. How malleable is it?

RM: Just malleable enough! I like it because it is NOT easy. It is hard, and you have to really commit yourself to the piece. I am most intuitive when I am working with existing fragments from my inventory, essentially collaging parts together. Starting with a collection of parts, I create connections, often heating a bar of bronze to just the right temperature and bending it to form a bridge or activate a space. I see the space around each volume as much as I see the volume itself.

MS: Please describe your latest piece, *The Oracle's Tears*.
RM: I've always been drawn to ancient cities and architectural forms, and have been working with mythological themes for the past six years, with a series of maidens, a minotaur, a Trojan horse, and several oracles completed so far. When I visit these ancient civilizations, it saddens me that they are gone, destroyed to make way for new civilizations.

This sculpture is made from six major parts. The column is the dominant feature, structurally and conceptually. Just above it, I have placed a form which has reappeared in my work for 30 years, the Oracle. It is like an image on a tarot card, the hanging man, perhaps. A smaller piece, based on a shape I found in a market in Athens, connects the oracle and the column. On the top, the "capitol" repeats the triangular spaces seen throughout the sculpture. The tears are created by the three descending lines. The base is the final element. It provides a stable support and adds a sense of completion.

MS: How was the sculpture made?
RM: I used a combination of fabrication and casting. The oracle form was made by cutting out shapes from a sheet of ⅛ inch bronze and welding them together. The tears and the column were cast in sections, then welded. A potassium dichloride patina, applied using a blowtorch, gives the piece its golden color.

MS: This is an especially important piece for you, I think.
RM: You always hope your latest piece is the best! But yes, it combines ideas I've been working on for three years, with an overall theme which first appeared in my work when I was in undergraduate school.

MS: What advice do you have for a beginning student?
RM: Well, there's the old cliché: Learn the rules before you break them. Always worked for me!

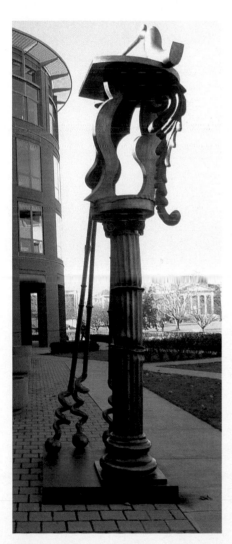
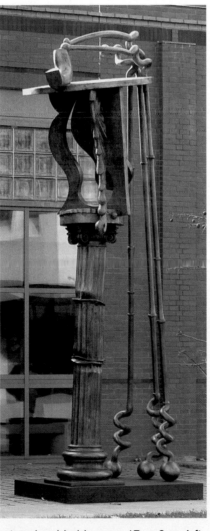

Rodger Mack, *The Oracle's Tears*, 1999. Cast and welded bronze, 17 × 6 × 4 ft (5.18 × 1.83 × 1.22 m)

Summary

- The first step in creating a design is to understand its purpose. A sculptor seeks to convey ideas and express emotions. A craftsperson or designer is equally concerned with the function and the beauty of an object. Form and function must match.

- The elements of three-dimensional design are line, plane, volume, mass, space, texture, and color and light.

- By accurately describing six views of an object, orthographic projection provides a way to develop accurate plans for three-dimensional designs.

- Artworks can vary in dimensionality—from relief, which uses a flat backing to support dimensional forms, to freestanding sculptures, which must be viewed from all sides. Exhibitions and installations push this effect even further, as the viewer must enter and physically explore the artwork.

- A line can connect, define, or divide a design. It can be static or dynamic, increasing or decreasing the stability of the form.

- A shape is created when a line connects to enclose an area; when an area of color or texture is defined by a clear boundary; or when an area is surrounded by a contrasting color, value, or texture. A plane is a shape that has been modified or combined to create a three-dimensional structure.

- A volume is an area of enclosed three-dimensional space. Volume is often created when planes are connected or multiplied to create an enclosure. A mass is an enclosed area of three-dimensional substance. Both volume and mass can be perceived through primary contours and secondary contours.

- Space is the partner to substance. Without it, line, plane, volume, and mass lose meaning.

- Texture refers to the visual or tactile surface of an object. It can be used to increase, decrease, or add complexity to our understanding of a physical object.

- Like texture, the color of, on, and within an object can increase or decrease our understanding of the form. Light can enhance our perception of a three-dimensional form, attract an audience, or be used as a material in itself.

Keywords

actual lines	function	negative shape	section
characteristic texture	harmony	orthographic projection	shape
contradictory texture	hue	plane	sight line
contrast	implied lines	plan view	space
contrasting colors	installation	polyhedra	symbolic color
elevation	intensity	primary contour	temperature
form	in the round	relief	texture
freestanding	kinetic form	saturation	three-quarter work
	light	secondary contour	value
	line		volume
	mass		walk-through

As you begin your studio work, consider:

1. What are the unique characteristics of each of the elements of three-dimensional design? How does a line contribute to the composition, compared to the contribution of a plane, volume, or mass?

2. Specifically, what role does each element play in your project?

3. What is the relationship between substance and space? Are they equally balanced, or does one dominate? What would happen if this relationship was substantially exaggerated—if the composition was 90 percent space and 10 percent mass, for example?

4. To what extent can texture, color, or light enhance, conceal, or add complexity to the form?

5. Is your object equally interesting on all sides? Are there any surprises?

Gaston Bachelard, *The Poetics of Space*, Maria Jolas, translator. Boston, Beacon Press, 1969.

Frank Ching, *Architecture: Form, Space, and Order*, 2nd edition. New York, Van Nostrand Reinhold, 1996.

John Lidstone, *Building with Wire*. New York, Van Nostrand Reinhold, 1972.

Charles Wallschlaeger and Cynthia Busic-Snyder, *Basic Visual Concepts and Principles for Artists, Architects and Designers*. Dubuque, William C. Brown, 1992.

Howard Hibbard, *Masterpieces of Western Sculpture from Medieval to Modern*. New York, Harper and Row, 1980.

Key Questions

Key Readings

chapter eight

Three-Dimensional Design:
Organization

The power of each element of design can be amplified through careful composition. In Alice Aycock's *Tree of Life Fantasy* (see 7.42, page 7-13), line, plane, and space have been combined to create an exuberant dance. Every element is both dependent on and supportive of every other element. Martin Puryear's *Seer* (8.1) consists of a closed volume at the top and an open volume at the bottom. The horn-shaped top piece is powerful and imposing, while the open construction at the bottom invites us to enter and visually explore the structure. Here, the contrast between open and closed volumes adds both power and mystery to the piece. And graceful metal lines have been combined with a series of contoured volumes to create the elegant and utilitarian form of Niels Diffrient's *Freedom Chair* (8.3).

Artists and designers use each element very deliberately. Extensive exploration and experimentation are used to determine the best means of integrating disparate parts into a cohesive whole. Dozens of drawings or three-dimensional models may be produced before an idea is finalized. As shown in Stan Rickel's *Teapot Sketches* (8.2), a physical object can be made manifest through an almost endless variety of forms.

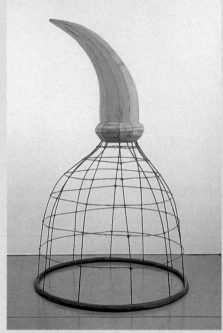

8.1 Martin Puryear, *Seer*, 1984. Water-based paint on wood and wire, 78 × 52¼ × 45 in. (198.2 × 132.6 × 114.3 cm).

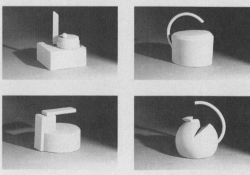

8.2 Stan Rickel, *Teapot Sketches*, 1991. Mixed medium, 12 × 12 in. (30.5 × 30.5 cm).

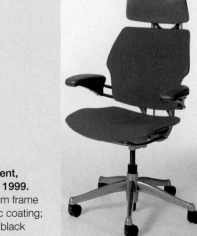

8.3 Niels Diffrient, *Freedom Chair*, 1999. Die-cast aluminum frame with fused plastic coating; four-way stretch black fabric.

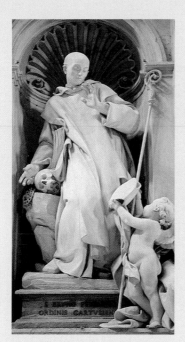

8.4 Michel-Ange Slodtz, *St. Bruno*, 1744. Marble.

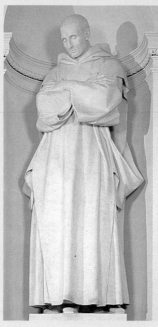

8.5 Jean-Antoine Houdon, *St. Bruno of Cologne*, 1766. Stucco.

Principles of Three-Dimensional Design

Balance

For the architect, sculptor, and industrial designer, physical balance is a structural necessity, while visual balance is an aesthetic necessity. As with physical balance, **visual balance** requires equilibrium, or equality in size, weight, and force. Especially in three-dimensional design, visual balance can be created through absence as well as presence. Space is always the partner to structure.

The expressive power of **balance** can be seen in two contrasting interpretations of a single subject. Figures 8.4 and 8.5 both represent St. Bruno, an eleventh-century Catholic saint who founded an austere, contemplative religious group known as the Carthusian Order. Members lived in caves and devoted their time to transcribing manuscripts, to meditation, and to prayer.

The first statue, completed by Michel-Ange Slodtz in 1744, dramatizes a pivotal moment in Bruno's life. Preferring his contemplative existence to the power and prestige of a more public life, Bruno rejects promotion to the office of bishop. Slodtz used **asymmetrical balance** to express this dramatic moment. Asymmetrical balance creates equilibrium between visual elements that differ in size, number, weight, color, or texture. In this case, the small bishop's hat, proffered by the angel in the lower right corner, is the focal point of the entire sculpture. The much larger figure of St. Bruno recoils when confronted by this symbol of authority. As a result, the small hat matches the power of the saint.

A very different interpretation of the life of St. Bruno is given in the second sculpture. Completed by Jean-Antoine Houdon in 1766, Figure 8.5 emphasizes the contemplative nature of the Carthusian Order and its founder. Using **symmetrical balance,** Houdon presents a dignified, introspective man. If we divide the figure in half from top to bottom, the two sides basically mirror each other. This saint is a philosopher, very much at peace with the choices he has made. Just as asymmetrical balance is appropriate for the dramatic moment represented by Slodtz, so symmetrical balance is ideal for the serenity shown by Houdon.

A third common approach to balance is shown in this mask of the Native American Bella Coola tribe (8.6). With **radial balance,** all visual elements in a composition are connected at a central point. Here,

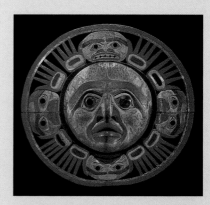

8.6 Bella Coola Mask Representing the Sun, from British Columbia, before 1897. Wood, diameter 24¾ in. (63 cm).

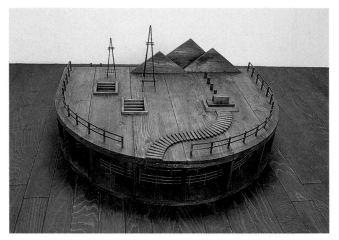

8.9 Akira Kamiyama, *This Is My Place, I Suspect,* **1984.** Japanese cedar, yarn, oil stain, 19⅞ × 39⅜ × 32¼ in. (50.5 × 100 × 82 cm).

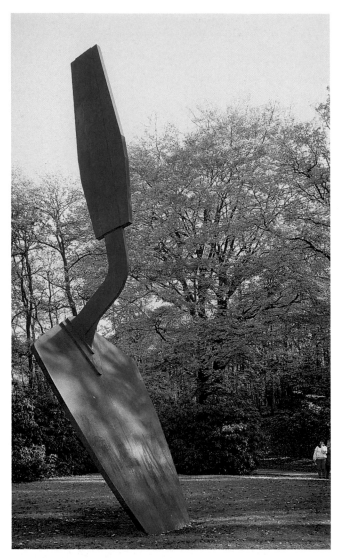

8.7 Claes Oldenburg, *Trowel,* **1971.** Steel, painted blue, 38 ft 4⅔ in. × 11 ft 11⅔ in. (11.7 × 3.7 m).

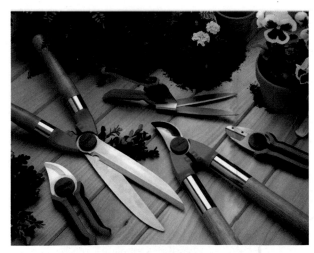

8.8 Home Pro Garden Tool Line. Designers: James E. Grove, John Cook, Jim Holtorf, Fernando Pardo, Mike Botich. Design Firm: Designworks/USA.

the center of the face creates the pivot point. Radiating outward in all directions, the composition is an effective representation of the sun.

Scale and Proportion

Scale is determined by the size of an object relative to its surroundings. Almost 40 feet tall, Claes Oldenburg's *Trowel* (8.7) is both witty and imposing. What manic gardener has left this giant tool in the park? We are familiar with gardening tools which can be handheld (8.8). Any change in the "normal" size of an object immediately attracts our attention.

A very different approach to scale transforms *This Is My Place, I Suspect* (8.9) by Akira Kamiyama. The small brown structure looks like an architectural model for an antiquated factory. When combined with the industrial site, this very personal title suggests a mystery. What can possibly occur in this place? Connecting the small scale with the evocative title, we may conclude that this is the place for almost anything, from meditation to murder. Unable to enter this miniature piece physically, we must explore the site conceptually, using the clues presented as a springboard for our imagination.

Proportion refers to the relative height, width, and length of visual or physical elements *within* a composition. Any change in proportion substantially affects all aspects of a three-dimensional form. Three variations of Constantin Brancusi's *Bird in Space* are shown in Figures 8.10 to 8.12. In *Maiastra* (8.10), the abstract bird form is dominated by the egg-shaped torso that tapers into the folded wings at the bottom and the raised head at the top. This bird is approximately 3 times taller than it is wide. Brancusi further abstracted *Golden Bird* (8.11) and elongated the body. The bird is now 7 times taller than it is wide and an elaborate base adds even more height to the sculpture. With *Bird in Space* (8.12), Brancusi elongated the form even more and added an expanding "foot" below the folded wings. This bird is almost 10 times taller than it is wide. By lengthening the columnar structure in this final version and carefully tapering the sculpture near the base, Brancusi made this simple sculpture fly.

In industrial design, changes in proportion can enhance or diminish function. The five gardening tools in Figure 8.8 are all based on the same basic combination of handle, blades, and simple pivot. Variations in proportion determine their use. The short-handled pruner in the lower-left corner is used to trim twigs and small branches from shrubs. It must fit comfortably in a single hand. The proportions of the lopper in the opposite corner are much different. Its 20-inch-long handle provides the leverage needed to cut heavier branches from small trees. For the industrial designer, function often determines proportion.

As with all design decisions, choosing the right scale and proportion greatly increases expressive power. Giovanni Bologna's *Apennine* (8.13) is scaled to overwhelm the viewer with a sense of the mountain spirit's presence. His human frame far exceeds human scale, and the surrounding trees and cliff appear to diminish in proportion to him.

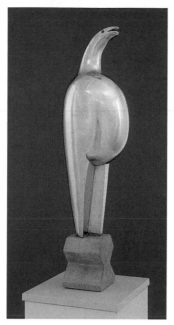

8.10 **Constantin Brancusi,** *Maiastra,* **1912.** Polished brass, 29⅞ × 7¼ × 7½ in. (75.7 × 18.5 × 19 cm).

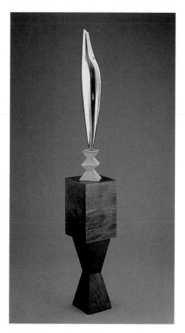

8.11 **Constantin Brancusi,** *Golden Bird,* **1919, pedestal c. 1922.** Bronze, stone, and wood, 37¾ in. h. (95.9 cm), base 48 in. h. (121.9 cm).

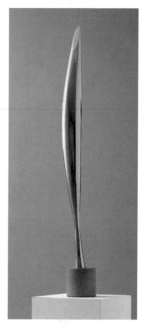

8.12 **Constantin Brancusi,** *Bird in Space,* **1928.** Bronze (unique cast), 54 × 8½ × 6½ in. (137.2 × 21.6 × 16.5 cm).

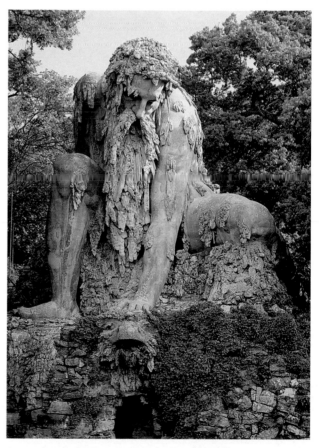

8.13 **Giovanni Bologna,** *Apennine,* **1580–82.** Stone, bricks, mortar. Villa di Pratolino, Florence region, Italy.

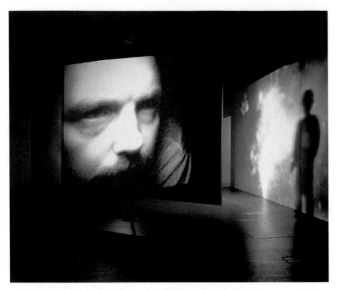

8.15 Bill Viola, *Slowly Turning Narrative*, 1992. Video/sound installation.

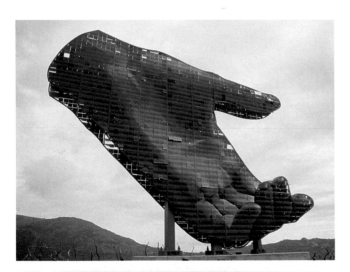

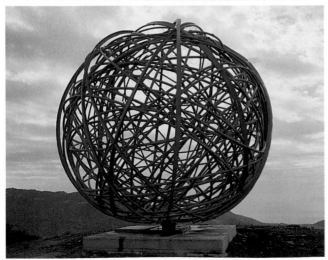

8.16 Todd Slaughter, *Mano y Balo* (details), 1997. Aluminum and steel, hand 27 × 40 × 4 ft (8.2 × 12.2 × 1.2 m), ball 20 ft (6 m) diameter. Overlooking the Straits of Gibraltar.

Proportional extremes can be equally expressive. Standing just over five feet tall, Alberto Giacometti's *Chariot* (8.14) offers a somber analysis of the human condition. The solitary figure is delicately balanced on gigantic wheels, which then rest on two small pedestals. The entire form is linear, as if distilled down to the barest essentials. Both the chariot and the figure it transports are precariously balanced and seem very vulnerable.

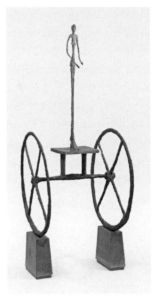

8.14 Alberto Giacometti, *Chariot*, 1950. Bronze, 57 × 26 × 26⅛ in. (144.8 × 65.8 × 66.2 cm).

Proximity

Physical impact and conceptual complexity can also be strengthened through **proximity,** the distance between the parts of a structure or between an object and the audience. While *This Is My Place, I Suspect* (8.9) conceptually pulls the viewer into a miniature world, the various components of Bill Viola's *Slowly Turning Narrative* (8.15) physically surround the viewer. This installation consists of a 9 × 12 ft screen, which slowly rotates on its central axis in a darkened room. Black-and-white projections of a man's face can be seen on one side; on the other, color images of children, people at a carnival, and other playful images are shown. One side of the screen is a mirror, which reflects distorted images back into the room. The combination of the moving images and moving screen is hypnotic. In close proximity to the viewer, the enormous faces have an overwhelming impact.

A combination of scale, proximity, and wind animates Todd Slaughter's *Mano y Balo* (8.16). Commissioned by the port city of Algeciras in Spain, the monumental sculpture rests on a bluff overlooking the Strait of Gibraltar. The 40-foot-long hand may be catching or throwing the 20-foot-tall ball which is positioned 50 feet away. Slaughter notes that, "The implied action of the hand . . . metaphorically

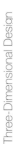

alludes to the history of exchange of religion, art, power and conflict between the European and African continents." To heighten the metaphor, the hand has been designed to disappear when the wind blows. On the front and back, one-thousand movable panels that are attached to the armature have been covered with the photographic image of a hand. A strong wind shifts the panels from their vertical position to a horizontal position, causing the hand to dissolve visually into the surrounding sky.

Contrast

Just as similarity in line, space, texture, volume, and color can be used to unify a sculpture, so **contrast,** or difference, can be used to create **variety.**

Contrast can appear in many forms and in varying degree. Two strongly opposing systems dominate Arnaldo Pomodoro's *Sphere* (8.17). The imposing spherical volume seems to have been eaten away by some external force, leaving a pattern of rectilinear teeth across its equator. This creates a strong contrast between the massive structure and the invading space, and adds rhythm and texture to the spherical form.

Loops (8.18), by Mary Ann Scherr, presents a contrast between movement and constraint. A curving plane encircles the user's throat, providing protection but restricting motion. Below, the suspended rings sway with every movement of the body, creating a dynamic counterpoint to the constraining collar.

Water animates Pol Bury's *Fountains at Palais Royal* (8.19). The design relies on three major elements. The site itself is dominated by the regularly spaced columns that are so characteristic of neoclassical architecture. The polished steel spheres, poised within the bowl of each foundation, reflect these columns and the shimmering water, which provides the third element in the design. In a sense, the spheres serve as mediators between the rigid columns and the silvery water. Like the columns, they are simple volumes, arranged in a group. Like the water, they seem fluid as they reflect the moving water and the passing clouds. In this project, unity and variety have been combined to create an elegant and intriguing sculpture.

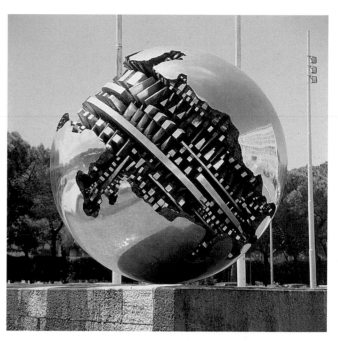

8.17 **Arnaldo Pomodoro, *Sphere,* 1965.** Bronze, 47 in. (119.4 cm) diameter. Ministero degli Esteri, Rome.

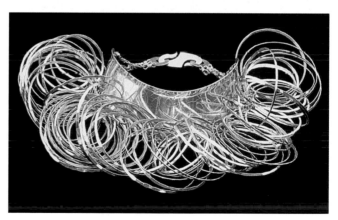

8.18 **Mary Ann Scherr, *Loops,* 1988.** Sterling silver neckpiece, 8½ × 4¾ × 5 in. (21.6 × 12.1 × 12.7).

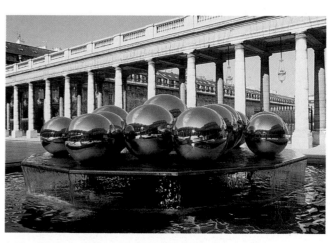

8.19 **Pol Bury, *Fountains at Palais Royal,*** Paris, 1985.

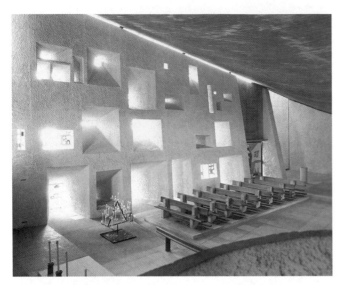

8.20 Le Corbusier, *Interior, Chapelle de Ronchamp*, Notre-Dame-du-Haut, Ronchamp, France, 1950–55.

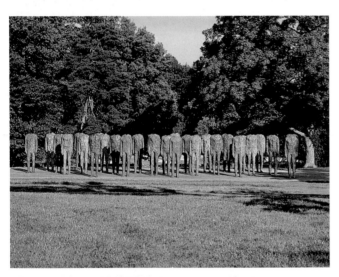

8.21 Magdalena Abakanowicz, *Standing Figures* (Thirty), **1994–99.** Bronze, overall 54 ft 3 in. × 19 ft 8 in. (16.55 × 6 m).

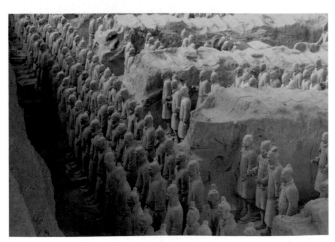

8.22 Tomb of Emperor Shih Huang Ti, 221–206 B.C. Painted ceramic figures, life size.

Finally, strong contrast between light and dark adds both visual and emotional impact to architect Le Corbusier's *Interior, Chapelle de Ronchamp* (8.20). Light enters the darkened church through the narrow, stained-glass windows. Expanding into broad beams as it passes through the thick walls, it pours into the spaces, as liberated as the spirit.

Repetition

Repeated use of any aspect of design is called **repetition.** Repetition is often used to unify elements within an artwork or to quantify an elusive idea. For example, the 30 statues in Magdalena Abakanowicz's *Standing Figures* (8.21) are unified by their similarity in size, shape, and solemnity. Variations in each cast bronze surface provide a degree of individuality. Often interpreted as victims of war, the hollow, headless figures seem frozen in time, offering a silent testimony to a tragic past.

The 6,000 clay soldiers filling the tomb of Emperor Shih Huang Ti (8.22) demonstrate a different use of repetition. The emperor, best known for unifying China and building the Great Wall, may have sought companionship as he faced his death, or wanted a memorial to his accomplishments. His large army of ceramic soldiers could serve either purpose.

Sherrie Levine's *La Fortune* (8.23) demonstrates a third use of repetition. Our sense of reality is challenged when we encounter these six billiard tables. The identical arrangement of the balls seems impossible: the balls would be randomly distributed in six actual games. Here, a very ordinary scene becomes mysterious, even nightmarish, due to relentless repetition.

Grids

Highly repetitive artworks can be mind-numbing or mind-expanding, depending on the intention and execution of the work and on the response of the audience. Let's start with a simple **grid.** It offers a matrix for thought, nothing more. The most patient viewer may begin to see subtle variations in space or imagine a game of tic-tac-toe. Less patient viewers will find the work meaningless.

To reach a broader audience, most artists add information to this basic structure.

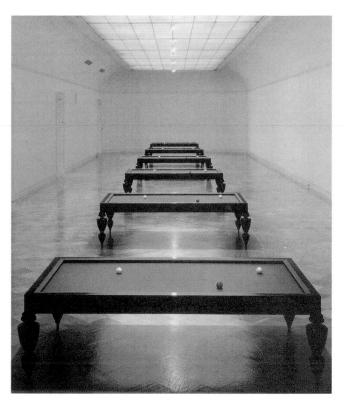

8.23 Sherrie Levine, *La Fortune* (After Man Ray) 1–6, 1990. Felt, mahogany, resin, 33 × 110 × 60 in. (84 × 280 × 153 cm).

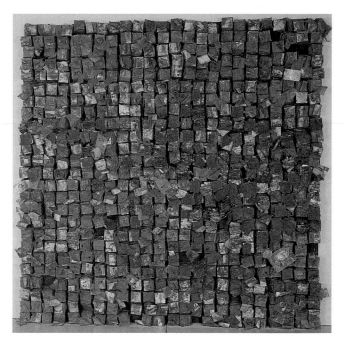

8.24 Leonardo Drew, *Number 56,* 1996. Rust, plastic, wood, 113 × 113 in. (287 × 287 cm).

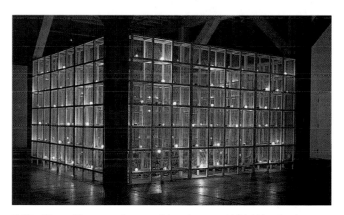

8.25 Mona Hatoum, *Current Disturbance,* 1996. Wood, wire mesh, lightbulbs, timed dimmer unit, amplifier, four speakers, 9 ft 2 in. × 18 ft × 16 ft 6 in. (279 × 550.5 × 504 cm).

In *Number 56* (8.24), Leonardo Drew poured rust into hundreds of plastic bags that were then connected to a wooden support. The rust, so suggestive of decay, and the relentlessly numbered plastic specimen bags present a dialog between order and chaos. On a purely visual level, the resulting order and disorder offer a hypnotic combination of monotony and mystery.

In *Current Disturbance* (8.25), Mona Hatoum used a grid for unity and a sequence of lights for variety. A single, clear lightbulb has been placed in each compartment within the structure. Controlled by a computer, these lights flicker in various patterns, from near darkness to a crescendo of illumination when all are lit. A single lit bulb in the center of the piece and the grid structure itself are the only constants.

Daniel Buren's *The Two Plateaus* (8.26) offers another variant on the grid. This public art project, located in the Palais Royal in Paris, covers a 1,000-square-foot plaza. The striped cylinders range in height from about two to six feet. Mimicking the columns in the building and organized on the pavement like players on a checkerboard, they bring both energy and humor to the site.

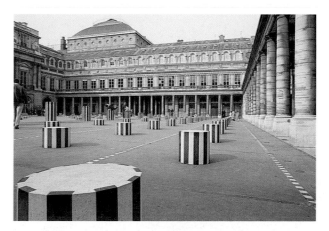

8.26 Daniel Buren, *The Two Plateaus,* 1985–86. 1,000-square-foot sculpture for the Cour d'Honneur, Palais Royal, Paris. Black marble, granite, iron, cement, electricity, water.

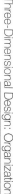

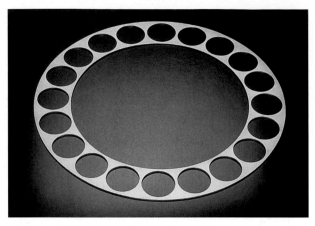

8.27 David Watkins, *Torus 280 (B2)*, 1989. Neckpiece, gilded brass, 11 in. (28 cm).

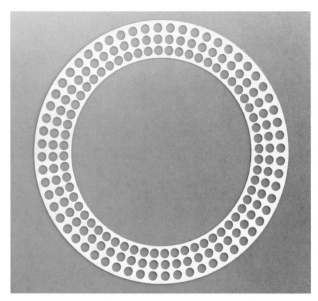

8.28 David Watkins, *Torus 280 (B1)*, 1989. Neckpiece, gilded brass, 11 in. (28 cm).

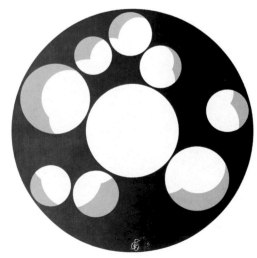

8.29

Rhythm

Repetition with variation creates rhythm. Most of us first encounter rhythm through music or dance. Musically, rhythm is defined as the organization of sound in time. Through a combination of sound and silence, rhythm can become amazingly complex. Meter (the basic pattern), accents (which emphasize specific notes), and tempo (the speed with which the music is played) can be combined to create a dazzling array of songs.

Just as a musician creates a deliberate pattern connecting sound and silence, so the artist can create rhythm using space and form. For a sculptor, **rhythm** can be defined as the sequential organization of multiple forms in space. Variations in the basic pattern and the rate of change combined with the use of accents can enhance or detract from the concept being communicated. As with music, the number and distribution of beats create the rhythm. In David Watkins's *Torus 280 (B2)* (8.27), the consistent order of the circular shapes creates a slow, regular pattern. When the number of circles multiplies in *Torus 280 (B1)* (8.28), the **tempo,** or pace, increases. As the neckpiece expands outward, the space between the circular openings also expands, creating greater variety in form. Variations in the size and location of the circles create a very different effect in Figure 8.29. With fewer openings in the circle and greater variety in the shapes, the rhythm becomes quiet and graceful.

The multiple views offered by physical objects accentuate the importance of rhythm. The fluid movement of the four women circling an exuberant musician creates a joyous dance in Jean-Baptiste Carpeaux's *The Dance* (8.30). Our eyes follow the turning heads, clasped hands, and swirling arms as they move in, out, and around in space. A similar rhythm animates Steve Woodward's *Model of Proposal for Concourse Commission* (8.31). The plywood vortex seems to rise out of the floor to collect in a spinning disk at the top, then descend again, in an endless pattern. When combined with the spinning effect, this up-and-down movement gives the design great vitality.

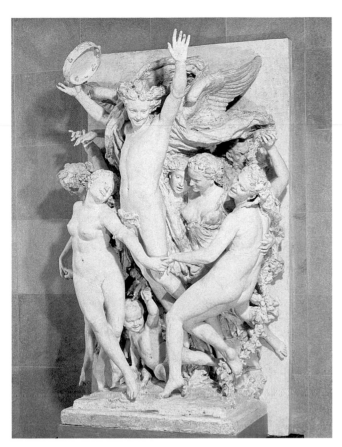

8.30 Jean-Baptiste Carpeaux, *The Dance* (after restoration), **1868–69**. Marble, 7 ft 6½ in. (2.3 m).

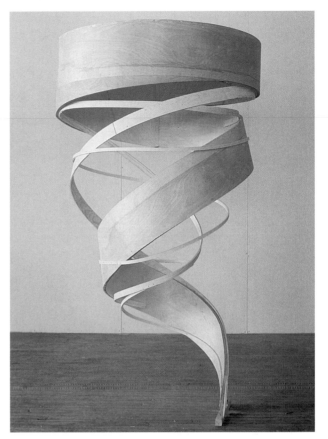

8.31 Steve Woodward, Model of Proposal for Concourse Commission, **1987**. Wood, 13¾ × 8 × 7½ in. (34.9 × 20.3 × 19 cm).

In contrast, the rhythm in Louise Nevelson's *Luminous Zag: Night* (8.32) is relentless and percussive. Within the grid, each box contains a highly agitated mix of diagonal and horizontal forms that open and close as decisively as pistons in an engine. Each rhythmic "beat" in this sculpture is sharp and distinct.

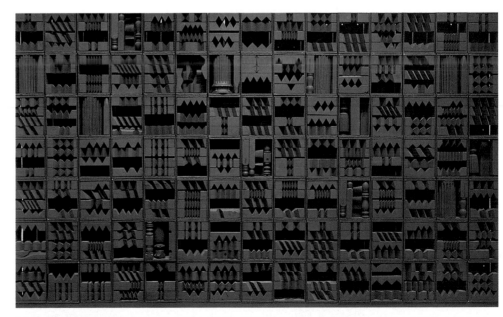

8.32 Louise Nevelson. *Luminous Zag: Night,* **1971**. Painted wood, 105 boxes, total 10 ft × 16 ft 1 in. × 10¾ in. (304.8 × 490.3 × 27.3 cm).

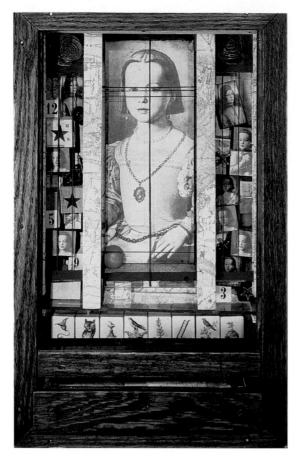

8.33 Joseph Cornell, *Untitled (Medici Princess)*, c. 1948. Construction, 17⅝ × 11⅛ × 4⅜ in. (44.8 × 28.3 × 11.1 cm).

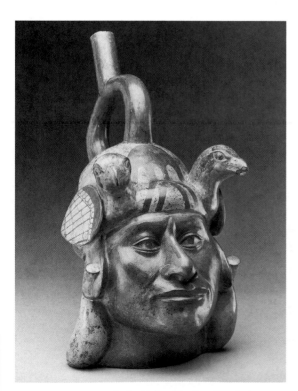

8.34 Portrait Vessel of a Ruler, Moche, 250–500 A.D. Ceramic.

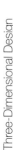

Composition and Construction

Choice of Materials

The materials used in a project may affect the range of possible solutions. In selecting a material, consider these qualitites in relationship to your intended design.

- *Strength*. How much weight can a given material support? What is its breaking point when stressed?

- *Workability*. How difficult is it to alter the shape of a material? Does it cut and bend easily?

- *Durability*. How long must an object last? In what context will a sculpture be shown? The hard basalt used for many Egyptian sculptures has endured for millennia, while the flexible fabric used in a temporary installation may last less than a year.

- *Weight*. A material that is too light for a given purpose can be as problematic as a material that is too heavy. What is the function of the design, and how can weight serve that function?

- *Cost*. Can the material chosen be obtained easily and at a reasonable cost? If your budget is limited, expensive materials will have to be removed from consideration.

- *Toxicity*. Many plastics produce toxic gases when cut, etched, or burned. Paints and solvent may require the use of masks and gloves and often present significant disposal problems. Is the ventilation of your workplace appropriate for your work process? Are less toxic materials available?

- *Function*. Most important, how appropriate is a given material for a particular purpose? A teapot will be useless if the material used is porous, and a chair that is too difficult to construct can never be mass-produced. Any material chosen must serve both the structural and aesthetic needs of the physical object.

Construction Methods

Compositional choices are strongly influenced by the construction method used. The two most common methods of construction are addition and subtraction.

In an **additive** process, the artwork is constructed from separate parts that have been connected using glues, joints, stitching, or welds. **Assemblage** is one additive method. Using objects and images that were originally created for another purpose, Joseph Cornell created a whole series of evocative box structures, such as Figure 8.33. Many of these assemblages were designed to honor specific people, past or present. **Modeling** is an additive process often used by ceramicists. Pinching and pushing this pliable material, skillful potters and ceramicists can make both functional and sculptural objects (8.34)

In a **subtractive** process, the artist removes materials from a larger mass, gradually revealing the sculpture within the stone or other material. **Carving** is the most common subtractive method. Traditional carvers, such as the Tlingit man shown in Figure 8.35, follow a methodical process, beginning with a drawing on the cedar pole, making a rough cut, then refining and finishing the totem pole.

Connections

Physical and visual **connections** are equally important in three-dimensional design. Visual connections can compositionally unify multiple surfaces, while physical connections can increase strength, flexibility, functionality, and stability.

Connections can be created

- Through **contact** (8.36A)

- Through **junctions** (8.36B)

- Through **joints** (8.36C)

Physical connections are critically important to woodworkers. Through years of experimentation, carpenters have developed dozens of specific joints and splices. Mary Miss' *Staged Gates*, shown

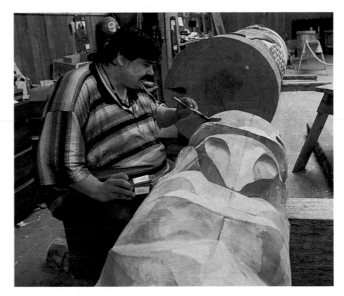

8.35   Tlingit Totem Carver, 1996. Southeast Alaska.

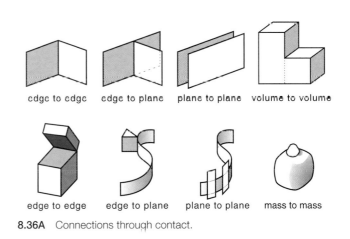

edge to edge   edge to plane   plane to plane   volume to volume

edge to edge   edge to plane   plane to plane   mass to mass

8.36A   Connections through contact.

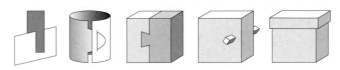

8.36B   Connections through junctions.

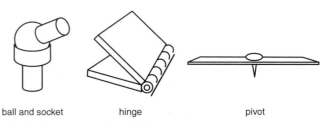

ball and socket   hinge   pivot

8.36C   Connections through joints.

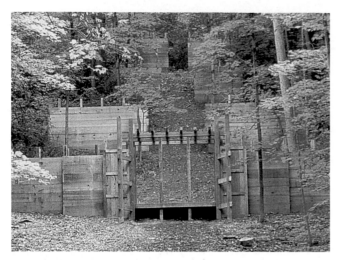

8.37A Mary Miss, *Staged Gates,* 1979. Wood, 12 × 50 × 120 ft (3.6 × 15.2 × 36.6 m).

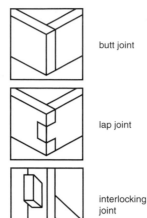

butt joint

lap joint

interlocking joint

8.37B Three types of joints.

in Figure 8.37A, was largely constructed using three types of joints (8.37B). Nails, screws, or bolts are required when lap or butt joints are used. Interlocking joints can be strengthened using nails or can create a simple connection without such additional reinforcement.

Employed to create functional objects, industrial designers pay particular attention to all types of connections. The junction between two flexible planes and a cylindrical volume creates a simple and elegant squeegee in Figure 8.38. The joints used in the *Tizio Table Lamp* (8.39) give it both versatility and grace. And, Robert Brunner and Ken Wood used a variety of hinges and pivots in *Sportscope*, a simple periscope for children (8.40).

Visual connections are just as important as physical connections. In Figure 8.41, a split yellow-orange circle dominates the center of the piece. Proximity between the two halves creates a visual connection despite the physical separation. A second split circle echoes the interior circle and creates a dynamic container for the composition as a whole. The two gold spheres at the upper left and

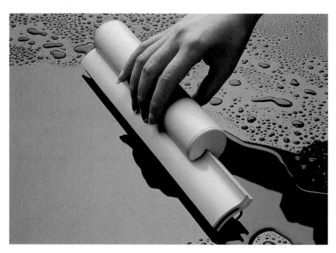

8.38 Ziba Design, Squeegee. Designers: Schrab Vossoughi, Christopher Alviar, Paul Furner. Design Firm: Ziba Design.

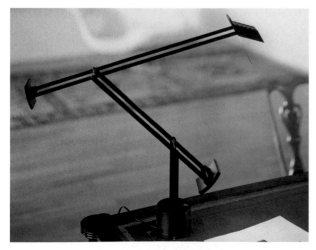

8.39 Artemide (R. Sapper), *Tizio Table Lamp.*

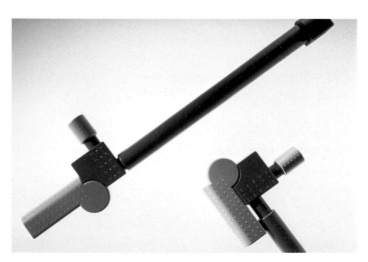

8.40 Lunar Design (Robert Brunner and Ken Wood), *Sportscope.* Pentagram Design.

lower right seem poised for movement. Every component is connected to at least one other component, either through contact or penetration.

Transitions

When the multiple surfaces of an object are varied, many types of **transitions** can be created. The various angles and joints in Eduardo Chillida's *Asbesti Gogora III* (8.43) create an abrupt transition from surface to surface, while a fluid transition helps to unify the various sections of Liv Blåvarp's neckpiece *Bird* (8.42). When a sculpture is composed of separate parts, an even wider range of transitions can occur. Mark di Suvero's *Gorky's Pillow* (8.44) is as complex and as playful as a children's playground. With a perimeter exceeding 64 feet in circumference, the sculpture presents a variety of transitions between the interior and exterior, from the top to the bottom, and from side to side.

Such transitions are often based on **gradation.** Gradation creates sequential change within a consistent system. Here are a few of the many options available.

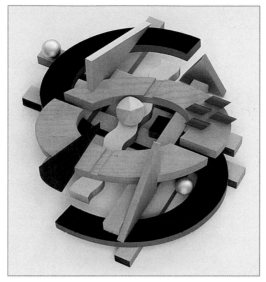

8.41 John Okulick, *Wind Wizard*, 1987. Painted wood, gold leaf, oil stick, 22 × 25 × 6 in. (55.9 × 63.5 × 15.2 cm).

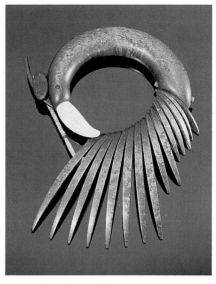

8.42 Liv Blåvarp, *Bird*, 1991. Neckpiece, birdseye maple, satinwood, whaletooth, 12½ × 10¼ in. (32 × 26 cm).

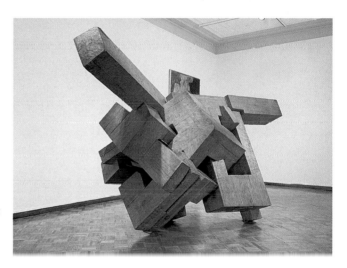

8.43 Eduardo Chillida, *Asbesti Gogora III*, 1962–64. Oak, 81½ in. × 136⅜ in. × 73⅛ in. (207.3 × 346.4 × 184.2 cm)

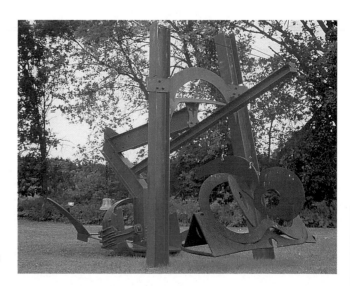

8.44 Mark di Suvero, *Gorky's Pillow*, 1969–80. Steel, painted steel, brass bell, 15 ft × 23 ft 1 in. × 9 ft 7 in. (457 × 703 × 292 cm).

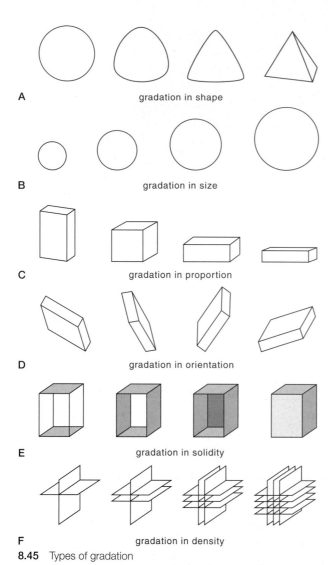

A

gradation in shape

B

gradation in size

C

gradation in proportion

D

gradation in orientation

E

gradation in solidity

F

gradation in density

8.45 Types of gradation

- Gradation in shape (8.45A)
- Gradation in size (8.45B)
- Gradation in proportion (8.45C)
- Gradation in orientation (8.45D)
- Gradation in solidity (8.45E)
- Gradation in density (8.45F)

Unity and Variety

Regardless of the design principles used, creating a design that is functional, cohesive, and structurally sound is a major challenge. Offering both interior and exterior surfaces and with multiple views, any three-dimensional object tends to be complex.

Finding the right balance between **unity** and **variety** is crucial. Too much unity can be monotonous, while too much variety becomes chaotic. Some designs require a high level of unity while other designs require more variety. Based on a grid, Sol LeWitt's *Wall/Floor Piece #4* (8.46) provides a methodical transition from the horizontal floor to the vertical wall. At the other extreme, the lines, shapes, volumes, and masses in Judy Pfaff's *Rock/Paper/Scissor* (8.47) ricochet off the floor, walls, and ceiling with exuberant energy. Just as extreme unity is right for the LeWitt piece, so extreme variety is right for Pfaff's installation.

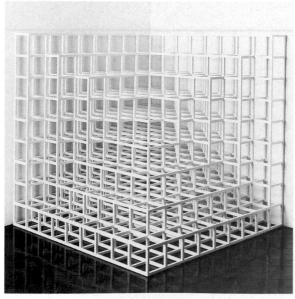

8.46 Sol LeWitt, *Wall/Floor Piece #4,* 1976. White painted wood, 43¼ × 43¼ × 43¼ in. (109.9 × 109.9 × 109.9 cm).

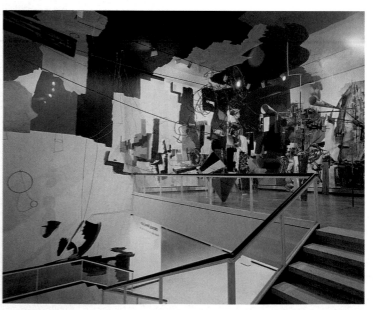

8.47 Judy Pfaff, *Rock/Paper/Scissor,* 1982. Mixed media installation at the Albright-Knox Art Gallery, Buffalo, NY, September 1982.

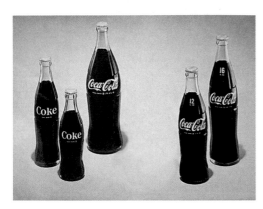

8.48 **Raymond Loewy, Coca-Cola Contour Bottle.** Coke, Coca-Cola, and the Dynamic Ribbon device and the design of the Coca-Cola Contour Bottle are registered trademarks of the Coca-Cola Company.

Similarity in any aspect of the design increases unity. Difference in any aspect of the design increases variety. Both are essential. The "feathers" in Liv Blåvarp's *Bird* (see 8.42, page 8-13) unify the design while gradation adds variety. Raymond Loewy's Coca-Cola bottles (8.48) retain a distinctive contour despite variations in proportion and size. Symmetrical balance unifies the mask from the Pacific island of New Ireland in 8.49. An underlying sense of order freed the artist to experiment with many textures, colors, and figures, resulting in a complex and energetic mask.

Finally, the tower of photographs in the Holocaust museum in Washington, DC (8.50) is unified by a dominant structure and its repeated contents. Designer James Ingo Freed filled the soaring structure with thousands of photographs of Jews massacred in the Polish town of Ejszyszki. Multiplied over and over, the wedding pictures, photographs of groups of school children, and family snapshots personalize the massacre and make the Holocaust more meaningful.

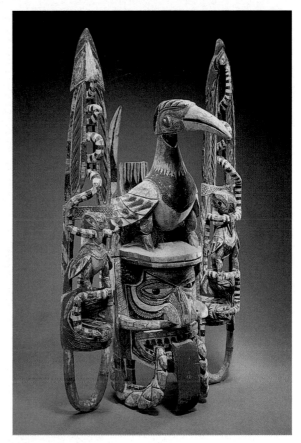

8.49 **Mask (Wanis), New Ireland.** 37 × 20⅞ × 19 in. (94 × 53 × 48.3 cm).

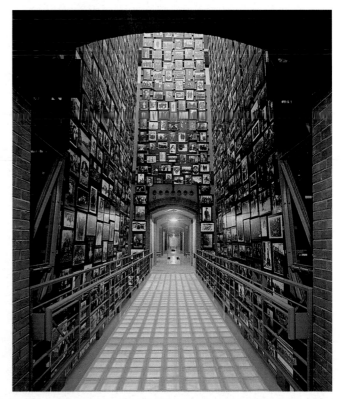

8.50 **Tower of Photos from Ejszyszki,** completed in 1993, United States Holocaust Memorial Museum, Washington, DC.

Profile:
David MacDonald, Ceramicist

A Passion for Pottery

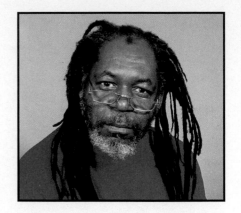

Internationally renowned ceramicist David MacDonald is best known for his work with utilitarian vessels. His work has been included in over 60 exhibitions, including the Torpedo Factory Art Center in Alexandria, Virginia; The Studio Museum in Harlem; and the Afro-American Historical and Cultural Museum in Philadelphia. He is also renowned as a teacher and community leader, with work in an adult literacy program, a summer ceramics intensive program for high school students, and work with inmates at the Green Haven Maximum Security Correctional Facility in New York State to his credit.

MS: How did you start making art?
DM: Initially, it was a way to create some private space. As the third in a family of nine children, I always shared a bedroom with at least three of my brothers. I would help my parents unpack the groceries, then unfold the paper bags so that I could use the inside as drawing paper. Through hours of drawing, I was able to create my own little world.

MS: In our conversations and in viewing your work, I am struck by your passion for ceramics in general and functional vessels in particular. What is special about clay?
DM: I was introduced to ceramics during my second year in college. I was immediately fascinated by clay: it is responsive to the slightest pressure and can record the finest impression. After my first mug came out of the kiln and I made my first cup of tea, I was hooked. The idea of turning a lump of dirt into a useful object amazed me. Since I grew up with very little material wealth, I loved the idea of transforming nothing into something.

Now, I am drawn to functional ceramics because I like playing with the interaction between the object and the user. Having to produce a functional object makes the creative act much more interesting and challenging for me. When a teapot has just the right weight, balance, and proportions, it makes the act of pouring tea a celebration of the physical world.

MS: What is the source of your ideas?
DM: Anything can become a conscious or unconscious inspiration. I can get lost in the produce section of the supermarket: the shapes and colors of the vegetables give me all sorts of ideas.

On a more scholarly level, I was influenced by Japanese and Chinese ceramics during college, and for

the past 20 years, I have been strongly influenced by African art and culture.

MS: Yes, I notice that a dramatic change in your work occurred around 1978. Before that time, your work was sculptural, representational, and highly charged politically; afterward, it became more utilitarian and abstract. What happened?
DM: At the opening for a solo show in Syracuse, I was asked a question by an elderly white woman that dramatically changed my attitude about my work. She innocently asked if there was anything positive about being black in America or was it just one frustration and humiliation after another. The question haunted me for months afterward. I realized that my creative work had been based on anger and a feeling of victimization. As I matured as an individual, I realized that my experiences weren't limited to anger—there is much more to my life than that! I then decided to tap the rich and varied cultural and artistic tradition to which I am heir. Now I am most interested in expressing the magnificence and nobility of the human spirit and in celebrating my African heritage.

MS: What distinguishes a great pot from a mundane pot?
DM: There is no simple answer to this question. We can talk endlessly about form, surface, line, and so forth, and still not gain any real insight into what makes one pot great and another mundane. Yet, we immediately feel it when the mixture of physical elements is just right. Out of the 30 similar bowls a potter produces, two or three always seem to stand apart, as something special.

The search for this elemental quality makes my art magical and compels me to make the next piece. Ironically, if I ever identify exactly what it is that makes

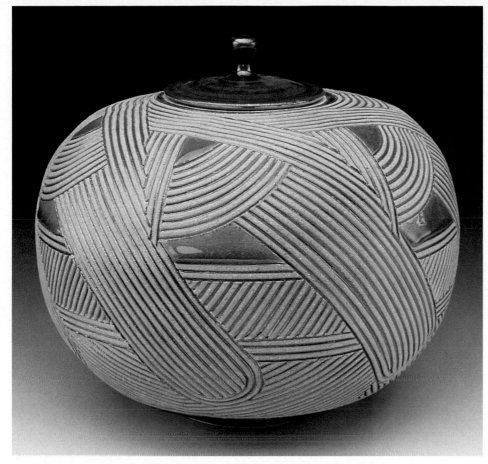

David MacDonald, *Carved Stoneware Storage Jar*, 1997. 15 in. (38.1 cm).

space. The slashing diagonal lines help to unify the design and move the viewer's eye around the form, reinforcing the spherical volume.

MS: What were the most valuable lessons you learned from your teachers?
DM: From Joseph Gilliard at Hampton University, I learned the history and technique of ceramics and gained greater patience and self-control. I developed my self-awareness and passion for communication through my work with Robert Stull at the University of Michigan. From Henry Gernhardt, my Syracuse University colleague for 24 years, I learned that teaching is also an art. In nearly 40 years of teaching, Henry's commitment to his art and his students never faltered.

MS: Is there any advice you would like to give to my students?
DM: An artist has to believe in him or herself. The dedication, courage, and energy my students bring to the classroom are more important than anything I can offer. If you want to stand above the crowd, your passion for your art must be manifest through a willingness to work harder than anyone else. The students who succeed see their art as a way of life and not simply as a way of earning a living. My job as a teacher is to help my students realize their potential and to bring eloquence to their unique voice.

an exceptional piece, the excitement will be sucked out of the creative process. The search is as compelling as the solution.

MS: Tell me about the vessel pictured here.
DM: *Carved Stoneware Jar* was inspired by the bulbous form of a melon or gourd. The body is full and round and the lid handle is suggestive of a stem. I like the sense of an internal force or energy stretching the outer shell almost to the point of bursting.

First, I considered the function of the jar. To a large extent, the function determines the form. A certain size range facilitates everyday use. If the size is increased, the object is more suitable for ceremonial use, or as a decorative object. Certain shapes offer more storage capacity and better accessibility to whatever is being stored. Finally, the base must be big enough to provide stability.

The surface was carved when the jar was leather-hard, a couple of days after being thrown on the potter's wheel. A form this large can "carry" a fairly complex pattern, composed of smaller shapes in combination with larger design areas. By leaving some areas uncarved, I was able to create an overlapping effect and increase the illusion of

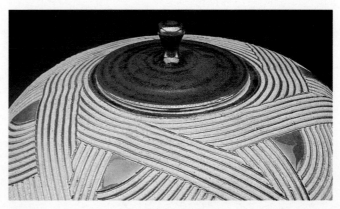

Detail.

Summary

- The power of each element of design can be amplified through careful composition. To determine the best way to combine multiple parts into a cohesive whole, designers often produce dozens of drawings or three-dimensional models before finalizing an idea.

- The three major types of balance are asymmetrical, symmetrical, and radial.

- Scale (the size of an object relative to its surroundings) and proportion (the size of one part of an object compared to another part) can enhance both function and communication.

- Proximity (the distance between structural components or between a sculpture and the viewer) can increase the impact of scale.

- Contrast in texture, dynamics, size, materials, or other variables can be used to emphasize a particular area in a design or to create an opposing visual system.

- Repetition increases design unity. Rhythm (repetition with variation) can create a transition from form to form or from surface to surface. Rhythm can be as graceful as a ballet or as percussive as a drumbeat.

- The native, or inherent, qualities of each material substantially affect both the structure and the concept in any design.

- Two primary construction methods are additive and subtractive.

- Connections and transitions can contribute compositional cohesion as well as structural strength.

- Finding the right balance between unity and variety is critical. Too much unity can be monotonous, while too much variety becomes chaotic. Similarity in any aspect of the design increases unity. Difference in any aspect of the design increases variety.

Keywords

additive	joints	subtractive
assemblage	junctions	tempo
asymmetrical	modeling	transition
balance	proportion	unity
balance	proximity	variety
carving	radial balance	visual balance
connections	repetition	
contact	rhythm	
contrast	scale	
gradation	symmetrical	
grid	balance	

As you begin your studio work, consider:

1. How many elements are being used in your design? What elements are being used most successfully?

2. If your design is strictly linear, consider using variations in the density, color, or proportion of the lines to add interest. If your design combines line, plane, and volume, consider using repetition, connections, and gradation to increase unity.

3. What is the most important characteristic of the composition? If it is essentially an exploration of movement in space, what is the rhythm, extent, and type of movement being created? When you understand the essential character of a design, you can more effectively invent ways to heighten its overall impact.

4. Try redesigning the project proportionally. A design that was first developed as a 6-inch cube will read very differently if it is redesigned to be 3 inches wide and 20 inches tall.

5. How do the various surfaces of the design relate to each other? What is the relationship between the interior and the exterior? To what extent can contrast between the various surfaces enhance meaning?

Key Questions

Oliver Andrews, *Living Materials: A Sculptor's Handbook.* Berkeley, CA, University of California Press, 1988.

Arline Fisch, *Textile Techniques in Metal.* Asheville, NC, Lark Books, 1996.

Paul Johnson, *Pop-Up Paper Engineering.* Bristol, Taylor & Francis, Inc., 1992.

Peter Lane, *Ceramic Form: Design and Decoration,* revised edition. New York, Rizzoli International Publications, Inc., 1998.

Susan Grant Lewin, *One of a Kind: American Art Jewelry Today.* New York, Harry N. Abrams, Inc., 1994.

Martha Dreyer Lynn, *Clay Today: Contemporary Ceramists and Their Work.* San Francisco, Chronicle Books, 1990.

Bonnie J. Miller, *Out of the Fire: Contemporary Glass Artists and Their Work.* San Francisco, Chronicle Books, 1991.

Rudi Stern, *Contemporary Neon.* New York, Retail Reporting Corporation, 1990.

Wucius Wong, *Principles of Form and Design.* New York, Van Nostrand Reinhold, 1993.

Key Readings

chapter nine

Physical and Cerebral

Constructed Thought

What is the difference between the pile of wood in Figure 9.1 and the sculpture in Figure 9.2?

The size, orientation, and location of the pile of wood are based on its purpose. It provides the raw material needed for building a house. Positioned at the edge of a construction site, the boards are arranged in a roughly parallel position so that workers can easily grasp and remove individual planks. The pile of wood is purely functional; it exists as an end in itself. Its organization has no aesthetic intention.

At first glance, Figure 9.2 may seem very much like a pile of wood. The rough planks are clustered together, in close proximity to the house and in a parallel position. On closer examination, we see the perpendicular boards that elevate the structure. Balanced on stilts, the mass of wood seems suspended and in transition. It continues around the house and into the windows. Is the house expelling or inhaling the boards? The entire structure seems poised, ready to shift at any moment.

How and why was this sculpture made? Sculptor Tadashi Kawamata begins by collecting scrap wood from demolished buildings. He then constructs temporary installations, which he describes as "cancers," on conventional buildings. With no predetermined end point, the structures grow like weeds, often enveloping the building. At the end of the exhibition, Kawamata continues onward, dismantling the construction to create another sculpture elsewhere. Using scrap material to build temporary structures, his work demonstrates the

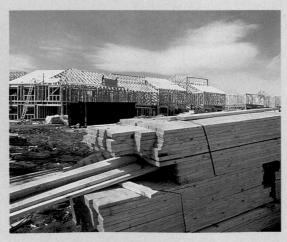

9.1 Pile of wood from a construction site.

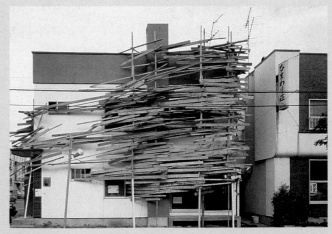

9.2 Tadashi Kawamata, *Tetra House N-3, W26 Project,* Sapporo, Japan, 1983.

fluidity and circulation of urban structures. His design is based on aesthetic rather than functional criteria.

All three-dimensional work gains power from its physical presence. Sculpture, however, is much more than brute force. It is through the transformation of tangible material into ideas and emotions that a sculpture gains significance. The planks in Figure 9.1 begin and end as physical material. A pile of wood is just a pile of wood. By contrast, sculpture such as *Tetra House N-3, W26 Project* uses physical material to explore and express ideas.

From Life to Art: Connection and Separation

Contemporary sculpture is constructed from a wide range of materials, including ice, fire, blood, spools of thread, and crushed automobiles. In her *Ceremonial Arch* (9.3), Mierle Ukeles combined the metal and wood used in traditional sculpture with gloves, lights, metal springs, and asphalt to create an artwork that is both visually exuberant and structurally sound. Sculpture is now shown in parks, subway stations, and public plazas as well as in galleries and museums. Because contemporary sculpture is so reliant on familiar materials and public settings, the relationship between art and life has become especially close.

This can be an advantage or a disadvantage. Connection to life gives art its vitality. For example, when a play expresses actual feelings in a compelling way, it connects to our personal experience. However, if the situations seem improbable and the acting contrived, the play is likely to fail. Authenticity is essential.

Made of tangible material, sculpture is inherently connected to reality. Too direct a connection, however, is deadly. A pile of wood is just a pile of wood. For art to have meaning, commonplace experiences must be distilled, re-examined, or transformed. It has often been said that a play is "life with the boring parts left out." A play that simply replicates everyday experience can never transport an audience beyond the commonplace. Likewise, sculpture requires a heightened experience, *beyond* everyday life. Through a combination of insight and hard work, the sculptor transforms even the most resistant material into compelling communication. When all elements in a sculpture work in harmony, the viewer is simultaneously connected by the reality of the material and transported by the power of the idea.

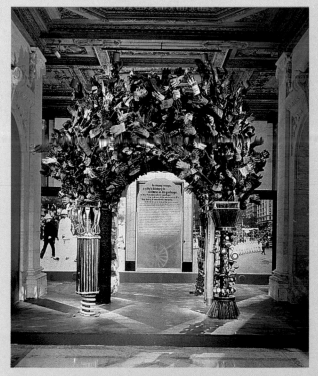

9.3 Mierle Ukeles, *Ceremonial Arch Honoring Service Workers in the New Service Economy*, 1988. Steel arch with materials donated from New York City agencies, including gloves, lights, grass, straps, springs, and asphalt; overall structure 11 ft × 8 ft × 8 ft 8 in. (3.35 × 2.43 × 2.44 m), plus glove branches ranging from 2 to 4 ft long (61 × 122 cm).

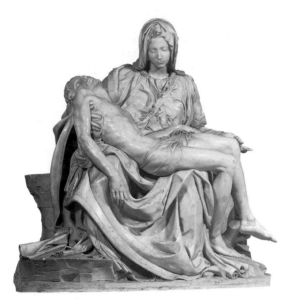

9.4 Michelangelo, *Pietà*, 1498–1500. Marble, 5 ft 8 in. (1.74 m) h.

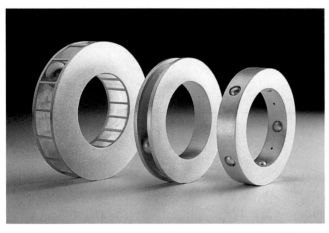

9.5 Sandra Enterline, *Caged Sphere Bracelet Series*, 1992. Sterling silver, 18-karat gold, hollow-formed, fabricated. Left to right, 5 × 5 × 1⅛ in. (12.7 × 12.7 × 3 cm), 4 × 4 × ¾ in. (10.2 × 10.2 × 1.9 cm), 4 × 4 × ¾ in. (10.2 × 10.2 × 1.9 cm).

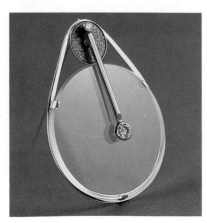

9.6 Myra Mimlitsch-Gray, *Timepiece*, 1988. Kinetic brooch, 14-karat gold, lens, diamonds, abrasive disk. Fabricated, 2¼ × 1½ × ¼ in. (6 × 4 × .5 cm).

Degrees of Representation

Representational sculptures often depict persons or objects in such exquisite detail that they seem to come to life. Michelangelo's *Pietà* (9.4) is a good example. In this massive sculpture, Mary grieves as she cradles the dead Jesus. Every crease in the fabric is defined and every nuance of gesture is deliberate. Mary's right hand extends Jesus' flesh as she gently lifts his right shoulder. His head is thrown back and his arms are limp. She tilts her head slightly and her left hand echoes the position of his feet. **Vitalistic** sculptures, such as the *Pietà*, seem to embody life. They engage our thoughts and emotions through their compelling realism and narrative implications.

Nonobjective sculptural objects can be appreciated for their pure physical form. For example, the simple metal rings Sandra Enterline constructed for her *Caged Sphere Bracelet Series* (9.5) work beautifully as ends in themselves. We can appreciate their economy and grace without knowing a story or pursuing any additional ideas they may suggest.

Most sculptural objects fall somewhere between these two extremes. These **abstract** sculptures have been distilled down from a recognizable source. Myra Mimlitsch-Gray's *Timepiece* (9.6) simultaneously suggests the mechanism and movement of a clock, a pendulum, and a musician's metronome. By reducing these familiar timepieces to their essential form, she was able to create an economical design that conveys a universal sense of time.

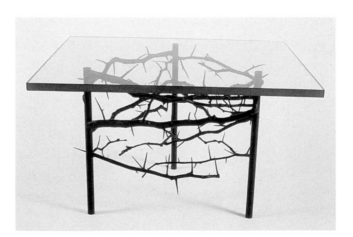

9.7 Michele Oka Doner, *Terrible Table*. Bronze and glass, 15¾ × 26 × 22 in. (40 × 66 × 56 cm).

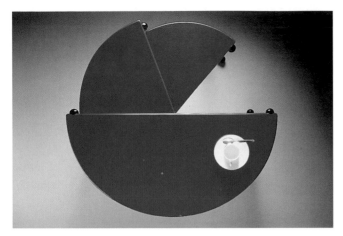

9.8 Gianfranco Frattini, *Tria Table*. Design firm: Morphos/Acerbis International. Opaque lacquered wood.

Each approach has advantages and disadvantages. The representational approach can stimulate the imagination or provide a fresh interpretation of a familiar object. For example, the thorny branches at the base of Michele Oka Doner's *Terrible Table* (9.7) are sure to change the emotional atmosphere of any room this table occupies. On the other hand, pure form is especially effective in situations in which universality, economy, or versatility is required. In contrast to Doner's table Gianfranco Frattini's *Tria Table* (9.8) is simple, straightforward, and highly adaptable.

Boundaries

Because the art/life connection is so important, sculptors must be especially attentive to the physical and psychological boundaries in each piece. As the dividing line between objects, images, or experiences, the **boundary** is charged with energy. It can serve three major purposes.

Boundaries Can Connect

A simple shape can create a boundary. To define *The Perfect Thought* (9.9), James Lee Byars painted two gold-leaf circles on the floor. The larger circle enclosed 23 separate works from earlier exhibitions while the smaller circle remained empty. This simple device gave cohesion to the existing body of work while leaving a second space open, to be filled by the viewer's imagination.

A physical boundary is used to create a psychological connection in *My Mother 3*, by Cho Duck-Hyun (9.10). The strip of fabric that extends out

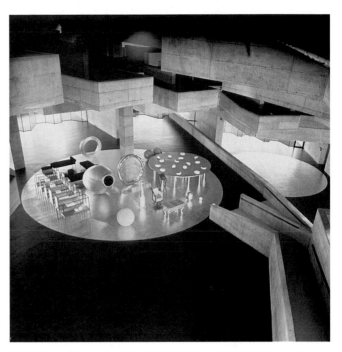

9.9 James Lee Byars, *The Perfect Thought*, 1990. (Installation shot). Various objects covered with gold leaf, composed in one of two circles of gold leaf, large circle 40 ft (12.2 m) diameter, small circle 27 ft (8.2 m) diameter.

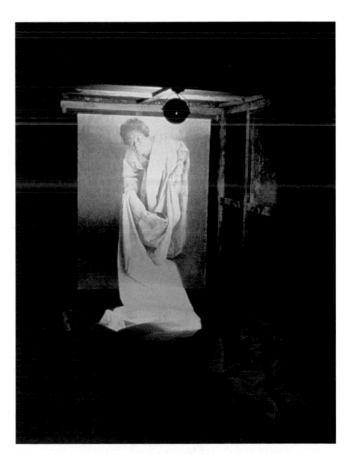

9.10 Cho Duck-Hyun, *My Mother 3* (Memory of the Twentieth Century), 1996. Graphite and charcoal on canvas, Halogen light, 48 × 57 in. (122 × 145 cm).

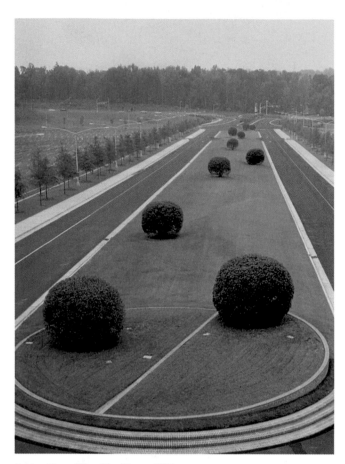

9.11 Maya Ying Lin, *Topo*, 1991.

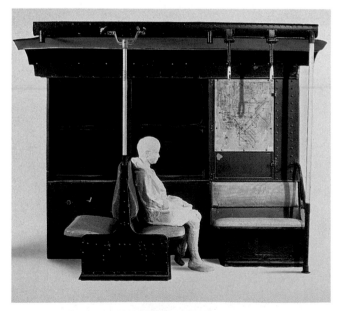

9.12 **George Segal, *The Subway*, 1968.** Plaster, metal, glass, rattan, electrical parts with lightbubs, and map. 7 ft 4 in. × 9 ft 5 in. × 4 ft 3 in. (2.25 × 2.88 × 1.3 m).

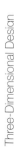
from the drawing and rolls onto the floor enters our space. Combined with the gentle gesture of the woman, the unfurled fabric invites our entry into her world. Here, the tangible world of sculpture and the illusory world of drawing work in perfect harmony.

Boundaries Can Separate

Constructed from nine 12-foot-wide bushes within the median of a busy highway, Maya Ying Lin's *Topo* (9.11) simultaneously relies on separation and connection for its power. Separated from the surrounding landscape, these particular bushes become sculptural objects. Enclosed within the mile-long median, they provide a series of visual stepping stones, inviting us to move down the line diagonally. Shifting circles at either end of the sculpture appear to rotate the last two bushes, directing our attention back down the line. Through this illusion of perpetual motion, the simple design becomes highly energized.

Psychological separation adds power to George Segal's *The Subway* (9.12). Developed as a three-dimensional painting, Segal's construction replicates a familiar setting, using actual subway seats, handrails, and a window, which flashes with the lights of "passing" trains. The ghostly white plaster figure seems familiar but remains distant, the shell of a living, breathing person. Here, a psychological boundary transforms the commonplace into an expression of alienation.

Indeed, physical and psychological boundaries are so important that some sculptures focus on this subject directly. Constructed from a series of translucent rooms, *Single Room Occupancy*, by Susan Schwartzenberg and Ali Sant (9.13), presents an examination of connection and isolation in contemporary life. Clustered together tightly and offering no real privacy, the eight-foot-long rooms suggest a connection among the residents in a budget hotel. On the other hand, a transparent telephone in one room, a sink in another, and a clear Plexiglas dresser in a third, particularize the rooms. As we explore the site more fully, we find that each resident is absorbed by his or her own hopes and fears. Lines of text, sound, and projected images

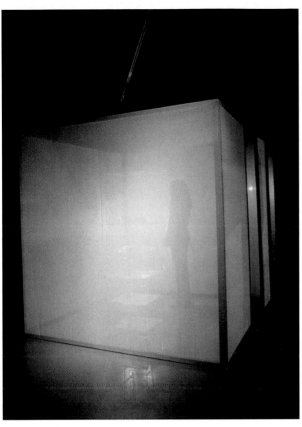

9.13 Susan Schwartzenberg and Ali Sant, *Single Room Occupancy* (detail), **1997.** Video and mixed media installation.

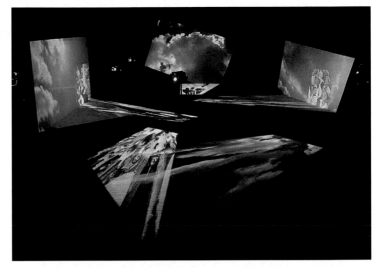

9.14 Susan Trangmar, *Blue Skies*, **1990.** Installation view.

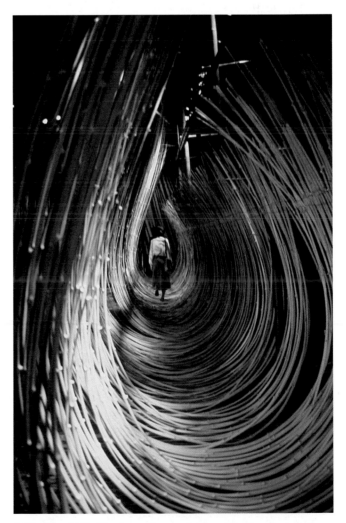

9.15 Hiroshi Teshigahara, One-man Show Bamboo Installation at Metropolitan Plaza in Ikebukuro, Tokyo, June 10–15, 1993.

add to the ghostly effect. There is no real sense of community among the people caught in this eerie labyrinth. Despite their close proximity, the inmates in the hotel remain isolated.

Boundaries Can Enclose

Increasingly, sculptors use every square inch of gallery space and surface to create complex installations. In *Blue Skies* (9.14), Susan Trangmar used the gallery walls as four large projection surfaces. Surrounded by the projections and by his or her own cast shadow, the viewer becomes a participant in the installation.

The sculpture itself can also envelop the viewer. The boundaries in Hiroshi Teshigahara's *Bamboo Installation* (9.15) create a passage through a bamboo maze. The patterns of light and shadow combined with the graceful arch entice and enchant the visitor. The physical sensation of enclosure brings magic to the delicate structure.

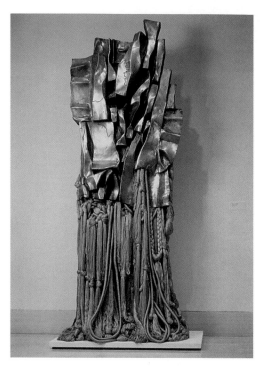

9.16 Barbara Chase-Riboud, *Malcom X #3*, 1970. Polished bronze and silk.

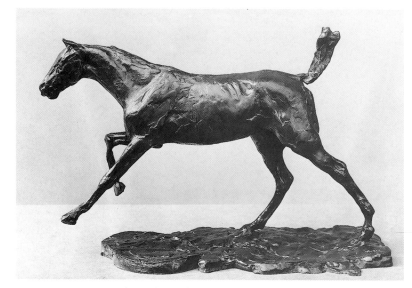

9.17 Edgar Hilaire Germain Degas, *Horse Galloping on Right Foot*, c. 1881. Bronze cast of wax model, 11⅛ in. (30 cm).

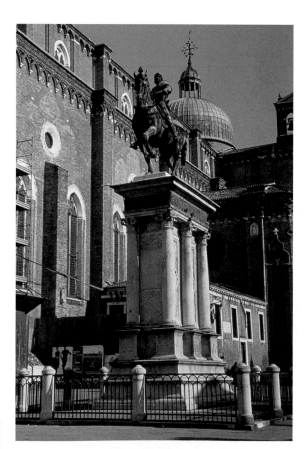

9.18 Andrea del Verrocchio, *Equestrian Monument of Colleoni*, c. 1483–88. Bronze, 15 ft (4.6 m). Cast by Alessandro Leopardi Campo.

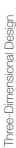

Bases and Places

Traditional sculpture is generally mounted on a **plinth,** which provides a horizontal base, or on a **pedestal,** which provides a vertical base. Either can serve three purposes:

- To physically separate the sculpture from the surrounding space.

- To provide strength and structural stability.

- To elevate an object psychologically, distinguishing it from its surroundings and increasing its impact.

Seemingly insignificant, the plinth or pedestal can actually become an essential component of three-dimensional design, both physically and aesthetically. In Figure 9.16, the marble base adds elevation as well as a marked contrast in material. As a result, Barbara Chase-Riboud's *Malcolm X #3* now has a solid platform from which to speak. The plinth in *Horse Galloping on Right Foot* (9.17), by Edgar Degas, provides a visual context for the galloping horse as well as physical stability. The sculpture would collapse, physically and aesthetically, if the base were removed. The pedestal for Andrea del Verrocchio's *Equestrian Monument* (9.18) elevates the heroic statue and creates an architectural connection to the surrounding buildings.

The traditional role of the base has been expanded by artists in the twentieth century. For Constantin Brancusi, the base was always an essential element of the artwork rather than a passive support. In *The Fish* (9.19), a circular mirror suggests the reflective quality of water while providing physical stability. Positioned on top of a graceful pedestal, both the fish and the water appear suspended. Seeking dynamism rather than stability, Umberto Boccioni split the base in half when he composed *Unique Forms of Continuity in Space* (9.20). The abstracted figure strides forward in space, too energetic to be contained by conventional boundaries. Pushing this idea even further, the base becomes the sculpture in Jude Lewis' *Family: Pride and Joined*. Constructed in response to a death in the family, the sculpture is dominated by warped and twisted floorboards, the site of an emotional trauma.

Indeed, in contemporary sculpture, the base often extends to include an entire architectural site. Resting directly on the surface of the plaza, the granite boulders in Elyn Zimmerman's *Marabar* (9.21) are intended to suggest continents, while the channel of water suggests the ocean. Combining large scale with a "baseless" design, the artist has dissolved the traditional boundary between the stones and the surroundings. As a result, the entire plaza is transformed into a sculptural site.

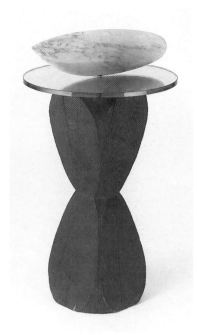

9.19 Constantin Brancusi, *The Fish*, **1922.** Marble, mirror, oak, 5¼ in. h. × 16⅞ in. w. (13.3 × 42.9 cm). Base mirror 17 in. (43.2 cm) dia., base wood 24 in. (61 cm) h.

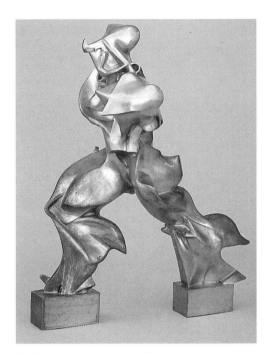

9.20 Umberto Boccioni, *Unique Forms of Continuity in Space*, **1913.** Bronze (cast in 1931), 43⅞ × 34⅞ × 15¾ in. (111.2 × 88.5 × 40 cm).

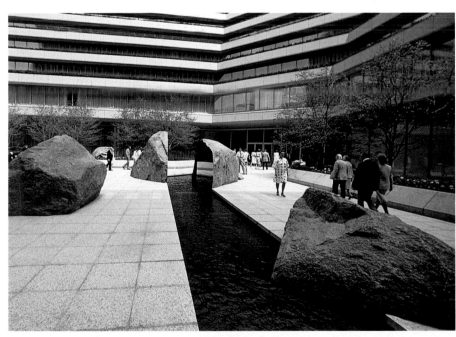

9.21 Elyn Zimmerman, *Marabar*, **1984.** Boulders (natural cleft and polished granite) and water. Plaza: 140 × 60 ft (42.7 × 18.3 m). Pool: 60 ft × 6 ft × 18 in. (18.3 m × 1.8 m × 45.7 cm). Boulders: 2 to 10½ ft. (61 cm to 3.2 m).

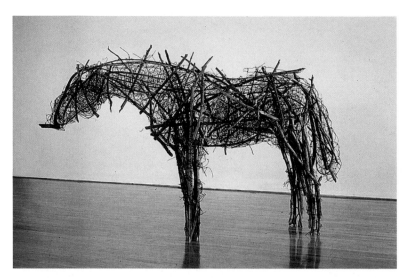

9.22 Deborah Butterfield, *Large Horse #4*, 1979. Steel, wire, sticks, 77 × 124 × 33 in. (195 × 315 × 84 cm).

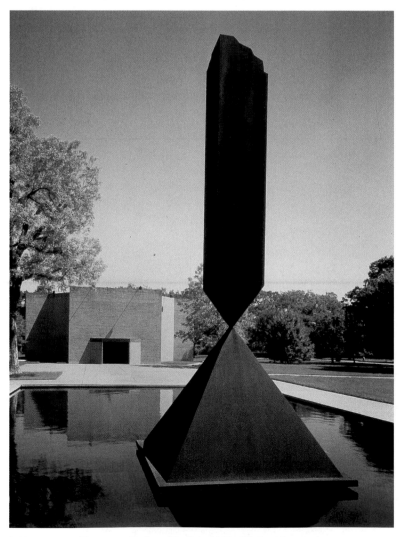

9.23 Barnett Newman, *Broken Obelisk*, 1963–67. Cor-Ten steel, 26 × 10¹/₂ × 10¹/₂ in. (66 × 26.7 × 26.7 cm).

Physical Qualities of Sculptural Objects

When we begin to work in three dimensions, physical reality replaces the illusions that dominate two-dimensional work. The movement of waves that is *suggested* in a painted seascape becomes a powerful force on an actual beach. We feel the wind and smell the salty air. Visual textures are replaced by the tangible textures. We can feel the sand and examine each seashell as we walk along the shore. All our senses come to life. The painted world we entered through imagination changes dramatically when physical entry is possible.

To create compelling sculpture, we must fully realize the physical potential of each object and each space. Physical forces, such as gravity, torsion, and tension create conceptual opportunities as well as structural limitations. Materials also affect meaning.

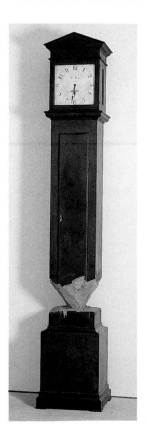

Deborah Butterfield's wood-and-wire *Large Horse #4* (9.22) has a mystery and power that is very different from the speed and grace of Degas' bronze horse. When all of the physical and material forces are fully engaged, the aesthetic impact increases.

9.24 Walter Martin and Paloma Muñoz, *Of Bodies Born Up by Water,* 1987. Plaster, oil paint, sheet metal, and wood, 111¹/₂ × 20 × 16¹/₂ in. (283 × 51 × 42 cm).

Physical Forces
Weight and Gravity

Of the forces of nature, **gravity** is the most immediately noticeable when we begin to construct a three-dimensional structure. Lines, spaces, and volumes must be organized according to the laws of physics while simultaneously meeting our aesthetic objectives. Balance becomes a structural necessity as well as a compositional force. After watching several prototypes collapse, it is easy to conclude that gravity is our enemy, to be conquered at all costs. But is it?

When we begin to analyze the uses of gravity in sculpture, we soon find that it is an asset rather than a liability. Just as a ballet dancer relies on gravity to provide a solid launching pad for each leap and a predictable support for each landing, so the sculptor uses gravity to express ideas and generate emotions.

Barnett Newman's *Broken Obelisk* (9.23) is a monochromatic structure constructed from a simple pyramid and an inverted obelisk. The point of contact between the two sections becomes charged with energy, as the top half seems to balance on the point of the pyramid. Caught in this moment of equilibrium, the sculpture is as carefully balanced as a ballerina on point.

Walter Martin's *Of Bodies Born Up by Water* (9.24) demonstrates how a similar structure can be used for a very different effect. The poised obelisk is now a grandfather clock. When it topples, time, memory, and family history may be erased.

The gravity in Beverly Pepper's *Ventaglio* (9.25) creates another kind of dance. The largest of the open cubic volumes leans to the left, while the three smaller volumes tumble forward. The movement is as energetic and as playful as a cartwheel. And, thanks to gravity, this dynamic activity contrasts sharply with the static base of the sculpture.

An even more forceful use of gravity animates *Device to Root Out Evil* (9.26). The inverted church structure seems to have been propelled aloft, finally driving into the ground upon landing. As noted by sculptor Dennis Oppenheim, this inversion of a familiar structure creates a reversal of content. The steeple is now pointing to hell rather than to

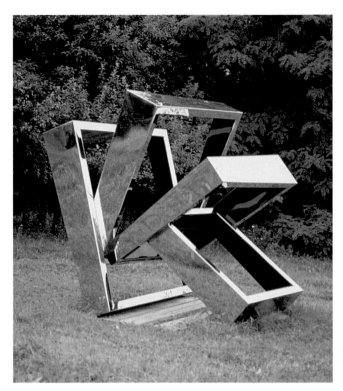

9.25 Beverly Pepper, *Ventaglio*, 1967. Stainless steel with blue enamel, 94½ × 78¾ in. (240 × 200 cm).

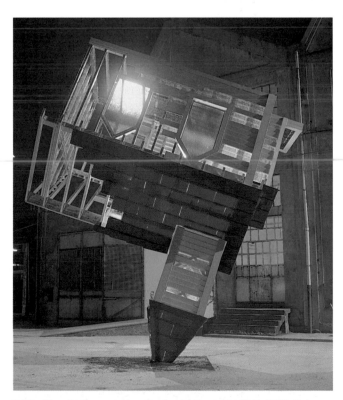

9.26 Dennis Oppenheim, *Device to Root Out Evil*, 1997. Galvanized structural steel, anodized perforated aluminum, transparent red Venetian glass, concrete foundations, 20 × 15 × 8 ft (6.1 × 4.57 × 2.44 m).

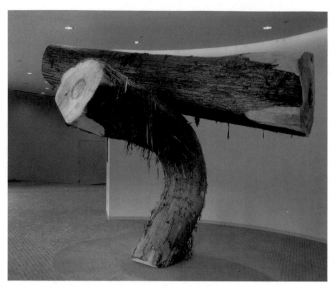

9.27 Chuichi Fujii, *Untitled*, 1987. Japanese cedar, 10 ft 6 in. × 13 ft ½ in. × 11 ft 6 in. (320 × 400 × 350 cm).

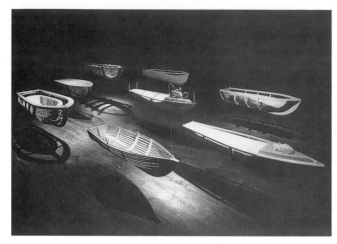

9.28 Patricia A. Renick, *Life Boats/Boats About Life*, 1979–80. 1 to 1½ ft high × 5 to 6½ ft long × 1 to 1½ ft deep (30.5 to 45.7 cm high × 152.4 to 198.1 cm long × 30.5 to 45.7 cm deep).

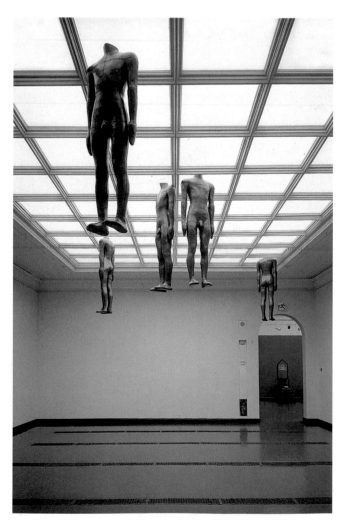

9.29 Antony Gormley, *Learning to Think*, 1991. Lead, fiberglass and air, 5 figures, each 68 × 41¾ × 122 in. (173 × 106 × 310 cm).

heaven. Even without any cultural associations, however, we would still respond to the improbable balance and intense color in this large piece.

Indeed, exaggerated or diminished gravity can change the meaning of any sculpture. In Chuichi Fujii's *Untitled* (9.27), a cedar log seems to have been crushed by the weight of a second log. The combination of the rough logs and the exaggerated weight seems to bring a powerful natural force into the pristine gallery. At the other extreme, Patricia A. Renick's *Life Boats/Boats About Life* (9.28) seems to float on air, as weightless as a dream. Dramatic lighting and elegant cast shadows heighten the magical effect. Here, it is the denial of gravity that gives the sculpture power.

A combination of weight and weightlessness gives Antony Gormley's *Learning to Think* (9.29) its impact. Constructed from a mold made from the artist's own body, the hollow lead figures are basically identical. Hovering 10 feet off the ground, they seem weightless. At the same time, because they are suspended from the ceiling, each figure seems as heavy as a convict at the end of a hangman's noose. This paradox gives the sculpture great physical force and communicates an elusive concept. Clearly, the knowledge embodied in this sculpture is not easy to attain!

Compression and Expansion

Most materials tend to **compress** as weight increases. As shown in Figure 9.27, physical com-

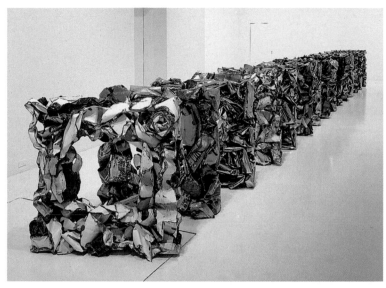

9.30A John Chamberlain, *The Hedge*, 1997. Painted milled steel, chromium-plated steel, and stainless steel, overall installed 44½ in. × 44½ in. × 46 ft 4 in. (113 cm × 113 cm × 14.12 m); 16 units, each 44½ × 44½ × 12 in. (113 × 113 × 30.5 cm).

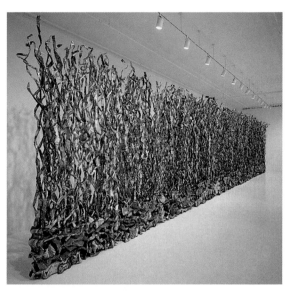

9.30B John Chamberlain, *The Privet*, 1997. Painted milled steel and chromium plated steel, 12 ft 6 in. × 61 ft 6 in. × 30 in. (3.81 m × 18.75 m × 76.2 cm).

pression can be used to evoke a visceral response. We feel the pressure as the top log pushes down on the log below. Compression plays an especially important role in the works of John Chamberlain, who began making sculptures from crushed automobiles in the sixties. In *The Hedge* and *The Privet* (9.30A–B), crushed pieces of metal have been transformed into an improbable garden. This contradiction between the materials and the meaning suggests a new definition of nature.

Expansion is an equally compelling force. Constructed from the charred fragments of a church that had been struck by lightning, Cornelia Parker's *Mass* (9.31) seems to present the event in suspended animation. Supported by fine steel wire and cotton thread, the hovering sculpture appears weightless, caught at the moment of explosion.

Tension and Torsion

Tension can be used to stretch or bend an object, while **torsion** creates a twisting movement. Either can add physical and cerebral strength to a sculpture. Stretched taut, the steel cables in Kenneth Snelson's *Free Ride Home* (see 7.14, page 7-5) provide the force needed to elevate the aluminum tubes which dominate the sculpture. Tension is equally important for the designer. It is the tension in the bent metal rods that creates the structure in the

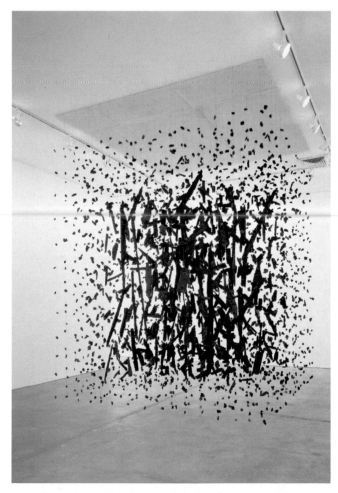

9.31 Cornelia Parker, *Mass (Colder Darker Matter)*, 1997. Charcoal retrieved from a church struck by lightning, suspended from steel wire and cotton thread, 10 × 10 × 10 ft (3.5 × 3.5 × 3.5 m).

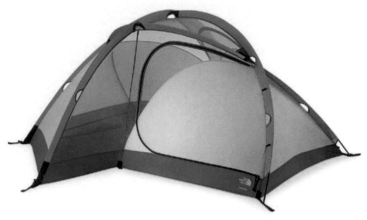

9.32 Peregrine Tent by The North Face, San Leandro, CA.

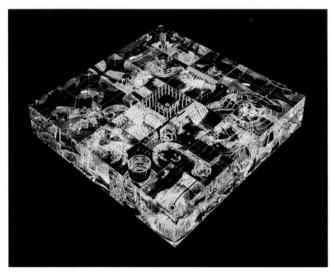

9.34 Eric Hilton, *Innerland*, 1980. Engraved by Ladislav Havlik, Lubomir Richter, Peter Schelling, and Roger Selander, cut by Mark Witter. Cast, cut, engraved, sandblasted, and polished, 3⁷/₈ × 19³/₈ × 19³/₈ in. (9.9 × 49.3 × 49.3 cm).

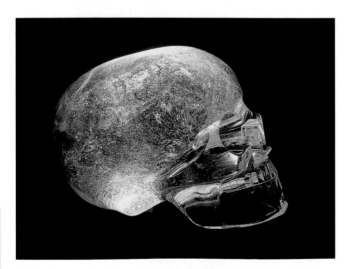

9.35 Human Skull Carved in Rock Crystal, Mexico (Aztec) Culture, 1300–1521 A.D.

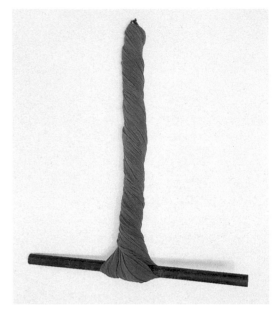

9.33 Giovanni Anselmo, *Torsion (Torsione)*, **1967–68.** Metal and material, 59 × 63 in. (150 × 160 cm).

Peregrine Tent from The North Face (9.32). In Giovanni Anselmo's *Torsione* (9.33), torsion provides both the form and the content of the artwork. Based on our experience in the physical world, we can feel the power of the twisted fabric and imagine the explosive result were this power released.

Material and Immaterial

Each of these physical forces is influenced by the materials the sculptor uses. Every material has unique physical properties as well as psychological associations. Mirrors are fragile, reflective surfaces commonly used for observation of the self and others. Blood is generally red, sticky, requires refrigeration, and provides evidence of both life and death. Bronze is malleable when heated and solid when cool, decays slowly, and can be colored gold, green, or copper-red, depending on the patina used. Depending on the weave and thread weight, silk can provide a shimmering, translucent veil or a solid, roughly textured barrier.

A love of materials and understanding of their characteristics is an essential aspect of all three-dimensional work. The transparency of glass is emphasized in Eric Hilton's *Innerland* (9.34). Constructed from 25 cubes of clear glass, the sculpture appears to shift with each change in the viewer's position. The transparency of rock crystal

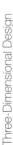

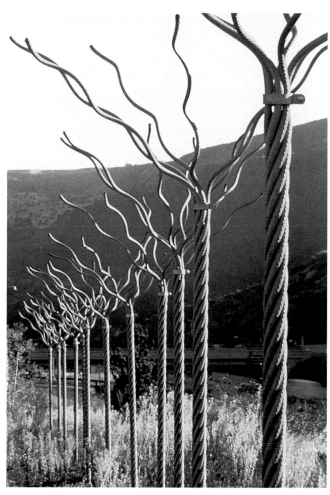

9.36 Maren Hassinger, *12 Trees No 2*, 1979. Galvanized wire rope, 10 × 150 × 5 ft (3.1 × 45.7 × 1.5 m).

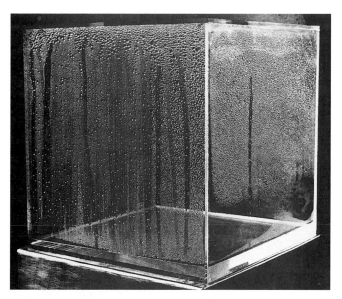

9.37 Hans Haacke, *Weather Cube*, 1963–65. Acrylic plastic, water, climate in area of display, 12 in. cube (30.5 cm).

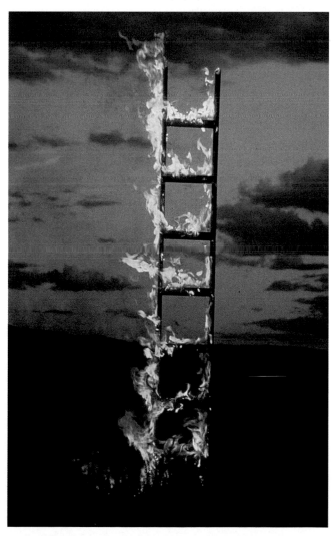

9.38 Ronald Dahl, *Seven Windows to a Sky on Fire*, 1982. Wood/flame, 9 × 12 × 3 in. (22.7 × 30.5 × 7.6 cm).

adds both visual and conceptual power to the carved Aztec skull in Figure 9.35. In Maren Hassinger's *Trees No 2* (9.36), the contradiction between the forms of the trees and the wire rope from which they were made provokes a question: Are these mechanical or natural objects?

In the past 50 years, sculptors have expanded their choice of materials to include many physical and chemical processes. These include:

- *Condensation.* Sealed inside the Hans Haacke *Weather Cube* (9.37), water evaporates or condenses based on the ambient temperature inside the gallery.

- *Oxidation.* Ronald Dahl transformed the familiar ladder when he placed his sculpture in the Nevada desert and set it aflame to create *Seven Windows to a Sky on Fire* (9.38).

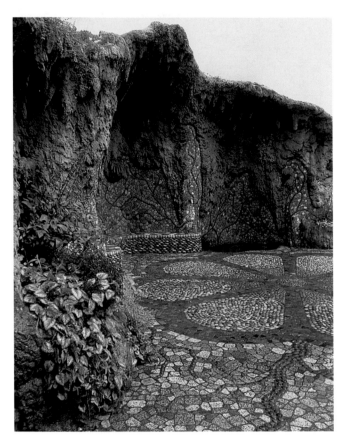

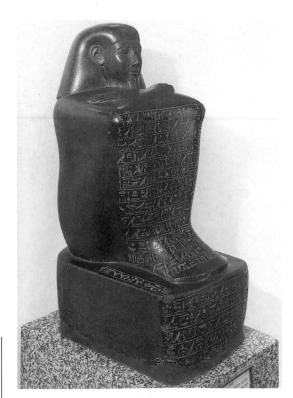

9.39 Lorna Jordan, *Waterworks Gardens: The Grotto*, 1996. Third of five public garden rooms in the King County East Division Reclamation Plant, Renton, WA.

- *Filtration.* Located next to a wastewater treatment plant, Lorna Jordan's *Waterworks Gardens: The Grotto* (9.39) purifies up to 2,000 gallons of oil-laced storm water per minute. The eight-acre site includes stone mosaics, natural filtration systems, and colorful bands of sedges, yellow iris, and red-twig dogwoods, which have been divided into five public gardens.

Permanence and Tangibility

The increasing use of diverse materials has also heightened awareness of the variations in permanence and tangibility of physical objects. **Permanence** refers to the durability of an object. **Tangibility,** derived from the Latin word for touch, refers to the substantiality of an object. Traditional sculpture, made of stone, metal, or wood, was intended to last for millennia. And, indeed, the solid black granite used in *Qennefer, Steward of the Palace* (9.40) has changed little since the statue was completed over 3,000 years ago. This sculpture is both tangible and permanent.

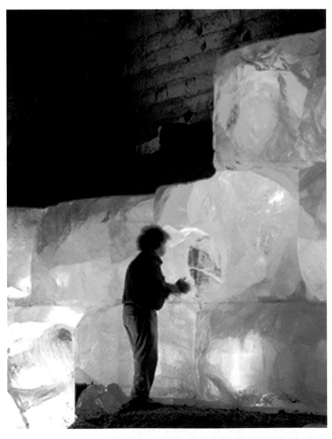

9.40 *Qennefer, Steward of the Palace*, c. 1450 B.C. Black granite.

9.41 Dale Chihuly, *Jerusalem Wall of Ice*, 1999. 54 ft (16.46 m).

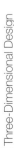

Jerusalem Wall of Ice (9.41), by American glass artist Dale Chihuly, was equally massive and tangible when first constructed in October 1999. Ice, however, is an unstable material. Erected outside the walls of the old city of Jerusalem, the 54-foot-long wall quickly melted in the hot, dry air. Designed to symbolize a melting of tensions between Israelis and Palestinians, the wall was tangible but impermanent.

Presence/Absence

Presence is another crucial aspect of physicality. When we actually confront a massive sculpture such as the Olmec portrait (7.38, page 7-12), it exudes a strength that is far beyond anything a small photograph can convey. Equally, the space surrounding a sculpture or the **absence** of an anticipated object can have great impact.

Many sculptors have used this quality of presence and absence to explore the passage of time and the nature of memory. British sculptor Rachel Whiteread explores presence and absence in many of her works. Using hundreds of gallons of cement to create a solid cast from an empty house, she creates a sense of absence by making the space within the house very solidly present (9.42). In his *Writing on the Wall* series, Shimon Attie used slide projections to remind us of shops and families destroyed during the Holocaust. Figure 9.43 shows one of the many slides from the 1930s that he projected onto a wall in Berlin. The actual bookstore depicted disappeared long ago.

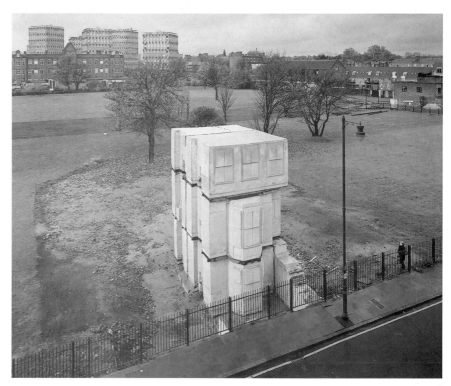

9.42   Rachel Whiteread, *House*, 1993. Commissioned by Artangel Trust and Beck's (corner of Grove Rd. and Roman Rd., London, destroyed 1994).

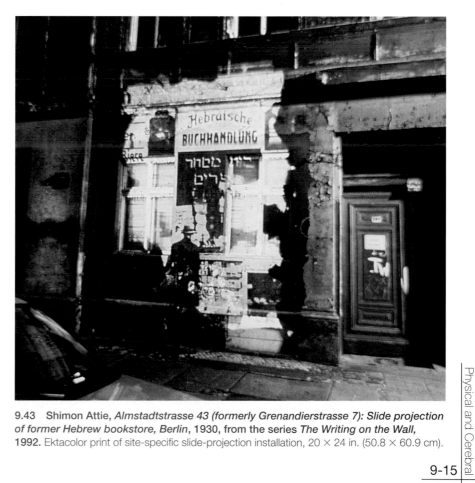

9.43   Shimon Attie, *Almstadtstrasse 43 (formerly Grenandierstrasse 7): Slide projection of former Hebrew bookstore, Berlin*, 1930, from the series *The Writing on the Wall*, 1992. Ektacolor print of site-specific slide-projection installation, 20 × 24 in. (50.8 × 60.9 cm).

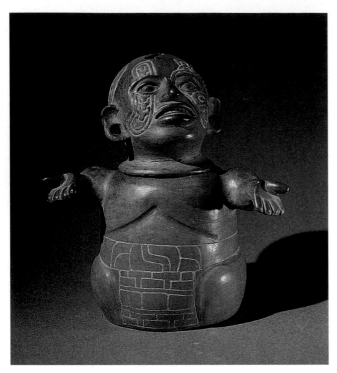

9.44 Covered Effigy Jar with Removable Head. From Teotihuacan, Mexico. Ceramic, 10¾ in. (27.3 cm).

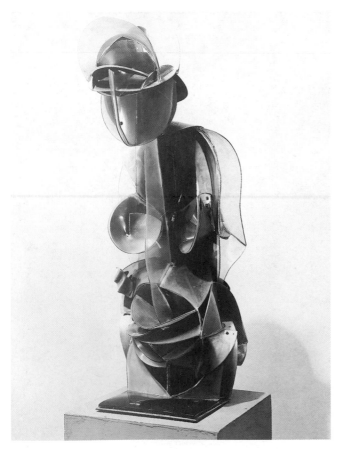

9.45 Antoine Pevsner, *Torso*, 1924–26. Construction in plastic and copper, 29½ × 11⅝ × 15¼ in. (74.9 × 29.4 × 38.7 cm).

Cerebral Qualities of Sculptural Objects

The combination of tangible material and aesthetic complexity gives sculpture a unique power. Like an alchemist, the sculptor transforms ordinary materials into conceptual gold. Tadashi Kawamata's pile of wood becomes a metaphor for urban change. In Mierle Ukeles' *Ceremonial Arch,* the gloves and lightbulbs used by sanitation workers are transformed into a sculpture. Scraps of metal become a garden in John Chamberlain's *The Hedge* and *The Privet.* Through a miracle of invention, the best sculptures simultaneously embrace and transcend their physical nature.

Building on a Tradition

As we study art history, we find that a remarkable range of ideas has been made manifest in physical form. Traditional sculpture has been characterized by four qualities.

- **Mass,** or solid substance, rather than open space, is the primary concern. Traditional sculptures, such as Michelangelo's *Pietà* (see 9.4, page 9-2), are relatively solid. In this masterpiece, a sense of profound resignation is created through the use of gravity. The mother has fully accepted her grief. The position of the limbs and the folds in the fabric create a dynamic surface on a stable pyramidal mass.

- The human figure is the primary subject. Sculptors have long sought to capture in wood, metal, or stone the vitality of a living person.

- As a means to this end, traditional sculpture is overwhelmingly representational. Indeed, attention to detail and the ability to animate marble has long been one of the hallmarks of Western sculpture, from the Renaissance to Romanticism. Even a less detailed pre-Columbian effigy jar (9.44) gains simple eloquence using a representational approach.

- Traditional sculptures tell stories. Public monuments have often been commissioned by kings or by communities of ordinary people to tell national stories. For example, the Statue of Liberty, designed to embody the democratic ideal shared by France and the United States, was financed through a public lottery, theatrical events, art exhibitions, and even prize fights. The poem describing "huddled masses yearning to breathe free" combined with the heroic figure distills the history of immigration to America into a few words.

Reinventing Sculpture

In Europe these four aspects of traditional sculpture reached their climax during the nineteenth century. Seeking fresh ideas and new approaches, artists in Russia, Italy, and France then began a process that would transform sculpture forever. Four major changes followed.

- Space, rather than mass, became a major concern. As shown in Antoine Pevsner's *Torso* (9.45), sculpture began to be constructed from the inside out rather than being carved from the outside in.

- Abstraction and transformation became more important than description and representation. For example, Raymond Duchamp-Villon's *The Great Horse* (9.46), constructed from a mix of organic and mechanical parts, bears little resemblance to an actual horse.

- While the human figure continued to dominate early twentieth-century sculpture, by midcentury almost any subject matter could be used. Indeed, many significant artworks from this period, including Mark de Suvero's *Ik Ook Eindhoven* (see 7.18, page 7-6), are **nonobjective,** without external subject matter. Weight, balance, and the dynamics of space are the only content such works require.

- Sculptors began to break down the traditional separation between art and life. Commonplace objects, such as Marcel Duchamp's *Bicycle Wheel* (9.47), were placed in galleries and defined as art.

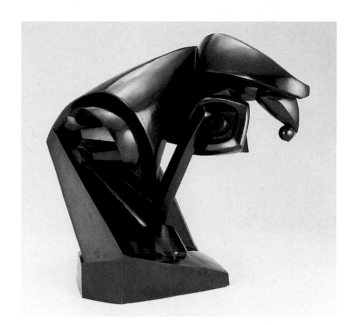

9.46   Raymond Duchamp-Villon, *The Great Horse*, 1957 version of a 1914 work. Bronze, 39¼ × 24 × 36 in. (99.7 × 60.9 × 91.4 cm).

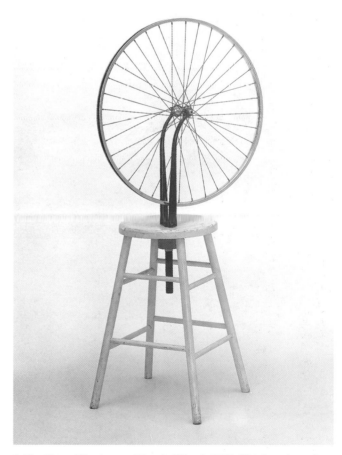

9.47   Marcel Duchamp, *Bicycle Wheel*, 1951. (Third version, after lost original of 1913). Assemblage, metal wheel, 25½ in. (63.8 cm) diameter, mounted on painted wood stool 23¾ in. (60.2 cm); overall 50½ × 25½ × 16⅝ in. (128.3 × 63.8 × 42 cm).

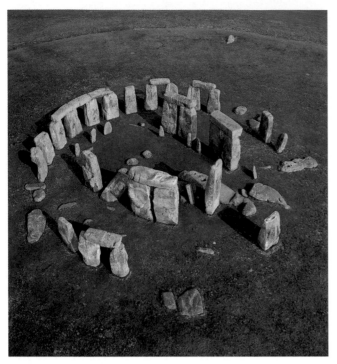

9.48 *Stonehenge* (aerial view), Salisbury Plain, England, c. 2800–1500 B.C.

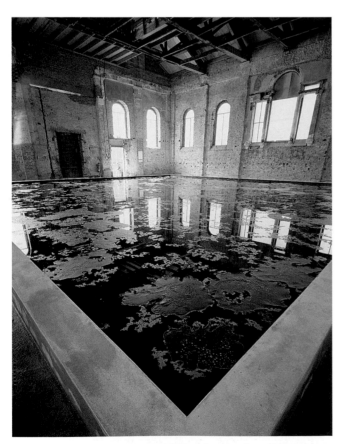

9.49 **Glen Onwin, *Nigredo*, 1992.** Installation view of exhibition *As Above, So Below*, at the Square Chapel, Halifax, 9 May–15 June, 1992. Exposed timbers of the roof reflected in an artificial concrete pool filled with black brine and wax.

Contemporary Questions, Contemporary Answers

The evolution of sculpture has accelerated in the past 30 years. **Earthworks,** which transform natural sites into sculptural settings, have become a powerful force in both art and ecology. An **installation,** which may combine time, space, and sound, can present both artist and audience with new opportunities for communication and expression. **Performance art** (which is discussed at greater length in Chapter 12), combines art, technology, and theater. The traditional has become the transformative. Four of the manifestations of change are described below.

Sculpture as Place

Traditionally permanent, sculpture has always been placed in a wide variety of significant settings. *Stonehenge* (9.48), constructed from massive limestone blocks weighing up to 50 tons, may have been used as a gigantic sundial by its Neolithic builders. The avenue approaching the stone circle is carefully aligned to the summer solstice while stones within the circle are aligned with the northernmost and southernmost path of the rising moon.

Likewise, contemporary sculptors add meaning to their work by exploring the physical, psychological, and temporal characteristics of each site. Glen Onwin's *Nigredo* (9.49) is one of four works in a series titled *As Above, So Below.* Placed in an abandoned chapel, this concrete pool, filled with water, black brine, and wax, seems especially ominous in the once-sacred site. The personal and the political are combined in Karen Giusti's *White House/ Greenhouse* (9.50). Placed in Battery Park in New York City, the transparent one-quarter scale model of the White House had both Wall Street and the Statue of Liberty in the background. Made of recycled steel beams, clear vinyl, and large paintings on Plexiglas, the structure presented a scathing commentary on American politics while simultaneously providing a greenhouse for 200 rosebushes.

Sculpture as Journey

As sculptures have expanded in size, the manner in which the viewer enters, exits, and explores the site has become increasingly important. When the audience participates, a sculpture can be transformed from an object into an experience.

Christopher Janney's *Sonic Plaza* (9.51) at Eastern Carolina University is an especially enticing example. Composed of four distinct sculptures, the site offers a wide range of sensory experiences to the viewer. Various melodic sounds greet participants at the *Sonic Gates*. The 64 water jets on the *Percussion Water Wall* spew forth complex patterns of water to a percussive accompaniment. Four additional sculptures emerge from the large doors of the *Media Glockenspiel* each day. And, the cloud of water vapor created by *Ground Cloud* hovers over the plaza, responding to pedestrian movement and wind direction.

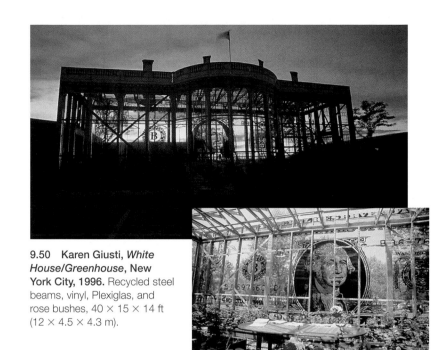

9.50 Karen Giusti, *White House/Greenhouse*, New York City, 1996. Recycled steel beams, vinyl, Plexiglas, and rose bushes, 40 × 15 × 14 ft (12 × 4.5 × 4.3 m).

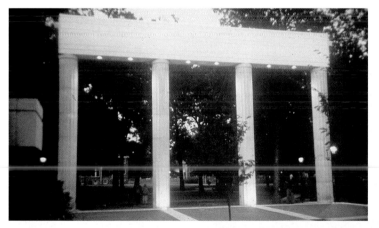

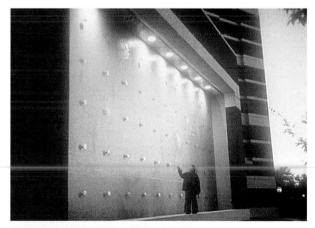

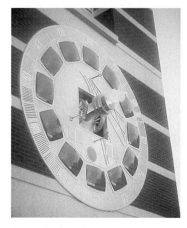

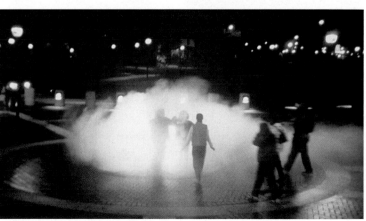

9.51 Christopher Janney, *Sonic Plaza*, Eastern Carolina University, 1998. Sound, light, water, and interactive elements, total length 400 ft (122 m). Top row, left to right: *Sonic Gates* and *Percussion Water Wall*; bottom row, left to right: *Media Glockenspiel* and *Ground Cloud*.

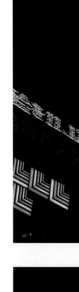

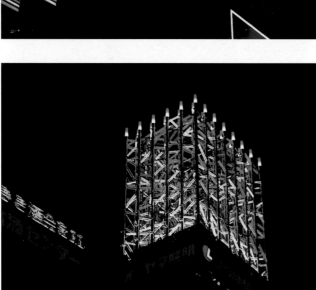

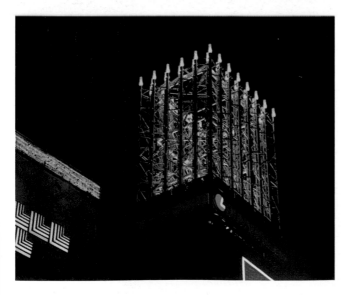

Sculpture as Time

A fascination with time pervades contemporary sculpture. Many sculptures demonstrate the changes that occur as time passes. The amount, frequency, and means of change vary widely. Placed atop the corporate offices of a lighting company, Fumaki Nakamura's *Light Communication* (9.52) presents a simple metamorphosis in a spectacular way. The 88 neon poles gradually illuminate the interior of the structure in three 30-second cycles. The beauty of the light combined with the hypnotic sequence of change simultaneously animates and illuminates the night sky.

Sculpture is also used to demonstrate the impermanence that is an essential characteristic of time. To create *curcuma sul travertino* (9.53), Shelagh Wakely covered the entrance hall to a British school with a thin layer of yellow turmeric spice. As visitors passed through the room, they gradually erased the dust. Thus, during the week-long exhibition, visitors were marked by their passage through the room, and with spice on their shoes, they subsequently marked each new room they entered.

Time itself is the subject of Jim Campbell's *Digital Watch* (9.54). An ominous ticking noise accompanies the installation. On the massive screen, viewers see themselves twice: in real time to the left of the clock and in a two-second delay on the clock face itself. The repetition and delay create a disturbing psychological effect. The persistent sound of the watch freezes time with each tick, while pushing time forward in a relentless pattern.

Sculpture as Self

It has often been said that all artwork is autobiographical. This is especially true of sculpture. As the physical manifestation of thought, sculpture has an immediacy similar to that of a living person.

Both traditional and contemporary sculptors have explored this theme in many marvelous ways.

9.52 Fumaki Nakamura, *Light Communication*, Oyama Lighting. Installed at Ginza 4-chome (main intersection). Eighty-eight poles on a box frame with 400 flashing lamps and projection lights underneath, front 26 ft 3 in. w. × 19 ft 8 in. d. × 29 ft 4 in. h. (8 × 6 × 12 m). Neon tube total length 546 ft 2 in. (1500 m).

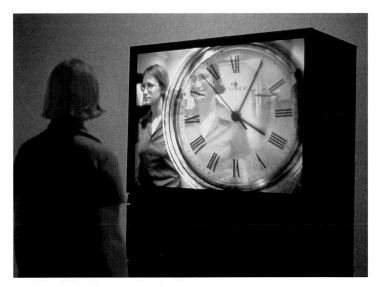

9.54 **Jim Campbell,** *Digital Watch,* **1991.** Watch, camera, video cameras, electronics. Dimensions variable.

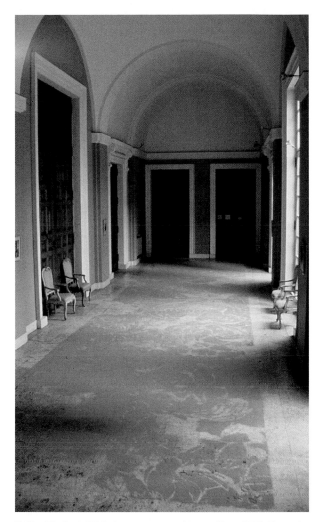

9.53 **Shelagh Wakely,** *curcuma sul travertino,* **1991.** Turmeric powder on travertine marble floor (smell of turmeric filled the space), swept up after 3 weeks, 46 ft × 11 ft 6 in. (14 × 3.5 m).

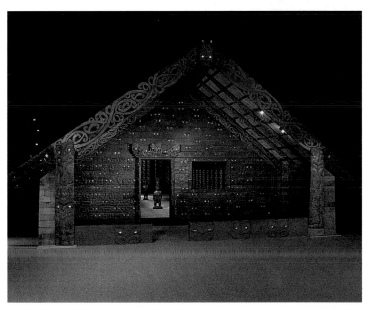

9.55 *Maori Meeting House,* **called "Rautepupuke," New Zealand, 1881.** 56 ft × 13 ft 10 in. (17 × 4 m).

The indigenous people of New Zealand, the Maori, have often combined sculpture with architecture to create a genealogical self-portrait. The face of a prominent ancestor is placed on the front gable of the sacred meeting house (9.55). The ridge at the top of the roof is his backbone, the rafters form his ribs, and the four corner posts represent his arms and legs. Faces of other ancestors are carved on the exterior of the building and on interior posts. Finally, carvings of the Earth Mother and Sky Father are placed over the porch. Through a combination of representation and symbolism, every aspect of the building is designed to honor the past and inspire the present people.

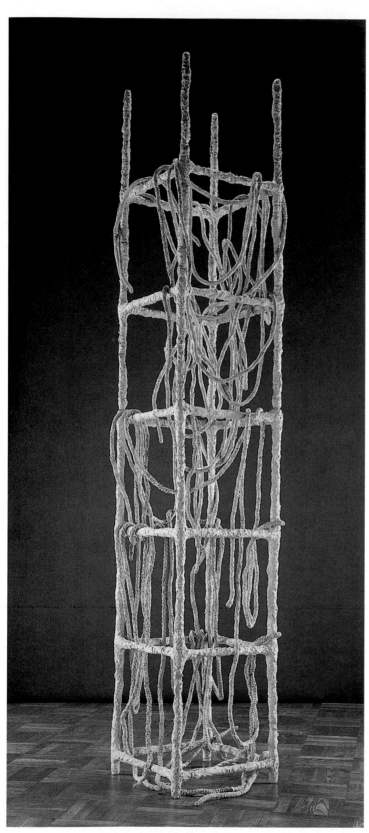

9.56 Eva Hesse, *Laocoön*, 1966. Acrylic paint, cloth-covered cord, wire, and papier-mâché over plastic plumber's pipe, bottom 130 × 23¹/₂ × 23 in. (330.2 × 59.7 × 58.4 cm), top 130 × 21¹/₂ × 21¹/₂ in. (330.2 × 54.6 × 54.6 cm).

Eva Hesse's *Laocoön* (9.56) is a more abstract self-portrait. As noted in Chapter Seven, the ancient Greek sculpture *Laocoön and His Two Sons* (see 7.23, page 7-7), depicts a scene from the Trojan War. Laocoön warns against accepting the large wooden horse the Greeks offer as a gift. The Greek goddess Athena sends two serpents to attack and kill Laocoön, thus gaining entry into Troy and victory in battle for the Greeks hidden in the horse.

Like the snakes that bind Laocoön and his sons, the cords in Hesse's sculpture are messengers of death. They choke the ladder structure and foreshadow Hesse's own death at age 34 from a brain tumor. As she noted, "My life and art have not been separated."[1]

Cornered (9.57), by Adrian Piper, offers a very different self-portrait. Piper, who identifies herself as African American, calmly discusses racial classifications in the 17-minute video, noting the prevalence of mixed ancestry in all Americans. Beginning with the statement, "I'm black. If you feel that my letting you know that I'm not white is making an unnecessary fuss, you must feel the right and proper course of action for me to take is to pass for white." In this installation, Piper's self-identity turns into a social statement.

Attention's Loop (9.58A–B), by Elizabeth King, offers yet another type of self-portrait. In this installation, six highly detailed mannequins are presented in a variety of poses. Carefully articulated arms and hands in three additional display cases line the back wall of the gallery, while an 11-minute video loop animates the mannequins. The combination of supreme craftsmanship, robotic machinery, and the fluid animation communicate a complex range of ideas. The mannequins are both fascinating and disturbing. It appears that human consciousness has been trapped in the mannequin's body.

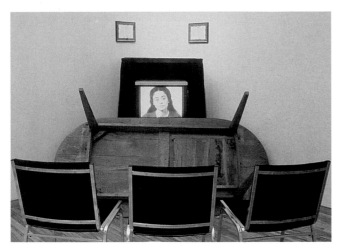

9.57 **Adrian Piper**, *Cornered*, **1988.** Seventeen-minute video installation with table, lighting, and birth certificates.

Expressing Ideas in Physical Form

Over the past century, the range of ideas, materials, and approaches used by sculptors has expanded. Any concept is now fair game, from the most personal to the most political. To express such complex ideas, contemporary sculptors use a wide range of materials and fully exploit the physical forces of gravity, tension, torsion, compression, and expansion. By exploring the meaning as well as the structural strength of each material, the sculptor can increase the conceptual complexity of each artwork.

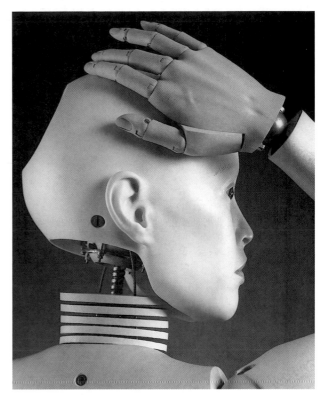

A

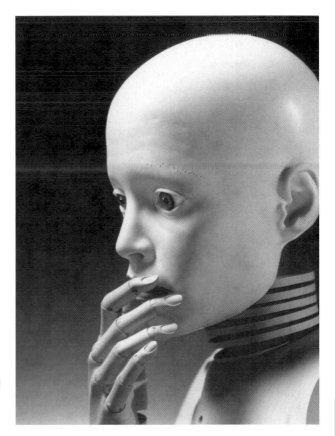

9.58A and B   **Katherine Wetzel** (photograph), **Elizabeth King** (sculpture), *Pupil* from *Attention's Loop,* **1987–90.** Installation at the Bunting Institute, Radcliffe College, 1997. Porcelain, glass eyes, carved wood, brass. One-half life size.

B

Profile:
Rick Paul, Sculptor

Physical, Virtual, and Cerebral

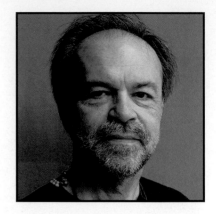

Rick Paul is a professor in the Department of Visual and Performing Arts at Purdue University and chairperson of the Art and Design division. Paul has been involved with foundations design courses throughout the entire 30 years of his teaching career, and for 10 years, he was foundations design coordinator at Purdue.

Paul received his BFA in sculpture from the University of Florida and his MFA in sculpture from Pennsylvania State University. During the 1980s, he made room-sized architectural installations, including exhibitions at The Contemporary Arts Center, Cincinnati; The Cultural Center, Chicago; The Fort Wayne Museum of Art; and The Institute of Contemporary Art, Philadelphia. In 1992, Paul was awarded a Master's fellowship by the National Endowment for the Arts.

Paul's earliest computer work dates from 1974. It was the advent of the personal computer and CAD software that prompted him to use computers to make sculpture. His current work is almost entirely virtual but still maintains many of the characteristics of earlier, site-related sculptures. The relationship between structure and form, the use of environmental context, and the significance of symbolic substitution continue to be issues addressed by his art.

MS: How and why did you start making art?

RP: I started making art as a sophomore in college. At that time I was majoring in another creative area, chemistry, and taking art courses as electives. The first two art courses I enrolled in were photography and three-dimensional design. I enjoyed these classes so much that I continued to take at least one art course each subsequent semester. It took me five years of undergraduate school to decide my major. Once I realized that art could be as creative and challenging as the sciences, I changed my major from chemistry to art and finished my BFA in two semesters.

MS: You have been making sculpture for some 35 years. What qualities attract you to three-dimensional art and design?

RP: As a child I found building my own toys much more interesting than playing with packaged toys. The raw materials for my projects came from the neighborhood trash cans. I had a large walk-in closet full of all sorts of mechanical and electrical parts cataloged and stored in columns of shoeboxes. I was totally fascinated with the variety of materials and forms used by industry and the many ways to combine the parts.

I also made large dioramas and miniature architectural structures. These were often based on the book I was reading at the time. My father forbade me to use his workshop and tools but that did not stop me from using them when he was not around. Looking back, I am convinced that these childhood experiences helped me to develop my intuitive sense of space and dexterity. It also led me to understand the specific physical properties of each material (strength, hardness, malleability, color, texture, grain), which every sculptor uses to advantage.

I have always enjoyed posing questions and solving complex problems. I enjoy the challenges of construction—how can I design an object which possesses structural integrity and withstands the forces of gravity? And, every sculptural question has an ideal as well as a pragmatic answer. When and where do you compromise the ideal solution to get the job done?

MS: Tell me about your creative process. How do you generate, develop, and implement an idea?

RP: My creative process starts with an initial spark—usually a response to an intriguing idea, site, material, or process. Ideas usually come from looking at an ordinary everyday experience from an unusual viewpoint. For example, my 10 years of working with Gatorfoam started with a scrap I carried with me in my truck for over a year. Occasionally I would examine it while stopped at a red light. I was convinced that it had very special properties that I could take advantage of to make very special sculptures. I was right. Gatorfoam, which is like foamcore with a hard surface, permitted me to construct very large, light structures very easily. *Kepler's Dream* at The Contemporary Arts Center in Cincinnati (1981) was the first piece I built with this material.

My virtual objects usually start as sketches. Some of my best ideas occur when I am traveling. During travel, I am physically and psychologically free of my usual daily routine and obligations. I have time for new ideas and more freedom to explore. I would never think of going to my studio to sketch. I like to sketch while in an unrelated, contrasting environment such as a restaurant. I have a collection of napkins and paper placemats from various eating establishments from around the world. I also have a sketchbook that I carry with me. I have one simple rule for using my sketchbook: there are no rules! Drawings are combined with text and computer pseudocode. My sketchbook is a record of where my head has been and where ideas might lead me in the future. Brainstorming on paper is a great way of generating new ideas. Other methods can be applied later to develop and refine what you started.

MS: What do you do when you hit a wall?
RP: I guess I am a contrarian. Often I deliberately turn left where other people would go forward. I make a point of

searching for the less obvious. In the process I am willing to obliterate or discard an approach I've worked on for hours.

MS: Why are your pieces so big?
RP: I enjoy orchestrating the movement of the viewers through a given space. I challenge them with spaces that are inviting but are at the same time too small to occupy, are physically inaccessible or uncomfortable. I ask them to conjure what it would be like to experience these spaces. I want the images invoked within the viewers to be more stimulating than the actual experience. This is why my work is large. Then too, many of the spaces where I have exhibited are also very large.

MS: What is the importance of scale?
RP: I consider two kinds of scale when building a sculpture. The first is the scale of the work itself. How big is it relative to the viewer or space it occupies? If I use architectural elements, they are two-thirds scale. This scale makes for a more intimate environment and can provide for more information within a limited space. Rarely is the viewer aware that such elements as stairs are subhuman in scale. In this way they accept the various architectural elements as larger than they really are.

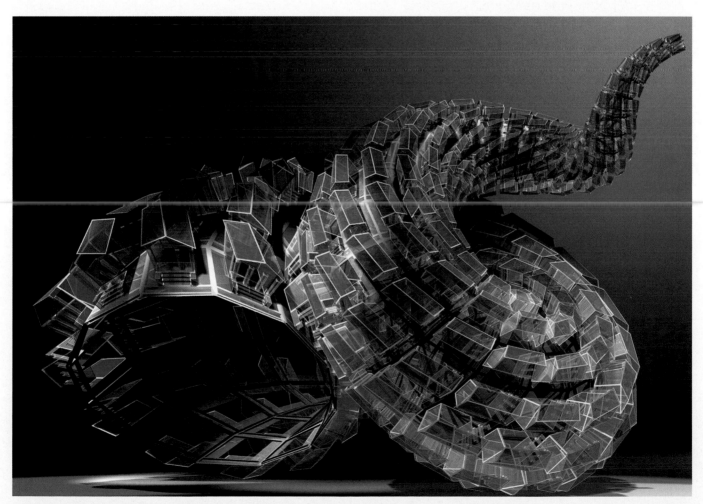

Rick Paul, *DC Object*, 1998. Virtual sculpture, wood and canvas (virtual materials), 36 × 13 × 13 ft (virtual size).

The second kind of scale is "material scale." Material scale is actually a scale range that is defined by the physical characteristics of the material. For example, corrugated cardboard works fine for small-scale constructions, but it is an unlikely material for a tiny matchbox sculpture or the construction of an object 20 feet tall. You learn what the scale range of a material is by working with it. Typically students are unaware of the potential of a material. This is why I encourage them to study and experiment with unfamiliar materials before using them.

MS: In our discussions of teaching, you talked a lot about the advantages of limitations, which can help students focus their energy and explore an idea more deeply. What are the limitations in your own work? How do you push past the boundaries?
RP: I accept the limits of a problem as a challenge rather than a hindrance. The most significant limits to creativity are self-imposed, rather than external. Humans often become inhibited with age. Many of these inhibitions are arbitrary. Knowing yourself and how to work around self-imposed limits is an important asset to creativity that takes a long time to develop.

MS: How do you compare your tangible art with your virtual objects?
RP: For me there is no boundary separating the material world from the virtual world. My work moves back and forth between the two, drawing from both. I am currently working on a series of virtual objects built for specific real environments. Compare *Object at Rest* and *DC Object*, for example. Both were conceived with a specific site in mind. They are roughly equal in size. They are made of the same materials (wood and fabric). Both were conceived as floating objects to be exhibited in an out-of-context environment. There are advantages and disadvantages to both ways of working.

MS: It is clear that you are equally committed to your teaching and your artwork. Do you have any advice for my students?
RP: Realize that there is no substitute for experience. Art and design require mastery of many skills, investigation of many emotions, and exploration of many ideas. There are no shortcuts. Persistence is much more important than talent. No matter how much talent you have, nothing will happen without a sincere and sustained commitment to your work.

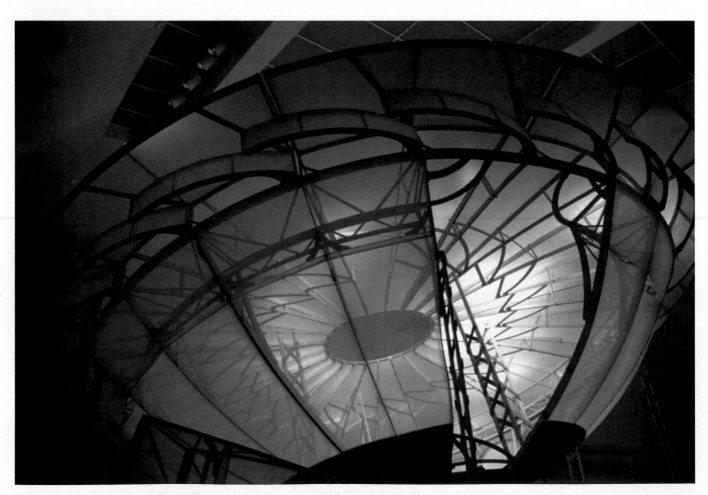

Rick Paul, *Querschnitt,* 1989 installation. Gatorfoam™, wood, and fabric, 36 × 24 × 20 ft.

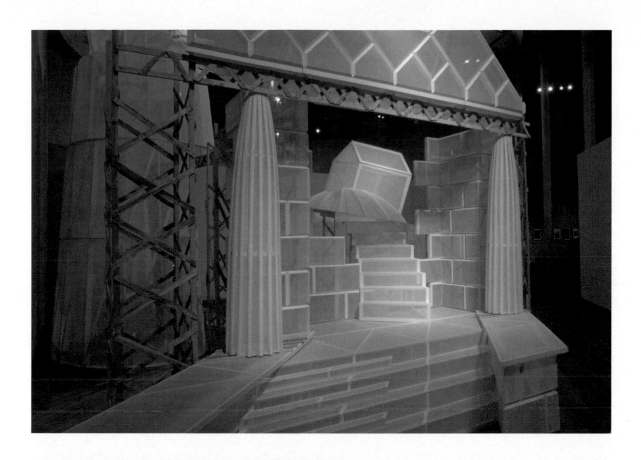

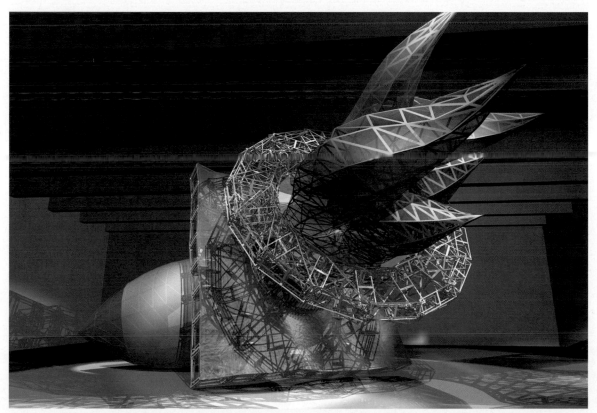

Top: Rick Paul, *Object at Rest,* 1994 installation. Wood and fabric, 24 × 24 × 12 ft. Bottom: Rick Paul, *Expanding History,* 2000. Virtual sculpture, wood and fabric (virtual materials) 36 × 26 × 14 ft (virtual size).

Summary

- A pile of wood at a construction site is stacked for convenience and accessiblity. A pile of wood in a sculpture is designed to communicate ideas and emotions.

- Art gains power from its connection to life. Through art, commonplace experiences are distilled, re-examined, and transformed.

- Physical and psychological boundaries can connect or separate art and life.

- A base can distinguish a sculpture from its surroundings, provide structural stability, and expand aesthetic content.

- Physical forces, such as gravity, compression, expansion, tension, and torsion, can be used to express ideas while providing structural strength.

- The materials a sculptor selects can both heighten and deepen the meaning of the artwork.

- Traditional Western sculpture is massive, representational, figurative, and narrative.

- Contemporary sculpture is generally more spatial, abstract, and nonfigurative. Many contemporary sculptors use specific sites, audience participation, temporal change, and explorations of the self to create powerful works.

Keywords

absence	gravity	presence
abstract	installation	representational
base	mass	tangibility
boundary	nonobjective	tension
compress	oxidation	torsion
condensation	pedestal	vitalistic
earthworks	performance art	weight
expansion	permanence	
filtration	plinth	

As you begin your studio work, consider:

1. How is your artwork similar to everyday life? And, what distinguishes it from everyday life?

2. Can a boundary or base add physical or conceptual strength to your work?

3. What can gravity, compression, expansion, tension, or torsion contribute to your design?

4. How would a change in material affect your artwork, both physically and conceptually?

5. What can happen when your project is placed in a specific setting?

6. What can the viewer learn or feel through an encounter with your artwork?

7. What does your artwork reveal about yourself and the world around you?

John Beardsley, *Earthworks and Beyond: Contemporary Art in the Landscape*. New York, Abbeville Press, 1998.

Jack Burnham, *Beyond Modern Sculpture: The Effects of Science and Technology on the Sculpture of This Century*. New York, George Braziller, Inc., 1968.

Nicolas de Oliveria, Nicola Oxley, and Michael Petry, *Installation Art*. Washington, DC, Smithsonian Institution Press, 1994.

Nicholas Penny, *The Materials of Sculpture*. New Haven, Yale University Press, 1993.

Arthur Williams, *Sculpture: Technique, Form, Content*. Worcester, MA, Davis Publications, Inc., 1993.

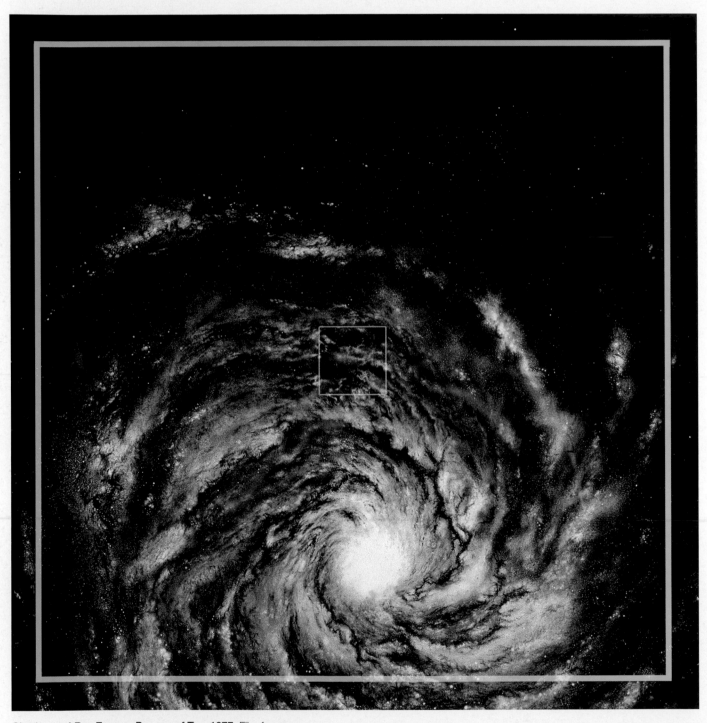

Charles and Ray Eames, *Powers of Ten,* **1977.** Film frame.

Time
Design

From prehistory to the present, artists have sought to create images, objects, and architectural works that embody and express the most profound aspects of human experience. Expressions of love and hate, life and death, dominance and subordination, and joy and sorrow fill the walls of any art museum. As we study art and design, we encounter an endless variety of images and objects that express thoughts and feelings in imaginative form.

This compulsion to create and communicate has always compelled artists to seek new avenues of expression and break conventional boundaries. In contemporary art, innovation and experimentation have become the rule, rather than the exception. Actions and ideas once considered taboo dominate many exhibitions. Separations between music, theater, and art become blurred when interdisciplinary artworks are created. Breadth of knowledge and a willingness to explore new forms of expression characterize the work of contemporary artists.

In this final major section we will consider time as a dimension of art and design. While all areas of visual communication are affected by time, it is the sequential arts—such as film, computer graphics, visual books, and performance art—that most depend on the manipulation of time. Each of these areas of study is very extensive and complex. Chapter Ten offers an overview of time design and a description of its basic aspects and elements. Various forms of storytelling are discussed in Chapter Eleven. The section ends with an exploration of interdisciplinary art and design, including an extended discussion of visual books, installation art, and performance art.

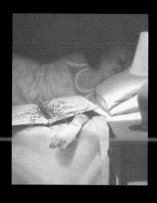

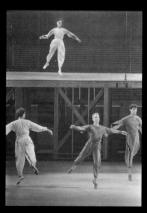

chapter ten

Aspects and Elements of Time

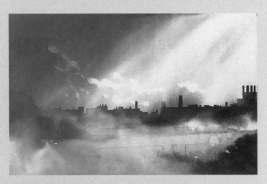

10.1 Alfred Leslie, *Bridge from Mill Creek Park, Youngstown, OH, #82* from *100 Views Along the Road*, 1983. Watercolor, 18 × 24 in. (45.7 × 61 cm).

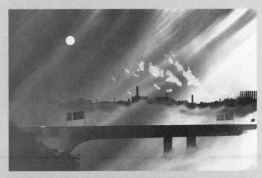

10.2 Alfred Leslie, *Bridge from Mill Creek Park, Youngstown, OH, #80* from *100 Views Along the Road*, 1983. Watercolor, 18 × 24 in. (45.7 × 61 cm).

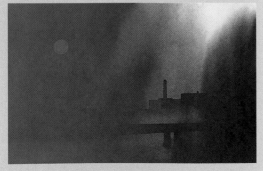

10.3 Alfred Leslie, *Bridge from Mill Creek Park, Youngstown, OH. #84* from *100 Views Along the Road*, 1983. Watercolor, 18 × 24 in. (45.7 × 61 cm).

Dan Graham installed *Past Continuous Pasts* in a New York City gallery in 1974. The walls were covered with mirrors, and time-delayed video monitors were positioned at either end of the room. Upon entering, viewers first viewed themselves in the present, then, watching the video monitors, viewed themselves in the past.

From 1978 to 1983, Alfred Leslie worked on a series of black-and-white watercolor paintings of the American landscape (10.1–10.3). In some cases, he studied a single landscape for several days. In other cases, he recorded the landscape, sequentially as he drove across the country.

In 1998, Nancy Callahan and Diane Gallo created *Storefront Stories* in Cherry Valley, New York. A combination of words, images, and everyday objects was installed in an unused storefront window. Every 10 days, the installation was changed, presenting the next chapter in a story. Over a six-week period, an entire narrative was revealed to the people in the town.

An unusual advertisement was shown during the 1984 Super Bowl game. The 60-second commercial begins as gray-faced workers in a futuristic city trudge into a huge theater and shuffle into their seats (10.4). From the screen, a grim "Big Brother" intones: "From today we celebrate the first anniversary of the information purification directions." A woman athlete is then shown, carrying a sledgehammer and sprinting toward the theater, with guards in hot pursuit (10.5). On arrival, she hurls the hammer into the screen, which explodes. As the words appear on the screen, an announcer reads, "On January 24, Apple Computer will introduce Macintosh. And you'll see why 1984 won't be like *1984*."

What is the connection? What do these artworks have in common?

In each case, an understanding of time is an essential aspect of the work. Like gravity, time itself is intangible. And, it is easy to overlook a force that we cannot see. Yet the *effects* of time are critically important in all areas of art and design. An illustrator working on a track meet poster seeks the most dramatic moment in each event. The action shown in a narrative painting such as *Raft of the Medusa* (see 3.51, page 3-17) is as important as the composition created. And, through variations in texture and color, a ceramicist invites us to examine a bowl slowly, revealing nuances as the form is turned.

Photographers, book artists, and filmmakers are especially sensitive to the importance of time. When news photographer Sam Shere captured the moment at which the dirigible *Hindenburg* exploded, he created an indelible image (10.6).

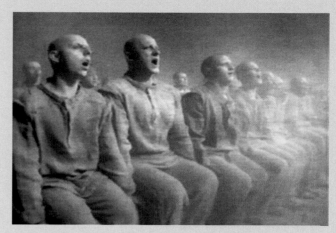

10.4 **Apple Computer television ad introducing the Macintosh computer.** Shown during the 1984 Superbowl game.

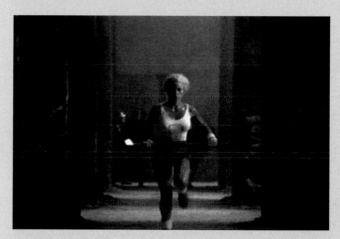

10.5 **Apple Computer television ad introducing the Macintosh computer.** Shown during the 1984 Superbowl game.

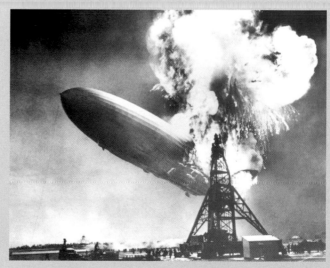

10.6 **Sam Shere, Explosion of the *Hindenburg*, Lakehurst, NJ, 1937.** Photograph.

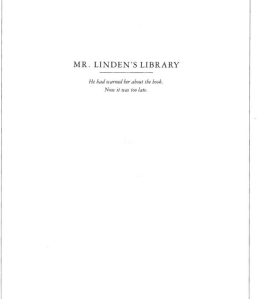

MR. LINDEN'S LIBRARY

He had warned her about the book.
Now it was too late.

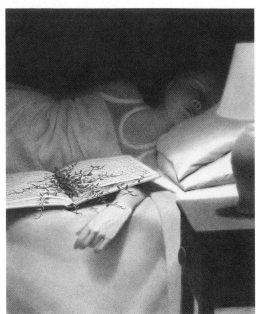

10.7 Chris van Allsburg, "Mr. Linden's Library" from *The Mysteries of Harris Burdick*, Houghton Mifflin, 1984.

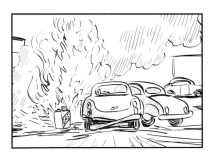

10.8A

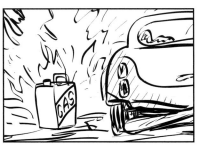

10.8B

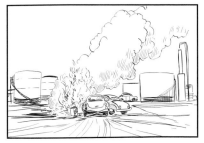

10.8C

In *The Mysteries of Harris Burdick,* illustrator Chris Van Allsburg suggested a series of complex stories using a single drawing and a fragment of text (10.7). And, after shooting many reels of footage, a filmmaker spends months editing the film down to the essentials.

Meanings unfold through the passage of time. Selecting and composing each moment is critical. Connections made through the juxtaposition of images can create a visual rhythm, express an idea, or tell a story. While these aspects of time are most clearly demonstrated through film and comic books, the implications for all areas of art and design are profound.

Building Blocks

Transforming temporal experience into expression or communication may seem daunting at first. The compositional skills needed for two-dimensional design and the spatial skills needed for three-dimensional design can become even more energized when time is added to the mix.

We are surrounded by time design, however, and with some basic definitions and a sense of direction, can build on our existing vocabulary and soon begin to work. We are all familiar with television, movies, and comic books. Each of these sequential structures is composed from four basic units: frame, shot, scene, and sequence. The **frame** is a single static image. Projected onto a flat screen, a film frame is governed by the same compositional criteria as a painting, a poster, or a photograph. As shown in Figure 10.8 A–C, the boundaries of the frame determine the meaning of the image. The

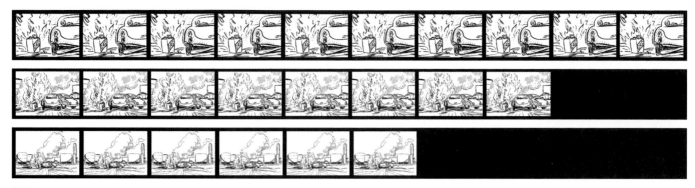

10.9

close-up in the first frame shows the gasoline can that is the source of the fire. The **medium shot** in the second frame shows the parking lot in which the fire has been set. The **long shot** in the final frame shows the fire in a larger context. We now see that this fire at an oil refinery could spark an explosion.

In filmmaking, a **shot** is a continuous group of frames. In Figure 10.9, the first shot consists of 10 frames, the second shot consists of 8 frames, and the third shot consists of 6 frames. By combining these shots, we can create a scene. A **scene** is usually constructed from continuous action in continuous time and continuous space.

A **sequence** is a collection of related shots and scenes that comprise a major section of action or narration. To understand the expressive potential of a sequence, we must examine four major ways in which shots can be related.

Relationships Between Shots

In *Film Art: An Introduction*, David Bordwell and Kristin Thompson describe four types of shot-to-shot relationships.

A **graphic relationship** connects two or more images through visual similarity. Because the images of doves, airplanes, and crosses in Figure 10.10A–C are graphically similar, a visual connection is made when they are shown together. In this case, a visual connection can be used to communicate a political idea.

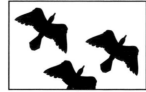

10.10A

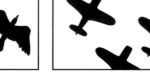

10.10B

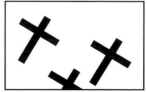

10.10C

Doves symbolize peace, bombers symbolize war, and crosses symbolize death. The juxtaposition of these shots shows that the transition from peace to war leads to death.

A **spatial relationship** can expand or compress the stage on which an action occurs (10.11A–C). Through a combination of close-ups and distance shots, the filmmaker can imply movement and can increase or decrease the connection between the actor and the audience.

A **temporal relationship** can establish **chronology,** the order in which events occur. A story may be told through a simple sequence of events, or reorganized, using **flashbacks,** which refer to previous events. The 1993 movie of *The Fugitive* uses flashbacks extensively. The film begins with the murder of Dr. Kimball's wife. Wrongly accused of the crime and sentenced to death, Kimball must discover the actual killer if he is to clear his name. Flashbacks to the murder, which occur throughout the story, show Kimball's recollection of the event that shattered his life.

When many shots are combined, a deliberate **rhythmic relationship** can be developed. Rhythm is often based on an interplay between static and dynamic, on a contrast between light and dark, or on a combination of shots of different duration (10.12).

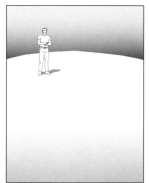
10.11A

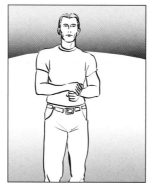
10.11B

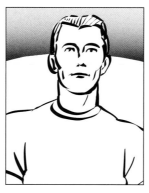
10.11C

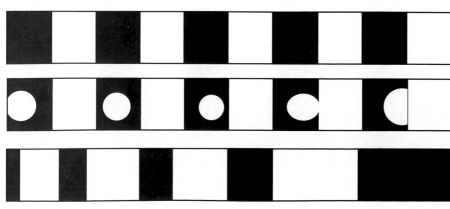
10.12

In *The Birds*, Alfred Hitchcock used all these relationships to create a suspenseful sequence that builds to an explosive climax (10.13A–K). In *Film Art*, David Bordwell and Kristin Thompson describe an especially impressive example.[1] Melanie, the central character in the sequence, watches in horror as a line of flaming gasoline advances across the pavement, then ignites a gasoline station. The shots of her face create one graphic relationship, while the shots of the flame create a second graphic relationship. By **crosscutting,** or alternating between the two, Hitchcock created a relentless rhythm and established a simultaneous temporal relationship: Melanie is watching the gasoline as it advances toward the gas station. In a final aerial view, we shift our spatial position to watch the final explosion from a seagull's point of view. Graphic, rhythmic, temporal, and spatial relationships have been combined to create a cinematic tour de force.

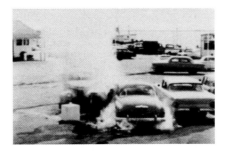
10.13A

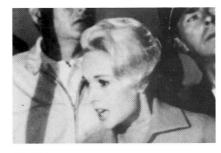
10.13B

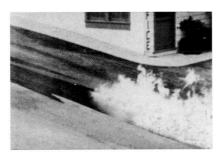
10.13C

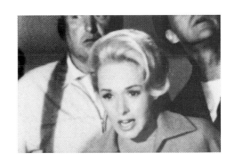
10.13D

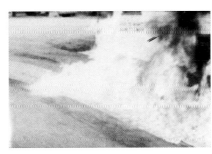
10.13E

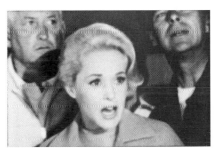
10.13F

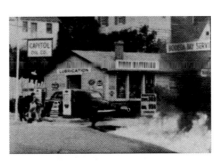
10.13G

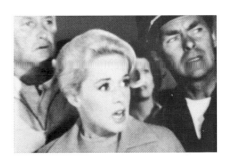
10.13H

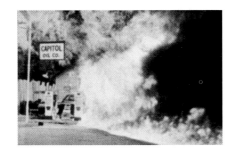
10.13I

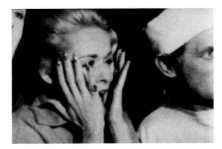
10.13J

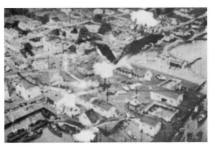
10.13K

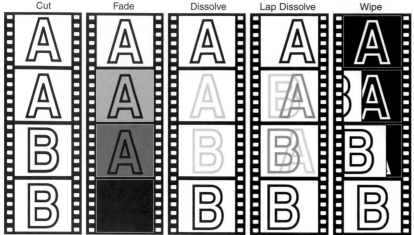

Cut	Fade	Dissolve	Lap Dissolve	Wipe
A	A	A	A	A
A	A	A	A	A
B	A	B	B	B
B		B	B	B

10.14

Transitions from Shot to Shot

The four most common transitions in film are the **cut, fade, dissolve,** and **wipe** (10.14). A cut is an abrupt transition that may connect very different images or very similar images, depending on the effect required. Fades and dissolves are gradual transitions. In a fade, the shot slowly darkens or lightens. In a dissolve, as one shot fades, another appears. Two shots are superimposed briefly in a **lap dissolve.** A wipe is more abrupt than a fade but softer than a cut. In a wipe, the first shot seems to be pushed off the screen by the second.

As described by Scott McCloud in *Understanding Comics,* comic books rely on six additional transitions.[2]

American comics rely heavily on **action-to-action transitions** (10.15). Capturing sequential moments within an event, the action-to-action transition is clear and straightforward.

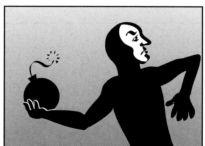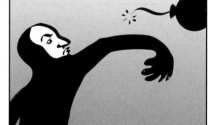

10.15 Action-to action transition.

In a **subject-to-subject transition** (10.16), two shots within the same scene are juxtaposed. The combination may provide crucial information, as in this explosive story.

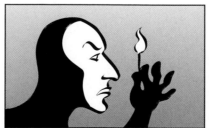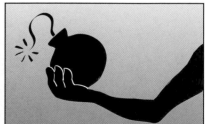

10.16 Subject-to-subject transition.

A **scene-to-scene transition** (10.17) requires more reader involvement. Depending on the images used, this type of transition can transport us across great distances in time and space.

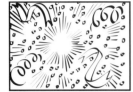 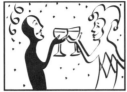 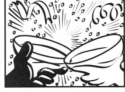 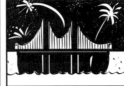

10.17 Scene-to-scene transition.

A **non-sequitur transition** (10.18) requires even more reader involvement. Because there is no logical relationship between shots, meaning must be invented.

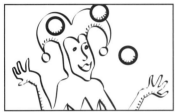 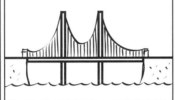

10.18 Non-sequitur transition.

Two additional transitions often appear in Japanese comic books.

A **moment-to-moment transition** (10.19) is used when a character or situation is simply being observed over time.

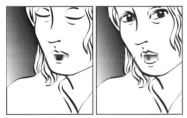

10.19 Moment-to-moment transition.

An **aspect-to-aspect transition** (10.20) is used to record different views within a scene. The passage of time is slowed as we scrutinize our surroundings.

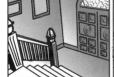 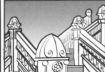 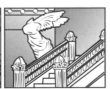

10.20 Aspect-to-aspect transition.

Six Elements of Time

Duration

Duration refers to the running time of a film, video, or performance; to the events depicted in the story (plot duration); and to the overall span of time the story encompasses (story duration). For example, the viewing time of *Star Wars* is 118 minutes, and the plot duration (from the capture of Princess Leia to the destruction of the Death Star) is about a month. The overall story duration, however, extends back to Darth Vader's betrayal of the Jedi warriors and his alliance with the dark side of the Force.

Matching the duration to the message is essential. Tolstoy's *War and Peace* cannot be fully communicated in a 20-minute film. Equally, a 10-second space shuttle launch may lose rather than gain power when the duration is increased. Every moment has its own power. A 15-second soft drink ad uses time just as carefully as a 2-hour film.

Determining the plot duration is equally important. Following the principles of drama described by Aristotle, ancient Greek plays generally occur over a one- or two-day period. Even though the characters often refer to previous events, the action on stage is brief. *Hamlet, Romeo and Juliet,* and most other Shakespearean plays are equally brief. By limiting the time frame, the playwright focuses our attention on a few events and thus increases the impact of the play.

Tempo

Tempo refers to the speed at which time passes. Despite the apparent constancy of real time, our perception of events in our lives varies widely, depending on the nature of the activity and the rate of change. Consider this story. Once upon a time, six coal miners were trapped by the collapse of a mine shaft. Based on the size of their shelter and the number of trapped men, the miners determined that there would be enough oxygen for a four-hour wait. Beyond that point, rescue would be futile: they would run out of oxygen. A miner with a fluorescent watch was asked to call out the hours as the time passed. He did so, but modified his report, cutting in half the actual length of time passed. Eight hours passed. All the miners were rescued, except the man with the watch. He alone knew that they were out of oxygen.

While all moments are fleeting, through editing and careful observation a filmmaker can compress, expand, or exaggerate time. The final shoot-out in *Bonnie and Clyde* provides a classic example. A combination of extreme slow motion and skillful editing produces a ballet of violence, as the two outlaws are riddled with machine-gun bullets at the end of the film.

Tempo is equally determined by the movement of the actors and by the editing of the film. In *Star Wars,* the fight between Darth Vader and Obi-Wan Kenobi began as staged combat between two actors (10.21). To provide director George Lucas with enough raw material, many versions, or **takes,** were filmed, using multiple cameras. The final tempo was determined through editing. By connecting fragments from many different views, Lucas was able to increase or decrease the fight tempo.

As with film, tempo in a comic book is largely determined by the organization of multiple images. Vertical panels placed in close proximity tend to speed up the tempo, while horizontal panels tend to slow down the tempo. The tragic conclusion to the myth of Orpheus is shown in a double-page spread from Essential Vertigo's *The Sandman* (10.22). To retrieve his dead wife, the musician Orpheus has descended into the Underworld. Through his song, he persuades the god Hades to release his beloved Eurydice. They may leave unharmed, but if Orpheus looks back

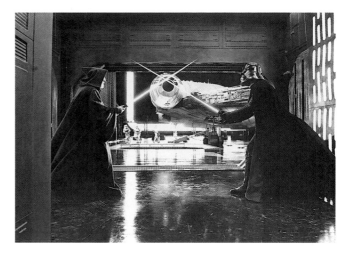

10.21 George Lucas, *Star Wars*, 1977.

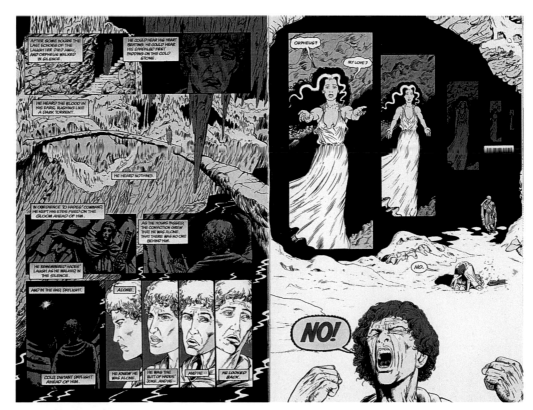

10.22 **Essential Vertigo,** *The Sandman Special #1*, 1991. TM and © DC Comics. All Rights Reserved. Used with Permission.

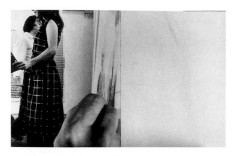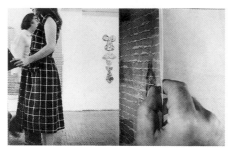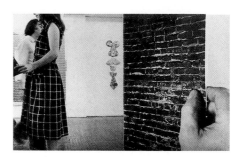

10.23 A–C   Michael Snow, from *Cover to Cover*, 1975. Press of the Nova Scotia College of Art and Design. New York University Press.

before they reach the surface, Eurydice will again be lost. At the bottom of the left page, multiple frames show his desire to look back. The frames at the top of the right page show the result. He looked, and Eurydice fell back into the void.

In a visual book, tempo can be created in two ways. First, by increasing the number and frequency of images, the artist can increase the tempo. Second, by turning the page, the reader controls viewing speed. In a flip book, actions can pass slowly or quickly, depending on the pace set by the viewer. In a more elaborate book called *Cover to Cover* (10.23A–C), Michael Snow presents multiple views of a room interior and the surrounding landscape. There is no text: photographs of walls, doorways, and streets re-create the environment within the book format. The viewer can run or stroll through the house, depending on the speed with which the pages are turned.

Intensity

Intensity refers to the level of energy in a performance or the quality of observation of an event. For example, to win an Olympic gold medal, an ice skater must spin rapidly, fully extend each move, and exude both athletic skill and emotional conviction. Likewise, even an ordinary glass of water becomes fascinating when observed closely. The glass itself offers a graceful interplay between line and shape, while light passing through droplets of water breaks into a prismatic array of color.

Intensity of performance is an essential aspect of theater. We can feel the concentration the actors bring to the stage and when a dramatic or dangerous event occurs, we can share their emotion. In *Cleaning the House* (10.24), Yugoslavian artist Marina Abramovic combined intensity with metaphor to make a political statement. Wearing a

10.24   Marina Abramovic, *Cleaning the House*, 1995. Performance at Sean Kelly Gallery, duration 2 hours.

white dress and sitting in a poorly lit New York City basement, she repeatedly scrubbed the dirt and blood off a collection of massive cow bones. Like the bones, various ethnic groups in her homeland have been "cleansed," bringing trauma and bleached bones to the once-prosperous country.

The opening sequence in Sergio Leone's *Once Upon a Time in the West* provides a cinematic example of observational intensity. Three bandits await the arrival of their leader by train. For nearly 15 seconds, the film focuses on the face of the most disreputable of the men, recording every twitch and swat as a fly repeatedly alights and investigates every florid detail (10.25). Finally, the train does arrive—and just in time, for the bandit has pulled his gun and is preparing to shoot the fly (and himself). No expansion or contraction of the actual running time is needed. The very act of filming the sequence in such detail gives it significance, as well as humor.

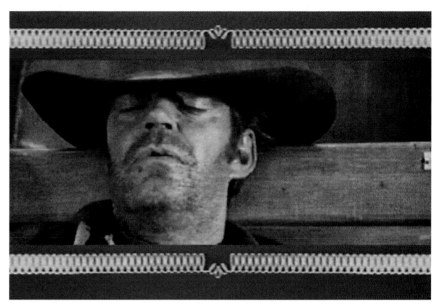

10.25 Sergio Leone, *Once Upon a Time in the West*, 1968.

Scope

Scope can be defined in two ways. Conceptually, it is the extent of our perception or the range of ideas our minds can grasp. Temporally, scope refers to the range of action within a given moment.

The earliest films, such as *The Arrival of a Train at La Ciotat Station* (10.26), are limited in scope. A single event is seen from a fixed viewpoint. By positioning his camera carefully, director Louis Lumière created a dynamic, diagonal composition. The train and passengers seem to come out of the screen and into the theater. Some audience members were so convinced of the illusion that they ran from the theater to avoid being hit by the train. In the early days of cinema, any moving image fascinated the audience, and the dramatic composition made this film especially popular.

As directors gained experience, they expanded the temporal scope of their films. In *The Great Train Robbery*, a gang of bandits holds up a train; a

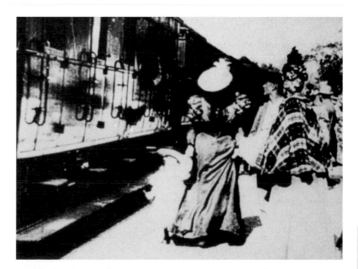

10.26 Louis Lumière, *The Arrival of a Train at La Ciotat Station*, 1897.

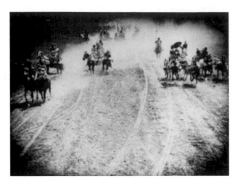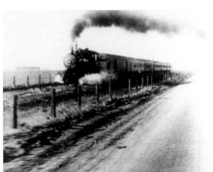

10.27A–B   D. W. Griffith, *Intolerance*, 1916.

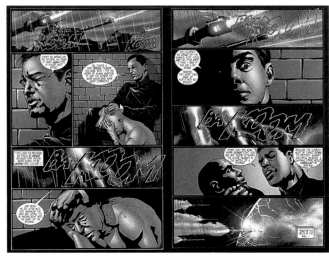

10.28   Paul Jenkins, writer, and Jae Lee, artist. *Inhumans: "First Contact," Volume 2, Issue 5, March 1999.* Marvel Comics.

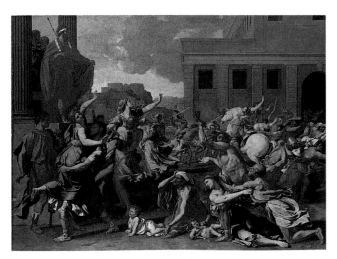

10.29   Nicolas Poussin, *The Rape of the Sabine Women*, 1634. Oil on canvas, 5 ft ⅞ in. × 6 ft 10⅝ in. (154.6 × 209.9 cm).

telegraph operator alerts the authorities; a posse is gathered from men attending a local dance; the posse captures the thieves. Director Edwin S. Porter used only 11 shots and the editing is quite simple. Nonetheless, it is clear that the robbery, the telegrapher's message, and the dance are roughly simultaneous events.

With *Intolerance,* director D. W. Griffith expanded conceptual scope to the limit. Using intolerance throughout history as a theme, Griffith developed four simultaneous stories: the fall of Babylon, Jesus' final days, the St. Bartholomew's Day Massacre in France, and a labor strike in modern-day America. These stories are intercut throughout the film, with the image of a woman rocking a cradle as a further recurrent theme. Each story concludes in an attempted rescue. Weaving the four narratives together in an accelerating rhythm (10.27A–B), Griffith brings the film to a breathtaking conclusion.

Complex stories require complex editing, and Griffith became a master of the art. By alternately showing two or more events, he created a connection between simultaneous actions. Comic book artists use many of the same skills. This technique of crosscutting is repeatedly used in *Inhumans* (10.28), by Paul Jenkins and Jae Lee. Moving from cannon fire to a quiet conversation between the two men, the artists show that the events are concurrent.

Scope is equally important in traditional narrative painting. In Nicholas Poussin's *The Rape of the Sabine Women* (10.29), a complex event is shown in a single image. Seeking wives, the Romans have invited the Sabines to a festival. They then attack their guests and abduct the women. Many actions occur at once. In the left corner, Romulus raises his cloak as a signal to attack. As the courtyard swirls with struggles between the women and their captors, an old woman and two children watch in terror.

Setting

Setting is one of the most complex aspects of time. It includes the physical and temporal location of a story, its props and costumes, and the use of sound.

The physical setting of an event has an extraordinary impact on meaning. An action that is appropriate in one context may be appalling in another. As a drum major, you will be applauded when you strut down mainstreet during the Fourth of July parade. At a different time of day (such as Monday morning rush hour) or in a different location (such as a synagogue), you are likely to be arrested.

The temporal setting is equally significant. Most of the action in *Gone with the Wind*, is derived from romantic conflict involving Scarlett O'Hara, Ashley Wilkes, and Rhett Butler. While each of the three characters is interesting, the love triangle itself is commonplace. It is the temporal setting of the novel during the American Civil War that shifts the story from soap opera to epic.

Likewise, Nancy Holt's *Sun Tunnels* (10.30) would be meaningless if removed from its site in western Utah. Constructed from four 22-ton concrete tunnels, this sculpture is aligned with the rising and setting sun during the winter and summer solstices. The arrangement of stars in four constellations is shown using holes cut in the walls of each tunnel. Designed to heighten awareness of our place in the universe, this work relies on both time and place for its impact.

Objects and Implications

Props and costumes can have an equally dramatic effect in a narrative. The top hat and tuxedo worn by Fred Astaire in many films helped convey a formal elegance, while the leather jacket worn by Michael Jackson in *Beat It* clearly placed him on a contemporary city street. In James Cameron's *Titanic*, the diamond known as the Heart of the Ocean and the drawing of Rose wearing this jewel are essential to the overall narrative.

Fifty Years of Silence (10.31 A–C), a visual book by Tatanya Kellner is even more dependent on objects and their meanings. The simple pine crate that houses the book seems innocuous, until we see the small, five-digit number burned into the lid. When the lid is removed, a papier-maché arm is revealed, bearing the same number. It is a cast of the arm of Kellner's mother, a survivor of Auschwitz. The book pages, cut out around the arm, tell the story of the family before and during the Holocaust. As

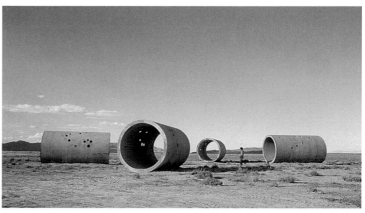

10.30 Nancy Holt, *Sun Tunnels*, 1973–1976. Great Basin Desert, Utah. Four tunnels, each 18 ft long × 9 ft 4 in. diameter (5.5 × 2.8 m), each axis 86 ft long (26.2 m). Aligned with sunrises and sunsets on the solstices.

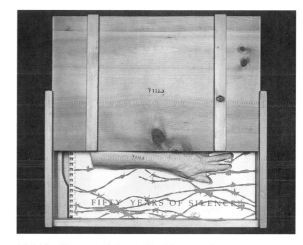

10.31A Tatanya Kellner, *Fifty Years of Silence*, 1992. Cover, 14 × 22⅝ × 3 in. (35.5 × 57.3 × 7.6 cm).

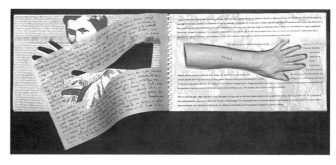

10.31B Tatanya Kellner, *Fifty Years of Silence*, 1992. 12 × 20 × 1½ in. (30.5 × 50.8 × 3.8 cm).

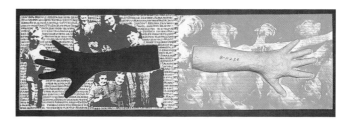

10.31C Tatanya Kellner, *Fifty Years of Silence*, 1992. 12 × 20 × 1½ in. (30.5 × 50.8 × 3.8 cm).

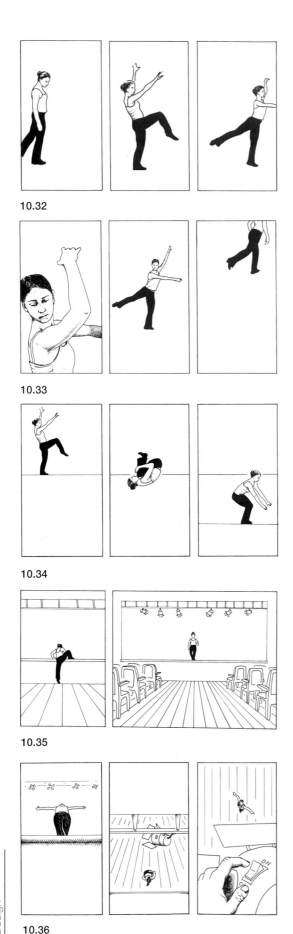

10.32

10.33

10.34

10.35

10.36

the pages are turned, the actual arm and the cut-out arm are as inescapable as the repressed memories of a Holocaust survivor. By placing it in such a prominent position in the book, Kellner provides us with a sculptural close-up of the indelible tattoo.

The wooden crate suggests a container for expensive wine or a shipping crate for a valuable object. The arm is an even more compelling sculptural object. By using these "props," Kellner gives her book greater immediacy, and transforms the familiar story of a Holocaust survivor into a highly personal event.

Setting and Actor

Relationships between an actor and a setting can substantially affect our interpretation of an action or event. Placement of a single figure within a setting can demonstrate a wide range of possibilities.

First we must decide where to place the dancer within the frame. Three alternatives are shown in Figure 10.32. Positioned at the far left edge, she looks into a large void, which invites more extensive movement from left to right. Positioned in the center, she commands attention. She can move to the right, left, forward, or back with ease. She is now in a more commanding position. Facing right, and moved to the right, she seems ready to leave the frame, perhaps to join other dancers offstage.

What happens when the size of the dancer is varied? As shown in Figure 10.33, changing the size of the figure in relationship to the frame helps to define the distance between the dancer and the viewer. When the dancer is reduced in size and placed in the upper half of the frame, she seems distant, far from the viewer. When she moves far into the foreground, with her torso filling the frame, she seems to push past the boundary and into our space.

The addition of an illusionistic setting (10.34) dramatically changes the amount of space available to our dancer. Even a simple line can be used in various ways. It may be the ground, providing a resting place for the dancer. When the dancer overlaps the line, it recedes, suggesting a horizon. The addition of a second line can expand the space even further. We can now show two grounds at the same time: the foreground and the background.

In Figure 10.35, the addition of perspective lines further enhances the space. A long corridor in one-point perspective gives the dancer an expansive stage that invites movement from the background to the foreground. A room corner in two-point perspective can enclose the background space while extending the space for movement to both the left and right. Combining these elements creates a complex and believable space in which the dancer can perform. The space is extended beyond the edge of the frame by the chairs and the lines in the floor. The chairs overlap and decrease in size, further defining the space. Despite her small size, the dancer's central placement makes her the focus of the image.

The setting can become even more significant when the dancer is viewed from above or below (10.36). Looking up from the front row gives the figure a commanding presence. Looking down from the balcony makes her seem insignificant.

Turning on the lights greatly increases the compositional and emotional possibilities (10.37). Side-lighting accentuates the dimensionality of both the figure and the setting. When we backlight the dancer, she becomes a silhouette. We lose information about her volume, but gain a striking graphic image and an impressive cast shadow. Spotlighting the dancer can direct attention to a specific part of her body or eliminate the rest of the stage altogether.

Variations in focus (10.38) can affect both spatial location and emotional impact. When the foreground figure is out of focus, she is less dominant and we quickly look past her into the more tightly focused corridor. A more traditional use of focus is shown in the second drawing. Clear focus in the foreground gradually diminishes as we approach the distant stage. However, do we really want to focus on this uncouth rabble? By focusing on the distant stage, we can watch the dancer end her performance and accept the applause.

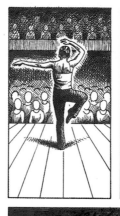
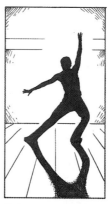
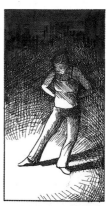
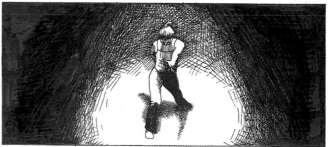

10.37

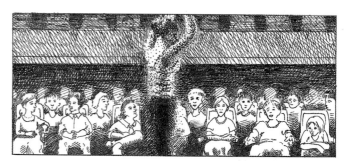
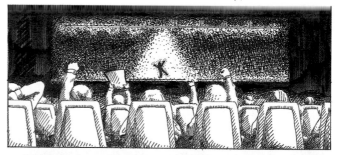
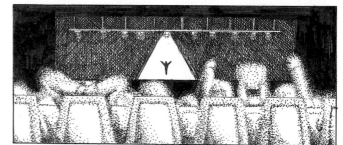

10.38

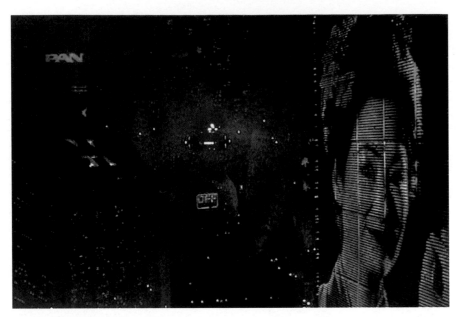

10.39 *Blade Runner.* The city.

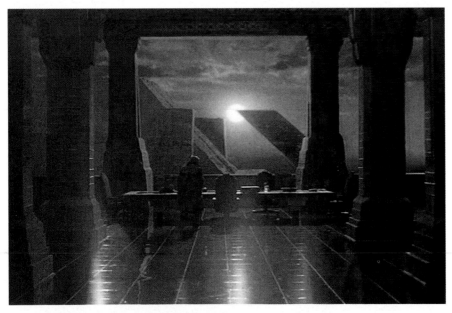

10.40 *Blade Runner.* Tyrell corporation offices.

Setting as Actor: Staging *Blade Runner*

A set provides an emotional context as well as a physical context for a film. Spaces can be magical, frightening, or inviting. Lighting can be used to obscure, illuminate, or exaggerate volume. Within a single scene, a character can be reduced to a silhouette through backlighting, can gain dimensionality and power through sidelighting, or can lose depth when extreme front lighting is used.

All these aspects of staging are critically important in the science fiction classic *Blade Runner* (1982). Set in Los Angeles in 2019, the film examines relationships between humans and machines, the manufactured and the real. Harrison Ford stars as a cop named Deckert who must hunt and destroy four androids, or "replicants," who have escaped from slavery on a distant colony.

Throughout the film, setting, lighting, props, and costumes are as important as any of the actors in creating the narrative. Three main settings are used. The first is the city itself—a grim, brooding place dominated by empty buildings and crowds of anonymous people. It is always dark, and it rains constantly. A moving image of a seductive geisha dominates the side of one building. She winks, gracefully places a pill in her mouth, and smirks at the viewer (10.39). An airship glides by, promising adventure on an offworld colony. Searchlights add restless movement and a sense of constant surveillance.

By contrast, the Tyrell corporation, which manufactures the replicants, is solid, stately, and seemingly invincible. It never rains in this second setting, and the pyramidal walls of the massive building gleam like bronze in the incessant afternoon light.

Inside, regular columns create a vast space, reminiscent of an Egyptian temple (10.40). Dr. Tyrell, godlike in his power, is often sidelit to increase his dimensionality.

A third major setting is the Bradbury Hotel, the home of genetic engineer J. F. Sebastian. This grand old hotel, with its massive cornices and deserted rooms, feels like a mausoleum, a city of the dead (10.41). Its endless staircases are obscured in mist, and searchlights rake the corridors. We enter Sebastian's apartment through an oversized door and are greeted by a pair of miniature robotic soldiers, two of his creations. A massive Greek vase dominates one room, while a collection of mannequins and mechanical toys fills another. This labyrinth is the perfect setting for the final battle between Deckert and Roy, the leader of the replicants.

10.41 *Blade Runner.* Bradbury Hotel.

Props in *Blade Runner*

These settings create an ominous world. In the director's cut, three origami figures play a pivotal role in the film. The first origami figure, a chicken, is made by another cop after Deckert accepts the assignment to kill the androids. The second, the figure of a man, is made after Deckert searches the apartment of one of the androids. The third, a tiny silver unicorn (10.42), has special significance. Halfway through the film Deckert has imagined a unicorn running through a forest. This pastoral scene, only seconds long, is totally unlike anything else that occurs in the film. Earlier in the film, we learned that the Tyrell replicants have been given memories, to increase their "humanness." With the introduction of the origami unicorn, we realize that the image in the forest was a memory planted in Deckert's brain when *he* was made. Deckert is a replicant himself.

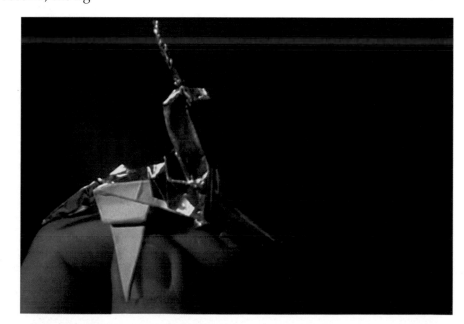

10.42 *Blade Runner.* Origami unicorn.

Sound: The Hidden Dimension

Two versions of a clip from *Chariots of Fire* were shown during the 1996 Academy Awards ceremony. In the first, a group of young men ran along a beach, accompanied by the sounds of their feet splashing in the water. It was a pleasant, but prosaic scene, showing ordinary men on an ordinary beach. The same footage was then shown as it appeared in theaters around the world. Accompanied by the famous theme music, these Olympic runners became graceful, even godlike. They were transformed by the music.

Despite its invisibility, the soundtrack is as important to a film as the images we see. Sound engages another of our senses and heightens emotion. A well-written score can set the stage for an action and help to unify a complex film. And, sound heightens our expectations. Consider the importance of squeaky doors in any horror movie or our feeling of expectation when the *Star Wars* theme is played. As we begin to study film, we find that the example from *Chariots of Fire* is not an isolated case. Sound can make or break a film.

Four types of sound dominate time design. They are speech (as delivered by an actor or generated from the audience), music, ambient sound, and sound effects. Each sound has seven qualities.

Loudness is determined by the size of the oscillations in a sound wave. Just as Beethoven varied the volume (or loudness) within his symphonies, so the astute filmmaker or performance artist learns to use a full range of sound, from a whisper to a scream.

Pitch is determined by wave frequency, as compression and expansion occur within the sound wave. The higher pitch of most female voices is generally less threatening than the lower pitch of most male voices. Not surprisingly, the hero is a tenor, while the villain is a bass or baritone in most operas.

Timbre refers to the unique quality of each instrument. For example, a note of the same volume and pitch is quite different when it is generated by a trumpet rather than a violin.

Duration refers to the length of time the sound can be heard. A sound that persists over a long period of time is often used as a bridge between two or more film clips, while a brief, explosive sound may jolt us out of our seats.

Rhythm is determined by three qualities: the **beat,** or pulse, of the sound; the **pace,** or tempo, at which the sound is played; and the **accents,** or areas of emphasis, within the sound. We encounter rhythm in every conversation as we listen to the speed of our friend's speech and note his emphasis on particular words. Rap music, which in some ways is a heightened form of speech, greatly emphasizes the beat, both through a rhythmic use of words and the strong definition of each syllable. A stand-up comic is especially dependent on rhythm. A great joke will fall flat if delivered poorly.

In film, **fidelity** refers to the connection between a sound and its source. The arrival of a helicopter at the end of the musical *Miss Saigon* is accompanied by the loud sound of a churning propeller. Here, the sonic and visual information matches. In *Apocalypse Now,* Wagner's "Ride of the Valkyries" is played as a group of helicopters arrives. As with *Chariots of Fire,* this mismatch between the visual and sonic information substantially changes our interpretation of the event.

Finally, all forms of sound operate within a **spatial context.** The bagpipe, designed to rally troops in war, is an excellent instrument to play outdoors. When played in a small room, the same instrument can very nearly blast plaster off a wall. Likewise, a whispered conversation in a small closet may be more compelling than a shouted conversation on a beach. Even when we have no image at all, sound alone can define space and create a sense of anticipation or dread.

In a film, the spatial dimension of sound becomes even more significant. **Diegetic** sound, or sound that is part of the world we see on the screen, can be generated by a visible event or can come from an invisible, offscreen source. Both onscreen and offscreen sound are critically important and in many cases, a director will shift between the two. For example, in *Titanic,* a quartet of musicians begins to play "Nearer My God to Thee" as the ship sinks lower and lower. The music continues as we see an elderly couple in their cabin, embracing (10.43) and a mother comforting her child. The combination of the music and the images heightens the emotion of the moment.

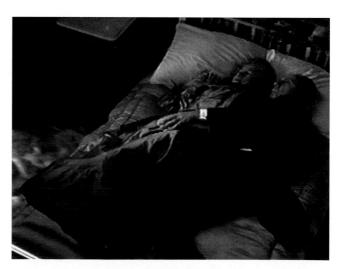

10.43 James Cameron, *Titanic*, 1997.

Chronology

Chronology refers to temporal order. In real time, a foot race begins with the athletes lining up in position (action A), the firing of the starting gun (action B), the running of the race (action C), and the conclusion at the finish line (action D). In a sequential art form, these actions can be organized in various ways, from a disorienting ABACADA pattern to the familiar ABCD pattern of the actual race.

Changes in chronology can completely change meaning.

In *Structure of the Visual Book,* Keith Smith demonstrates beautifully the narrative possibilities of multiple images. Here is a distilled version of his example (10.44–10.53).[3]

In each case, relationships between the images create the sequence of events needed to tell a story.

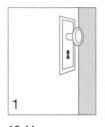

Start with a door.

10.44

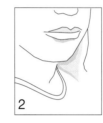

Add a figure. Here, a woman opens the door.

10.45

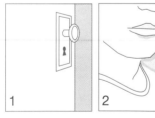

Here, the door opens and we meet a woman.

10.46

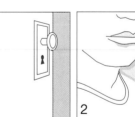

Adding a close-up of a hand creates a confrontation.

10.47

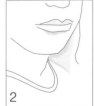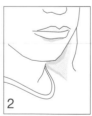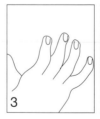

. . .while this order creates a sense of anticipation.

10.48

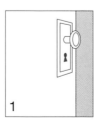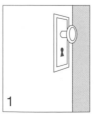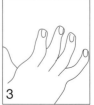

Here, we create a mystery.

10.49

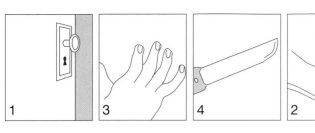

1 3 4 2

With the introduction of a fourth image, a new meaning emerges. It is now becoming threatening.

10.50

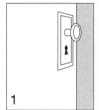 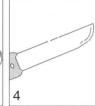 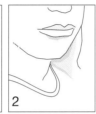 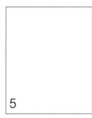 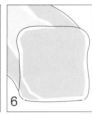

1 3 4 2 5

And now even more so. Our imaginations provide a wide range of horrors for panel five.

10.51

1 3 4 2 5 6

Addition of the sixth image, however, diffuses the tension. It is not a murder after all, just a sandwich being made.

10.52

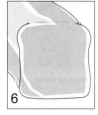 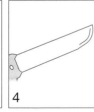 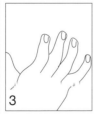 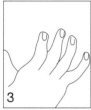

6 2 4 3

The woman still has to take care, however: this final version suggests that she has cut herself!

10.53

10.44–10.53 Keith Smith, from *Structure of the Visual Book,* 1995.

Editing

Chronology is created when shots are combined. A filmmaker combines shots through **editing.** Editing serves six basic purposes.

First, the film editor must select the most compelling images from the total footage shot. No matter how carefully a scene is rehearsed, variations in performance quality do occur, especially when there are many actors on the set. Even more footage is shot for a documentary film. In filming the 1936 Olympic Games in Berlin, Leni Riefenstahl devoted 10 solid weeks of work just to watching the raw footage. Editing this material down to a three-and-one-half-hour film took another two years!

Second, these images must be organized into a cohesive whole. Multiple cameras are often used to provide plenty of rough footage. Constructing a coherent conversation using both close-up and distant shots is often the first step.

Third, through editing, a temporal framework for the film is developed. Time can expand, contract, or move in a dizzying spiral. When using crosscutting, the editor shifts back and forth between two or more events, thus suggesting the simultaneous occurrence of multiple actions.

A Tale of Two Cities, by Charles Dickens, is a literary example of crosscutting. The narrative reaches a climax as Sydney Carton, in Paris, is led to the guillotine, while his double, who was actually condemned to die, is drugged and transported to London. Chapter after chapter, the story shifts between the two men, increasing the sense of urgency while presenting the simultaneous events. This novel offers simultaneous action at its best. Indeed, pioneer film director D. W. Griffith used Dickens as an example when challenged for his innovative editing of *Intolerance.*

Fourth, tempo in a film is largely determined by the number of cuts made. For example, an introspective drama may be constructed from 1,000 shots, while an action film may be made of 2,000 shots or more. Variations in tempo help sustain interest. If there is too little variation, a fast-paced film is just as monotonous as a slow-paced film. To develop momentum gradually, many filmmakers use a slow-paced beginning, which builds to a fast-paced climax, which returns to a slow-paced conclusion.

Fifth, connections made through editing can heighten emotion and suggest the real motivation for a character's actions. In a famous experiment, early Soviet filmmaker Lev Kulesov demonstrated the emotional impact of editing. He combined a neutral shot of an actor's face with four very different images, including a bowl of soup, scenes from nature, a baby, and a dead woman.[4] When the film was shown, the audience praised the actor's skill: he looked hungry when the soup appeared, longed for freedom when the landscape was shown, was filled with joy at the sight of the baby, and felt grief at the sight of the woman. In each case, however, the shot of the actor's face was exactly the same. The emotions were created by the audience's response to the editing, not by any change in the actor's expression.

Finally connections made through editing can substantially change or enhance the meaning of a film. By cutting from a bone spinning in the air to a space station orbiting the earth (10.54A–B), Stanley Kubrick connected prehistory to space travel in *2001: A Space Odyssey*.

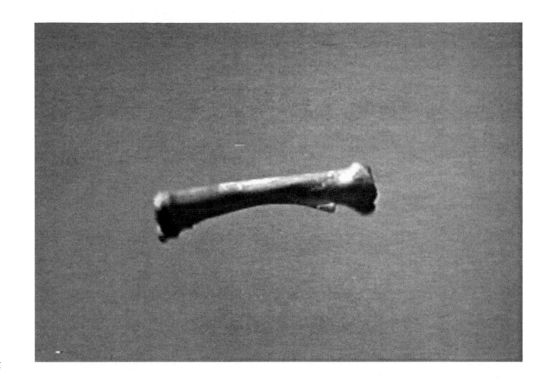

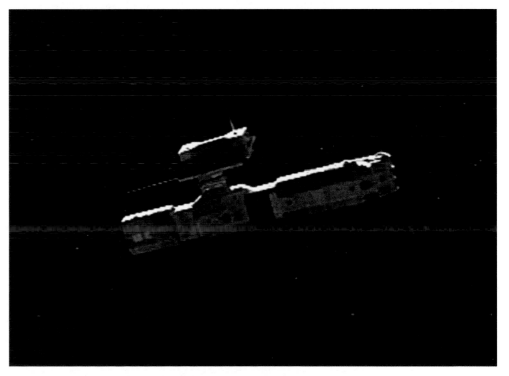

10.54A–B   Stanley Kubrick, *2001: A Space Odyssey*, 1968.

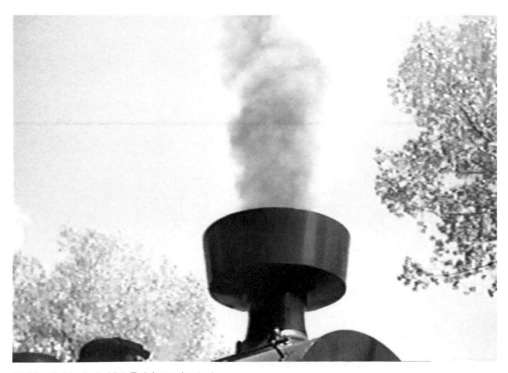

10.55 *Schindler's List.* Extinguished candle.

Schindler's List: Content and Composition

All these aspects of editing are used brilliantly in *Schindler's List*. Mixing contemporary images with black-and-white images of wartime Poland, director Steven Spielberg tells a harrowing tale of the survival of over 1,000 Jews during the Holocaust. Based on historical events, the film shows the transformation of Nazi Oskar Schindler from a single-minded war profiteer to a compassionate man who finally bought the lives of his enslaved workers. It is an incredible story, and any skillful filmmaker could have made a good film based on this event. However, to show the complexities of each character and to turn the story into a truly compelling film required another level of insight. Spielberg and his collaborators had that insight.

The critical importance of editing is apparent from the start. A contemporary scene of a Jewish family at home ends with a trail of smoke rising from an extinguished candle (10.55). We cut to the smokestack on a train in wartime Krakow (10.56) and are transported back in time.

Two opposing forces in the film are then established. The Nazi bureaucrats, assigned to register the Jewish inhabitants of the city, carefully set up tables, typewriters, and rubber stamps (10.57). Lines of Jews awaiting registration establish the second major force. While many individual characters will be developed as the tale unfolds, these groups of angry and frightened

10.56 *Schindler's List.* Train's smokestack.

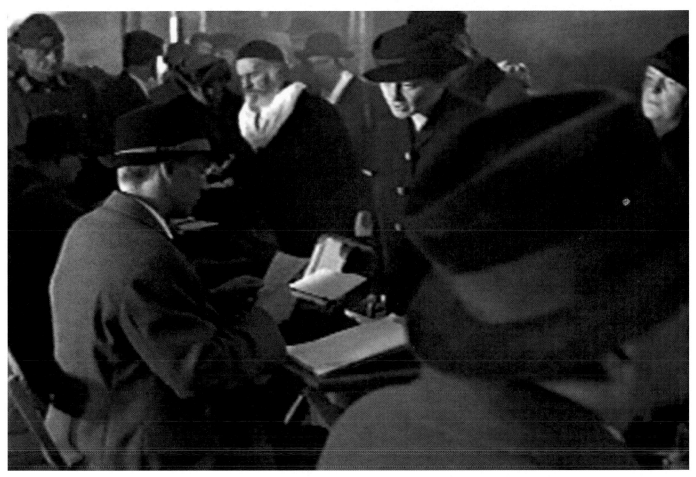

10.57 *Schindler's List.* Nazi bureaucrats.

people recur throughout the film. Regardless of individual ability or virtue, in genocide, every member of the targeted group is equally doomed.

The character of Oskar Schindler is established next. In a small hotel room, he pours a drink, lays out three good suits on the bed, selects his cuff links, and counts his money (10.58). This sequence ends with an extreme close-up as he attaches a Nazi Party pin to his lapel. Just as the bureaucrats carefully laid out their ink pads and rubber stamps in a series of close-ups, so too close-ups provide an inventory of the tools of Schindler's trade.

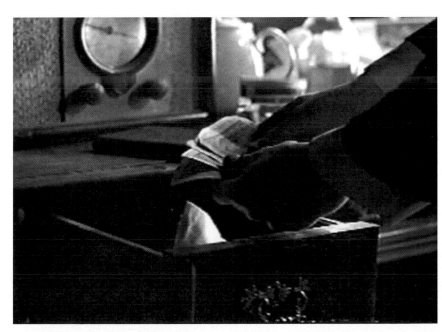

10.58 *Schindler's List.* Schindler counting his money.

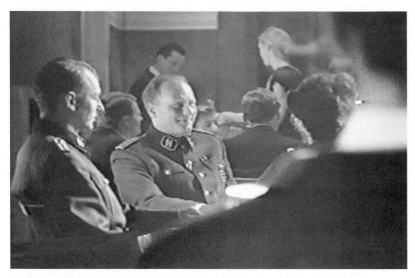

10.59 *Schindler's List.* Schindler in a cafe.

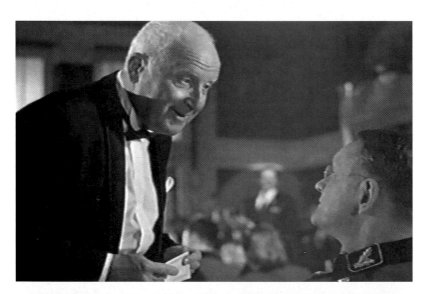

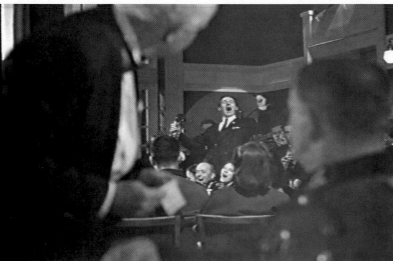

10.60A–B *Schindler's List.* Maitre d'.

In the next sequence, Schindler puts his tools to good use. When he arrives at a cafe favored by Nazi officers, the maitre d' seats him, then asks a waiter who he is. Neither one knows his name. Schindler sits at the center of the room. Through a series of close-ups, we follow his gaze, as he notes the SS insignia on an officer's uniform and assesses the importance of the reserved table across the room. Using Schindler as the axis, the camera pans around the room (10.59). Positioned just over his shoulder, we watch Schindler as he watches the action. He did not come to this restaurant for a meal. He intends to meet the most influential Nazis in the area and establish himself as a man of consequence. At the end of the sequence, the highest-ranking officer asks the maitre d' about this newcomer. He now enthusiastically replies, "Why, that is Oskar Schindler!" (10.60A). Schindler (who entered the restaurant as a nobody) is now well defined: he has become the center of attention. The evening has been a success (10.60B).

Crosscutting is used throughout the film, both to establish a connection and to emphasize separation. Eviction of a Jewish family from their spacious home is immediately followed by images of Schindler surveying the same space, now his new home. He reclines on a large bed and exclaims, "It couldn't be better!" (10.61). We then cut to the evicted family, struggling up the stairs of their new house, which will be shared with many other families. As they sit down in the single room they have been assigned, the wife notes, "It could be worse." Her angry husband replies, " How could it *possibly* be

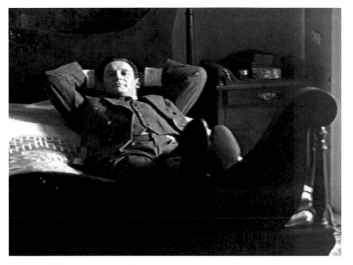

10.61 *Schindler's List.* New home.

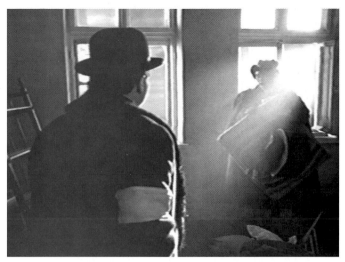

10.62 *Schindler's List.* New home.

worse?" (10.62). Just then, another large family apologetically moves into the cramped space. It is now worse.

The destruction of the Krakow ghetto is a masterpiece of storytelling. Sound is especially important in this sequence, and variations in pacing substantially increase the visual impact. The sequence begins as Nazi commandant Goeth gives his assembled troops a brief history lesson (10.63). As he describes the arrival of the Jews in Poland in the fourteenth century, we cut from the soldiers to scenes of ghetto families quietly eating and preparing for the day ahead, unaware of the terror to follow. We return to Goeth as he concludes his speech, noting that "by this evening, those six centuries are a rumor. They never existed."

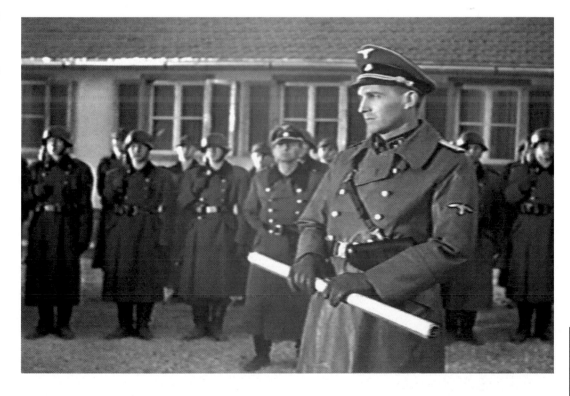

10.63 *Schindler's List.* Commandant Goeth.

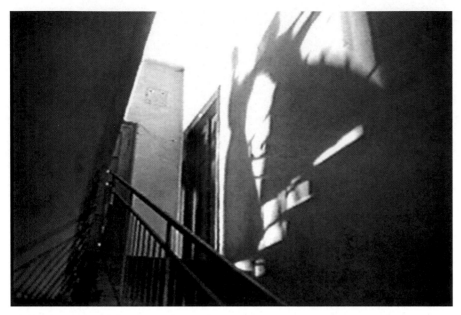

10.64 *Schindler's List.* Staircase.

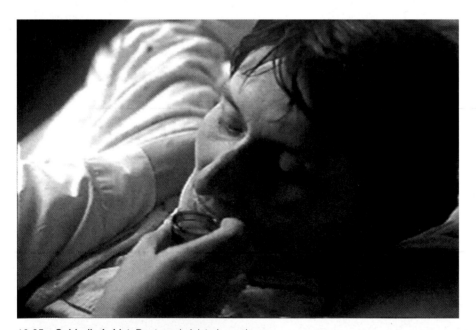

10.65 *Schindler's List.* Doctor administering poison.

An explosion of violence follows. The family at breakfast is now wrapping jewels in bread and eating them, in the hope of retaining something of value when the pogrom ends. Stern, the overworked accountant upon whom Schindler depends, desperately searches his pockets for his identity papers as a soldier screams in his face. The camera is jostled as terrified people are evicted from their apartments. Diagonal staircases and extreme camera angles increase compositional dynamism (10.64).

A contrast between violence and compassion, fast and slow pace, heightens the impact of this sequence. An old woman, walking slowly down a foggy street, is ignored by the soldiers who run past, determined to clear the ghetto. A doctor methodically adds poison to cups of water, then gently administers it to his patients (10.65) rather than leave them for the soldiers to kill. A young Polish boy, assigned to report any survivors, instead saves the life of a woman and her daughter.

We now see a small girl in a red coat walking through the streets (10.66) and observed by Schindler, who surveys the action from a nearby hill. Accompanied by angelic music, she is the symbol of all the innocent deaths on this horrible day. We last see her as she scoots under a bed, seeking a place to hide. We will not see her again until much later in the film when her red coat appears again as the corpses from the ghetto liquidation are gathered to be burned.

Quiet finally descends on the city. The soldiers are now using stethoscopes to listen for survivors who may have hidden in apartment walls. In a

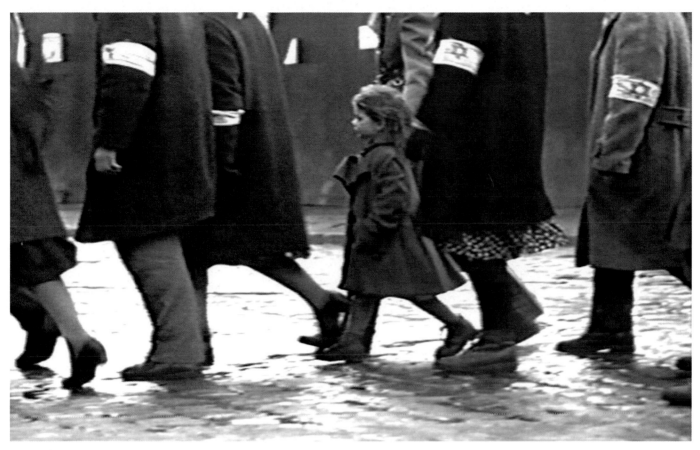

10.66 *Schindler's List.* Girl in a red coat.

final burst of violence, one soldier plays a vigorous Bach toccata while other soldiers explode into action, firing their machine guns into the walls and urging their dogs to attack (10.67).

The calm before the storm makes this sequence even more frightening. It would be impossible to sustain a fast pace throughout the film. Incessant horror would have simply left us numb. The editing and use of contrast has greatly enhanced the power of the ghetto sequence, leaving us with an indelible impression.

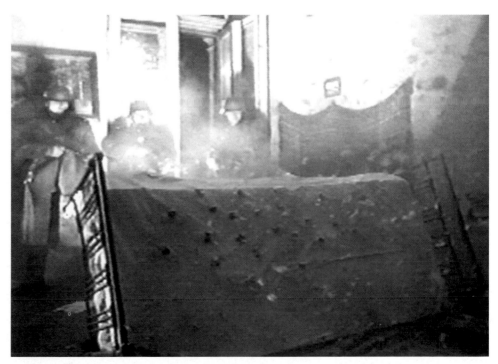

10.67 *Schindler's List.* The soldiers.

Profile:
Sharon Greytak, Filmmaker
Resilient Spirit

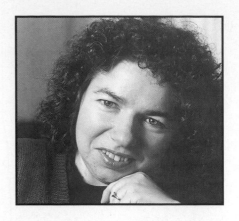

Sharon Greytak is writer, producer, and director of two award-winning features *The Love Lesson* (1996) and *Hearing Voices* (1990), as well as the documentary *Weirded Out and Blown Away* (1985). Her films have been screened theatrically and at numerous festivals and showcases, including the Museum of Modern Art, Walter Reade Theater, Kennedy Center for the Performing Arts, George Eastman House, WNET-13, The Wexner Center, and Films de Femmes in Creteil, France. She won a Silver Award at the Houston International Film Festival and first prize at the Athens International Film Festival. She has recently finished *Losing It,* a feature-length documentary, and is now writing her third fiction screenplay.

MS: You studied painting at CalArts and were always interested in literature. How, then, did you become a filmmaker?

SG: Film seemed to suit my personality. I was beginning to feel that art shown primarily in galleries reached a specific audience, but not the general public where discussion and change should occur. I felt an urgency about the social issues I wanted to address, and the unconventional stories I knew only I could tell. I knew as a filmmaker I could reach a very wide audience.

Furthermore, the process of painting is mainly solitary, while filmmaking is absolutely a collaborative art. There's an energy in film production that doesn't exist anywhere else, an energy toward what the mind's eye sees, toward what the camera will record. I guess I'm able to hold an idea and an image in my mind for a very long time. Communicating my vision and staying on track as the piece becomes more refined is the essence of what drives any artist.

MS: You write the screenplay, hire the crew, produce and direct the film, then market the result. Yet it all seems to start with a story you want to tell. What stories interest you most?

SG: All of my screenplays are original. A film is a visual story—very different than a written story. I write pictures. The script is the blueprint, providing the visual and emotional tone as well as the dialog.

I explore unconventional human relationships in my stories—relationships that are overlooked by the mass media. I am interested in stories that haven't been told. In any film, I am always aware of the facet or angle of a story that is unique. The space between one's public and private identity has always fascinated me. I want to give voice to people whose voices are rarely heard.

MS: You've said that you are good at spotting the nuggets, the most telling images and human interactions. What makes an image or an exchange of dialog compelling?

SG: It's very hard to explain. For me it's a combination of all the senses, plus one or two unnamed senses; maybe instinct. I guess you're looking for the essence of what you're trying to communicate, but never naming it precisely. If you name it directly, it's dead. It comes back to trusting the viewer and leaving space for interpretation. When I'm directing actors and doing several takes, I look for something that shimmers, or wavers in the air around them; where all of us, cast and crew, have created an ephemeral moment aside from the actor's lines or anything tangible. It's something that lingers in the air for a moment. It is resonant, yet unsaid.

MS: Film constantly changes, and if the viewer doesn't "get" it the first time, the story can be lost. How do you determine what to say? What is essential?

SG: In any artform, it is so easy to overstate an idea. When I was in my twenties, I studied with painter David Salle. At that time I was painting and drawing. I showed a series of mixed media works in David's experimental studio class. David cocked his head, stared a long time, then turned and said, "What do you think I am, stupid?" I was stunned. He went on about signs and symbols, the indexical and the iconic, a priori knowledge, and underestimating your audience. He then rattled off a list of books and articles I should be reading.

I made no art for three months. I read. I read aesthetics and politics, semiotics. I skulked around the edges of my classes, listening and watching. It was the turning point in my life as an artist. Exactly the right thing. And I picked up the camera. Super-8 at first. I realized I had been always talking about my abstract drawings in a very narrative way. I wondered what I would do if I had to choose an image in the world. Inspiration had never come from life before. It had always been formal properties of line and color, mark-making, and the gesture. It was from that point that my films and drawings began to have an undertone, something of their own, combined with a respect for the intelligence of my audience.

MS: I am impressed by the immediacy of film. A good film draws me in: I feel that I am right there.
SG: A base in reality is essential: when you have that, anything is possible to write. And, small things can illuminate big ideas. When I screened my short films at a festival in Krakow, Poland, we were invited to visit Auschwitz. Since I have a physical disability, I was not able to follow the tour group to the second level of the barracks. The irony of the situation was comical, and powerful. Had it been 50 years earlier, I wouldn't have lasted a day there. Just by fate the scenario would have been very different.

As the rest of the tour went upstairs, I stayed alone on the ground floor of the barracks. In silence I was able to look at the scratches on the door. Scratches that had been made by human hands. By sitting still, alone, I could touch where so many other lives had been. I could make a more authentic connection through the remnants of a real life, through the energy I did not expect to find.

MS: Tell me about your current film.
SG: *Losing It* is an international film exploring the quality of life for people with disabilities. It's about how people navigate social stereotypes within their culture to carve out a sense of purpose and worth despite physical limitations. I traveled in the U.S., Brazil, Hong Kong, Russia and Italy to interview people about the way they view themselves and the way in which society views them. It's also a story of personal search and human nature with regard to disability.

MS: What advice do you have for my students?
SG: Cultivate a diverse circle of friends and colleagues. Build a career slowly. Making art means a life in the arts. Not a year or two, but a lifetime of observing and questioning in order to create something unique. When I find myself having to do something or go somewhere out of obligation, a thing that at the time seems totally a waste of time, fate often finds a way of adding that experience or person to further my creative work. Most of the time I end up seeing an angle I wouldn't have recognized before. I guess what I'm saying is, stay open enough for life to show you things. Let life take you where you're supposed to go.

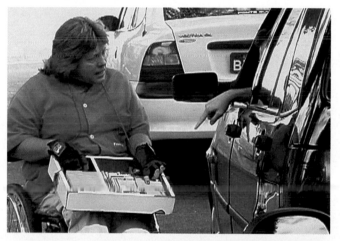

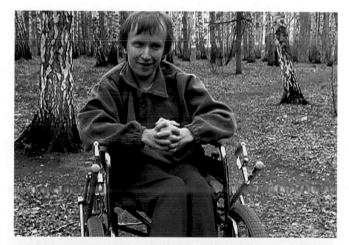

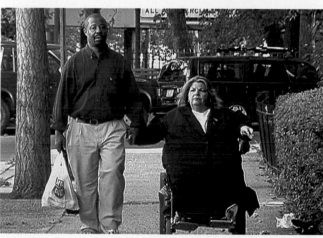

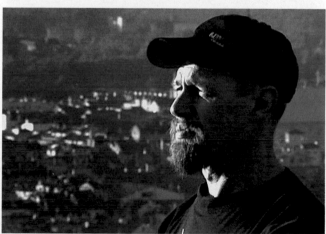

Stills from *Losing It*, documentary film by Sharon Greytak, writer, producer, director, 2000.

Summary

- An understanding of time is an essential aspect of any artwork. Photographers, filmmakers, and performers use time directly; painters, illustrators, ceramicists, and other artists generally use time indirectly.

- The building blocks of film are the frame, the shot, the scene, and the sequence.

- Shots can be related graphically, spatially, temporally, and rhythmically.

- The cut, fade, dissolve, and wipe are the most common transitions in film.

- Comic books use six additonal transitions: action-to-action, subject-to-subject, scene-to-scene, moment-to-moment, non-sequitur, and aspect-to-aspect.

- Duration, tempo, intensity, scope, setting, and chronology are the six major elements of time design.

Keywords

accent
action-to-action
  transition
aspect-to-aspect
  transition
beat
chronology
close-up
crosscut
cut
diegetic
dissolve
duration
editing
fade
fidelity
flashback

frame
graphic relationship
intensity
lap dissolve
long shot
loudness
medium shot
moment-to-moment
  transition
non-sequitur
  transition
pace
pitch
rhythm
rhythmic
  relationship
scene

scene-to-scene
  transition
scope
sequence
setting
shot
spatial context
spatial relationship
subject-to-subject
  transition
take
tempo
temporal
  relationship
timbre
wipe

When you begin your studio work, consider:

1. What is the duration of the actual event you are using for your artwork? What duration is best for the edited version? How does a change in duration affect the meaning or change the emotion in a film?

2. How quickly does time pass in the artwork? Are there any changes in tempo? What happens when time is compressed or expanded? When do these changes occur, and what do they contribute?

3. What is the intensity level of your performance? How are you communicating this intensity to the audience? How will a change in intensity affect the expressive power of the artwork?

4. Is your artwork limited or broad in scope? What is the advantage of each approach?

5. What is the setting for your project? Consider sound and lighting as well as physical structures. What is the effect of a change in setting?

6. In what order do events occur? Will your project benefit from a change in chronology?

David Bordwell and Kristin Thompson, *Film Art: An Introduction*, 5th edition. New York, McGraw-Hill, 1997.

Lincoln F. Johnson, *Film: Space, Time, Light and Sound*. Holt, Rinehart and Winston, Inc. 1974.

Scott McCloud, *Understanding Comics*. New York, HarperPerennial, 1994.

Keith A. Smith, *Structure of the Visual Book*. Fairport, NY: The Sigma Foundation, Inc. 1992.

chapter eleven

Narrative and Non-Narrative

As with any other form of art or design, a film, performance, or installation is designed to communicate ideas, express emotions, record action, and explore vision. Since the verbal and visual information is distributed over many images, ideas and emotions can be expanded when sequential art is used. Just as a poet uses a few words to evoke a complex idea, so artists can communicate a wide range of thoughts and feelings through a single image. On the other hand, the sequential artist can act like a novelist. Through editing and careful organization, a collection of images can be developed into extended narrative and non-narrative structures.

Tell Me a Story

Like the novelist, many sequential artists use collections of images to tell stories. Storytelling is one of the most ancient and effective forms of communication. It can serve four basic purposes.

- *Stories can increase self-awareness.* When we record our own story in an autobiography, we become more conscious of the patterns in our lives and can gain a better understanding of the individual events that break or confirm these patterns.

- *Stories can provide inspiration.* By researching the life of another artist or discussing the past with an elderly relative, we find that our personal problems and conflicts are not unique. Everyone experiences a wide range of emotions, from exhilaration to despair. In reading another person's story, we can learn from his or her solution to a problem.

- *Stories can supply information.* News stories and documentary films provide us with information on current events and analysis of their implications. Art never occurs in a vacuum. Developing an understanding of the world around us can strengthen our ideas.

- *Stories can encourage understanding.* Abstract numbers and dry statistics are rarely as compelling as concrete examples. When we hear the story of a particular refugee in a specific war, the horrible effect of combat on civilians becomes personal. Such stories can help us to understand the emotional meaning of an event.

To increase our understanding even further, we may explore the biggest questions of all, through myths. A **myth** is a traditional story collectively composed by many members of a society. The creation of the world, sources of evil, the power of knowledge, and even the nature of reality may be explained through these grand expressions of the imagination. The *Star Wars* series, most comic books, and many types of performance art are based on myths.

Working with Multiple Images

In all forms of storytelling, multiple images can provide many advantages over an individual image. In Jacques-Louis David's *Oath of the Horatii* (11.1), both the action and the emotion must be expressed within a single frame. To avoid mass slaughter, two warring Roman clans, the Horatii and the Curatii, have each agreed to send three warriors into a fight to the death. This heroic moment of self-sacrifice is demonstrated by the three young Horatii warriors on the left. A tragic complication to this plan is borne by the wives of the warriors, who are huddled together in a triangular shape on the right. They are members of the opposing Curatii clan, and will lose either their brothers or their husbands in the battle. The children in the background are caught in the middle.

Through skillful composition and careful selection of an emotionally charged moment in the narrative, Jacques-Louis David created a masterpiece that caused a sensation when it was first shown in 1786 and continues to be studied today. The use of gesture, composition, and technique in this painting is stunning. Nonetheless, it is difficult to appreciate the painting fully or to understand the story without explanation. With only a single image, David had to rely on his audience for some knowledge of the event shown. Without this information, the audience understands only part of the story.

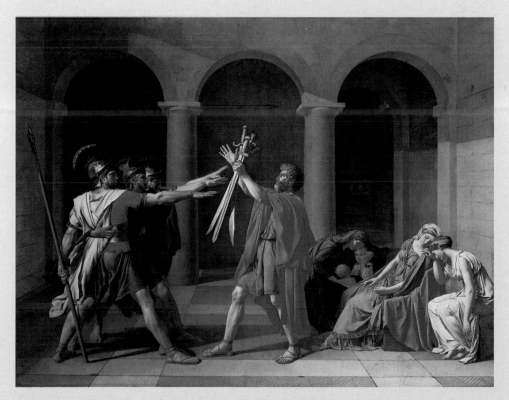

11.1 **Jacques-Louis David, *Oath of the Horatii*, 1784–85.** Oil on canvas, 14 ft × 10 ft 8¼ in. (4.27 × 3.26 m).

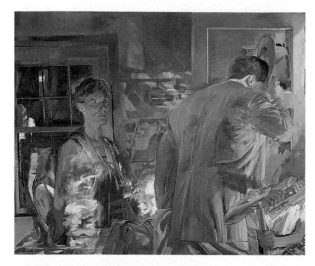

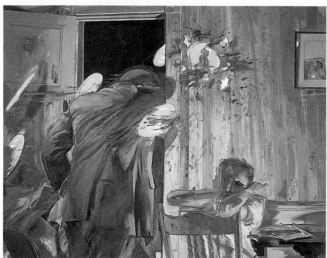

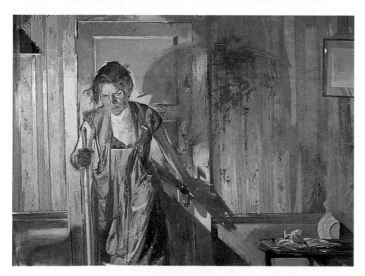

11.2 Jerome Witkin, *Division Street* [A story told in 3 panels], **1984–85.** Oil on canvas, triptych. Top panel, 75⅛ × 63¼ in. (190.9 × 160.7 cm); middle panel, 81⅛ × 63 in. (206.2 × 160 cm); bottom panel, 87⅛ × 63 in. (221.3 × 160 cm). Also see triptych as designed by the artist on page 11-29.

By contrast, in the three paintings which comprise *Division Street* (11.2), Jerome Witkin tells a story sequentially. Like David, he selected the colors, gestures, and actions most appropriate to the narrative and composed each frame with great care. Unlike *Oath of the Horatii,* however, *Division Street* requires little explanation. The argument in the first frame, the man's explosive departure in the second frame, and the angry woman in the third frame tell the story. This multiple-image narrative can speak for itself.

Multiple-Image Structures

In *Structure of the Visual Book,* Keith Smith describes three multiple-image structures commonly used by printmakers, photographers, and book artists.[1]

A **group** is a collection of images that are related by subject matter, composition, or source. In Figure 11.3, images of a pyramid, the letter A, and a pair of praying hands can be grouped compositionally. Each is dominated by a triangular shape. The individual illustrations in Figures 11.4, 11.5, and 11.6 can be grouped by subject. All are part of the *Frog Folio,* a calendar produced by Dellas Graphics to showcase the work of contemporary illustrators. In a group, image order is unimportant.

A **series** links multiple images together sequentially. Each image builds on the previous image and leads to the subsequent image. As a result, events are linked together like boxcars on a train. *Chance Meeting,* by Duane Michals (11.7), is a series of photographs. Like a short film, it tells a simple story using multiple images.

Simple narratives, such as fairy tales and fables, often use serial construction. Indeed, numerical repetition may be an essential part of the story. For example, when Goldilocks enters the house of the three bears, she samples three bowls of porridge.

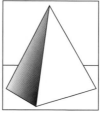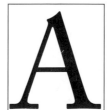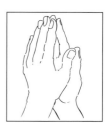

11.3

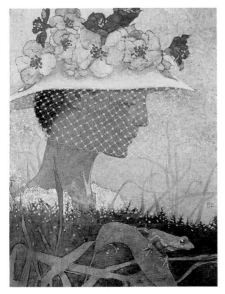

11.4 Bart Forbes, _Landmark_, 1999. Oil on canvas, 14 × 19 in. (35.6 × 48.3 cm).

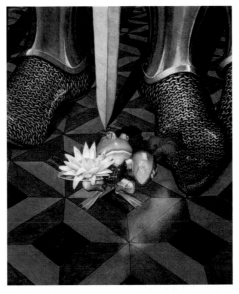

11.5 Charles Santore, cover of _William the Curious, Knight of the Water Lilies_, 1997. Watercolor, front cover 9 × 12 in. (22.8 × 30.5 cm).

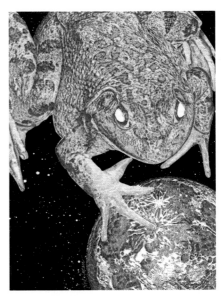

11.6 Murray Tinkelman, _The Frog Jumps over the Moon_. Colored ink crosshatch, 9 × 12 in. (22.9 × 30.5 cm).

One is too hot, the second is too cold, the third is just right. She tries sitting on the three chairs, with a similar result. Finally, when she decides to take a nap, she finds the first bed too hard, the second too soft, and the third just right. As a story for children, Goldilocks and other such tales are simple and straightforward. Flashbacks, crosscutting, or other narrative complexities are avoided.

A **sequence** is the multiple-image structure used by most popular filmmakers and comic book artists. In a sequence, multiple images are organized by _cause and effect_. In a simple sequence, action number two is caused by action number one. In a complex sequence, there may be a considerable delay between the cause and the effect. Actions five, six, and seven may all be caused by

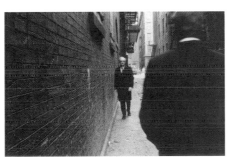
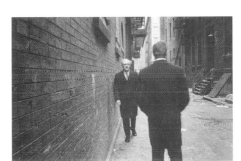
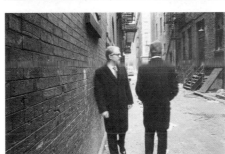
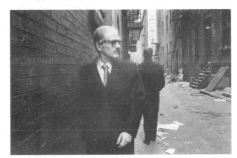
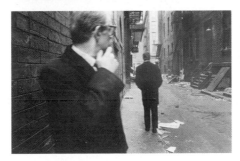
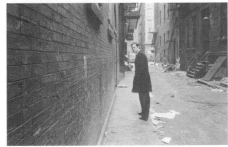

11.7 Duane Michals, _Chance Meeting_, 1969. 6 prints, each 4⅞ × 3¼ in.(12.4 × 8.3 cm).

action number one. Rather than film a simple line of boxcars in a train, we may now move among the cars, showing the conductor napping, two passengers playing cards, the engineer steering, and another passenger reading. These human actions may be combined with images of the landscape through which the train is traveling, the setting sun, or even images of the construction of the original train track. To understand a sequence, viewers may have to mentally connect many disparate fragments of information.

From Scene to Screenplay

With a run time of an hour or more, a film or television show is constructed from many sequences, each building the story using cause and effect. Let's analyze one example.

Jeremy and Angela are spending their honeymoon on the Orient Express. On the third morning of the trip, they awake to the sound of drunken singing in the adjoining cabin. Angela wants to confront the revelers, while Jeremy cautions her against getting involved. They begin to argue. Angela accuses Jeremy of indifference, while Jeremy says Angela is overreacting. Now focused on their own quarrel, they ignore the singers and instead continue their argument over breakfast in the dining car. Finally, Angela threatens to leave. Jeremy ridicules her threat, saying that she isn't capable of traveling alone in a foreign country. Angela punches Jeremy in the nose. Jeremy then shoves his grapefruit into her face. Their fight disrupts the dining car. At the next stop, the conductor throws both of them off the train. Sitting in a deserted train station they both begin to laugh at their ridiculous response to the drunken singers.

As described in *Story* by Robert McKee, the **beat** is the most basic element in a story.[2] A beat is an exchange of behavior, based on action and reaction. There are five beats in this story.

1. Angela responds to the singers: "I am not going to listen to those drunken louts for one more minute!" Then, Jeremy responds to Angela: "Oh, take it easy. Let's get some breakfast; I bet they will be asleep when we return."

2. As they walk to the dining car, Angela says to Jeremy: "You really don't care, do you? If some-

one punched you in the nose, you would just walk away." Jeremy responds to Angela: "Don't be such a hothead. There is no reason to get angry about every little thing."

3. Over breakfast, Angela retorts : "If you can't take the heat, get out of the kitchen! I suggest we split up at the next station." Jeremy responds: "Are you kidding? You wouldn't last a day on your own."

4. Angela punches Jeremy, who shoves his grapefruit into her face.

5. The conductor reacts by throwing both of them off the train. Sitting on their suitcases in the empty station, they finally respond to the situation by laughing.

Beats build **scenes.** Scenes generally occur in a single space in continuous time. There are four scenes in this story: the cabin, the corridor, the dining car, and the deserted train station. Scenes build sequences. In filmmaking, a sequence is made from a series of scenes, which generally increase in emotional impact. In this story, a minor disagreement escalates into a major battle. Each action results in a stronger reaction, culminating in the couple's ejection from the train. Sequences build **acts.** An act is an even longer sequential structure. The **screenplay,** which is the written blueprint for the film, is constructed from multiple acts.

Establishing Boundaries

When just starting college, few of us have the time, money, or expertise necessary to write a screenplay or direct a film. However, we can use the same storytelling principles to develop shorter visual stories. By carefully choosing the right aspect of an event or idea, we can develop effective stories, regardless of the medium.

Conceptual Boundaries

It is wise to begin by defining the conceptual breadth of an idea. An idea that is overly ambitious or is ill-defined will be impossible to communicate well.

You already have extensive experience with conceptual framing. Just consider the questions you face when planning a 10-page art history paper.

- *What is the topic?* What historical period interests you most? In a course devoted to Western art from the Renaissance to Impressionism, you have many excellent choices and a dazzling array of images. Choosing a topic that is manageable and interesting is essential.

- *How should the topic be approached?* If the paper is on Impressionism, you could:
  - Analyze the work of a single artist, such as Cassatt or Degas.
  - Compare and contrast paintings by Cassatt and Degas.
  - Explore the impact of photography on Impressionist painters.

By focusing on one aspect of a complex topic, you can develop an effective research strategy and complete the paper on time.

Defining conceptual boundaries is equally important in sequential art. Just as Impressionism is too big a topic to explore thoroughly in a 10-page paper, so reality is too big to record fully in a 10-minute video. The following questions can help you define the conceptual frame of an artwork.

- *What to see?* Start with an interesting and easily accessible site. Explore several of the buildings on campus, then select one and begin your research. Find out the history of the building, look for distinctive architectural details, and find out what happens each day in the building.

- *When to see it?* Each time of day is distinctive, both visually and emotionally. How does the building look at sunset? What is its appearance at midnight? Select the moments in time that are charged with meaning; then watch closely.

- *And then, what happens?* To answer this question, you must become a storyteller.

Developing a Story

In 1908, the White Star Line began construction of three identical Atlantic ocean liners. The Olympic *was launched in 1910; the* Titanic *was launched in 1911; the* Gigantic *was never completed. The* Titanic *struck an iceberg during her maiden voyage and sank on April 15, 1912. She had lifeboat capacity for 1,178 people; there were 2,201 on board. The* Californian, *less than 10 miles away, did not respond to her distress signals. The* Carpathia, *58 miles away, sped to the scene. Arriving four hours later,* Carpathia *rescued 711 people from the freezing lifeboats. The* Olympic, Titanic's *sister ship, provided reliable service until she was scrapped in 1937.*

These are the basic facts. No narrative, however, is limited to facts. Even a newspaper reporter must make choices about the organization of events and determine the most important aspects of a story. Fiction offers even more options. Using a familiar journalistic device, let's list the most basic questions.

- *Whose story is it?* That of ship designer Thomas Andrews, who perished? Of J. Bruce Ismay, director of the White Star Line, who survived? Of the captain of the *Carpathia*, who became a hero? Of the captain of the *Californian*, who was reviled?

- *When should the story begin and end?* We know that the iceberg was spotted at 11:40 P. M. and that the collision occurred soon after. A storyteller, however, can start at any point in time. How does the story change when we begin with initial planning of the "unsinkable" ship? What happens when we start the story just as a survivor comes to consciousness after being rescued?

- *Where does the story occur?* Each cabin, deck, and lifeboat contains its own specific characters and its own particular story.

- *Why did the tragedy occur?* Was the captain pressured to complete the crossing in record time, which caused him to increase the ship's speed, despite the danger? Was faulty construction the cause?

- *What is the story really about?* Courage? Arrogance? Injustice? Sixty-two percent of the

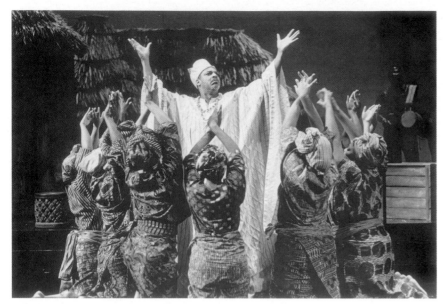

11.8 Scene from *Death and the King's Horseman*, 1999.
Performed by Syracuse Stage.

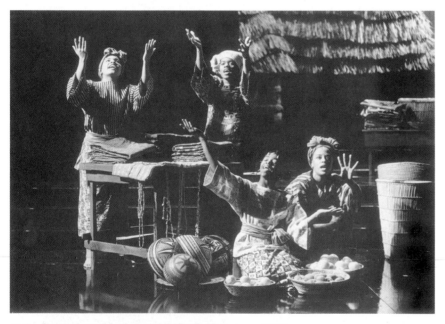

11.9 Scene from *Death and the King's Horseman*, 1999.
Performed by Syracuse Stage.

325 first-class passengers survived, while only 25 percent of the 706 third-class passengers survived. While the sinking itself is the most obvious event, this tale contains many stories.

Knowing where to start the story is essential. If the story is devoted to the construction of the ship and the arrival of the passengers, the most dramatic events (the sinking itself, the rescue, and the inquiry into the cause) will be lost.

Emotional Boundaries

In theater and performance art, communication often depends on a connection between the imaginary world on stage and the tangible world of the audience. This was demonstrated beautifully in Wole Soyinka's *Death and the King's Horseman,* performed by Syracuse Stage in 1999. The play explores a range of cultural conflicts between the native Yoruba population of Africa and a group of British colonizers. The king has died, and the king's horseman, a powerful leader in his own right (11.8), must commit suicide, so that he can guide the king in the world beyond life. Attempts by the British government to stop this essential ritual are disruptive and tragic.

To feel the full impact of the event, the audience must emotionally connect to the Yoruba world, which revolves around a village market. As we enter the theater, a dramatically lit stage piled with fruit, colorful baskets, and bolts of fabric invites us into this world. One by one, seven female actors enter, assume the poses of various vendors, then freeze. The play begins with the sound of drumming coming from behind the audience. As the women become animated and the market comes to life (11.9), we are enveloped in the Yoruba world. Additional actors sing and dance down the aisles, finally joining the company on stage.

Establishing an emotional connection between the image and the audience is even more important in filmmaking. In a film, the image is created by a flickering beam of light rather than by a live actor. When we see a play, the entire stage is visible and each member of the audience frames the scene a bit differently. In a film, the frame is defined by the director. By using a close-up, the director can place the actor directly in front of us. A distance shot pushes the actor away, reducing the emotional connection. Realizing the importance of framing, the best directors select shots that are especially compelling, both emotionally and visually.

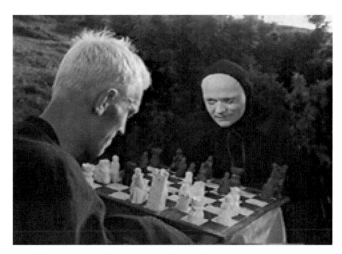

11.10 *The Seventh Seal.* Chess game with Death.

Boundaries in *The Seventh Seal*

Throughout *The Seventh Seal*, Swedish film director Ingmar Bergman used framing to create a strong emotional connection between actors and audience. A medieval knight tries to win his life in a chess game with Death (11.10), while his cynical squire tries to find some meaning in a world beset by the Black Plague. Movement from background to foreground is used repeatedly, and close-up shots relentlessly push the actors into our emotional space. Framing creates three types of relationships in this film.

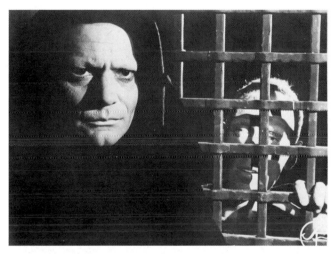

11.11 *The Seventh Seal.* The knight's confession.

- *Actor to actor.* In the middle of the film, the knight visits a confessional, little realizing that the priest to whom he confides his fears is actually Death, his opponent in the game (11.11). Death is first seen in the background, then moves behind the knight, then finally winds up in the foreground, with his true identity revealed. Despite the grill separating them, Death thus circles around his opponent, pouncing when the knight unwittingly reveals the strategy behind his game.

- *Actor to audience.* A naive young actor is later forced to dance on a burning table in a tavern. We see his feet surrounded by flames, then his head as he becomes more and more terrified and exhausted (11.12). Close-ups place us on

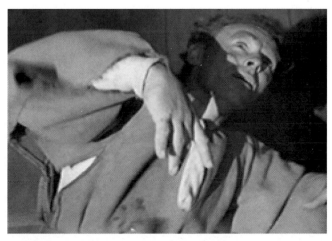

11.12 *The Seventh Seal.* Young actor dancing.

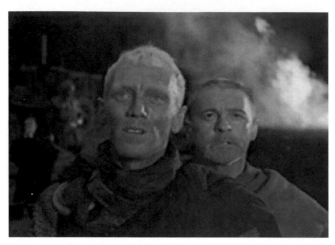

11.13 *The Seventh Seal.* The knight and his squire watching the fire.

the table, right next to the tormented man. We may not *become* this character, but through compositional proximity, we stand next to him as he dances.

- *Actor speaking to audience.* Toward the end of the film, an innocent young girl is tied to a tree and burned as a witch. The knight and his squire watch in horror and pity (11.13), speculating on the presence or absence of any deity at this awful event. These questions are addressed even more directly as the film ends. Facing the camera, all the major characters confront Death and describe what they have learned. Through skillful framing, Bergman transformed a form of popular entertainment into a philosophical discussion.

Style

Just as any setting offers a wide range of compositional possibilities, so any story can be told in many ways. Three cinematic interpretations of William Shakespeare's *Romeo and Juliet* provide a striking example of the importance of style. Zeffirelli's *Romeo and Juliet* (11.14) is closest to the written play in style and interpretation. There is some editing of the original text, but the lines spoken were written by Shakespeare. While the musical score is a distinctly modern interpretation of Renaissance music, the beautiful settings, opulent costumes, and graceful dancing that fill the screen are based on historical models.

West Side Story (11.15) offers a very different interpretation of the story of Romeo and Juliet. Set in contemporary New York City, this film uses warfare between rival gangs to create the tragedy, rather than the familiar conflict between the Capulets and the Montagues. While the story is based on Shakespeare's play, the dialog is distinctly American. The spirit and emotion of the original were retained, but the dialog, setting, and specific actions

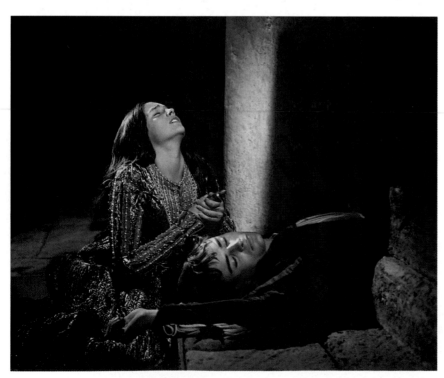

11.14 Franco Zeffirelli, *Romeo and Juliet,* 1968. Romeo and Juliet.

are contemporary. Even the characters have new names, as Romeo becomes Tony, the leader of the Polish Jets, and Juliet becomes Maria, affiliated with the Puerto Rican Sharks.

An unusual combination of these two sensibilities occurs in *William Shakespeare's Romeo and Juliet* (11.16). Now set in contemporary California as a struggle between the skinhead Montagues and the leather-clad Capulets, the film begins with a prologue delivered from a television screen by a newswoman. The words of Shakespeare are often delivered as a scream, and familiar characters are transformed in amazing ways. For example, when we first meet Mercutio, he is wearing high heels, a silver-sequined miniskirt with a halter top, and a white wig. The words of Shakespeare have been retained, but the setting, characters, and action have been shifted to create a bizarre contemporary version of a sixteenth-century play.

Degrees of Definition

Every story is constructed using a chain of events. In traditional narrative, the first event causes the second, which results in the third, and so on until the conclusion is reached. Like a crossword puzzle, the storyteller presents us with various clues, which we construct into meaning.

When the relationship between cause and effect is clear, the puzzle is easy to solve. When there is an extended delay between cause and effect, or when relationships among events seem arbitrary, the solution becomes much more elusive.

Un Chien Andalou (An Andalusian Dog), by Salvador Dali and Luis Bunuel, presents such a puzzle. A quarrel between two lovers is presented through a bizarre sequence of illogical events. As the film opens, a man smoking a cigarette calmly sharpens a straight razor. A sliver of cloud passes across the full moon. The man grasps a woman's face (11.17) and slits her left eye with the razor. He then bicycles down the street wearing a nun's uniform. The uninjured woman welcomes him to her apartment. Ants crawl out from a hole in his hand. A severed hand appears on the street below. A crowd gathers. A policeman gives the severed hand to a woman, who places it in a box. The crowd disperses.

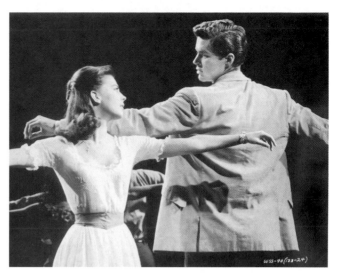

11.15 *West Side Story*, 1961. Tony and Maria.

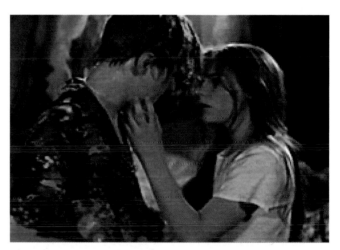

11.16 *William Shakespeare's Romeo and Juliet*, 1996.

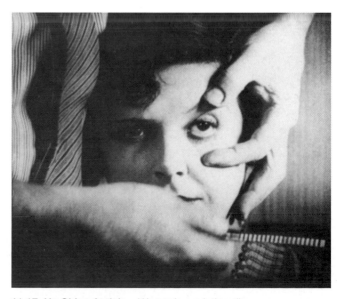

11.17 *Un Chien Andalou.* Woman's eye being slit.

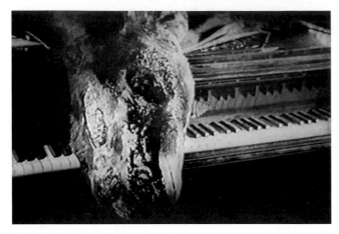

11.18 *Un Chien Andalou.* Mule's head on piano.

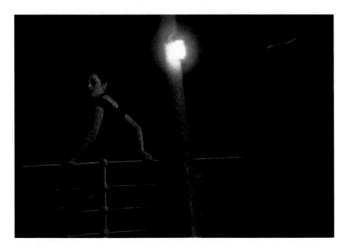

11.19 *Titanic.* Young Rose preparing to jump.

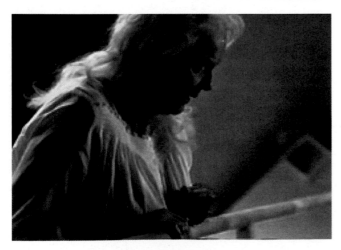

11.20 *Titanic.* Elderly Rose at ship's railing.

The woman, still standing in the street, is then hit by a car. As the film continues, the man harnesses himself to a piano filled with slaughtered mules (11.18), shoots a double image of himself, and strolls along a beach with the woman, collecting, then discarding, debris. While these two characters dominate the story, and hands appear repeatedly, the film as a whole is as mysterious and disturbing as a surrealist painting.

In contrast, a series of very clear cause-and-effect relationships fuels the lovers' quarrel in James Cameron's *Titanic.* The film begins with a prologue showing a contemporary expedition to salvage a precious diamond from the sunken wreck. Rose, an elderly woman who survived the disaster, then describes the voyage she remembers. Through her memories, we meet the primary characters. Young Rose is a pampered society woman betrothed to the rich and arrogant Cal. Jack is an independent but impoverished artist who has won his passage back to America in a poker game.

Conflicts between Cal and Rose are apparent from the start. Rose is intelligent and strong-willed, with a love of art and ideas. Cal is arrogant and domineering; he demands obedience. Rose feels trapped, and in despair, she climbs over a railing on the ship and prepares to jump (11.19). Jack saves her. The resulting romance develops through a sequence of cause-and-effect events, and reaches a climax with a battle between Cal and the lovers on the sinking ship. Rose survives, and in a classic **denouement,** or summation, the film ends as the elderly Rose again climbs a ship's railing and flings the diamond back into the sea (11.20). Beautifully filmed and carefully edited, the three-hour film easily sustains our interest. In this case, the traditional narrative structure served the director's purpose. There is no ambiguity: the actions and emotions of all of the characters are shown clearly.

Each film has its own purpose and its own power. *Un Chien Andalou* is suggestive, rather than descriptive, and mystery is an essential part of its meaning. *Titanic* gains meaning and emotion from the escalating conflict between Cal and Rose. In each case, the director made the right choice for the film content.

Story and Style in *Citizen Kane*

Basic Construction

The Opening Sequence

Because most narratives are so dependent on **causality,** or the interplay between cause and effect, the first image shown substantially affects each subsequent action. Furthermore, in a culture saturated by images, a powerful opening may determine whether the viewer even stays with the story long enough to become involved. As a result, many directors use the opening sequence to create a sense of anticipation that will pull the viewer into the story.

Citizen Kane, widely hailed as one of the finest films ever made, actually uses three opening sequences to set the story in motion. Each builds on the previous sequence, creating a powerful domino effect. From the very beginning, we are swept into a complex story.

In the first opening, we see the dim silhouette of a castle behind a gate dominated by a "No Trespassing" sign. Through a series of dissolves, we move in closer (11.21), accompanied by slow, ominous music. As the music reaches a climax, a light in a window blinks off. The camera zooms in on a glass globe containing a tiny cabin in a snowy landscape. In an extreme close-up, we now see a man's lips move (11.22), as he whispers the word "rosebud." The globe falls to the floor and scatters. A nurse enters the distorted room, and after taking his pulse, pulls a sheet over the face of the man. Charles Foster Kane is dead.

The second opening is dramatically different, in style, narration, and pacing. It is a newsreel, showing the major events in Kane's life (11.23). All the basic information about the man is presented through the narrator's brisk voice-over: Kane's fortune

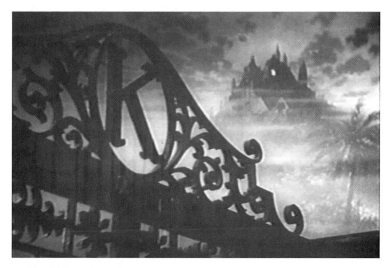

11.21 *Citizen Kane.* Castle gate.

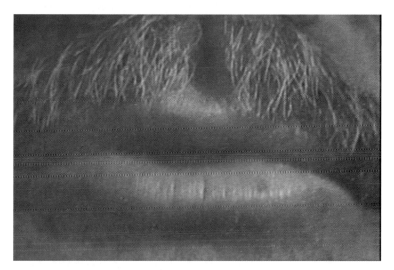

11.22 *Citizen Kane.* Kane's lips.

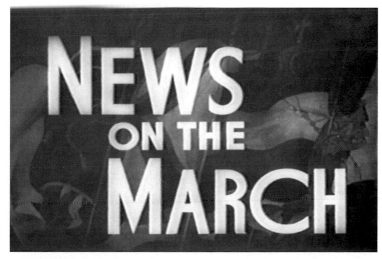

11.23 *Citizen Kane.* Newsreel.

came from a Colorado gold mine, he was a powerful newspaper editor, he had an affair with a shopgirl, he failed in his attempt to be elected governor. This sequence presents the facts of his life, but misses the meaning. A reporter named Thompson is sent to solve the mystery, to determine who, or what, was "rosebud."

We get closer to Kane in the third opening. Thompson begins his search at the Thatcher library, a forbidding place of echoing rooms and silent sentries. Walter Thatcher was both Kane's guardian and his nemesis. As Thompson reads Thatcher's journal, the words dissolve into a snowy scene in Colorado. When the scene ends, young Charlie is taken from his parents and his impoverished life in the wilderness to begin his new life in Chicago. Each of the openings tells us more about Kane and each expands the sense of anticipation.

A Personal Perspective

Different characters offer different perspectives on the same event. Harper Lee's novel, *To Kill a Mockingbird,* is narrated by "Scout," a six-year-old girl. As a child, she interprets events in a particular way. When her father, the lawyer Atticus Finch, is confronted by a lynch mob at the jail holding an accused rapist, Scout defuses the tense situation by asking one of the mob leaders about his young son, who is her playmate. The man finds he cannot attack the father of an innocent child. Scout's perspective is essential: no adult would ask such a question. In the climax of the story, Scout is pursued though the woods by a man who seeks revenge for Finch's defense of the accused rapist. Only Scout could be in such a situation, especially in her costume as a ham, which she had worn during a school play. Without her innocent voice and unique perspective, the novel would lose its power.

Four different characters provide the narrative perspective in *Citizen Kane*. Our only direct contact with Kane is in the opening sequence, as he dies. All the remaining information on him comes from the memories of others—his guardian, Thatcher; his ex-wife, Susan; his manager, Bernstein; and Leland, once his best friend. Each provides a unique perspective.

Developing Characters

Characters play a variety of roles within a narrative. As an egocentric species, we are immediately drawn to images of humans and fascinated by the choices a complex character makes. Just as we seek to understand the actions of our friends, so we seek explanations for the actions we see on a film screen.

The most memorable characters offer a combination of vulnerability and strength. We admire a character for her strengths and may wish to emulate her fortitude. However, vulnerability makes the character human and therefore accessible. Without the paralyzing power of kryptonite, Superman would win every battle. With the outcome assured, there could be no conflict, and thus, no story.

Inner conflict or conflicts between characters usually generate the cause-and-effect relationships on which a narrative is built. *Citizen Kane* relies on both types of conflict. The pivotal mystery, which is set in motion by Kane's death, is reinforced when Thompson is given his assignment to "find rosebud: dead or alive." Who was Kane, and why was "rosebud" so important to him? As the story unfolds, we are offered a wide variety of opinions.

1. In "News on the March," Kane is called a communist by Thatcher, a fascist by a man in a labor rally, and finally is described as "an American" by Kane himself.

2. The Thatcher diaries, read by Thompson and shown in close-ups on the screen, include a confrontation between the newspaperman and the banker. Thatcher is appalled by Kane's support for the working class, and points out that as a capitalist, Kane has much to lose if reforms occur. Here, Kane defines himself more emphatically: "You don't realize that you're talking to two people. As Charles Foster Kane, who has two thousand, six hundred and thirty-one shares of Metropolitan Transfer, I sympathize with you. Charles Foster Kane is a dangerous scoundrel; his paper should be run out of town. . . . On the other hand, I am the publisher of the *Inquirer.* As such, it is my duty

to see that decent hardworking people are not robbed blind by a bunch of money-mad pirates." Kane clearly realizes that his motivations are contradictory. Welles uses a series of increasing close-ups to demonstrate the increasing tension between Kane and Thatcher (11.24–11.26).

3. Thompson next visits Bernstein, Kane's business manager. His memories reveal two critical aspects of Kane's character. First, with the publication of his first edition of the *Inquirer,* Kane inserts a "Declaration of Principles" pledging honest reporting and support for the working man. For Bernstein, Kane was a man of principles. This is reinforced by a second story, in which Bernstein describes Kane completing a scathingly honest review of his wife's dreadful singing.

4. This review had been started by Leland, once Kane's best friend. He offers quite a different assessment of the man. Kane, he says, "wasn't a brutal man—he just did brutal things." Kane "never had a conviction, besides himself." Kane "never actually gave you anything—he just left you a tip." At the end of the interview, Leland offers a more compassionate assessment: "He did everything for love. All he ever wanted was love. He just didn't have any to give."

5. Two final interviews complete our picture of Kane. His former wife, Susan Alexander, focuses on Kane's attempt to transform her into an opera singer. Susan is initially excited by this prospect, but is soon overwhelmed by the gap between her modest ability and the demands of the profession. It is only after she attempts suicide that Kane allows her singing lessons to end. Raymond, the butler, offers a final

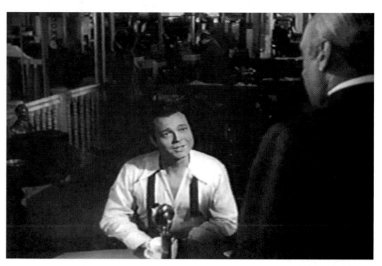

11.24 *Citizen Kane.* Kane and Thatcher.

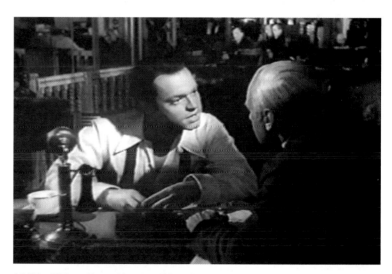

11.25 *Citizen Kane.* Kane and Thatcher.

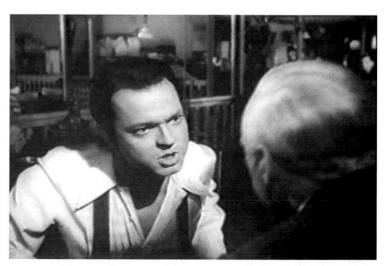

11.26 *Citizen Kane.* Kane and Thatcher.

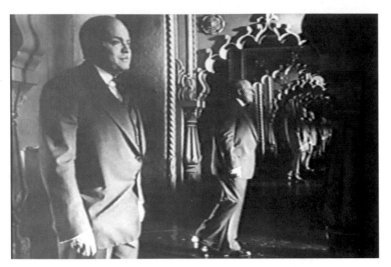

11.27　*Citizen Kane.* Mirror.

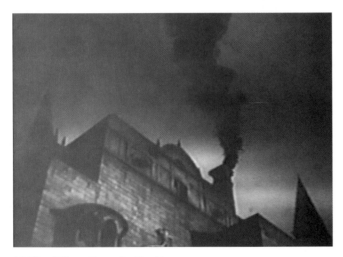

11.28　*Citizen Kane.* Castle chimney.

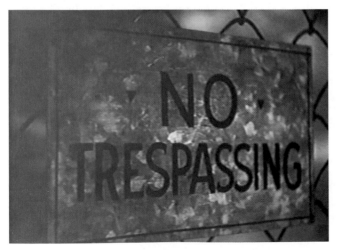

11.29　*Citizen Kane.* "No trespassing."

memory. When Susan walks out on him, the elderly Kane awkwardly lunges around her bedroom, ferociously destroying mirrors and hurling books to the floor. He stops only when he picks up the snow globe seen at the beginning of the film, and for a second time in the film, he utters the word "rosebud." He then departs, endlessly mirroring himself as he walks through his monolithic castle. (11.27)

While the mystery is revealed to the audience at the end of the film, Thompson never does learn the meaning of "rosebud." Nonetheless, the memories of Kane's associates have deepened his understanding of a complex and contradictory character and provided us with a remarkable film.

The Closing Sequence

Especially with a mystery story, the closing sequence is as important as the opening sequence. A powerful closing can reveal an elusive truth, resolve outstanding conflicts, pose a question, or hammer home an important point.

In *Citizen Kane,* three closing sequences mirror the film's beginning. In the first, Thompson summarizes his search for Kane. In the second, the true identity of "rosebud" is revealed to the viewer. The third ending is a reprise of the opening shot. The mysterious outline of Kane's castle is shown, now with smoke billowing from the chimney (11.28). This change is significant. To clear out the castle, workmen are burning most of Kane's possessions, including Rosebud. The camera slowly tilts downward, resting once more on the "No Trespassing" sign (11.29). After two hours of film, the mystery is only partially resolved: we can never fully enter another person's life.

Visualizing *Citizen Kane*

No matter how inventive the narrative, without effective visualization any form of art or design is sure to fail. This is especially true of a complex character study such as *Citizen Kane*. There is none of the action of a film like *Star Wars* and the basic plot can be summarized as "a powerful newspaper

editor dies; a reporter seeks to write a comprehensive obituary." If the film had been shot in a
conventional manner, there would be no reason for us to study it now.

The visualization of *Citizen Kane*, however,
is one of its most spectacular assets. Manipulation of time, complexity of composition, use
of setting, and inventive use of sound distinguish the film. Three compositional aspects
are especially prominent.

Composing the Shot

One of the innovations in *Citizen Kane* is its
extreme depth of field. **Depth of field** refers to
the range of spatial focus within an image. In a
photograph with limited depth of field, the
foreground is sharply focused while the background is blurred. In a photograph with great
depth of field, foreground, middle ground, and
background all remain focused.

Cinematographer Gregg Toland used a special lens to retain a remarkable level of focus
throughout *Citizen Kane*. Director Orson Welles
then used this effect to compose images combining action in the background with action in
the foreground.

The separation of young Charlie from his
parents provides an early example. Filmed
inside the cabin, his mother and Thatcher dominate the foreground while his father restlessly
prowls around in the middle ground (11.30).
Charlie, who is playing outside in the snow, is
framed by a window in the background.
Compositionally and emotionally, he is the center of attention, yet removed from the action and
powerless to act. Despite Charlie's cheerful cries of
"The Union forever!" as he plays, his mother is
determined to separate Charlie from his father.

A similar composition is used during a staff
party at the *Inquirer*. Bernstein, his manager, and
Leland, his best friend, sit in the foreground, discussing Charlie's independence and incorruptibil-
ity. Kane, dancing with a group of showgirls, is
framed by a mirror in the background (11.31). How
noble is he, really? In this scene, he comes across as
the sinner Leland fears rather than the saint that
Bernstein sees.

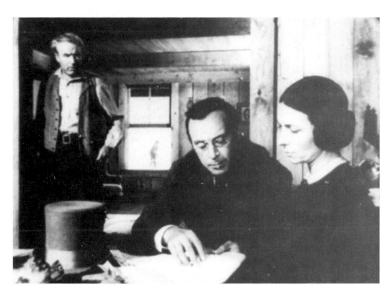

11.30 *Citizen Kane.* Thatcher and Kane's parents.

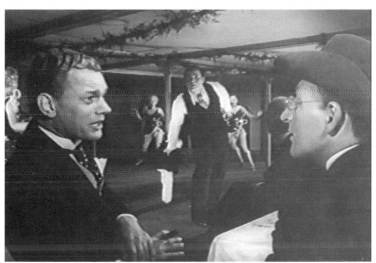

11.31 *Citizen Kane.* Kane dancing.

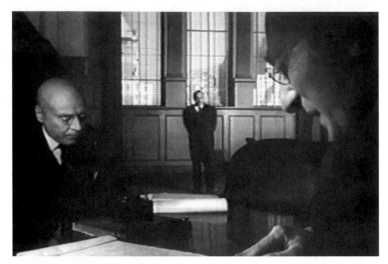

11.32 *Citizen Kane.* Bernstein, Kane, and Thatcher.

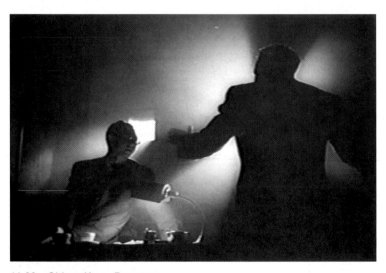

11.33 *Citizen Kane.* Reporters.

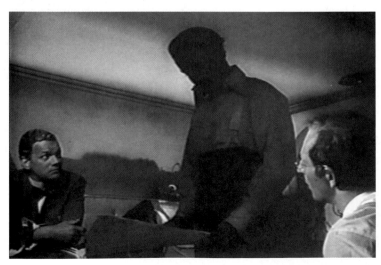

11.34 *Citizen Kane.* "Declaration of Principles."

The final use of this compositional structure occurs later in his life, as Bernstein and Thatcher sign a contract stripping Kane of direct control over his newspapers. Despite his central position within the frame, Kane is powerless and distant once again, as his future is decided by others (11.32). Each of these compositions strongly supports the specific event shown. Repetition of a similar composition in these recurrent situations creates a powerful pattern. Kane, the great newspaper tycoon, has never had real power over the most important events in his life.

Staging the Shot

Unusual camera angles appear throughout the film. In a break with theatrical and cinematic convention, Welles had the ceilings constructed for all the interior sets. Since ceilings are rarely shown and cost more to build, set designers usually leave them out. Welles, however, used the ceilings very deliberately. By placing the camera on the floor and shooting upward, he gave Kane great stature, while trapping him under the low ceilings. Kane may be the richest man in America, but he is still confined by his environment. As with the use of framing, composition and conception mesh perfectly.

The lighting in the film is also distinctive. At the end of the "News on the March" segment, when Thompson and the other reporters discuss the "rosebud" mystery, they are silhouetted by the glare of the film-projector light (11.33). They are visually and conceptually "in the dark" as they try to understand Kane's actions.

This unusual lighting continues as Ralston, the boss, further describes the lack of emotional depth in the newsreel and assigns the "rosebud" hunt to Thompson. His abdomen, rather than his face is lit during this monologue: it is his "gut" feeling that the story is incomplete.

Most important, Kane himself is shown in silhouette as he reads his lofty

"Declaration of Principles" to Bernstein and Leland after his first day at the *Inquirer* (11.34). His head is completely in the dark. Later in the film, we learn that Kane is willing to compromise his principles for personal gain; looking back at the earlier shot, we begin to wonder just how solid were his beliefs. The lighting used casts doubt on Kane's declaration from the beginning.

Uses of Sound in *Citizen Kane*

Having established his reputation through such radio programs as "The War of the Worlds," Welles was especially aware of the power of sound. In *Citizen Kane*, sound is used to connect shots, punctuate dialog, and express emotion. Every sound is deliberate. Threatening music accompanies the opening shots of Xanadu, Kane's castle, while lively, brassy music plays during the exuberant early days at the *Inquirer*. Sound accentuates space, especially during Thompson's visit to the cavernous Thatcher library and during the remote conversations between the elderly Kane and his wife Susan, who is bored by the vast emptiness of Xanadu (11.35).

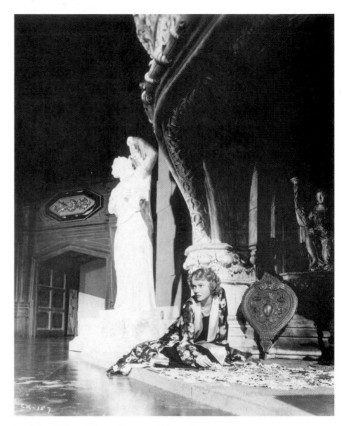

11.35 *Citizen Kane.* Susan at Xanadu.

Sound consistently expands the film's content. At the height of his popularity, Kane falls in love with Susan, a struggling singer and music store clerk. In a visit to her apartment, he persuades her to sing for him and applauds enthusiastically at the end of her timid performance. This applause is carried over to the next shot, showing a small audience gathered outside a political rally. The applause continues further, into a vast hall packed with supporters of a Kane campaign (11.36). However, Kane's affair with Susan will soon lead to his defeat at the polls. The recurrent applause accentuates the close connection between Kane's romance and his political career.

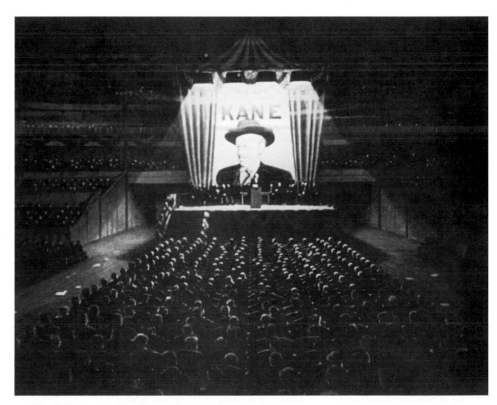

11.36 *Citizen Kane.* Kane campaign.

Editing and Emotion

The editing of Citizen Kane is equally complex. This film is told almost entirely through flashbacks. Welles had to convey emotional content, maintain momentum, and keep the various stories straight. The transitions between shots and the manipulation of time are especially notable.

Transitions

Four common types of transitions occur within the first 10 minutes of the film. The film opens with a close-up of a "No Trespassing" sign on the fence at Xanadu. The camera slowly tilts upward to reveal Kane's castle. Dissolves are used for the opening sequence showing the darkened silhouette of Xanadu. It is a foggy night, and mist rises from the silent ponds surrounding the castle. Nothing is certain, but based on the clues, we anticipate the worst.

As the music reaches a crescendo, a light in the tower blinks off. The screen again dissolves, now into an image of falling snow. The camera zooms in on the globe and in an extreme close-up, we hear and see Kane say "rosebud." The globe shatters and Kane dies.

After the slow, dreamlike exploration of the Kane estate, an abrupt cut to the "News on the March" obituary is especially jarring. It, too, opens with dissolves of Xanadu, now in daylight. Wipes are used while the range of Kane possessions is enumerated: "the beasts of the field, the birds of the air, the monsters of the deep—the largest private zoo since Noah's Ark." Each of these transitions is inextricably woven into the content of the film.

Time Compression

Seventy years of a man's life are shown in this film, and some of the events are shown repeatedly. Time compression is repeatedly used to move the narrative forward. One example occurs early in the film. Thatcher wishes Kane a "Merry Christmas" as he gives a shiny new sled to young Charlie; he then concludes with the phrase ". . . and a Happy New Year" as he dictates a letter to the adult Charles Foster Kane. Fifteen years have been compressed into one second.

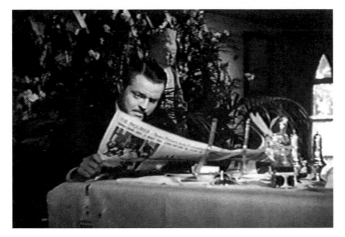

11.37 *Citizen Kane.* Charles.

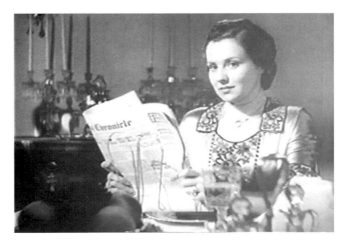

11.38 *Citizen Kane.* Emily.

Later in the film, time compression is combined with repetition in order to demonstrate the gradual discord in Kane's first marriage to a socialite named Emily. In the first shot, Charles and Emily are shown sharing breakfast together, very much in love. As the sequence continues, they move further and further apart. Through crosscutting, Charles and Emily are shown alternately (11.37, 11.38). It is like watching a tennis match. Disagreements dominate their dialog. When the sequence ends, they silently sit at opposing ends of the table, with Charles reading the *Inquirer* while Emily reads the rival *Chronicle* (11.39).

Citizen Kane is a sixty-year-old, black-and-white film with limited use of special effects. No one gets shot; there are no car crashes; no buildings explode. It is very different from most popular films today. Yet, we remain intrigued: this old film consistently tops the charts when critics choose their favorite films. A sense of mystery, an exploration of character, brilliant cinematography, and extraordinary editing all add to the appeal of *Citizen Kane*.

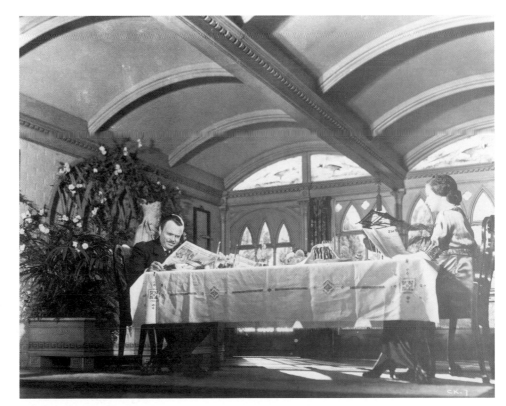

11.39 *Citizen Kane.* Breakfast.

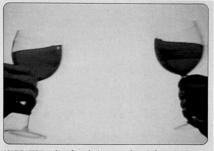

NARRATOR: When friends don't stop friends from drinking and driving

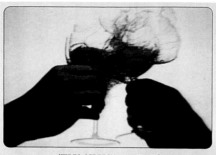

[TIRES SCREECH AND CRASH]

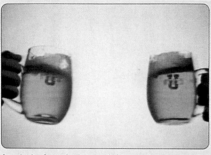

friends die from drinking and driving.

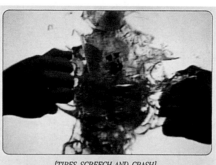

[TIRES SCREECH AND CRASH]

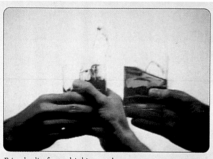

Friends die from drinking and—

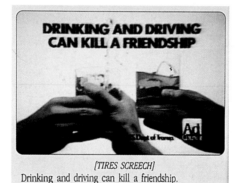

[TIRES SCREECH]
Drinking and driving can kill a friendship.

11.40 Agency: Leber Katz Partners, New York. Production: Phil Marco Productions, New York. Editing Company: Cinemetric, New York. Music Production: Roy Eaton Productions, New York. Details: TV, 30 seconds, color. First appearance: December 12, 1983. Advertiser's Supervisor: Eleanor Hanley. Account Supervisor: Susan Wershba. Creative Director: Jack Silverman. Copywriter: Lou Linder. Art Director: Len Fink. Agency Producer: Herb Miller. Producer: Catherine Bromley. Director/ Cameraman/Lighting Director: Phil Marco. Editor: Larry Plastrik. Music Director: Roy Eaton. Music Composers: Roy Eaton/Joe Hudson. Performers: Jon Carthay, Laurence White, Bobby Hudson. Voice: Doug Jeffers.

The 15-Second Sales Pitch

Duration, framing, editing, and narration become especially charged with meaning when a television commercial is designed. Lasting only 15 seconds, the ad must immediately command attention, make a favorable impression, and influence consumer behavior. Whether you are selling soap or discouraging smoking, your approach must be clear, concise, and compelling.

Ads must appeal to the emotions as well as the intellect. The **hard-sell** approach, shown in Figure 11.40, relies on rational argument and clearly presents one major point. The narrative is linear, and the message is explicit: drinking and driving can kill a friendship. Words underscore the ideas that are being communicated visually.

Soft-sell ads focus on emotion. While the message is still sharply focused, the designer may seek a sensory response rather than a rational response. An ad for a Jeep Cherokee (11.41) shows a car driving through the woods. The song "Row, row, row your boat" provides the sound track. There is no obvious connection between the song and the car, but the words "life is but a dream" certainly imply that a Jeep can provide a carefree vacation.

Feeling good is not enough: the viewer must feel good about the specific product being sold. Because viewer response is triggered by clues rather than literal content, designers using the soft-sell approach pay particular attention to details such as the soundtrack and lighting.

Ad Design Strategies

All ads rely on a clear message, strong imagery, and simple communication. However, very different strategies can be used to convey an idea, and the skillful designer carefully matches the communication style to the message content. Here are six contrasting strategies.

Rational: A rational ad provides the viewer with specific information. When the message is compelling in itself or the product is truly unique, a straightforward demonstration can be effective. A 1985 commercial for Cheer detergent (11.42) combined a rational demonstration with deadpan humor, which attracts our attention while conveying the message.

Emotional: When the product is not unique or the message lacks urgency, an emotional approach may be more effective. For example, to a dog owner, all dog food is pretty much alike. Neither the product nor the message is compelling in itself. When the dog food becomes a manifestation of love for the dog, however, the appeal is heightened. In Figure 11.43, the emotion of love is more powerful than any rational argument.

Serious: A serious approach is often best when you have a serious message. Public service announcements dealing with AIDS, drunk driving, or drug abuse are rarely funny. However, the ad will succeed only if it is seen. Horrific images of starving children or tortured prisoners may so repel viewers that they change the channel and lose the message. Finding the right balance between serious content and engaging imagery is crucial.

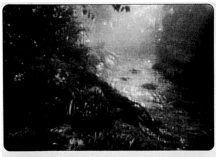

[BIRDS CHIRPING]

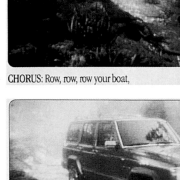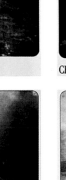

CHORUS: Row, row, row your boat,

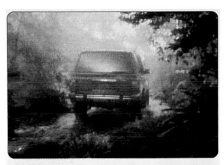

gently down the stream.

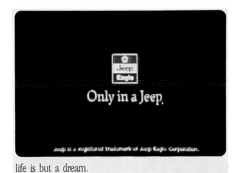

Merrily, merrily,

merrily, merrily,

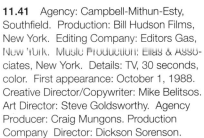

Only in a Jeep.

Jeep is a registered trademark of Jeep Eagle Corporation.

life is but a dream.

11.41 Agency: Campbell-Mithun-Esty, Southfield. Production: Bill Hudson Films, New York. Editing Company: Editors Gas, New York. Music Production: Elias & Associates, New York. Details: TV, 30 seconds, color. First appearance: October 1, 1988. Creative Director/Copywriter: Mike Belitsos. Art Director: Steve Goldsworthy. Agency Producer: Craig Mungons. Production Company Director: Dickson Sorenson.

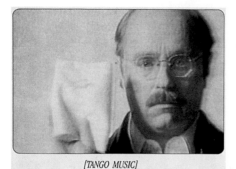
[TANGO MUSIC]

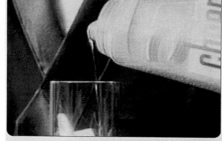

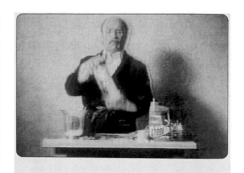

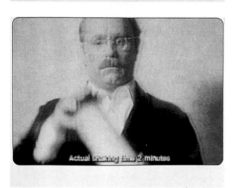
Actual cracking time 2 minutes

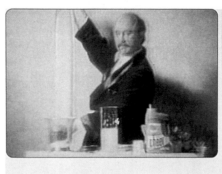

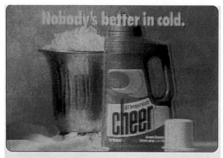
Nobody's better in cold.

NARRATOR: Nobody's better in cold, than All-Temperature Cheer.

11.42 Agency: Leo Burnett, Chicago. Production: Leroy Koetz Company, Chicago. Editing Company: Cutters, Chicago. Music Production: Colnot-Fryer Music, Chicago. First appearance: 1988. Account Supervisor: Ray DeThorne. Creative Director: Gerry Miller. Associate Creative Director/Copywriter: Alex Goslar. Art Director: Bob Ribits. Agency Producer: Angelo Antonucci. Production Company Producer: George Lakehomer. Production Company Director: Leroy Koetz. Editor: R. J. Music Composer: Cliff Colnot. Casting Director: Bonnie Murray. Performer: Jobe Cerny. Voice: Jim McCance.

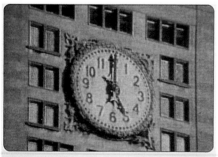
[SFX: CLOCKS CHIMING 5 PM]

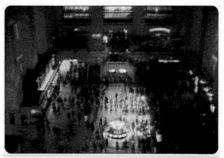
[MUSIC]

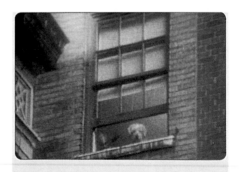

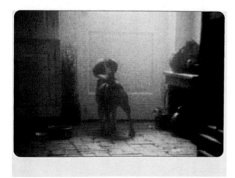

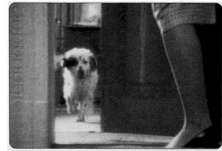
NARRATOR: When you think about the unique joy your dog brings you, why would you ever want to feed him anything less than America's finest dog food? New Reward,

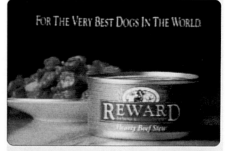
FOR THE VERY BEST DOGS IN THE WORLD

REWARD

for the very best dogs in the world. What may just be the very best dog food.

11.43 Agency: Goodby, Berlin & Silverstein, San Francisco. Production: Griner, Custa & Associates, New York. Editing Company: Straight Cut, Los Angeles. Music Production: Piece of Cake, Los Angeles. Details: TV, 60 seconds, color. First appearance: July 18, 1988. Advertiser's Supervisor: Tom Branky. Account Supervisor: Pam Malone. Creative Directors: Jeff Goodby, Rich Silverstein. Copywriter: Jeff Goodby. Art Director: Rich Silverstein. Agency Producer: Debbie King. Production Company Producer: Chris Stefani. Production Company Director/Cameraman: Norm Griner. Lighting Director: William Coleman. Editor: Tom Schacte. Music Director/Composer: Don Pierstrup. Casting Director: Kathy Sorkin.

Humorous: In a society saturated with sales pitches, an ad that makes us laugh is an ad we will remember. Since any ad is designed to encourage a change in behavior, memory is important. The message we receive while watching the nightly news must be retained when we buy a tube of toothpaste two days later. To be effective, however, a humorous ad must truly be funny, without insulting the viewer or demeaning the product. By showing the strength as well as the weakness of an elderly runner, the ad in Figure 11.44 strikes just the right balance.

Realistic: Communication requires connection. For a commercial to succeed, the viewer must feel a connection to the ideas and images presented. For example, few adults will pay attention to an ad for the latest rock band, while few teenagers will pay attention to an ad for denture adhesive. In either case, there is no connection to the message conveyed. Similarly, when we feel a connection to a character in an ad, we are more likely to listen to his argument.

A common form of realism is **testimonial.** In a testimonial, a trustworthy character (often a celebrity) addresses us directly. The 1998 Aleve medicine commercial is a good example. An ordinary-looking, middle-aged man wearing blue jeans tells us that two Aleve pills do the same job as a fistful of pills from a competing company. When he ends the ad by saying simply, "It works for me," we assume that it will also work for us.

A very different approach is used in Figure 11.45. The Marlboro Man, exemplar of the rugged cowboy so admired in American culture, has been realistically reinterpreted. The ad, which begins like a cigarette commercial, quickly shifts from the heroic image to the hacking cough of a sick smoker. Using

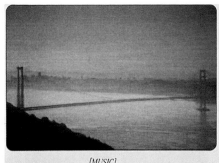
[MUSIC]

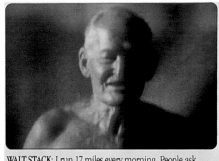
WALT STACK: I run 17 miles every morning. People ask

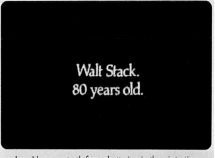
Walt Stack.
80 years old.
me how I keep my teeth from chattering in the wintertime.

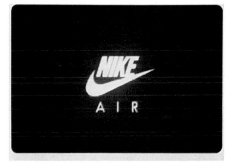
I leave them in my locker.

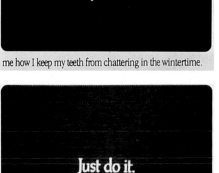
Just do it.

NIKE
AIR

11.44 Agency: Wieden & Kennedy, Portland. Production: PYTKA, Venice. Details: TV, 30 seconds each, color. First appearance: August, 1988. Advertiser's Supervisor: Scott Bedbury. Creative Directors: Dan Wieden, David Kennedy. Copywriters: Dan Wieden, Jim Riswold. Art Director: David Jenkins. Agency Producers: Bill Davenport, Elinor Shanklir. Production Company Director: Joe Pytka. Editor: Steve Wystrach.

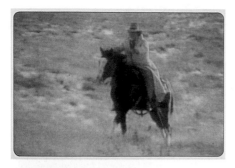

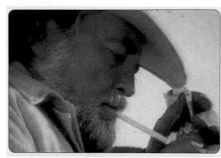

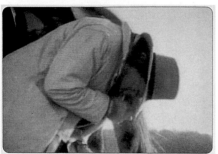

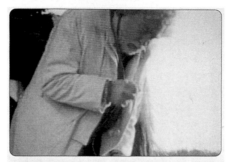

NARRATOR: No wonder cowboys are a dying breed. If

you need help quitting, tune into project QUIT, and take

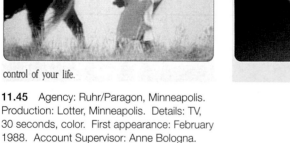

control of your life.

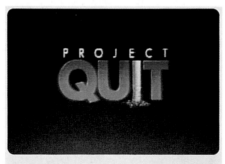

11.45 Agency: Ruhr/Paragon, Minneapolis. Production: Lotter, Minneapolis. Details: TV, 30 seconds, color. First appearance: February 1988. Account Supervisor: Anne Bologna. Creative Director/Art Director: Doug Lew. Associate Creative Director/Copywriter: Bill Johnson. Agency Producer: Arleen Kulis. Production Company Director: Jim Lotter.

this strategy, the designers attracted the viewer's attention and strengthened the nonsmoking message at the end.

Exaggerated: Exaggeration can be a great strategy when the product is commonplace or the message is uninteresting, To be effective, an ad must be seen and remembered. Exaggeration tends to be memorable. Even if the event shown is ludicrous, the ad can be effective if the basic message is believable. We know that the snails shown in Figure 11.46 are not literally stuck in traffic; they represent frustrated drivers who are moving at a "snail's pace." The metaphor is unexpected, and when combined with the voice-over, becomes humorous. Through exaggeration, a mass transit message becomes memorable.

Non-Narrative

Despite its unusual structure, *Citizen Kane* is a familiar type of popular film. It tells a fictitious story, based on a series of actions and reactions. The opening and closing sequences provide an effective framework for the multiple narratives presented by Kane's associates. The characters are believable, and the plot is plausible.

Many forms of sequential art, however, are non-narrative in structure. For example, the elegant contours and gleaming chrome of an expensive car provide both the form and the content in Figure 11.47. There is no story: viewers are simply shown a series of beautiful close-ups. Evocative artworks of this kind often require more audience participation and encourage an open-ended response.

Three common approaches to non-narrative are described below.

A **categorical** approach is based on exploration of a single concept, action, or emotion.

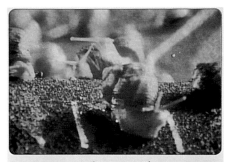

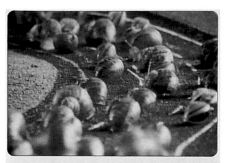

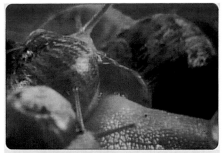

[TRAFFIC NOISE]
TRAFFIC REPORTER: I've never seen traffic like this. The traffic down there today is unbelievable.

[OTHER DRIVERS' VOICES]
NARRATOR: Remember what it was like the last time you drove yourself to the airport. Next time take Massport's

Logan Express Bus from Quincy or Framingham. It's fast, convenient, and comfortable. For more information, call Massport, at 1-800-23LOGAN.

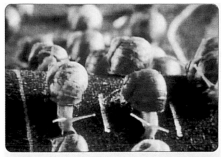

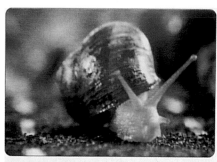

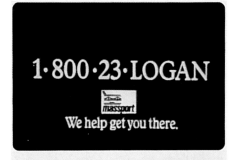

MAN: Move it, buddy!

WOMAN: I can walk faster than this.

11.46 Agency: Rossin, Greenberg, Seronick and Hill, Boston. Production Company: Cavanaugh & Co., Boston. Details: TV, 30 seconds, color. First appearance: November 1988. Advertiser's Supervisor: Teresa McAlpine. Account Supervisor: Neal Hill. Creative Directors: Gary Greenberg, Peter Seronick. Copywriter: Peter Seronick. Art Director: Gary Greenberg. Agency Producer: Julie Lauerman. Production Company Producer: David Norman. Production Company Director: Steve Cavanaugh. Set Designer: Bob Field. Cameraman/Lighting Director: Dan Stoloff. Editor: George Mauro. Voice: Chris Murney.

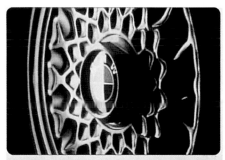

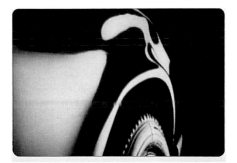

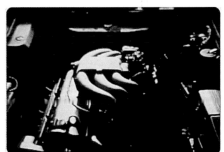

[MUSIC]

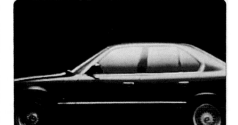

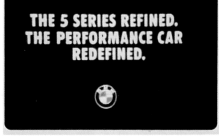

11.47 Agency: WCRS Mathews Marcantonio, London. Production: Park Village Productions, London. Music Production: Jeff Wayne Music, London. Details: TV, 60 seconds, color. First appearance: June 3,1988. Country: England. Language: English. Advertiser's Supervisor: Martin Hainge. Account Supervisor: Hugh Smiley. Creative Director: Alfredo Marcantonio. Art Director: Paul Garret. Agency Producer: Simon Wells. Production Company Producer: Chris Harvey. Production Company Director: Roger Woodburn. Cameraman: Joe Coe. Lighting Director: Keith Goddard. Editor: Patrick Moore. Music Composer: Trevor Jones.

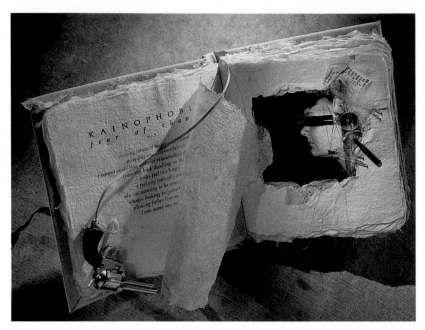

11.48 Susan Kae Grant, *Kainophobia, Fear of Change*, from *Giving Fear a Proper Name: Detroit*. **The Black Rose Press, 1982–85.** Edition of 15, printed letter press with silver prints. Mixed media, handmade paper, simulated bullet-proof case, 5 × 5 in. (12.7 × 12.7 cm).

Giving Fear a Proper Name, a visual book by Susan Kae Grant, uses text from a diary to explore fear. Contained within a clear plexiglass box, the book itself is like a fetish. Handmade paper and inserted objects cause the book to open on its own, and the tiny toy revolver that dangles from a bookmark string simultaneously suggests self-protection and self-annihilation.

This catalog of terror begins with kainophobia, the fear of change (11.48). From the diary, we learn that Grant has moved to Detroit, a profoundly foreign environment for her. On the first page of a double-page spread, she writes of "moving forward looking backward . . . I can never say good-bye." On the facing page, she is shown in profile, facing left, with her face pierced by straight pins and accompanied by a tiny compass and a plastic groom, suggesting a wedding cake. Topophobia, the fear of place, comes next. Grant now writes that she "stares in disbelief out smashed vacant beauties/violet oppressive depression surrounds me/people are angry, filled with hate." Her face in the photograph has now become a target. Eremophobia, the fear of solitude, follows. A close-up of her ear is shown, pierced by pins, while a plastic toy phone dangles like an earring. The book continues, with pages devoted to the fear of sleep, fear of being alone, fear of being observed, and so forth. In each case, increasingly painful words accompany a photographic self-portrait of some kind. The book ends with the fear of infinity. Now in profile facing right, Grant is accompanied by a pair of dice and a map of Texas, which will become her new home. Using fear as a category, then relentlessly exploring various types of fear, Grant transformed her personal experience into powerful communication.

In a **rhetorical** approach, sequential images are used to present an argument. One example is *Powers of Ten* by Charles and Ray Eames (11.49A–C).This nine-and-one-half-minute film provides an elegant exploration of "the relative size of things in the universe." The central image is framed by a dark border that includes information on the spatial position of each shot on the right and its numerical equivalent on the left. Beginning with a shot of a man asleep in a park, the camera gradually moves out to the farthest reaches of the known universe. Physicist Philip Morrison provides the narration, describing the meaning of the image at each step.

The process is then reversed, and the speed is greatly accelerated. Returning to the sleeping man, the camera now moves through his skin, into his blood, down to a cell, and finally, into an atom in the man's right hand. The beautiful images entice us while the mathematical narration teaches us. Moving from astrophysics to nuclear physics, this film presents an analysis of the distance between the largest and smallest spaces known.

Words for the World by Ed Hutchins, presents a social argument using equally simple means. By filling a small metal pencil box with 16 special pencils, he makes a plea for tolerance and peace. A map of the world is printed on the top of the box. Various texts are printed on the pencils, in languages ranging from Arabic to Zulu, each accompanied by an English translation. The phrases are simple: "It doesn't hurt to listen." "The time is always right for justice." "We all live under the same sky." The message, however, is compelling. What words will we write with these pencils? What words can we say to each other? Hutchins is promoting a change in behavior rather than knowledge of the cosmos.

Finally, sequential art may be purely **abstract.** In a well-designed book or film, changes in colors, shapes, textures, and movement can provide all the information needed for a compelling piece. *Blacktop,* another experimental film by Charles and Ray Eames, provides one example. An outdoor basketball court has been washed. As the residue is rinsed away, the film records the movement of soap bubbles and water over the asphalt surface. The delicate Bach harpsichord music that is used as the sound track suggests that this act of washing the asphalt is as elegant as a Balanchine ballet. And, in the hands of these inventive filmmakers, it is.

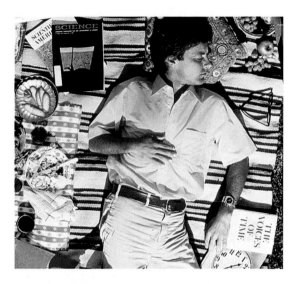

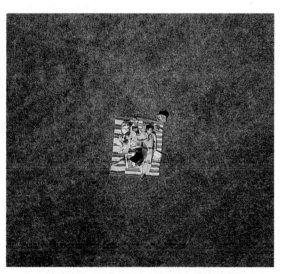

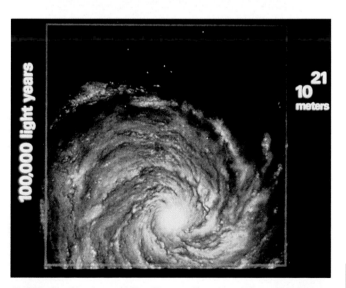

11.49A–C Charles and Ray Eames, *Powers of Ten***, 1977.** Film frames.

Profile:
Jerome Witkin, Painter

Life Lessons: Exploring the
Human Condition

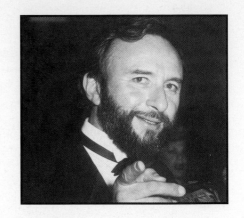

Jerome Witkin is an internationally renowned figurative painter. He has had over 40 solo exhibitions, including shows at Greenville County Museum of Art in South Carolina; Delaware Art Museum; Columbia College Art Gallery in Chicago; Arkansas Art Center; Munson-Williams-Proctor Institute in Utica, New York; and three shows at Sherry French Gallery in New York City. Witkin is the recipient of numerous awards, including a Guggenheim Fellowship and two Ford Foundation fellowships. His work is in over 40 public collections, including the Butler Institute of American Art in Youngstown, Ohio; Hirshhorn Museum and Sculpture Garden in Washington, D.C.; the Cleveland Museum of Art; and the Metropolitan Museum of Art in New York City. Witkin's work has been reviewed extensively in major periodicals, and a book on his work titled *Life Lessons: The Art of Jerome Witkin,* by Sherry Chayat, was published in 1989.

Three aspects of Witkin's work exemplify the importance of narrative in painting. First, there is a theatrical use of setting, character, and movement. Using a stage he has constructed in his studio, Witkin uses space and lighting as deliberately as a film director. Second, he has a heightened awareness of time, often focusing on the "decisive moment" as described by photographer Henri Cartier-Bresson. Witkin often makes narratives of four or more paintings, which help him convey complex ideas dramatically. Third, Witkin is a technical virtuoso, using light, color, and illusionistic space with extraordinary energy.

MS: To what extent is painting a narrative art form?
JW: It depends on the painter. For me, the story is very important. As a child, I was fascinated by the stories I heard on the radio. They occurred in episodes, and while waiting for a week between programs, I could image settings, situations, and characters. The words provided the beginning point, then my imagination took over. I approached comic books in the opposite way. I tended to ignore the word balloons and instead made up my own dialog to accompany the images.

MS: What is the advantage of multiple images?
JW: I really think Francis Bacon was right when he said that a painting should attack the nervous system. With multiple pictures, you can create an emotional overcharge based on the interplay between images. The viewer gets more fully involved. This can extend the meaning of the painting.

MS: To what extent are you influenced by other forms of narrative, such as films or novels?

JW: As a painter, I shouldn't separate myself from other media such as dance or theater. My world involves choreography, human gesture, human physicality, all of which is integrated into the play I am creating in paint. The trouble with art today is that we have so taken the meat off the bones that there is often nothing left. I am drawn to paintings that have a real emotional depth as well as a breadth of ideas.

MS: How did *Division Street* evolve, both as an image and as an idea?
JW: *Division Street* is based on an actual and very, very psychologically charged memory. I saw my father turn to leave, I saw my mother launch plates at him, I saw her come back through the door. I wanted my father to be fairly anonymous: his face remains hidden. The color in the first two images is heightened. It is the color of night, or of a nightmare.

MS: Why was it done as a triptych?
JW: A triptych can be like a symphony, with the first

image presenting the essential theme, the second developing the theme, and the third providing a conclusion. The center is especially important in each of these paintings. The center of the first panel is at the edge of my father's tricep. To the left, there is a gap, a division. In the middle panel, the division occurs at the space between the door jamb, the father, the plates, and the kid. In the last panel, the center of gravity has shifted, to the edge of the closed door.

The space also shifts from panel to panel. It is fairly deep in the first, begins to flatten in the second, and becomes very shallow in the third. You are finally confined, closed in. While working on the paintings, I wrote in my notebook that "the use of telephoto can crush the form to help express the boy's emotional take on the scene, his surprise and shock."

MS: So many visual storytellers use film or video to express their ideas. Why do you use paint?
JW: At its core, painting is an exploration of the mystery of reality. Painting can make the world real: if I paint it, I can see it, if I can see it, I can hold it. With each mark of the brush, you respond to reality and create a new reality.

Painting is a summation of experience, requiring a level and degree of sustained attention that is unlike anything else. It offers us a dialog with reality. A still life is a meditation on order, at very close range. Figurative painting engages us in a different way: in effect, we are always seeing ourselves, whether we are painting a self-portrait or working from the model.

Painting requires an appreciation of intonation—the nuances of light, space, and gesture. It is so much more than the accumulation of perceptual detail.

MS: What advice do you have for my students?
JW: Choose your images carefully. We are inundated by millions of images, on television, in magazines, on city streets. In this age of careless images, seek and produce your images with care. It is when painting becomes a necessity rather than a diversion that you begin to become an artist.

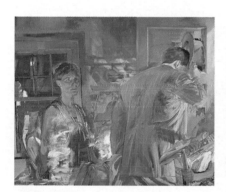 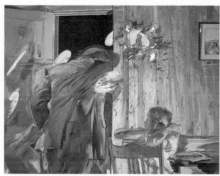 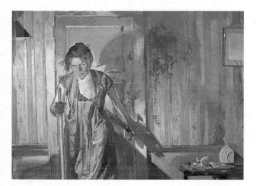

Jerome Witkin, *Division Street* [A story told in 3 panels], 1984–85. Oil on canvas, triptych. Left panel, 75⅛ × 63¼ in. (190.9 × 160.7 cm); middle panel, 81⅛ × 63 in. (206.2 × 160 cm); right panel, 87⅛ × 63 in. (221.3 × 160 cm).

Summary

- Multiple-image structures can be used to express complex ideas using narrative and non-narrative approaches.

- Storytelling is one of the most ancient and effective forms of communication. Stories can increase self-awareness, provide inspiration, supply information, and encourage understanding.

- The group, series, and sequence are the multiple-image structures most commonly used by printmakers, photographers, and book artists.

- The beat, scene, sequence, and act are used by filmmakers and playwrights to create screenplays.

- By establishing effective boundaries, we can develop more effective stories. Common questions include: Whose story is it? When should the story begin and end? Where does the story occur? Why did it happen? What is the underlying theme or message in the story?

- A change in style can substantially affect communication.

- Ideas and emotions can be communicated through a straightforward series of causes and effects or through a series of seemingly unrelated images.

- The opening and closing, personal perspective, and characters used can make or break a story.

- Television advertisements can present complete ideas in 15 seconds. Hard-sell, soft-sell, rational, emotional, serious, humorous, realistic, and exaggerated approaches are the most common strategies.

- Categorical, rhetorical, and abstract are common non-narrative approaches.

Keywords

abstract	exaggerated advertising	scene
act	group	screenplay
beat	hard-sell advertising	sequence
categorical narrative	humorous advertising	series
causality	myth	serious advertising
denouement	rational advertising	soft-sell advertising
depth of field	realistic advertising	testimonial advertising
emotional	rhetorical narrative	

As you begin your studio work, consider:

Setting
1. What is the geographical location? China? Italy? Iowa? How much do you need to know about that location to be convincing?
2. On what day, year, or century does the story occur? How does it change when set in 1066, 1941, or 2001?
3. What season is it? What time of day is it? What does the sky look like?
4. What are the characteristics of the location? Is it arid? A jungle? Noisy? Silent?
5. Where does the story occur? Dentist's office? Child's tree house? A slaughterhouse?

Characters
1. Whose story is it? A 9-year-old girl? A 16-year-old boy? A priest? A thief?
2. What is the point of view? Does the main character tell his or her own story (first-person narrative), or does someone else tell the story? How does this affect the result?
3. What are the strengths and weaknesses of each of your characters?

Conflict
1. What problems occur? Why? How do the characters deal with problems? Is it more comic or tragic?
2. Are the conflicts between the characters, or between human and animal, human and god, human and machine, or human and nature?
3. To what degree is the conflict resolved at the end?

Chronology and Editing
1. What is the duration of the story? An afternoon? A month? A century?
2. Will an expansion or compression of time improve the story?
3. What are the most significant moments in the narrative? How can they be presented most effectively?

Medium
1. What is the best medium for your narrative? A video? A visual book? A performance?
2. How will your idea change when it is expressed in a different medium?

Huntley Baldwin, *How to Create Effective TV Commercials*, 2nd edition. Lincolnwood, IL, NTC Business Books, 1989.

Stephen D. Katz. *Film Directing, Shot by Shot: Visualizing from Concept to Screen*. Studio City, CA, Michael Wiese Productions, 1991.

Robert McKee, *Story: Substance, Structure, Style and the Principles of Screen Writing*. New York, HarperCollins, 1997.

Keith A. Smith, *Structure of the Visual Book*. Fairport, NY: The Sigma Foundation, Inc., 1992.

Christopher Vogler. *The Writer's Journey: Mythic Structure for Storytellers and Screenwriters*. Studio City, CA, Michael Wiese Productions, 1991.

Steve Riordan, editor. *Clio Awards: A Tribute to 30 Years of Advertising Excellence, 1960–1989*. Glen Cove, NY, PBC International, 1989.

chapter twelve

Interdisciplinary Arts: Books, Installations, Performances

In this final chapter, we explore three forms of interdisciplinary art. In **interdisciplinary art,** two or more different disciplines are fused to create a hybrid art form. The first section focuses on visual books, which combine words and images in a wide variety of structures. The next section is devoted to **installation art,** which presents an ensemble of images and objects within a three-dimensional environment. The final section is devoted to **performance art,** which may be broadly defined as live art performed by artists.

Exploring the Visual Book

What is a visual book?

A **visual book** is an experimental structure that conveys ideas, actions, and emotions using multiple images in an integrated and interdependent format. Every image is connected in some way to every other image. In a sense, there are no single pages in a visual book. It is the combination of the multiple pages that creates the complete artwork.

Any material may be used for pages, from the bags of tea Nancy Callahan used for her *Daybook* (12.1 A–B) to sheets of lead Anselm Kiefer used for *Breaking of the Vessels* (12.2). Pages may be of any size or shape, from the three-inch triangles Daniel Kelm and Tim Ely used in *Rubeus* (12.3) to eight-foot-tall screens. The subject

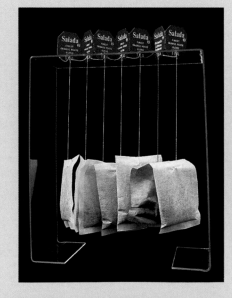

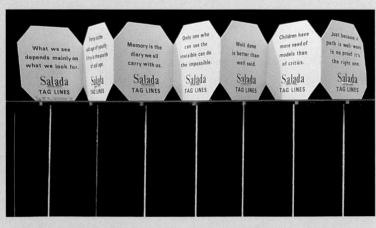

12.1A–B Nancy Callahan, *Daybook*, 1988. Artist's book, screen printing and hand-fabricated tea bags, 16 × 12 × 6 in. (40.6 × 30.5 × 15.3 cm).

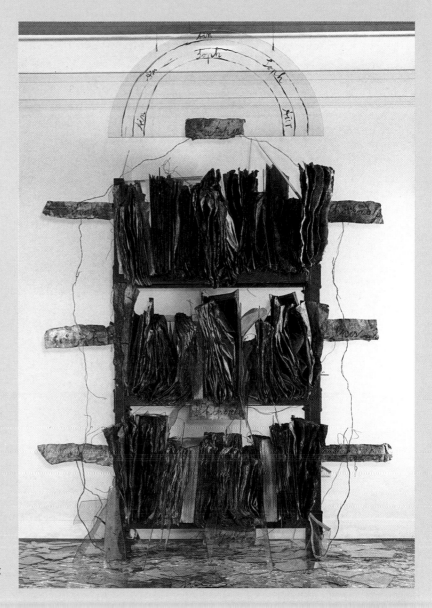

12.2 Anselm Kiefer, *Breaking of the Vessels*, 1990. Lead, iron, glass, copper wire, charcoal, and aquatec. 12 ft 5 in. × 11 ft 3 in. × 4 ft 9 in. (378.5 × 343 × 144.8 cm).

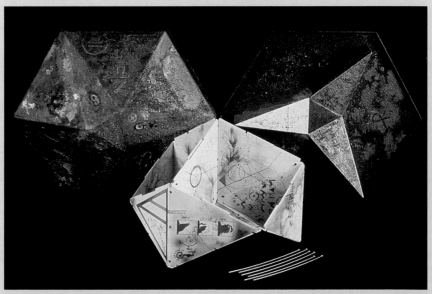

12.3 Daniel E. Kelm and Timothy C. Ely, *Rubeus*, 1990. Book: Flexahexahedron (6 cyclically linked tetrahedra with a circular axis of rotation), Arches paper, museum board, stainless steel wire, aluminum tubing, brass beads, cotton-covered polyester thread, with drawings using airbrush acrylics and ink, 5 × 10½ × 10½ in. (12.7 × 26.7 × 26.7 cm). Box: High faceted structure with hexagonal base and felt pad; paper consolidated paperboard and medium-density fiberboard, finished with polymer medium, copper leaf, plastic, metal bits, and sand from sacred sites, 6.25 in. (15.9 cm) high, 13 × 13 in. base (33 × 33 cm).

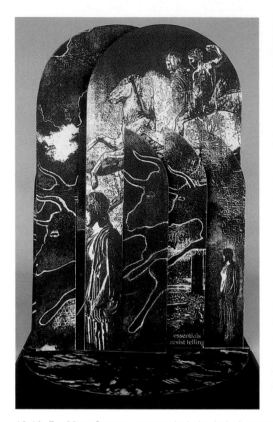
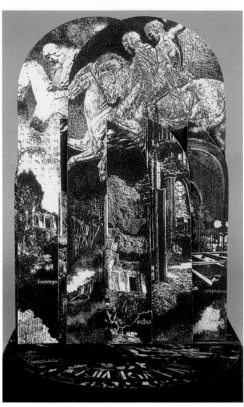

matter can be painfully personal, as in Susan Kae Grant's *Giving Fear a Proper Name* (see 11.48, page 11-26), profoundly philosophical, or highly political. Images can be generated using photography, printmaking, drawing, or other techniques.

Visual books combine two-dimensional composition and three-dimensional structure. For example, each page in my own *Labyrinth* (12.4 A–B) was composed individually, then slotted together to create a complex three-dimensional object. Even when a more traditional bound-edged

12.4A–B Mary Stewart, a page in *Labyrinth*, front and side view, 1999. Intaglio, 13 × 18 × 39 in. (33 × 45.7 × 99 cm).

codex structure is used (as shown in Figure 12.5A–C), variations in the page length and shape can substantially affect meaning.

Visual books may be entirely visual, as in Michael Snow's *Cover to Cover* (see 10.23, page 10-10); primarily verbal, as in Tom Phillips' *A Humument* (12.6); or entirely conceptual, as in Keith Smith's *Book 50* (12.7). Generally seen by one person at a time, a visual book can create a very direct connection between the audience and the artist. This contact is especially important with pop-up

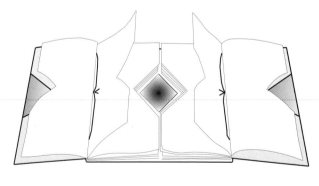

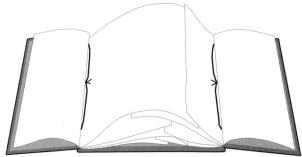

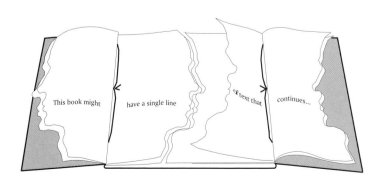

12.5A–C Keith Smith, Bound-Edged Codex Structure.

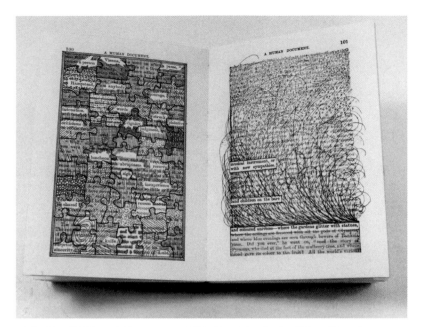

12.6 Tom Phillips, *A Humument*, 1980. From *The Cutting Edge of Reading: Artists' Books*, R. R. Hubert and J. D. Hubert. Granary Books, NY, 1999.

BOOK NUMBER 50
(Turning the page creates and destroys the image.)
Autumnal Equinox 1974

Construct a Western Codex book consisting of images on thirty transparencies. Process the film-positives by developing, short stop but no fix. Wash, dry and under proper safelight, hand bind as a leather case bound book. Place completed book in light-tight box.

Present the boxed book to the viewer. Upon opening the box and viewing, the entire book will not fog at once. Opening to the first page, the viewer will glimpse the image as it quickly blackens. The black will protect the remainder of the book from light. Upon turning each page, the viewer will momentarily see the image as it sacrifices itself to protect the remaining pages.

KE⊙TH

12.7 Keith Smith, *Book 50*, 1974. An entirely conceptual book.

books, which come to life when the pages are turned and the tabs are pulled.

Selecting a Text

Generative Potential

An evocative text can act as a springboard for the book artist, while an overly descriptive text may become a trap. More than verbal polish, a text must provide an opening for further development.

The labyrinth book project I assign to my students provides such generative potential, both visually and conceptually. The students begin by developing a labyrinthine drawing of a neo-Gothic building on campus (12.8). Because this drawing will act like a stage set for the narrative, careful use of lighting, balance, and the illusion of space is encouraged.

After a critique of the work, students expand their ideas and refine their images, finally creating two rough drawings, one on the front and one on the back of a 22 × 30 in. sheet of sturdy paper. This sheet is then cut apart to create four 7 ½ × 22 in. strips, which are finally folded and sewn to create sixteen 7 ½ × 11 in. pages.

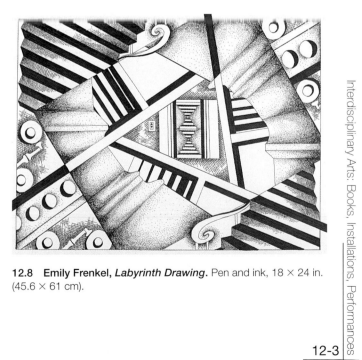

12.8 Emily Frenkel, *Labyrinth Drawing*. Pen and ink, 18 × 24 in. (45.6 × 61 cm).

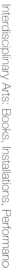

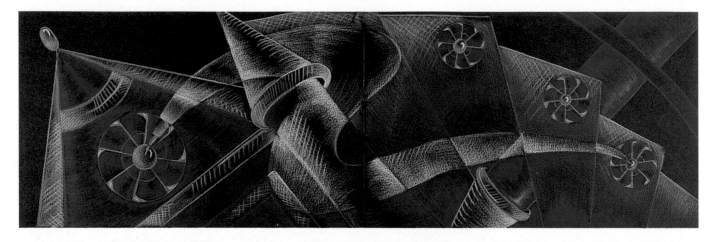

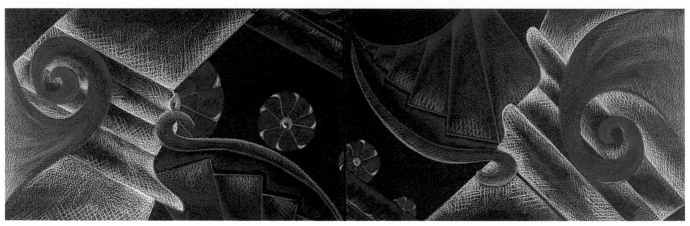

12.9A–B Emily Frenkel, *Labyrinth Book*, **two double-page spreads.** Colored pencil on black paper, 11 × 7½ in. (28 × 19 cm).

The book is developed from this raw material. We consider dictionary definitions:

lab·y·rinth: 1: a structure full of intricate passageways that make it difficult to find the way from the interior to the entrance or from the entrance to the center (for example, the labyrinth constructed by Daedalus for Minos, king of Crete, in which the Minotaur was confined); 2: a maze in a park or garden formed by paths separated by high, thick hedges; 3: something bewilderingly involved or tortuous in structure: a complex that baffles exploration; 4: a situation from which it is difficult to extricate oneself; 5: the internal ear, or its bony or membranous part; 6: a body structure made up of a maze of cavities and channels; 7: intricate, sometimes symbolic pattern, spec. such a pattern inlaid in the pavement of a medieval church; 8: in metallurgy, series of troughs in a stamping mill through which water passes for washing pulverized ore.[1]

We read the story of Theseus, the Greek hero who conquered the half-man, half-bull Minotaur, and meet the princess Ariadne, who provided him with a ball of golden thread that aided in his escape from the maze. We investigate labyrinths as described by archaeologists, physiologists, and psychologists.

This assignment consistently results in an astonishing array of inventive books. Some students introduce characters into the setting, creating a simple narrative. Others use the illusion of space to move the viewer through mysterious corridors and down precipitous staircases. Others use light and pattern to create a world of enchantment and beauty (12.9 A–B). All are valid solutions to the problem. Because the word *labyrinth* is so open to interpretation, the generative potential of the assignment is great.

Divisions and Connections

A text that easily breaks apart can suggest connections or divisions between book pages. An alphabet provides the page divisions in Edward Gorey's *The Gashlycrumb Tinies or, After the Outing* (12.10 A–B). Each letter is accompanied by a rhythmic and rhyming text describing assorted accidents and childhood fatalities, beginning with "A is for Amy who fell down the stairs, B is for Basil assaulted by bears, C is for Clara who wasted away, D is for Desmond thrown out of a sleigh," and so forth. The alphabet provides a sense of anticipation, as we wonder what wild expression of humor we will encounter on the next page, while the singsong rhythm and clever rhymes help to unify the separate pages.

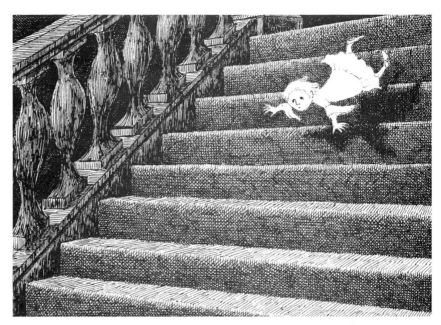

12.10A Edward Gorey, *A is for Amy who fell down the stairs.* Illustration from *The Gashlycrumb Tinies or, After the Outing.*

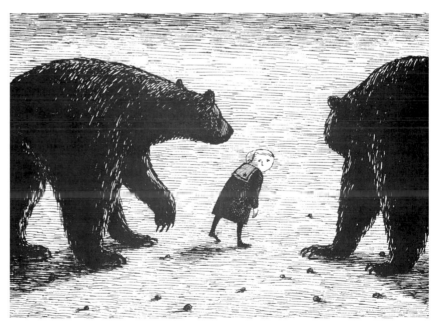

12.10B Edward Gorey, *B is for Basil assaulted by bears.* Illustration from *The Gashlycrumb Tinies or, After the Outing.*

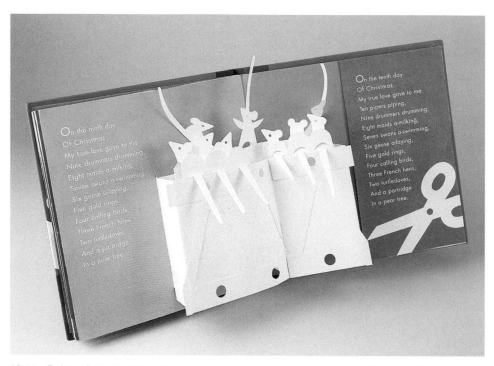

12.11 Robert Sabuda, "Nine Drummers Drumming." Reprinted from *The 12 Days of Christmas, a Pop-up Celebration*. Simon & Schuster.

Similarly, a traditional song provides the structure for *The Twelve Days of Christmas*, by Robert Sabuda. This song has become a holiday cliché, and a conventional drawing of the familiar partridge in a pear tree would have been deadly. Sabuda overcame the cliché by using a lively imagination combined with elegant and elaborate pop-ups. The "six geese-a-laying" sit atop a slice of gooseberry pie, while the "seven swans-a-swimming" fill a crystal ball. Nine graceful figures dance atop a music box: a mirror is used to multiply some of the figures, finally producing the necessary "eleven ladies dancing." And, the "nine drummers drumming" (12.11) are mice, with their tails tapping out a lively beat! Imagination conquers cliché, every time.

Music

Each language has a distinctive aural quality, or music, as well as a distinctive grammatical structure. English, which is dominated by words derived from Latin and Germanic languages, provides at least two ways to say almost anything. For example, a Viking warrior is *strong* (a word that is derived from the Anglo-Saxon word for strength), while a Roman warrior is *vigorous* (a word that is derived from the Latin word for strength). Spanish provides great grammatical clarity, and similar word endings encourage rhyme, while Chinese is literally musical—the meaning of words changes when the inflection and the tone of voice change.

Each text also has music. When words are poorly chosen, the text is discordant and painful to read. When the words are used thoughtfully, however, both the meaning and the music improve. *Kubla Khan*, by Coleridge, uses wonderfully musical language.

> In Xanadu did Kubla Khan
> A stately pleasure dome decree:
> Where Alph, the sacred river, ran
> Through caverns measureless to man
> Down to a sunless sea.[2]

You simply must read this aloud. A combination of rhyme, repetition, and alliteration makes the words sing.

Rachel Carson's *Under the Sea Wind* provides many examples of musical prose:

> By September the eels of the sound country had begun to drop downstream to the sea. The eels came down from the hills and the upland grasslands. They came from cypress swamps where black-watered rivers had their beginnings; they moved across the tidal plain that dropped in six giant steps to the sea. In the river estuaries and in the sound they joined their mates-to-be. Soon, in silvery wedding dress, they would follow the ebbing tides to the sea, to find—and lose—themselves in the black abysses of mid-ocean.[3]

As with an alphabetic or a traditional song, the music of the text may suggest page divisions while simultaneously providing conceptual unity to the book as a whole.

Writing a Text

At some point, most book artists and illustrators decide to generate their own texts. The ideas and emotions they want to express are not available in a traditional text and copyright laws may limit use of a contemporary text.

Taking a creative-writing course is a good place to start. As with art courses, a well-designed writing course can provide a solid base of information and encourage the beginner to try various approaches. Try writing a page or two in response to any of these assignments:

- *Memory Amplifier.* Describe an object, sensation, or setting that summarizes or epitomizes an event, a feeling, or an idea in your life. Looking at family photographs, childhood toys, or everyday objects is a good place to start.

- *Moment of Truth.* Describe an event that clarified or transformed your life.

- *Homeworld.* Describe the physical or psychological place that is your home. Is it a particular house? A forest? The World Wide Web?

- *Build a Memory Bank.* These triggering questions can help you start. Just fill in the blanks. (a) "the first time I ever____" (b) "the best day of my life was___" (c) list memorable events, such as theater, trips, concerts (d) companions in triumph and adversity (e) consider the greatest gift you ever received or ever gave.

- *Concept Generator.* Take a single word. Research it, using a thesaurus, dictionary, encyclopedia, the Internet, and so on. Collect all of the resulting meanings into a book.

The Best Texts

Selecting or writing an appropriate text can increase the impact of the book. The best texts are of personal interest, offer room for experimentation in the book format, and are meaningful to your audience. Ask yourself the following questions as you assess the potential of several texts.

- *What is the conceptual, psychological, or political power of the text?* Does it embody ideas and emotions you find personally compelling? The stronger your connection to the text, the more effective the book will be.

- *Does the text include any verbal patterns that can help unify the book?* Rhythm, repetition, and rhyme can be used to create a stronger connection among the pages.

- *How resonant are the words?* Do they gain or lose strength through multiple readings?

- *How accessible is the text?* Is the language comprehensible to the intended audience? How wide an interest is there in the book's subject matter?

- *How long is the text?* Generally, texts of 30 words or less are easiest to use effectively. Extended texts can get long-winded and crowd out the images.

Any source, from graffiti to Shakespeare, can be used. Indeed, many visual books derive their power from an unexpected selection of words.

Text and Typestyle

After a text is chosen, book construction can begin. Each page you design raises many questions. Let's concentrate on three major questions, using an 11 × 17″ double-page spread. Ask yourself the following questions.

- *What typestyle and type size is most appropriate to the ideas expressed?*

Each typestyle has a significant effect on communication. Let's experiment with a simple phrase: "Footsteps echoed emptiness."

Impact type has an industrial look: perhaps it is the echo of boots descending a factory staircase that we hear (12.12).

FOOTSTEPS ECHOED EMPTINESS

12.12

Garamond type, especially when italicized, is flowing and graceful. The footsteps we now hear may be those of a child descending a staircase in a Victorian house on Christmas Eve (12.13).

footsteps echoed emptiness

12.13

Madrone type paints a much grimmer picture. A gang war has concluded, and the survivors are slowly leaving the deserted parking lot where it occurred (12.14).

FOOTSTEPS ECHOED EMPTINESS

12.14

- *Can more than one typestyle be used effectively?*

Multiple texts are used in many books to communicate the distinctive voices of multiple speakers or to convey multiple perspectives on the same event. *Sticky Buns: An Overnight Roll* uses this approach (12.15). This book was developed by a team of 12 artists during a workshop organized by the Paper and Book Intensive, a national book-arts group. An actual recipe for cinnamon buns is provided near the top of each page, while a **gloss,** or commentary on the text, is written in italics along the bottom. Words carefully selected from the recipe are thereby reinterpreted, suggesting a romantic afternoon in the kitchen as emotions (as well as dough) begin to rise.

A very different approach to text is used in *Holding Together,* by Judite dos Santos (12.16). A translucent sheet of paper with one or two words printed on each side has been inserted between opaque pages showing primitive clay sculptures. Some of the text is always easily readable while other words are reversed. The book moves from this opening page to an evocation of the senses: touch, smell, taste, vision, hearing. Through an effective use of 22 words and 16 images, this quiet book explores our connections to the earth.

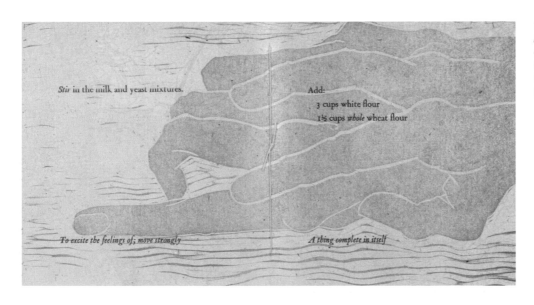

12.15 *Sticky Buns: An Overnight Roll,* **1996.** A collaborative book developed by 12 artists participating in a letterpress workshop at the Paper and Book Intensive. Kathy Keuhn, instructor.

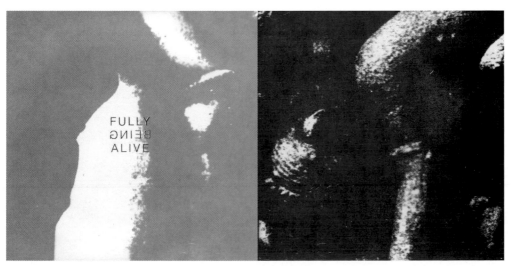

12.16 **Judite dos Santos,** ***Holding Together.*** Images, design and poem by artist. (Limited edition artist's book.)

- *How should the words be positioned on the page?*

In the first example, position combined with size emphasizes the acute hearing we develop in threatening situations (12.17).

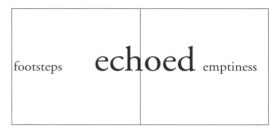

12.17

The mysterious implications of the phrase are emphasized in the second example (12.18).

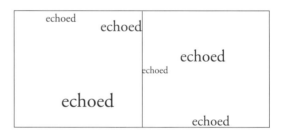

12.18

With the addition of two more pages, the final example communicates the loneliness of the journey (12.19).

footsteps echoed emptiness

12.19

Image-to-Page Relationships

Just as the size, position, and style of type can enhance or destroy the power of a text, so also can the position, size, and kind of image substantially affect visual communication.

Positioned at the far left edge, the door invites us into the book (12.20).

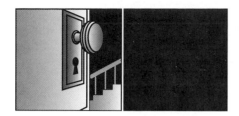

12.20

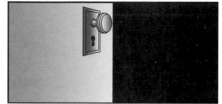

12.21

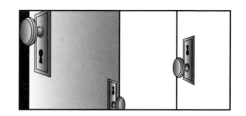

12.22

Reduced in size and positioned along the **gutter** (that is, the center line), the door now suggests an opening into an alternative world located beneath the surface of the book (12.21).

Multiplied and mirrored, the door now creates an entry into a dream (12.22).

Word and Image Relationships

Things get even more interesting when words and images are used together.

This organization suggests the woman's memory of a past event (12.23).

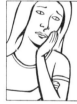 footsteps 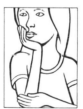 echoed 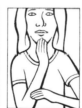 emptiness

12.23

Here, the same phrase describes a walk into the future (12.24).

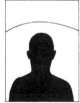 footsteps 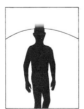 echoed 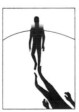 emptiness

12.24

And, this combination of word and image puts us back into a labyrinth (12.25).

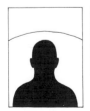 footsteps 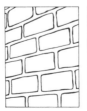 echoed 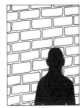 emptiness

12.25

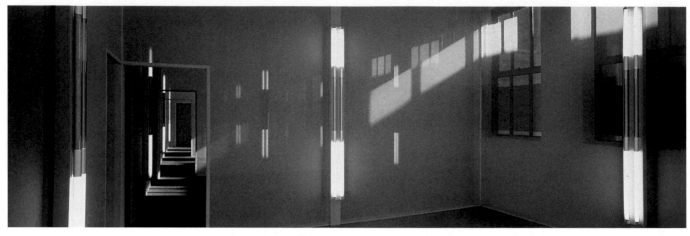

12.26 Robert Irwin, *Part II: Excursus: Homage to the Square³*. Installation at Dia Center for the Arts, NY, September 1998–June 1999.

Advantages of Visual Books

Through a combination of words and images, visual books can convey complex ideas and emotions to a broad audience. In some books, the words provide direct, explicit communication while the images are more implicit and evocative. In other books, the words are evocative while the images are explicit and direct. In either case, layers of meaning can be created through a contrast between the visual and the verbal. Instead of over-explaining an image, words can be used to suggest alternative ideas and implications. For artists with big ideas, this interplay between words and images greatly expands communication.

Installation Art

An installation may be defined as an ensemble of images and objects that are presented within a three-dimensional environment. Because we occupy the actual time and space of the artwork, we become physically engaged in an installation, and the aesthetic experience becomes heightened.

Uses of Space and Time

Some installations are primarily spatial in nature. For example, many installations by Robert Irwin emphasize direct experience within a constructed space. By creating a series of entrances, exits, and environments, Irwin creates a framework that is activated by each visitor. His *Part II: Excursus: Homage to the Square³* (12.26) was installed at the Dia Center in New York in 1999. This structure consisted of nine cubic rooms, defined by delicate walls of translucent cloth. The opacity and transparency of the fabric varied, depending on the amount and location of the light. Two vertical fluorescent lights illuminated each cube, creating subtle changes in color from room to room.

Entering the installation was both inviting and disorienting. From any point, all of the rooms were visible, yet veiled. The translucent layers of cloth and the variations in light made the most distant rooms dissolve. The vertical fluorescent lights, which always remained visible, first read as individual, then as mirror images, creating a hallucinatory experience similar to a carnival fun house. All activity within the space was created by the visitors themselves, who entered, and explored, the installation like ghostly silhouettes.

By contrast, *Floodsong,* by Mary Lucier, was primarily, temporal in nature. Six video monitors, were installed in a narrow room at the Museum of Modern Art. Each showed an interview with a survivor of the 1995 Grand Forks flood. A young girl, an old woman, an old man, a minister, and a farmer told the story of the terrifying event. In the enclosed space, the individual voices were

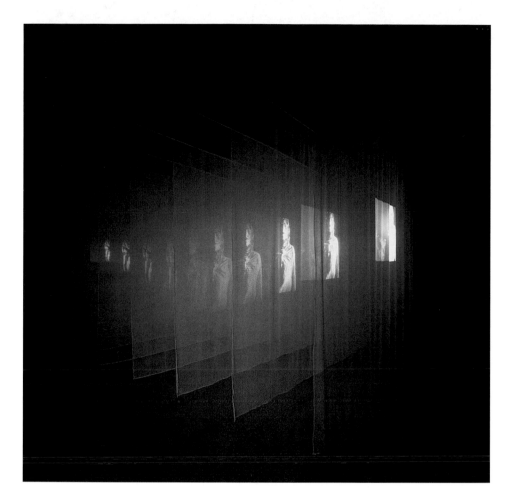

indistinct. They echoed and merged, creating a
litany of fortitude and grief, resilience and fear. In
sharp contrast to the straightforward interviews, an
enormous projection on the back wall of the gallery
took the audience through wrecked houses and
piles of debris.

Using a combination of the spatial and the temporal, Bill Viola has created installations that
envelop the viewer physically, emotionally, and
intellectually. In *The Veiling* (12.27), thin sheets of
translucent fabric were hung on parallel lines
across the center of a darkened room. An image of
a man was projected from one end, while an image
of a woman was projected from the opposite end.
These projections became increasingly diffused as
they passed through the multiple layers of cloth.
Finally, the two figures merged on the central veil
as pure presences of light.

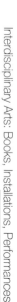

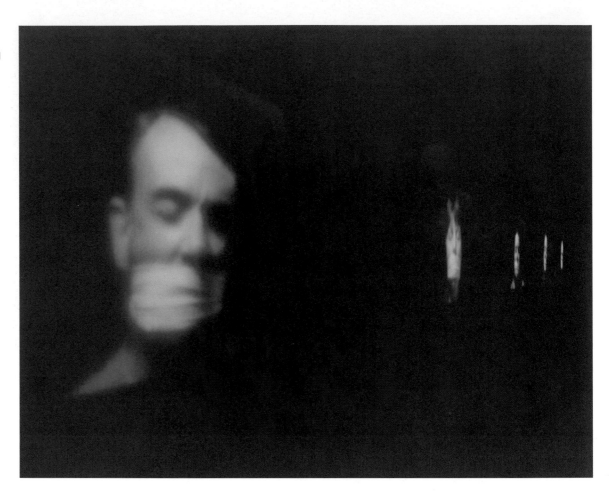

A very different effect was created in *Hall of Whispers* (12.28). In his catalog for a retrospective exhibition of Viola's work, David Ross wrote:

> Viewers enter a long, narrow, dark room, and must pass between ten video projections arranged in two rows along the side walls, five on either side of the room. The projections are life-sized black and white images of people's heads facing the viewer, with their eyes closed and their mouths tightly bound and gagged. They are straining to speak, but their muffled voices are incomprehensible, and mingle in the space in a low, indecipherable jumble of sound.[4]

This installation, while similar to *Floodsong* in layout, created an entry into a nightmare. Lucier's installation evoked a range of emotions: fear, pity, and respect; while Viola's *Hall of Whispers* evoked terror.

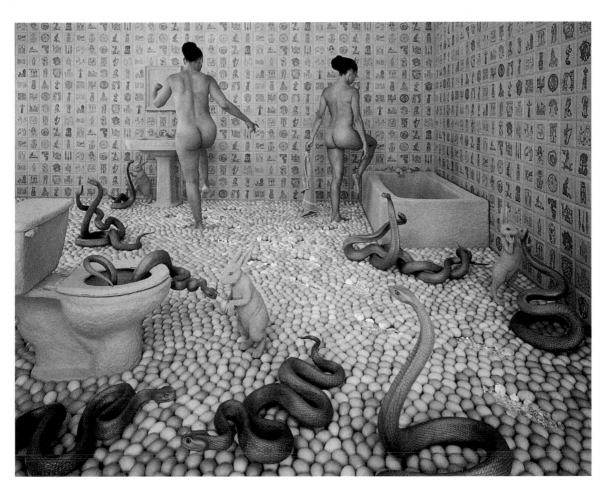

12.29 Sandy Skoglund, *Walking on Eggshells*, 1997. Cibachrome print. 47 × 60 in. (119 × 152 cm).

The Importance of Context

Installations must be seen in context. Spatial variations from site to site require changes in an installation whenever it is moved. More importantly, each site adds its own meaning to the artwork. No site is neutral. Each imparts its own emotional and spatial charge.

When the context is used fully, a powerful connection can be made between art and life. For example, our associations with the interior and the objects used in Sandy Skoglund's *Walking on Eggshells* (12.29) are essential to the meaning of the piece. For most of us, there is no place more private than a bathroom and there are few animals more insidiously frightening than snakes. This combination alone is sure to create tension. Addition of a floor covered with delicate eggshells, twin female figures, and playful rabbits expands the expressive range

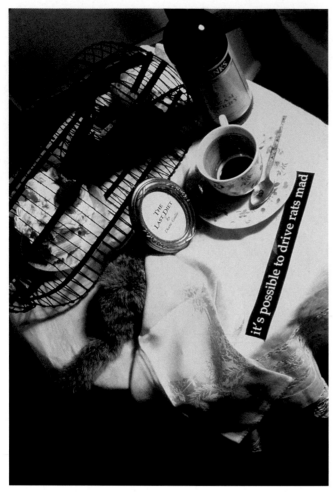

12.30 Diane Gallo and Nancy Callahan, *Storefront Stories*, 1999. Mixed medium installation 6 × 6 × 6 ft (1.83 × 1.83 × 1.83 m).

further. Even the wall tiles are deliberate. Dominated by hieroglyphics from the Egyptian Book of the Dead and other ancient images, they add to the sense of mystery. The women in this space seem like goddesses from antiquity, and the bathroom becomes loaded with conflicting emotions.

A site may also be used to expand the audience for art. In *Storefront Stories* (12.30), Nancy Callahan and Diane Gallo (see Chapter 4 "Profile," page 4-10) transformed empty shop windows in several small towns into a series of vignettes based on childhood memories. When shown in Cherry Valley, New York, a single window was changed every day over a six-week period. In this project, personal experience became public communication through the use of a nontraditional exhibition space.

Through *Truisms* (12.31), Jenny Holzer brought public art to an urban audience for a more political purpose. Printing various proverbs on posters, flyers, t-shirts, hats, and finally, on electronic signs, Holzer used mass-marketing techniques to convey messages such as "Abuse of Power comes as no Surprise" and "Raise Boys and Girls the Same Way." Shown next to the flashing neon signs in New York City's busy Time Square, these seemingly banal messages took on new importance and reached many viewers unfamiliar with contemporary art.

Advantages of Installation Art

For the artist seeking new and expanded means of expression, installation art offers:

- *A fresh perspective on a familiar setting or situation.* The site itself is an essential component of the piece. We must see familiar settings afresh. Any aspect of reality can become a staging area for art. Our expectations may become shifted, inverted, or upended.

- *A large scale.* Most installations are made in a size that invites physical entry. Thus, the distance between viewer and image is eliminated: we become one with the artwork. The principles of time, space, and gravity that rule our everyday life can be used deliberately in an

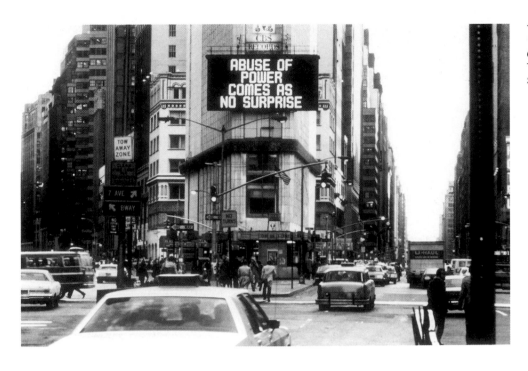

installation to heighten impact or to create a sense of disorientation.

- *Increased viewer involvement.* No longer a bystander, the viewer must physically enter and consciously interact with the artwork.

Performance Art

Mixing dance, theater, music, and art with politics, philosophy, and other disciplines, performance art pushes the possibilities of interdisciplinary work even further. As with any other art form, performance art is designed to communicate ideas and express emotions. Unlike traditional art forms, performance art is immediate and direct. Rather than paint an image on a canvas, the performers generally present images directly, on a stage, in a gallery, or outdoors. The wood, bronze, or marble of traditional figurative sculpture is replaced with the flesh and blood of the artist's own body. The stage becomes a laboratory for aesthetic experimentation and the audience, as much as the artist, may determine the outcome of an event.

Historical Background

Performance art has become especially prominent in the past ten years. The current surge in interest is often traced to the Happenings developed by Allan Kaprow and others in the fifties and sixties. In a **Happening,** the time, place, materials, and general theme for the event were determined by the artist. Upon arrival, the audience created the artwork through their actions. Unrehearsed, these events were often chaotic as well as exhilarating.

The roots and rationale for contemporary performance art actually extend back in time to the Futurists, a group of Italian poets, musicians, and artists most active from 1911 to 1915. Determined to develop a new approach to art, they created revolutionary paintings and sculptures based on dynamism, wrote inflammatory manifestos, and staged theatrical performances that were both frenetic and shocking. In word and deed, the Futurists rebelled against good taste, traditional subject matter, compositional rules, and established institutions, such as museums.

Characteristics of Performance Art

To some extent, contemporary performance art shares many of the basic characteristics of Futurism. Four qualities are most notable.

The Element of Time

Just as a symphony ceases to exist as soon as the last note fades, so performance art is inherently ephemeral. While a piece may persist in the memory of each member of the audience, the full force of the event disappears as soon as the audience leaves the site. While any well-trained classical violinist can perform a given Beethoven sonata, roles in performance pieces are rarely played by new actors. Generally, a piece written by Laurie Anderson must be performed by her. Even when a new production is planned, difficulty in transferring information about the role may make it impossible to restage the piece.

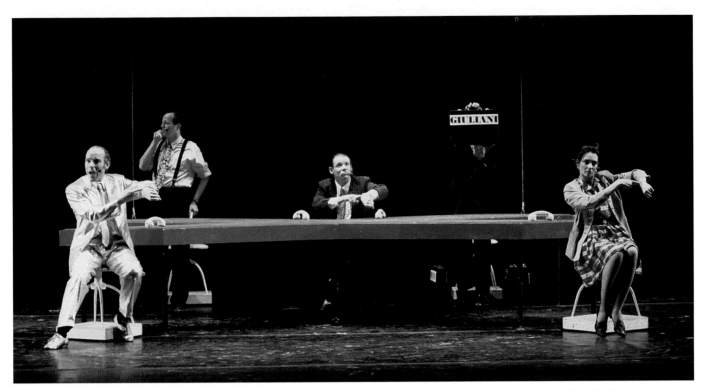

12.32 Karole Armitage, *Predator's Ball,* **1996.** Brooklyn Academy of Music. Sets by David Salle, animation videos by Erica Beckman, costumes by Hugo Boss, Pila Limosner & Debra Moises Co.

As a result, time is always of particular importance in performance art. In 1952, musician John Cage deleted pitch, timbre, and loudness from one composition, leaving duration as the only remaining aspect of the music. The resulting work, titled *4 minutes 33 seconds* (4'33") was therefore silent for four minutes and thirty-three seconds.

Time was also a major component of Dan Graham's *Past Continuous Pasts,* installed in a New York City gallery in 1974. The walls were covered with mirrors, and time-delayed video monitors were positioned at either end of the room. Upon entering, viewers first viewed themselves in the present, then, watching the video monitors, viewed themselves in the past.

Multidisciplinary Collaboration

Working collaboratively, artists can expand their ideas and explore new modes of expression. Despite their interest in live art, few visual artists have extensive training in dance and theater. It may be physically impossible for them to perform a movement themselves. And, just as an amateur's drawing is very different from a drawing done by a professional, so amateur dance differs greatly from professional dance. By working collaboratively, artists, actors, musicians, and dancers can combine forces to create powerful new pieces.

Furthermore, a collaboration tends to extend the ideas generated by each of the participants. Despite their similarities, art, theater, music, and dance are also distinctively different. Each has a long and complex history, an extensive theoretical background, and particular aesthetic values. By sharing information and discussing alternative approaches to an idea, each participant in a performance has an opportunity to rethink his or her their own creative process.

Many disciplines have been combined successfully. In *Predator's Ball* (12.32), Karole Armitage combined her choreography with sets by painter David Salle and videos by Erica Beckman. This tale about Wall Street junk bond dealer Michael Milken is both stark in its staging and frenzied in its energy.

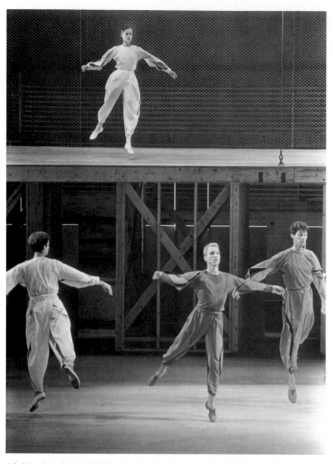

12.33 Lucinda Childs, Image from *Available Light*, 1983. Performed at the Brooklyn Academy of Music.

In *Available Light* (12.33), choreographer Lucinda Childs sought a pulse in the spaces designed by architect Frank Gehry and the music composed by John Adams. And, in *L.O.W. in Gaia* (12.34), Rachel Rosenthal presented a meditation on art, feminism, and ecology.

Blurred Boundaries

During a performance, separations between art and life are often dissolved. For some artists, performance art is a way to work outside the rarefied world of the art museum or the competitive world of the commercial gallery. Viewing art as a creative process and a life-affirming philosophy rather than as a product, such artists seek new venues and new audiences. Separations between high art and mass culture may become blurred. Graffiti, popular music, or television advertisements may provide more inspiration than a masterpiece in a museum. Indeed, in describing his approach to a Happening, Allan Kaprow said that "the line between art and life should be kept as fluid and perhaps as indistinct as possible."

Many contemporary artists pursue this goal with a vengeance. In John Cage's *First Construction in Metal,* automobile brake drums, cowbells, and

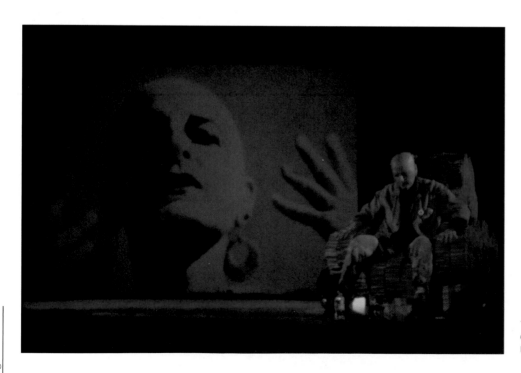

12.34 Rachel Rosenthal, *L.O.W. in Gaia.* First performance, Marquette University, WI. 1986.

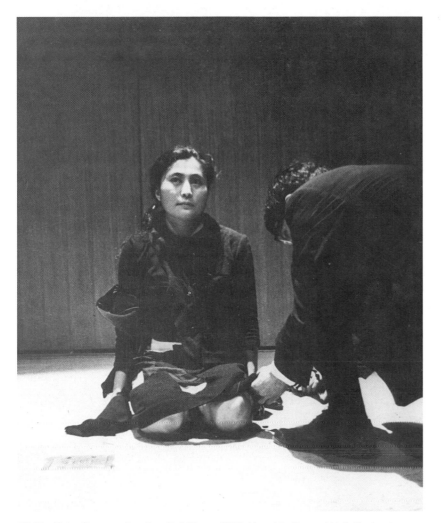

12.35 **Yoko Ono, performing *Cut Piece*, 1964.** Yamaidu Concert Hall, Kyoto, Japan.

involve the audience in the work. In *Performance/Audience/Mirror,* Dan Graham confronted his audience directly, describing their appearance and commenting on their participation in the performance. In *Cut Piece* (12.35), musician Yoko Ono knelt on the stage, as a traditional Japanese woman. Throughout the half-hour performance, members of the audience approached, and using a large pair of scissors provided, cut off her clothing. And with *Pull,* Mona Hatoum created a humorous interaction between audience and artist. Viewers were invited to pull on an actual braid of hair, then watch the artist's reaction on the video monitor. No longer an observer, each member of the audience helped create the artwork.

The Advantages of Interdisciplinary Art

Visual books, installations, and performance art all require interdisciplinary integration. The connections created offer new opportunities for creative thinking and complex communication. Ideas and emotions outside the mainstream can become accessible to both artists and audiences. Furthermore, because each of these new media requires a substantial amount of audience participation, relationships between artist and audience become redefined. An active audience can contribute more to the experience than a passive audience. When artist and audience share the same time and space, as in a performance piece, this connection is especially strong.

With performance art, boundaries dissolve, not only between art and theater, but also between art and life.

sheets of metal are used along with conventional percussion instruments in a highly rhythmic piece. In *Imaginary Landscape #4,* Cage broke the concert-hall barrier even more vigorously. Twelve ordinary radios, tuned to various stations, were the major instruments played. Any advertisement, news, or music each radio played became part of the concert.

The Artist and the Audience

When barriers between art and life are removed, separations between artist and audience also become blurred. Indeed, many artists deliberately

Profile:
Bonnie Mitchell, Internet Artist

As Worlds Collide: Collaborative
Creativity Using the World Wide Web

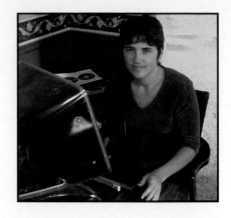

Bonnie Mitchell is an internationally renowned Internet artist. Since 1992, she has explored collaborative creativity through five major Internet projects. Her work has been exhibited in the United States as well as in the United Kingdom, the Netherlands, Germany, and Siberia. She has shown work at the SIGGRAPH Art Show, International Symposium of Electronic Arts, Digital Salon, and ArcadeII as well as at other computer art shows. Mitchell has lectured widely on creativity and computer art, including presentations at conferences and symposia around the world. She is currently an assistant professor at Bowling Green State University, where she teaches interactive multimedia and 3D computer animation.

MS: A commitment to collaboration is a major aspect of both your artwork and your teaching. Why collaborate?
BM: Artists do not operate in a vacuum. They are inspired and influenced by other artists, the visual environment, human interaction, and experience. Collaboration enables artists to better understand their own creativity by forcing them to engage in a situation where they must work cooperatively. When collaborating, the artist can't have complete control over the artwork. Instead, he or she must consider alternative ways to solve visual problems. For instance, if I were given a white canvas or blank computer screen and asked to create a work of art, I would create something very different than if I were asked to manipulate an image that had been drawn by someone else. In my collaborative Internet art projects, each artists' visual response was affected by the image that they were given or chose to manipulate. Collaboration also helps to form communities of people that have similar interests.

MS: *Chain Art*, in 1992, was your first major Internet project. How did it start, and what were the results?
BM: It began with a call for participation, sent via e-mail to six people. These people forwarded the message to many other people around the globe. Within a week, I received over 200 responses. Participants were then divided into 22 groups, based on their computer capabilities and geographical location. I tried to make each team as diverse as possible. We started with six members per group, but as people dropped out and others joined, this number fluctuated. Overall, participants from 10 countries contributed a total of 136 images.

Each group was given a starter image which consisted of an incomplete composition. A member of the team downloaded the image from my site, manipulated the image, and returned it to the site. The next team member downloaded the changed image, manipulated that, and

returned it to the site. This continued over a six-week period. All of the images were available on my site at the end.

The World Wide Web was not really developed in 1992. It was very difficult to transfer images using FTP [file transfer protocol], and you could not view the images directly from the Internet. Also, there were not nearly as many artists using the Internet as there are today. Nevertheless, the *Chain Art* project increased my interest in creativity and when the World Wide Web was better developed in 1993, I decided to expand my work.

MS: *Digital Journey* (1993) seems much more open-ended, allowing people to submit more than just images.
BM: Yes. Rather than a simple starter image, participants were offered 20 starter Web pages, each with a different theme. Each page provided images, poetic text, and instructions on how to contribute. Since successful multimedia projects often combine visual art, writing, animation, and audio, participants were encouraged to send contributions which would be connected to any element on the page that inspired them. I developed the *Virtual Self* page, which received numerous images, poems, and videos from individuals around the world.

MS: What was the result?`
BM: The submissions were extremely varied. For example, one participant submitted a URL to link up to the word "quest," whereas another person submitted images to link up to phrases such as "electronically altered ego," etc. We received small animations and lots of poetic text and images, but no audio files. I was amazed to find that "fashion" and "tattoos" were the two most popular Web-page themes.

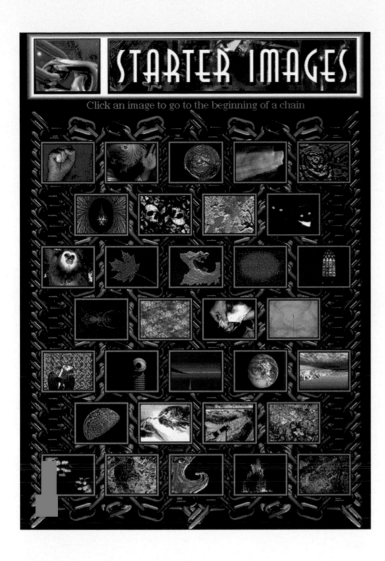

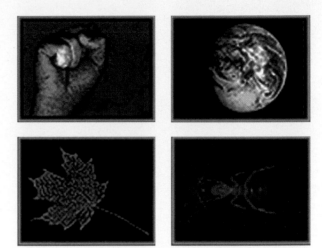

Bonnie Mitchell, Images from Websites entitled *Chain Art* (top left) and *Digital Journey* (below left). Above, detail from *Chain Art*.

MS: After *Digital Journey,* you created two more collaborative WWW art projects based on the *Chain Art* concept. Could you describe your most recent project?

BM: *As Worlds Collide,* developed in fall 1997, added the element of space and time. Using Apple Quicktime VR, I was able to create panoramic virtual reality artworks, or "worlds," which the viewer could explore by zooming in and out or by moving right and left. The images could be animated interactively, thus revealing themselves over time. As with the previous projects, participants wishing to manipulate a "world" downloaded a digital image to alter. When the image was returned to my server, it was automatically converted into a panoramic world and published on the World Wide Web.

MS: What did you and your collaborators gain from these Internet experiences?

BM: With each project, virtual communities were formed. Participants collectively developed ideas and shared experiences over the Internet. Cultural and social boundaries disappeared. Influence and inspiration, combined with personal insight, provided the building blocks for further creative collaboration. We all learned from each other.

MS: It's amazing. This is so unlike traditional artwork, both in process and result. One last question: do you have any advice for my students?

BM: Think big! The WWW provides new possibilities for creativity as well as communication. Reach out beyond the confines of your own school and community and always look for ways of improving your understanding of your own creativity as well as the world in general.

Summary

- A visual book is an experimental structure that conveys ideas, actions, and emotions in an integrated and interdependent format. Each page is connected in some way to the preceding page and the following page.

- Visual books combine two-dimensional composition with three-dimensional structure and may use time and narrative very deliberately. They may be entirely visual, entirely verbal, or may mix words and images.

- In selecting a text, consider its potential to generate ideas, how a text will be divided and distributed over multiple pages, the rhythm and music of the words, and the significance of the ideas.

- Every typestyle has its own distinctive quality, which can add or detract from the meaning of the book.

- The combination of words and images in a visual book can encourage the development of complex ideas using layers of meaning.

- An installation may be defined as an ensemble of images and objects that is presented within a three-dimensional environment. When the viewer enters an installation, he or she is physically surrounded and aesthetically engaged.

- An installation may be primarily spatial in nature, primarily temporal, or may use both equally. The context in which an installation occurs can add to, subtract from, or expand its meaning.

- Installation art offers a fresh perspective on a familiar setting or situation, is usually done in large scale, and requires some viewer involvement.

- Performance art is live art designed by artists. Combining aspects of theater, music, art, and dance, it offers both the artist and the audience a laboratory for aesthetic experimentation.

- Many performance artists use time very deliberately, expand their ideas through collaboration, and seek to blur the boundaries between art and life.

- Each of the interdisciplinary arts described in this chapter requires substantial audience participation. As a result, relationships between the artist and the audience are constantly being redefined by contemporary artists.

Keywords

gloss	installation art	typestyle
gutter	interdisciplinary art	visual book
Happening	performance art	

When designing a visual book, consider:
1. What thoughts and emotions do you most want to express?
2. What thoughts and emotions are best expressed in words? Which are better expressed through images?
3. What balance between words and images is best? It is wise to make one prototype that is primarily verbal, one that is primarily visual, and several that use words and images equally.
4. How many pages are needed? Crowding all the words and images onto a few pages is rarely effective. Try distributing this information over 10 or more pages, using the fronts and backs of pages equally and creating a continuous flow. Try adding some blank pages for emphasis.

When designing an installation, consider:
1. What ideas do you want to express? What emotions do you want to evoke?
2. Viewers actively explore installations. How will you invite them into your artwork? What will they discover as they explore the space? What may they know on leaving that they didn't know on entering? What is the nature of the experience you are offering?
3. What is the advantage of a confined space as opposed to an expansive space?
4. Is a well-lit environment appropriate, or should the space be dark, possibly threatening?
5. What sounds will you provide, and what sounds can be generated by the audience?

When designing a performance, consider:
1. What ideas and emotions are best explored through live art?
2. Do you have the acting, dancing, speaking, or musical skill needed for your project, or do you need to find performers?
3. When working collaboratively, what can you offer to your partner and what can your partner offer to you? What similarities and differences are there in your creative processes? What is the best way to handle differences of opinion?
4. How, when, and where can rehearsals occur?
5. How many performers are needed? A monologue by a solo performer is very different from a duet or a performance involving 20 people.
6. What is the relationship between the performer(s) and the set? Should all the performers appear live, or can some appear via slides or video projections?
7. How can sound and light heighten emotion or expand meaning?
8. What role will the audience play?

Roselee Goldberg, *Performance: Live Art Since 1960*. New York, Harry N. Abrams, 1998.

Nicolas de Oliveria, Nicola Oxley, and Michael Petry, *Installation Art*. Washington, DC, Smithsonian Institution Press, 1994.

David Ross, *Bill Viola*. New York, Whitney Museum of American Art, 1998.

Keith A. Smith, *Structure of the Visual Book*. Fairport, NY, The Sigma Foundation, Inc., 1992.

Keith A. Smith, *Text in the Book Format*. Fairport, NY, The Sigma Foundation, Inc., 1991.

Glossary
by Mary Stewart and Peter Forbes

A

abstract form In film, a multiple-image structure, in which the parts are related to each other through their visual characteristics, such as shape, color, scale, or direction of movement.

abstract shape A shape that is derived from a perceptual source but is so transformed that it bears little visual resemblance to that source.

abstraction The reduction of an image or object to an essential aspect of its form or content.

accent A specific note in music that has been emphasized, or a shape, volume, color, and so on in visual art that has been emphasized. Using an accent, a designer can bring attention to a specific part of a composition and increase rhythmic variety in a pattern.

accent color A color that stands out from its surroundings. Often used to attract attention to a specific part of a design.

act A major division in a film or theatrical event. Acts are generally constructed from a group of sequences that gradually increase in intensity.

action-to-action transition In comic books, the juxtaposition of two or more panels showing a sequence of specific actions. This is the most common transition in American comic books.

actual lines Lines that are physically present in a design.

additive color Color created by combining projected beams of chromatic light. The additive color primaries are red, green, and blue; the secondaries are cyan, magenta, and yellow.

additive sculpture A physical object constructed from separate parts that have been connected using glues, joints, stitching, welds, and so on.

afterimage In visual perception, a ghostly image that continues to linger after the actual image has been removed.

amplified perspective The exaggerated use of linear perspective to achieve a dramatic and engaging presentation of the subject. Amplified perspective is often created using an unusual viewing position, such as a bird's-eye view, accelerated convergence, or some form of distortion.

analogous color A color scheme based on hues that are adjacent on a color wheel, such as red, orange, and yellow.

analogy A similarity or connection between things that are apparently separate and dissimilar. Analogies are often used to explain a difficult concept or unfamilar skill. For example, when a teacher describes wet plaster as having the "consistency of cream," she is using an analogy.

angle of framing The position of the frame in relation to the subject it shows. The frame may be above the subject, creating a bird's-eye view, straight on, or below the subject, creating a worm's-eye view. Also known as the camera angle.

anomaly An obvious break from norm in a design. Often used to emphasize an aspect of a design.

aspect-to-aspect transition In comic books, the juxtaposition of two or more panels showing different views of a single setting or event. This transition is often used in Japanese comic books.

assemblage An additive method in which the artist or designer constructs the artwork using objects and images that were originally created for another purpose. Essentially, assemblage can be defined as three-dimensional collage.

asymmetrical balance An equilibrium among visual elements that differ in size, number, weight, color, or texture. Asymmetrical balance is generally nonaxial and highly dynamic.

atmospheric perspective A visual phenomenon in which the atmospheric density progressively increases, hazing over the perceived world as one looks into its depth. Overall definition lessens, details fade, and contrasts become muted. In a landscape, a blue mist descends.

attached shadow A shadow connected to the surface of an object that defines its form through tonal modulation.

B

backlight A light source positioned behind a person or object that can create a silhouette or separate the person or object from the background.

balance An equilibrium among interacting and/or opposing forces in a visual composition.

base A horizontal support for a physical object, such as a marble block for mounting a bronze sculpture.

beat 1. A unit of musical rhythm that creates the pulse of a sound. 2. In acting, the most basic element in a story. A beat is an exchange of behavior, based on action and reaction.

boundary The point of division between objects, images, or experiences.

brainstorming Any of a number of problem-solving techniques that are designed to expand ideas and encourage creativity. List-making, mapping, associative thinking, and metaphorical thinking are common strategies used.

C

calligraphic line Derived from the Greek words for beautiful and writing, a flowing, and expressive line that is as personal as handwriting. Calligraphic lines generally vary in thickness and apparent velocity.

carving The removal of materials from a larger mass, gradually revealing an image or object. Carving is a subtractive process.

cast shadow A dark shape, created by the absence of light, that results from placement of an opaque object in the path of a light source.

categorical form In film, a multiple-image structure that is organized based on categories, or subsets, of a topic. For example, a film on Hawaii might focus first on the sea, then on the volcanoes, then on the plant life, then on indigenous animals.

causality The interrelation of cause and effect, based on the premise that nothing occurs without cause.

cause-and-effect A critique in which the viewer seeks to determine the cause for each visual or emotional effect in a design. For example, the dynamism in a design may be caused by the diagonal lines and asymmetrical balance used. Also known as formal analysis.

centrifugal balance Balance created when visual forces in a composition imply an outward expansion.

centripetal balance Balance created when visual forces in a composition imply an inward movement, suggesting a compression of space.

characteristic texture The inherent, or familiar, texture of a material. The gleaming reflective surface of a steel teapot and the gritty texture of clay are two examples.

chroma The purity, intensity, or saturation of a color.

chromatic gray A gray made from a mixture of color plus white rather than simply using black and white.

chronology The order in which events occur.

close-up In film, a type of framing in which the scale of the object shown is relatively large, as in a close-up of an actor's face.

closure The mind's inclination to connect fragmentary information in order to create a completed form. Closure is an essential aspect of Gestalt psychology.

collage An image constructed from visual or verbal fragments initially designed for another purpose.

color key A color that dominates an image and provides an overall visual or emotional effect.

compare/contrast critique A critique in which similarities and differences between two designs are analyzed. Often used in art history classes to demonstrate connections and divisions between historical periods.

comparison Recognition of similarity in two or more compositions. Often used in art history to demonstrate connections between images done by different artists or in different periods. The images being compared may be similar in balance, color, content, style, and so on.

complementary colors Hues that oppose one another on a traditional color wheel. When juxtaposed, complementary colors create contrast; when mixed, complementary colors neutralize each other, creating a variety of browns.

composition The combination of multiple parts to create a harmonious whole.

compression The forcing or crushing of material into a smaller, denser condition and its visual dynamics and implied psychological effects.

concentric balance The repetition of a boundary in diminishing size to create a bull's-eye effect. Concentric balance can harness both the expanding energy of centrifugal balance and the compressive energy of centripetal balance.

concept A well-developed thought or a comprehensive generalization.

condensation To be reduced to a denser form, as with the transition from a vapor to a liquid

cone of vision In perspective drawing, a hypothetical cone of perception originating at the eye of the artist and expanding outward to include whatever he or she wishes to record in an illusionistic image, such as a perspective drawing. The cone's maximum scoping angle is 45 to 60 degrees; anything outside of the cone of vision is subject to distortion.

connection 1. A unifying relationship in a composition. 2. A physical joining, through joints, welds, stitching, and so forth.

contact The meeting point between visual or structural elements in a design.

content The emotional and/or intellectual meaning or message of an artwork.

continuity A fluid connection among compositional parts.

contour line A line that describes the edges of a form and suggests three-dimensional volume.

contradictory texture The unfamiliar use of a texture or the addition of an unusual texture to the surface of an object. Meret Oppenheim's *Object*, a cup, plate and spoon covered with fur, is a familiar example.

contrast The degree of difference between compositional parts or between one image and another. High contrast tends to be eye-catching and is often used by graphic designers to create dynamic, highly readable images.

contrasting colors Colors that are substantially different in hue, value, intensity or temperature.

convergent thinking A problem-solving strategy in which a predetermined goal is pursued in a linear progression using a highly focused problem-solving process. Six steps are commonly used: (1) define the problem, (2) do research, (3) determine your objective, (4) devise a strategy, (5) execute the strategy, (6) evaluate the results.

critique Any means by which the strengths and weaknesses of designs are analyzed. Common strategies include comparision, description, formal analysis, and inventing alternatives.

cropping The manner in which a section of an image or a fragment of observed reality has been framed. For example, photographers select a fragment of reality every time they look through the viewfinder of the camera. Part of the scene is included, while the remainder is cut away. Photographs are often cropped further in the darkroom, leaving only the most significant information.

cross contour Multiple, curving, parallel lines running over the surface of an object horizontally and/or vertically that describe its surface configuration topographically, as in mapping. This process is much like wireframing in three-dimensional computer modeling. Cross contours can also be used in drawing to suggest three-dimensional form through tonal variation.

crosscut In film, an abrupt alternation between two or more lines of action.

cross-hatching A technique used in drawing and printmaking to shade an object using two or more networks of parallel lines. Darker values are created as the number of line networks increases.

curvilinear shape A shape whose contour is dominated by curves and flowing lines.

cut In film, the immediate change from one shot or frame to another

D

definition 1. The degree to which a shape is distinguished from both the ground area and from other shapes within the design. 2. The degree of resolution or focus of an entire image. Sharply focused shapes tend to advance while blurred shapes tend to recede.

denouement The outcome, solution, or point of clarification in a story.

density The extent to which compositional parts are spread out or crowded together. The visual connections that occur easily in a high-density composition are often less obvious in a low-density composition.

depth of field The range of focus in a photographic image, from foreground to background. In a photograph with great depth of field, an object that is 15 feet from the camera is in focus, as well as an object that is 5 feet from the camera.

descriptive critique A critique in which the viewer carefully describes what he or she sees when observing a design. Descriptive critiques are used to heighten awareness of visual relationships, for both the artist and the viewer.

descriptive shape A shape that is derived from specific subject matter and strongly based on perceptual reality.

diegesis The world created in a film or video.

dissolve A transition between two shots during which the first image gradually disappears while the second image gradually appears.

dissonance The absence of harmony in a composition; often created using disharmonious colors.

distribution The manner in which colors, shapes, or other visual elements are arranged within the format.

divergent thinking An open-ended, problem-solving strategy. Starting with a broad theme, the designer explores in all directions, expanding ideas in all directions.

duration 1. The length of time required for the completion of an event, as in the running time of a film, video, or performance; 2. the running time of events depicted in the story (plot duration); 3. and the overall span of time the story encompasses (story duration).

dynamic Energetic, vigorous, forceful; creating or suggesting change or motion.

E

earthwork An artwork that has been created through the transformation of a natural site into an aesthetic statement.

editing In film, selecting and sequencing the details of an event to create a comprehensive whole.

elevation In orthographic projection, the front, back, and side views of an object or architectural structure.

emotional advertising Use of emotion to sell a service, product, or idea. This strategy is often used when a product is neither unique nor demonstrably better than a competing product.

emphasis Special attention given to some aspect of a composition, which gives it prominence.

exaggerated advertising Pushing an idea to an extreme to make a point.

expansion The extending outward of a material to fill more space.

eye level In linear perspective, the eye level is determined by the physical position of the artist. Sitting on the floor creates a low eye level while standing at an easel creates a higher eye level. Also known as the horizon line. All vanishing points in one- and two-point perspective are positioned on the eye level.

F

fade A gradual transition used in film and video. 1. Fade-in: commonly, a dark screen that gradually brightens as a shot appears. 2. fade-out: a shot that gradually darkens until the screen goes black.

fidelity The degree of connection between a sound and its source. For example, when we hear the sound of a helicopter and see a helicopter on the screen, the sound matches with the image, creating close fidelity.

figure The primary or positive shape in a design; a shape that is noticeably separated from the background. The figure is the dominant, advancing shape in a figure-ground relationship.

figure/ground reversal An arrangement in which positive and negative shapes alternatively command attention. Also known as positive and negative interchange.

fill light In cinematic and theatrical lighting, a diffused light that is used to decrease contrast between light and dark areas.

filtration The process of separating a solid from a liquid by passing it through a porous substance such as cloth, charcoal, or sand.

flashback In film, an alternation in chronology in which events that occur later in a story are shown first.

floodlight A softly defined light with a broad beam.

form 1. The physical manifestation of a design as opposed to the content, or the idea behind a design. 2. The organization or arrangement of visual elements to create a unified art form.

format The type of shape used for the outer edge of a design.

frame A single static image in film or video.

freestanding sculpture Sculpture that is self-supporting and is designed to be viewed from all sides.

function The purpose of a design or the objective that motivates the designer. For an industrial designer, the primary purpose of a design is often utilitarian. For example, he or she may be required to design a more fuel-efficient automobile. For a sculptor, the primary purpose of a design is aesthetic: he or she seeks to create an artwork that engages the viewer emotionally and philosophically. However, a sculpture, like an automobile, must be physically well-constructed, and a car, like a sculpture, must have aesthetic appeal.

fusion The combination of shapes or volumes along a common edge.

G

geometric shape A shape derived from or suggestive of mathematics. Geometric shapes are characterized by crisp, precise edges and mathematically consistent curves.

gestalt A German word for "form." A complete configuration that we perceive through psychological closure. This configuration is more complete than the sum of its parts. In a gestalt, all elements operate in relation to the whole.

gesture drawing A vigorous drawing that captures movement and the overall orientation of an object, rather than describing specific detail. Often used as a basis for figure drawing.

gloss 1. In writing, words of explanation or translation inserted into a text. 2. A secondary text within a manuscript that provides comments on the main text.

gradation Any gradual transition from one color to another or from one shape or volume to another. In drawing, shading created through the gradation of grays can be used to suggest three-dimensional form.

graphic relationship In film, the juxtaposition of two or more separate images that are compositionally similar. For example, a graphic relationship can be created when a basketball is shown in the first panel, an aerial view of the round free-throw zone is shown in the second, and the hoop of the basket itself is shown in the third.

gravity The force that tends to pull all bodies toward the center of the Earth.

grid A visual or physical structure created from intersecting parallel lines. A grid can provide the compositional framework for a design.

grisaille A gray underpainting, often used by Renaissance artists, to increase the illusion of space.

group In sequential structure, a collection of images that are related by subject matter, composition, or source.

gutter In bookbinding, the center line of a book, where the two pages meet.

Happening An assemblage of improvised, spontaneous events performed by the artist and audience alike, based on a general theme. There is no rehearsal, and any location, from a parking lot to a factory interior, can be used. The Happening is most commonly associated with Allan Kaprow and is a precursor to performance art.

hard-sell advertising An advertising approach in which a major point is presented in a clear, direct manner. The narrative is usually linear, and the message is usually explicit.

harmony A pleasing or soothing relationship among colors, shapes, or other design elements.

hatching A technique used in drawing and printmaking to shade using a range of gray tones created from multiple parallel lines.

high definition Sharply focused visual information that is highly readable.

horizon line In linear perspective, the line on which all vanishing points are positioned. More accurately described as the eye line or eye level.

hue The name of a color, such as red or yellow, that distinguishes it from others and assigns it a position in the visual spectrum and on the color wheel.

humorous advertising Use of humor to sell a service, product, or idea. By entertaining the viewer, the designer can make the product memorable.

illusionary space The representation of an object or scene on a two-dimensional surface so as to give it the appearance of three-dimensionality.

implied line 1. A line that is suggested by movement or by a gesture rather than being physically drawn or constructed. 2. A line that is suggested by the positions of shapes or objects within a design. With either form of implied line, the viewer mentally connects the points.

installation art An artwork or a design that presents an ensemble of images and objects within a three-dimensional environment.

intensity 1. The purity, saturation, or chroma of a color. For example, fire engine red is a high-intensity color, while brick red is a low intensity color. 2. In theater, the power, concentration, and energy with which an action is performed or the quality of observation of an event.

interdisciplinary art The combination of two or more different disciplines to create a hybrid art form.

interdisciplinary thinking Use of skills and knowledge from more than one discipline.

in the round A three-dimensional object that is self-supporting and is designed to be viewed from all sides, as in freestanding sculpture.

joint A physical connection between elements or parts in a three-dimensional object. Some joints are fixed, such as ones that are bolted together, while others can be moved, as with a hinge or a ball-and-socket joint.

junction 1. A conceptual intersection between ideas or events. 2. A physical intersection between elements or parts in a three-dimensional object.

K

key light The primary source of illumination used by filmmakers and set designers.

kinesthetic Bodily perception of position, balance, movement, tension, and so on.

kinetic form A static form that suggests motion or a form that actually moves.

L

lap dissolve In film, a dissolve in which two shots are temporarily superimposed.

layers of space Separating compositional space into foreground, middle ground, and background to intensify expressive possibilities and spatial complexity.

line 1. A point in motion. 2. A series of adjacent points. 3. A connection between points. 4. An implied connection between points. Line is one of the basic elements of design.

linear perspective A mathematically based system for projecting the apparent dimensions of a three-dimensional object onto a two-dimensional surface called the picture plane. Developed by artists during the Renaissance, linear perspective is one strategy for creating the illusion of space.

long shot In film, a type of framing in which the scale of the subject shown is relatively small, as with an image of a human figure within a landscape.

loudness The amplitude of a sound wave; the strength of a sound.

low definition Blurred or ill-defined visual information that is difficult to read.

M

maquette A well-developed, three-dimensional model, comparable to a two-dimensional thumbnail sketch.

mass A volume that has weight, density, and bulk.

medium shot In film, a type of framing in which the scale of the subject shown is of moderate size, as in a view of an actor from the waist up.

metaphor A figure of speech in which one thing is directly linked to another dissimilar thing. Through this connection, the original word is given the qualities of the linked word. For example, when we say, "she's a diamond in the rough," we attribute to a woman the qualities of an unpolished gem.

meter The basic pattern of sound and silence in music or of positive and negative in design.

model In three-dimensional design, a model is a technical experiment or a small-scale version of a larger design.

modeling An additive sculptural process by which a plastic material is formed into an artwork or design.

moment-to-moment transition In comic books, a transition in which a character or situation is simply being observed over time. This transition is often used in Japanese comic books but rarely in American comic books.

monochromatic color system A color system based on variations in a single hue. For example, a light, pastel blue, a medium navy blue, and a dark blue-black may be used in a monochromatic design.

myth A traditional story collectively composed by many members of a society. The creation of the world, sources of evil, the power of knowledge, and even the nature of reality may be explained through these grand expressions of the imagination.

N

negative shape 1. Any clearly defined area around a positive shape; the receding shape or ground area in a figure-ground relationship. 2. A shape created through the absence of an object rather than through the presence of an object.

nonobjective shape Circles, squares, and other shapes that are not based on a specific perceptual source.

non-sequitur transition In comic books, the juxtaposition of two or more frames or shots that have no obvious conceptual relationship.

O

objective criticism The assessment of strengths and weaknesses in a design based on the visual information presented. Essentially, objective criticism focuses on the ways in which lines, shapes, textures, volumes, and so forth are combined to create a cohesive whole.

one-point perspective A form of linear perspective in which the lines receding into space converge at a single vanishing point on the eye level or horizon line.

opponent theory An explanation for the electric glow that occurs when two complementary colors are placed side by side.

organic shape A shape based on forms from the natural world or suggestive of living organisms. Also known as biomorphic shape.

orientation The angle at which a visual element is positioned.

orthographic projection A drawing system widely used by artists and designers to delineate the top, bottom, and four side views of a three-dimensional object. Orthographic means "true picture." Unlike perspective drawing, which is designed to create the illusion of space, an orthographic projection is constructed using parallel lines that accurately delineate the object.

overlap Placement of one shape in front of another to create the illusion of space.

oxidation A common form of chemical change used in creating a patina, or colored surface, on a metal sculpture.

P

panel A single frame in a comic book.

pattern A design composed of repeated elements that are usually varied to produce interconnections and implied movement.

pedestal A vertical support for a sculptural object.

performance art A live presentation which may combine elements from a variety of art forms, such as film, video, theater, and dance.

permanence The degree of durability, or resistance to decay, in a given material or design.

perspective A graphic system used to create the illusion of space on a two-dimensional surface.

picture plane The flat surface on which an artist creates a pictorial image.

pitch In music, the relative highness or lowness of a sound. Pitch is determined by wave frequency, as compression and expansion occur within the sound wave.

plane In three-dimensional design, an area with measurable width and height. Shapes that have been combined to create three-dimensional structures are called planes.

plan view The bottom view of a three-dimensional object or architectural structure, drawn orthographically or freehand.

plinth A horizontal support for a sculptural object.

polyhedra Multifaceted volumes, such as tetrahedrons.

positive shape The principal or foreground shape in a design; the dominant shape or figure in a figure-ground relationship.

primary colors Colors from which virtually all other colors can be mixed. The additive (or light) color primaries are red, green, and blue. The subtractive (or pigment) color primaries are yellow, magenta red, and cyan blue.

primary contour The outer edges of a physical object, such as the extremities of a carved sculpture.

principles of design The strategies most commonly used by artists and designers to unify disparate visual information into a cohesive whole, including balance, emphasis, rhythm, and proportion.

proportion A comparative relationship between the parts to a whole. For example, in figure drawing, the model's head is often compared to the overall height of the body.

prototype A well-developed model, as with the fully functional prototype cars developed by automobile companies.

proximity The distance between the parts of a structure or between an object and the audience.

R

radial symmetry A form of balance that is created when shapes or volumes are mirrored both vertically and horizontally, with the center of the composition acting as a focal point.

rational advertising A type of advertising in which logic and comparisons of quality are used to sell a service, product, or idea. A rational approach is most effective when the message is compelling in itself or the product is truly unique.

realistic advertising Use of a familiar setting or situation to involve the viewer and relate a product, service, or idea to use in everyday life.

rectilinear shape A shape whose edges are created by straight lines and angular corners.

relief Sculpture in which forms project out from a flat surface. The degree of projection ranges from low to high relief.

repetition The use of the same visual element or visual effect a number of times in the same composition. Can be used to increase unity in a composition, produce a rhythmic movement, or emphasize the importance of a visual idea.

representation The lifelike depiction of persons or objects.

representational shape A shape that is derived from specific subject matter and strongly based on perceptual reality.

rhetorical form In filmmaking, a type of sequential organization in which the parts are used to create and support an argument. Often used in documentary films.

rhythm 1. The repetition of multiple parts in a composition to create a pattern of sound and silence, positive and negative, or other contrasting forces. 2. In filmmaking, the perceived rate and regularity of sounds, shots, and movement within the shots. Rhythm is determined by the beat (pulse), accent (stress), and tempo (pace).

rhythmic relationship The juxtaposition of multiple images to create a deliberate pulse or beat.

saturation The purity, chroma, or intensity of a color.

scale A size relationship between two separate objects, such as the relationship between the size of Mount Rushmore and a human visitor to the monument.

scene In film, continuous action in continuous time and continuous space.

scene-to-scene transition In comic books, the juxtaposition of two or more frames showing different scenes or settings.

scope Conceptually, the extent of our perception or the range of ideas our minds can grasp. Temporally, scope refers to the range of action within a given moment.

screenplay The written blueprint for the film; commonly constructed from multiple acts.

secondary colors Hues mixed from adjacent primaries. In paint, the secondary colors are violet, green, and orange.

secondary contour The inner edges of a physical object, such as the internal design and detailing of a carved sculpture.

section In orthographic projection, a slice of an object or architectural structure that reveals its internal structure and detail.

sequence 1. In filmmaking, a collection of related shots and scenes that comprise a major section of action or narration. 2. In narrative structure, any collection of images that have been organized by cause and effect. In a simple sequence, action number two is caused by action number one. In a complex sequence, there may be a considerable delay between the cause and the effect.

series In sequential structure, a collection of images that are simply linked together, as with cars in a train.

serious advertising Advertising that treats a topic in a somber or solemn manner. Often used for public service announcements, such as drunk driving commercials.

setting In time design, the physical and temporal location of a story, the props and costumes used in a story, and the use of sound.

shade A hue that has been mixed with black.

shading In drawing, a continuous series of grays that are used to suggest three-dimensionality and to create the illusion of light.

shape A flat, enclosed area created when 1. A line connects to enclose an area. 2. An area of color or texture is defined by a clear boundary. 3. An area is surrounded by other shapes.

shot In film, a continuous group of frames.

sidelight A light positioned to the side of a person or object. Can be used to increase the sense of dimensionality.

sight line 1. In perspective, a viewing line that is established by the arrangement of objects within one's field of vision. 2. A straight line of unimpeded vision.

simile A figure of speech in which one thing is linked to another dissimilar thing using the word *like* or *as*. Through this connection, the original word is given the qualities of the linked word. For example, when we say, "He's as strong as a lion," we attribute to a man the strength of an animal.

simultaneous contrast The optical alteration of a color by a surrounding color. For example, when a square of blue is placed on a yellow background, the blue appears dark and cool. The same blue will appear much lighter when it is placed on a black background.

soft-sell advertising An advertising approach that uses emotion, rather than reason, to sell a service, product, or idea. The narrative is often nonlinear, and ideas or actions may be implied.

space One of the basic elements of three-dimensional design. The distance between images or points in a design. The artist/designer physically contains and thus defines space when constructing a three-dimensional object.

spatial relationship In film making, the juxtaposition of two or more images that are spatially different, such as a close-up, a medium shot, and a long shot.

split complementary A complementary color plus the two colors on either side of its complement on the color wheel.

spotlight A light that produces a small, clearly defined beam.

static An equilibrium of forces. In design, a composition that is at rest or an object that appears stationary.

style The distinctive artistic treatment of an image or idea.

subject The person, object, event, or idea on which an artwork is based.

subjective criticism The assessment of strengths and weaknesses in a design based on nonobjective criteria, such as the narrative implications of an idea, the cultural ramifications of an action, or the personal meaning of an image.

subject-to-subject transition In comic books, the juxtaposition of two or more frames showing different subject matter.

subtractive color Color created when light is selectively reflected off a pigmented or dyed surface. For example, when an object is painted red, the molecular makeup of the red pigment absorbs (subtracts) all of the spectral light except the red wavelength, which is reflected back to the viewer's eyes. The subtractive primaries are yellow, magenta red, and cyan blue.

subtractive sculpture Any process by which an artist or designer removes materials from a larger mass, gradually revealing the form within.

symbolic color A color that has been assigned a particular meaning by the members of a society. For example, in the United States, the white color of a wedding gown symbolizes purity, while in Borneo it symbolizes death.

symmetrical balance A form of balance that is created when shapes are mirrored on either side of an axis, as in a composition that is vertically divided down the center.

tactile texture Texture that can be felt physically.

take In film or video, one version of an event.

tangibility The substantiality of an object or the degree to which an object or a force can be felt.

temperature The physical and psychological heat generated by a color.

tempo The pace at which music and time-based art occur. A fast tempo is generally used in action films while a slow tempo is usually used in a dramatic film.

temporal relationship How the shots in a film relate in time.

tension The distortion of an object through stretching or bending.

tertiary color A hue that is mixed from a primary color and an adjacent secondary color.

testimonial advertising Use of a trustworthy character or celebrity to provide endorsement for a product, service, or idea.

texture The surface quality of a two-dimensional shape or a three-dimensional volume. Texture can be created visually, using multiple marks; physically, through surface variation; or through the inherent property of a specific material, such as the texture of sand as opposed to the texture of polished glass.

three-point perspective A form of linear perspective in which the lines receding into space converge at two vanishing points of the eye level (one to the left of the object being drawn and one to the right of the object being drawn), plus a third vanishing point above or below the eye level. Used when the picture plane must be tilted to encompass an object placed above or below the eye level.

three-quarter work A physical object that is designed to be viewed from the front and sides only.

timbre The unique sound quality of each instrument. For example, a note of the same volume and pitch is quite different when it is generated by a trumpet rather than a violin.

tint A hue that has been mixed with white.

tone A hue that has been mixed with black and white.

torsion The distortion of an object through a twisting movement.

transition The process of changing from one state or form to another. For example, the surface of a metal sculpture as it shifts from a smooth to a rough surface or the manner in which a computer drawing morphs from one form to another.

triadic harmony A color scheme based on three colors that are equidistant on a color wheel.

tromp l'oeil A French term meaning "to fool the eye." A flat illusion that is so convincing the viewer believes the image is real.

two-point perspective A form of linear perspective in which the lines receding into space converge at two vanishing points of the eye level (or horizon line), one to the left of the object being drawn and one to the right of the object being drawn. Used when the object being drawn is placed at an angle to the picture plane.

typestyle The distinctive quality of the letterforms within a given font. For example, Helvetica type has a very different look than Palatino type.

U

unity The oneness, or wholeness, in a design that occurs when all parts work together to create a cohesive whole.

V

value 1. The lightness or darkness of a color. 2. The relative lightness or darkness of a surface.

value scale A range of grays that are presented in a mathematically consistent sequence.

vanishing point In linear perspective, the point or points on the eye level at which parallel lines appear to converge.

variety The differences that give a design visual and conceptual interest; notably, use of contrast, emphasis, differences in size, and so on.

visual book An experimental structure that conveys ideas, actions, and emotions using multiple images in an integrated and interdependent format. Also known as an artist's book.

visual texture 1. A surface treatment that simulates an actual physical texture. 2. Any covering of a surface with multiple marks.

visual weight 1. The inclination of shapes to float or sink based on their solidity and compositional location. 2. The relative importance of a visual element within a design.

vitalistic sculpture A sculpture that appears to embody life in an inanimate material, such as plastic, stone, or wood.

volume 1. In three-dimensional design, a volume is an enclosed area of three-dimensional space. 2. In two-dimensional design, basic volumes such as cubes, cones, and spheres are created through the illusion of space. 3. In time design, volume refers to the softness or loudness of a sound.

volume summary A drawing that communicates visual information reductively, using basic volumes, such as sphere, cubes. and cylinders to indicate the major components of a figure or object.

W

walk-through work An artwork or a design that presents an ensemble of images and objects within a three-dimensional environment. The viewer must walk through the space in order to experience the artwork fully.

weight The visual or physical heaviness of an object.

wipe In film, a transition in which the first shot seems to be pushed off the screen by the second. Wipes were used extensively in *Star Wars*.

Introduction

Books Consulted

Berger, Arthur Asa. *Seeing Is Believing: An Introduction to Visual Communication*, 2nd ed. Mountain View, CA: Mayfield Publishing Company, 1998.

Berger, John. *Ways of Seeing*. London: British Broadcasting Corporation, 1987.

Conran, Terance. *Terance Conran on Design*. Woodstock, NY: The Overlook Press, 1996.

Dondis, Donis. *A Primer of Visual Literacy*. Cambridge, MA: MIT Press, 1973.

Myers, Jack Fredrick. *The Language of Visual Art: Perception as a Basis for Design*. Orlando, FL: Holt, Rinehart and Winston, 1989.

Chapter One

Works Cited

1. David A. Lauer and Stephen Pentak, *Design Basics* (Orlando: Harcourt, Brace & Company, 2000), p. 132.

Books Consulted

Behrens, Roy R. *Design in the Visual Arts*. Englewood Cliffs, NJ: Prentice Hall, 1984.

Block, Jonathan; and Gisele Atterberry. *Design Essentials*, 2nd ed. Englewood Cliffs, NJ: Prentice Hall, 1999.

Cheathan, Frank; Jane Hart Cheathan; and Sheryl A. Haler. *Design Concepts and Applications*. Englewood Cliffs, NJ: Prentice Hall, 1983.

Escher, M. C. *The Graphic Works of M. C. Escher*. New York: Ballantine Books, 1971.

Hill, Edward. *The Language of Drawing*. Englewood Cliffs, NJ: Prentice Hall, 1966.

Lauer, David A.; and Stephen Pentak, *Design Basics*, 5th ed. Orlando, FL: Harcourt, Brace and Company, 2000.

Myers, Jack Fredrick. *The Language of Visual Art: Perception as a Basis for Design*. Orlando, FL: Holt, Rinehart and Winston, 1989.

Torczyner, Harry. *Magritte: Ideas and Images*. Richard Miller, trans. New York: Harry N. Abrams, 1977.

Zettl, Herbert. *Sight, Sound, Motion: Applied Media Aesthetics*, 3rd ed. Belmont, CA: Wadsworth Publishing Company, 1999.

Chapter Two

Works Cited

1. Johannes Itten, *The Art of Color* (New York: Van Nostrand Reinhold, 1974), p. 16.
2. Itten, op. cit., p. 18.
3. Alexander Theroux, *The Primary Colors: Three Essays* (New York: Henry Holt and Company, 1994), p. 6.

Books Consulted

Albers, Josef. *Interaction of Color.* New Haven, CT: Yale University Press, 1963.

Birren, Farber. *Light, Color and Environment.* New York: Van Nostrand Reinhold, 1982.

Constantine, Michael; and Jack Lenor Larsen. *Beyond Craft: The Art Fabric.* New York: Van Nostrand Reinhold, 1972.

Gerritsen, Frans. *Theory and Practice of Color.* New York: Van Nostrand Reinhold, 1975.

Itten, Johannes. *The Art of Color.* New York: Van Nostrand Reinhold, 1974.

Kilmer, Rosemary; and W. Kilmer. *Designing Interiors.* New York: Harcourt, Brace and Jovanovich, 1992.

Kuppers, Harald. *Color: Origin, Systems, Uses.* New York: Van Nostrand Reinhold, 1972.

Linton, Harold. *Color Model Environments.* New York: Van Nostrand Reinhold, 1985.

Munsell, Albert. *A Color Notation.* Munsell Color, 1981.

Munsell, Albert H. *A Grammar of Color: A Basic Treatise on the Color System of Albert H. Munsell.* New York: Van Nostrand Reinhold, 1969.

Norman, Richard B. *Electronic Color.* New York: Van Nostrand Reinhold, 1990.

Ocvirk, Otto G.; Robert E. Stinson; Philip R. Wigg; Robert O. Bone; and David L. Cayton. *Art Fundamentals: Theory and Practice,* 9th ed. New York: McGraw-Hill Companies, 2002.

Pile, John F. *Interior Design.* New York: Harry N. Abrams, 1988.

Zelanski, Paul; and Mary Pat Fisher. *Color.* Englewood Cliffs, NJ: Prentice Hall, 1989.

Chapter Three

Books Consulted

Arnheim, Rudolph. *Art and Visual Perception: A Psychology of the Creative Eye*. Berkeley, CA: University of California Press, 1974.

Behrens, Roy R. *Design in the Visual Arts*. Englewood Cliffs, NJ: Prentice Hall, 1984.

Berger, Arthur Asa. *Seeing Is Believing: An Introduction to Visual Communication*, 2nd ed. Mountain View, CA: Mayfield Publishing Company, 1998.

Berger, John. *Ways of Seeing*. London: British Broadcasting Corporation, 1987.

Cheathan, Frank; Jane Hart Cheathan; and Sheryl A. Haler. *Design Concepts and Applications*. Englewood Cliffs, NJ: Prentice Hall, 1983.

Dantzic, Cynthia Maris. *Design Dimensions*. Englewood Cliffs, NJ: Prentice Hall, 1990.

Dondis, Donis. *A Primer of Visual Literacy*. Cambridge, MA: MIT Press, 1973.

Feinstein, Roni. *Robert Rauschenberg: The Silkscreen Paintings, 1962–64*. New York: The Whitney Museum of American Art, 1990.

Friend, David. *Composition: A Painter's Guide to Basic Problems and Solutions*. New York: Watson-Guptill Publications, 1975.

Graham, Donald W. *Composing Pictures*. New York: Van Nostrand Reinhold, 1970.

Kepes, Gyorgy. *Language of Vision*. Chicago: Paul Theobald, 1944.

Lauer, David A.; and Stephan Pentak. *Design Basics*, 5th ed. Orlando, FL: Harcourt, Brace and Company, 2000.

Martinez, Benjamin; and Jacqueline Block. *Visual Forces: An Introduction to Design*. Englewood Cliffs, NJ: Prentice Hall, 1995.

Myers, Jack Fredrick. *The Language of Visual Art: Perception as a Basis for Design*. Orlando, FL: Holt, Rinehart and Winston, 1989.

Smith, Lawrence. *Contemporary Japanese Prints: Symbols of a Society in Transition*. London: British Museum Publications, 1985.

Wilde, Richard. *Problem: Solution: Visual Thinking for Graphic Communicators*. New York: Van Nostrand Reinhold, 1986.

Chapter Four

Works Cited

1. Mihaly Csikszentmihalyi, *Creativity: Flow and the Psychology of Discovery and Invention*, (New York: HarperCollins), pp. 55–76.
2. George Prince, "Creativity and Learning as Skills, Not Talents," *The Philips Exeter Bulletin*, June–October 1980.
3. Anne Lamott, *Bird by Bird: Some Instructions on Writing and Life* (New York: Anchor Books, 1998), pp. 18–19.

Books Consulted

Bayles, David; and Ted Orlando. *Art & Fear: Observations on the Perils (and Rewards) of Art Making.* Santa Barbara, CA: Capra Press, 1993.

Bohm, David. *On Creativity.* New York: Routledge, 2000.

Briggs, John. *Fire in the Crucible: Understanding the Process of Creative Genius.* Grand Rapids, MI: Phanes Press, 2000.

Csikszentmihalyi, Mihaly. *Creativity: Flow and the Psychology of Discovery and Invention.* New York: HarperCollins, 1996.

Dewey, John. *Art as Experience.* New York: Capricorn Books, 1958.

Gardner, Howard. *Art, Mind and Brain: A Cognitive Approach to Creativity.* New York: Basic Books, 1982.

Gardner, Howard. *Creating Minds: An Anatomy of Creativity Seen Through the Lives of Freud, Einstein, Picasso, Stravinsky, Eliot, Graham, and Gandhi.* New York: Basic Books, 1993.

Gardner, Howard. *Frames of Mind: The Theory of Multiple Intelligences.* New York: Basic Books, 1985.

Lamott, Anne. *Bird by Bird: Some Instructions on Writing and Life.* New York: Anchor Books, 1998.

LeBoeuf, Michael. *Imagineering: How to Profit from Your Creative Powers.* New York: McGraw-Hill, 1980.

Shekerjian, Denise. *Uncommon Genius: How Great Ideas Are Born.* New York: Penguin Books, 1991.

Wallace, Doris B.; and Howard E. Gruber, eds. *Creative People at Work.* New York: Oxford University Press, 1989.

Chapter Five

Works Cited

1. Keith A. Smith, *Structure of the Visual Book* (Fairport, NY: The Sigma Foundation, 1991), pp. 17–18.
2. Henry M. Sayre, *A World of Art*, 3rd ed. (Upper Saddle River, NY: Prentice Hall, 2000), p. 496.

Books Consulted

Adams, James L. *Conceptual Blockbusting*. Reading, MA: Addison-Wesley, 1986.

de Bono, Edward. *Lateral Thinking*. London: Ward Educational Limited, 1970.

Grear, Malcolm. *Inside/Outside: From the Basics to the Practice of Design*. New York: Van Nostrand Reinhold, 1993.

Johnson, Mary Frisbee. *Visual Workouts: A Collection of Art-Making Problems*. Englewood Cliffs, NJ: Prentice Hall, 1983.

Lakoff, George; and Mark Johnson. *Metaphors We Live By*. Chicago: University of Chicago Press, 1981.

Shahn, Ben. *The Shape of Content*. Cambridge, MA: Harvard University Press, 1957.

Von Oech, Roger. *A Kick in the Seat of the Pants*. New York: Harper and Row, 1963.

Von Oech, Roger. *A Whack on the Side of the Head*. New York: Harper and Row, 1986.

Chapter Six

Works Cited

1. Henry M. Sayre, *A World of Art*, 3rd ed. (Upper Saddle River, NY: Prentice Hall, 2000), pp. 298–99.

Books Consulted

Barnet, Sylvan. *A Short Guide to Writing About Art*, 6th ed. Reading, MA: Addison-Wesley Longman, 2000.

Barrett, Terry. *Criticizing Photographs: An Introduction to Understanding Images,* 2nd ed. Mountain View, CA: Mayfield Publishing Company, 1996.

Ocvirk, Otto G.; Robert E. Stinson; Philip R. Wigg; Robert O. Bone; and David L. Cayton. *Art Fundamentals: Theory and Practice,* 9th ed. New York: McGraw-Hill Companies, 2002.

Sayre, Henry M. *Writing About Art*, 3rd ed. Upper Saddle River, NJ: Prentice Hall, 1999.

Smagula, Howard, ed. *Re-visions: New Perspectives of Art Criticism.* Englewood Cliffs, NJ: Prentice Hall, 1991.

Tucker, Amy. *Visual Literacy: Writing About Art.* Burr Ridge, IL: McGraw-Hill Companies, 2002.

Chapter Seven

Works Cited

1. John Beardsley, *Earthworks and Beyond: Contemporary Art in the Landscape* (New York: Abbeville Press, 1998), p. 31.
2. Jonathan Fineberg, *Art Since 1940: Strategies of Being* (Englewood Cliffs, NJ: Prentice Hall, 1995), p. 383.
3. Alexander Theroux, *The Primary Colors: Three Essays* (New York: Henry Holt and Company, 1994), p. 86.
4. Theroux, op. cit., p. 6.

Books Consulted

Bachelard, Gaston. *The Poetics of Space.* Maria Jolas, trans. Boston: Beacon Press, 1969.

Ching, Frank. *Architecture: Form, Space, and Order,* 2nd ed. New York: Van Nostrand Reinhold, 1996.

Hibbard, Howard. *Masterpieces of Western Sculpture from Medieval to Modern.* New York: Harper and Row, 1980.

Lidstone, John. *Building with Wire.* New York: Van Nostrand Reinhold, 1972.

Wallschlaeger, Charles; and Cynthia Busic-Snyder. *Basic Visual Concepts and Principles for Artists, Architects and Designers.* Dubuque: William C. Brown, 1992.

Wong, Wucius. *Principles of Form and Design.* New York: Van Nostrand Reinhold, 1993.

Zelanski, Paul; and Mary Pat Fisher. *Shaping Space: The Dynamics of Three-Dimensional Design,* 2nd ed. Orlando, FL: Harcourt, Brace and Company, 1995.

Chapter Eight

Books Consulted

Andrews, Oliver. *Living Materials: A Sculptor's Handbook.* Berkeley, CA: University of California Press, 1988.

Dormer, Peter; and Ralph Turner. *The New Jewelry: Trends and Traditions.* London: Thames and Hudson, 1985.

Fong, Wen, ed. *The Great Bronze Age of China*. New York: The Metropolitan Museum of Art and Alfred A. Knopf, 1980.

Frantz, Suzanne. *Contemporary Glass: A World Survey from the Corning Museum of Glass*. New York: Harry N. Abrams, 1989.

Johnson, Paul. *Pop-Up Paper Engineering*. Bristol: Taylor & Francis, 1992.

Lane, Peter. *Ceramic Form: Design and Decoration*. rev. ed. New York: Rizzoli International Publications, 1998.

Lewin, Susan Grant. *One of a Kind: American Art Jewelry Today*. New York: Harry N. Abrams, 1994.

Lynn, Martha Dreyer. *Clay Today: Contemporary Ceramists and Their Work*. Los Angeles: Los Angeles County Museum of Art and San Francisco: Chronicle Books, 1990.

Miller, Bonnie J. *Out of the Fire: Contemporary Glass Artists and Their Work*. San Francisco: Chronicle Books, 1991.

Stern, Rudi. *Contemporary Neon*. New York: Retail Reporting Corporation, 1990.

Wong, Wucius. *Principles of Form and Design*. New York: Van Nostrand Reinhold, 1993.

Chapter Nine

Works Cited

1. Lucy R. Lippard, *Eva Hesse* (New York: New York University Press, 1976), p. 5.

Books Consulted

Beardsley, John. *Earthworks and Beyond: Contemporary Art in the Landscape*. New York: Abbeville Press, 1998.

Burnham, Jack. *Beyond Modern Sculpture: The Effects of Science and Technology on the Sculpture of This Century*. New York: George Braziller, 1968.

Hammacher, A. M. *Modern Sculpture: Tradition and Innovation*. New York: Harry N. Abrams, 1988.

Koplos, Janet. *Contemporary Japanese Sculpture*. New York: Abbeville Press, 1991.

Manzini, Ezio. *The Material of Invention: Materials and Design*. Cambridge, MA: The MIT Press, 1989.

Oliveria, Nicolas de; Nicola Oxley; and Michael Petry. *Installation Art*. Washington, DC: Smithsonian Institution Press, 1994.

Penny, Nicholas. *The Materials of Sculpture*. New Haven, CT: Yale University Press, 1993.

Schmidt, Jeremy; and Laine Thorn. *In the Spirit of Mother Earth: Nature in Native American Art*. San Francisco: Chronicle Books, 1994.

Sculpture Inside Outside. Introduction Martin Friedman. Essays by Douglas Dreishpoon, Nancy Prinenthal, Carter Ratcliff, Joan Simon. Profiles of the Artists by Peter W. Boswell and Donna Harkary. New York: Rizzoli International Publications, 1988.

Selz, Peter Howard. *Barbara Chase-Riboud, Sculptor*. New York: Harry N. Abrams, 1999.

Waldman, Diane. *Transformations in Modern Sculpture: Four Decades of American and European Art*. New York: The Solomon R. Guggenheim Foundation, 1985.

Watson-Jones, Virginia. *Contemporary American Women Sculptors*. Phoenix, AZ: Oryx Press, 1986.

Williams, Arthur. *Sculpture: Technique, Form, Content*. Worcester, MA: Davis Publications, 1993.

Wyatt, Gary. *Spirit Faces: Contempoary Native American Masks from the Northwest*. San Francisco: Chronicle Books, 1994.

Chapter Ten

Works Cited

1. David Bordwell and Kristin Thompson, *Film Art: An Introduction*, 5th ed. (New York: McGraw-Hill Companies, 1997), pp. 277–278.
2. Scott McCloud, *Understanding Comics* (New York: HarperPerennial, 1994), pp. 70–74.
3. Keith A. Smith, *Structure of the Visual Book* (Fairport, NY: The Sigma Foundation, 1991), pp. 102–104.
4. David Bordwell and Kristin Thompson, op. cit., p. 281.

Books Consulted

Bordwell, David; and Kristin Thompson. *Film Art: An Introduction*, 5th ed. New York: McGraw-Hill, 1997.

Johnson, Lincoln F. *Film: Space, Time, Light and Sound*. Orlando, FL: Holt, Rinehart and Winston, 1974.

McCloud, Scott. *Understanding Comics*. New York: HarperPerennial, 1994.

Zettl, Herbert. *Sight, Sound, Motion: Applied Media Aesthetics*, 3rd ed. Belmont, CA: Wadsworth Publishing Company, 1999.

Chapter Eleven

Works Cited

1. Keith A. Smith, *Structure of the Visual Book* (Fairport, NY: The Sigma Foundation, 1991), p. 106.
2. Robert McKee, *Story: Substance, Structure, Style and the Principles of Screen Writing* (New York, HarperCollins, 1997), pp. 37–41.

Books Consulted

Baldwin, Huntley. *How to Create Effective TV Commercials*, 2nd ed. Lincolnwood, IL: NTC Business Books, 1989.

Gordon, Stephen F. *Making Picture-Books: A Method of Learning Graphic Sequence*. New York: Van Nostrand Reinhold, 1970.

Hubert, Renee Riese; and Judd D. Hubert. *The Cutting Edge of Reading: Artists' Books*. New York: Granary Books, 1999.

Katz, Stephen D. *Film Directing, Shot by Shot: Visualizing from Concept to Screen*. Studio City, CA: Michael Wiese Productions, 1991.

La Plantz, Shereen. *Cover to Cover*. Asheville, NC: Lark Books, 1995.

McKee, Robert. *Story: Substance, Structure, Style and the Principles of Screen Writing*. New York: HarperCollins, 1997.

Riordan, Steve, ed. *Clio Awards: A Tribute to 30 Years of Advertising Excellence, 1960–1989*. Glen Cove, NY: PBC International, 1989.

Smith, Keith A. *Structure of the Visual Book*. Fairport, NY: The Sigma Foundation, 1992.

Vogler, Christopher. *The Writer's Journey: Mythic Structure for Storytellers and Screenwriters*. Studio City, CA: Michael Wiese Productions, 1991.

White, Minor. *Mirrors/Messages/Manifestations*. New York: Aperature, 1982.

Chapter Twelve

Works Cited

1. *Webster's New Universal Unabridged Dictionary*, 2nd ed. (New York: Simon & Schuster, 1983), p. 1011.
2. Maynard Mack, ed. *World Masterpieces* (New York, W.W. Norton & Company, 1965), p. 478.
3. Rachel Carson, *Under the Sea Wind* (New York: Viking Penguin, 1996), p. 23.
4. David Ross, *Bill Viola* (New York: The Whitney Museum of American Art, 1998), p. 116.

Books Consulted

Drucker, Johanna. *The Century of Artists' Books*, New York: Granary Books, 1995.

Goldberg, Roselee. *Performance: Live Art Since 1960*. New York: Harry N. Abrams, 1998.

Lyons, Joan. *Artists' Books: A Critical Anthology and Sourcebook*. Rochester, NY: Visual Studies Worskhop Press, 1985.

Oliveria, Nicolas de; Nicola Oxley; and Michael Petry. *Installation Art*. Washington, DC: Smithsonian Institution Press, 1994.

Ross, David. *Bill Viola*. New York: The Whitney Museum of American Art, 1998.

Smith, Keith A. *Structure of the Visual Book*. Fairport, NY: The Sigma Foundation, 1992.

Smith, Keith A. *Text in the Book Format*. Fairport, NY: The Sigma Foundation, 1991.

General Art Historical Sources

Arnason, H. H. *History of Modern Art, Painting, Sculpture, Architecture*, 3rd ed. New York: Harry N. Abrams, 1986.

Fineberg, Jonathan. *Art Since 1940: Strategies for Being*. Englewood Cliffs, NJ: Prentice Hall, 1995.

Maltin, Leonard. *Of Mice and Magic: A History of American Animated Cartoons*. New York: New American Library, 1980.

Newhall, Beaumont. *The History of Photography: From 1839 to the Present Day*, 5th rev. ed. New York: Museum of Modern Art, 1982.

Preble, Duane; Sarah Preble; and Patrick Frank. *Artforms: An Introduction to the Visual Arts*, 6th ed. Reading, MA: Addison-Wesley Educational Publishers, 1999.

Sayre, Henry M. *A World of Art*, 3rd ed. Upper Saddle River, NJ: Prentice Hall, 2000.

Schneider-Adams, Laurie. *Art Across Time*, 2nd ed. New York: McGraw-Hill Companies, 2002.

Stokstad, Marilyn. *Art History, Volumes One and Two*. New York: Harry N. Abrams, 1995.

Thompson, Kristin; and David Bordwell. *Film History: An Introduction*. New York: McGraw-Hill, 1994.

Townsend, Richard F., ed. *The Ancient Americas: Art from Sacred Landscapes*. Chicago: The Chicago Art Institute, 1992.

The 20th Century Art Book. New York: Phaidon Press, 1996.

Wallis, Brian, ed. *Art After Modernism: Rethinking Representation*. New York: New Museum of Contemporary Art, 1984.

1.25, Random House Vintage Books. Art Director: Edith Loeser. Agency: Carin Goldberg.

1.26, Courtesy Bantam Books.

1.27, Galleria Moderna Venice, Italy. Cameraphoto/ Art Resource.

1.28, American Numismatic Association, Colorado Springs.

1.30, © Bill Brandt/Bill Brandt Archive Ltd., London.

1.31, Museum of Modern Art, NY. Acquired through the Lillie P. Bliss Bequest. © 2001 Artists Rights Society (ARS), NY/ADAGP, Paris. Photo © 2002 Museum of Modern Art, NY.

1.32, © 2002 Cordon Art B. V. Baarn, Holland.

1.33, The Department of Theater Arts, California State University, Los Angeles, David McNutt, 1985.

1.34, © 1970 The Imogen Cunningham Trust.

1.35, The Stapleton Collection, Bridgeman Art Library.

1.36, Private collection. © Robert Rauschenberg/Licensed by VAGA, NY.

1.37, © Valerie Jaudon/Licensed by VAGA, N.Y.

1.38, San Francisco Museum of Modern Art, gift of the Women's Board.

1.39, © Ansel Adams Publishing Rights Trust/CORBIS.

1.40, Courtesy Joseph Helman Gallery, NY (# BH 1912).

1.41, Art Institute of Chicago, gift of Georgia O'Keeffe (1948.650). Photograph © 2001, The Art Institute of Chicago. All rights reserved.

1.42A, Magnum Photos, Inc.

1.43, Copyright Robert Frank, courtesy Pace/MacGill Gallery, NY. Museum of Fine Arts Houston: Target Collection of American Photography, museum purchase with funds provided by Target Stores.

1.44, Collection, Museum of Modern Art, NY. Gift of Mr. and Mrs. Walter Bareiss. Photo © 2002 Museum of Modern Art, NY.

1.45, Chronicle Books, 1993.

1.46, Collection of David Geffen, Los Angeles. © Jasper Johns/Licensed by VAGA, NY.

1.47, Museum of Modern Art, NY. Blanchette Rockefeller Fund. © Romare Bearden Foundation/Licensed by VAGA, NY. Photo © 2002 Museum of Modern Art, NY.

1.48, Courtesy George Eastman House.

1.49, Brooklyn Museum of Art, NY, gift of Mrs. Horace O. Havermeyer.

1.51, Honolulu Academy of Arts.

1.52, Collection of the artist. Courtesy D'Amelio Terras Gallery.

1.53, Reproduced by kind permission of the Trustees of the Edward James Foundation, West Dean Estate, West Dean, Chichester, England. Courtesy of the Edward James Foundation. © 2001 Charly Herscovici/Artists Rights Society (ARS), NY.

1.54, Client GSX Corporation. © Douglas Smith 2002.

1.55, Gabinetto Disegni e Stampe degli Uffizi, Florence. © 2001 Artists Rights Society (ARS), NY/SIAE, Rome. Photo: Index/Tosi, Florence, Italy (105933).

1.56, Courtesy Fogg Art Museum, Harvard University Art Museums, Louise E. Bettens Fund. Photographic Services. © President and Fellows of Harvard College, Harvard University.

1.57, © Richard Haas/Licensed by VAGA, NY. Photo: Peter Mauss/Esto Photographics.

1.59, Photo © 2002 Museum of Modern Art, NY.

1.60, National Gallery of Art, Washington, DC. Ailsa Mellon Bruce Fund. Photo: Bob Grove.

1.62, © Deborah Remington/Licensed by VAGA, NY.

1.64, Cathedral of Saint-Bavo, Ghent, Belgium. © St. Baafskathedraal Ghent/© Paul M. R. Maeyaert.

1.65, Smithsonian American Art Museum, Washington, DC/Art Resource.

1.66, Courtesy, the Colorado Historical Society (978.06/P871es).

1.67A–D, Reprinted with permission of Wadsworth, an imprint of the Wadsworth Group, a division of Thomson Learning, fax 800-730-2215.

1.68A–E, Photofest.

Chapter 2

2.1, Stedelijk Museum, Amsterdam. © 2001 Artists Rights Society (ARS) NY/Beeldrecht, Amsterdam.

2.2, Vatican Museums, Vatican State. Scala/Art Resource, NY.

2.8, Museum of Modern Art, NY. Gift of the Celeste and Armand Bartos Foundation. © Jasper Johns and ULAE/Licensed by VAGA, NY. Photo © 2002 Museum of Modern Art, NY.

2.11, Courtesy GreytagMacbeth, New Windsor, NY.

2.12, Collection of Louis, Susan, and Ari Meisel. Courtesy of Louis K. Meisel Gallery, NY.

2.13, School of Art, Ohio University.

2.15, Courtesy of Nicora Gangi.

2.16, © David Hockney/Gemini G. E. L.

2.17, Statens Museum for Kunst, Rump Collection, Copenhagen, Denmark. © 2001 Succession H. Matisse, Paris/Artists Rights Society (ARS), NY.

2.18, Smithsonian American Art Museum, Washington, D.C./Art Resource, NY.

2.20, Collection of the National Trust for Historic Preservation, Pocantico Historic Area, NY.

2.21, Collection, Albright-Knox Art Gallery, Buffalo, NY. Gift of Seymour H. Knox, 1956. © 2001 Estate of Arshile Gorky/Artists Rights Society (ARS), NY.

2.22, Philadelphia Museum of Art: Gift of Mrs. Iwao Setsu, Tokyo. Photo: Graydon Wood.

2.23, Philadelphia Museum of Art: Gift of Hilda K. Watkins. Photo: Lynn Rosenthal , 1997.

2.25, Private collection. © Kenneth Noland/Licensed by VAGA, NY.

2.27, © Wolf Kahn/Licensed by VAGA, NY.

2.28, University Art Museum, University of California, Berkeley, gift of the artist.

2.31, School of Art, Ohio University. Courtesy of the artist.

2.33, National Gallery of Art, Washington, DC. Collection of Mr. and Mrs. Paul Mellon. Photo: Richard Carafelli.

2.35, Chester Dale Collection, National Gallery of Art, Washington, DC. Photo © 2001 Board of Trustees.

2.36A, Honolulu Academy of Arts, gift of the Honorable Clare Booth Luce, 1984 (5311.1). © 2002 Victor Vasarely/Artists Rights Society (ARS), NY/ADAGP, Paris. Photo: Tibor Franyo.

2.38, National Gallery of Art, Washington, D.C., Alfred Stieglitz Collection, Bequest of Georgia O'Keeffe. © 2001 Georgia O'Keeffe Foundation/Artists Rights Society (ARS), NY. Photo: Bob Grove.

2.40, Joel Katz Design Associates, Philadelphia, PA. Photos © Peter Olson, digital illustration © Joel Katz Design Associates.

2.41, Musée d'Orsay, Paris. Reunion des Musees Nationaux/Art Resource, NY. Photo: Herve Lewandowski.

2.42, South Australia Museum, Adelaide. © 2001 Artists Rights Society (ARS), NY/Viscopy, Sidney.

2.43, © 2001 Estate of Francis Bacon/Artists Rights Society (ARS), NY. Photo © Tate Gallery, London/Art Resource, NY.

2.44, Photo: J. Kevin Fitzsimons.

2.46, Astor, Lenox, and Tilden Foundation. Spencer Collection, The New York Public Library/Art Resource, NY. © 2001 Succession H. Matisse, Paris/Artists Rights Society (ARS), NY.

2.47, © Wolf Kahn/Licensed by VAGA, NY.

2.48, Design firm: Louis Nelson Associates, Inc., NY. Art Director: Louis Nelson, Graphic Designer: Jennifer Stoller, Client: Port Authority/Port Authority Trans Hudson.

2.50, Minneapolis Institute of Arts, Minneapolis, MN, gift of the P. D. McMillan Land Company (54.30) .

2.52, Art Institute of Chicago, The Alfred Stieglitz Collection (1949.706). Photo © 2001 Art Institute of Chicago.

2.53, An oiran is the highest ranking courtesan. Courtesy of the Trustees of the Victoria and Albert Museum, London.

2.54, Signed at upper right. © Andrew Wyeth. Lent by Professor and Mrs. Charles H. Morgan, Amherst, MA. Mead Art Museum, Amherst College, on extended loan to the Museum from the Estate of Charles H. Morgan (AC EL.1984.51).

2.55, Nelson-Atkins Museum of Art, Kansas City, MO, gift of the Friends of Art (F63-15). Photo: E. G. Schempf.

2.56, © Sandy Skoglund/Superstock.

2.57, Repainted by Jim Kewanwytewa. Oraibi. Museum of Northern Arizona.

2.58, Copyright Maya Lin. Photo: Mark Segal/Panoramic Stock Images, Chicago.

2.59, Unsigned. Staatliche Kunstsammlungen der DDR. Kupferstichkabinett Dresden.

2.60, Signed lower right: Kollwitz. Staatliche Kunstsammlungen der DDR. Kupferstichkabinett Dresden. © 2001 Artists Rights Society (ARS), NY/VG Bild-Kunst, Bonn.

2.61, Staatsgalerie Stuttgart. © 2001 Artists Rights Society (ARS), NY/VG Bild-Kunst, Bonn.

2.62, National Gallery of Art, Washington DC. Gift of Robert and Chris Petteys. © 2001 Artists Rights Society (ARS), NY/VG Bild-Kunst, Bonn. Photo © 2001 Board of Trustees, National Gallery of Art.

Chapter 3

3.1, Courtesy Scott Hull Associates, Dayton, OH.

3.2, Philadelphia Museum of Art; purchased with a grant from the National Endowment for the Arts and matching funds contributed by Marion Boulton Stroud, Marilyn Skinbright, J. J. Medveckis Foundation, David Gwinn, and Harvey S. Shipley Miller. Photo: Graydon Wood, 1991.

3.76, © 1984 by Chris van Allsburg. Reprinted by permission of Houghton Mifflin Co.

3.77, The Historical and Interpretive Collections of The Franklin Institute, Philadelphia, PA.

3.79, Carlo Ponti. © 2001 Estate of Francis Bacon/Artists Rights Society (ARS), NY.

3.80, TM & © 2001 Marvel Characters, Inc. Used with permission.

3.81, Metropolitan Museum of Art, NY, George A. Hearn Fund, 1956 (56.78). Photo © 1984 Metropolitan Museum of Art.

3.82, Albright-Knox Art Gallery, NY, gift of Seymour H. Knox, 1967.

3.83, Photo: David Caras.

3.84, Philadelphia Museum of Art, PA, Bridgeman Art Library. © 2001 Artists Rights Society (ARS), NY/ADAGP, Paris/Estate of Marcel Duchamp.

3.85, Museum of Modern Art, NY, gift of the photographer. Reprinted with permission of Joanna T. Steichen. Copy Print © 2002 Museum of Modern Art, NY.

3.86, Collection, Whitney Museum of American Art, Gift of Mr. and Mrs. B.H. Friedman (75.1). Photograph © 2000: Whitney Museum of American Art. © 2001 Pollock-Krasner Foundation/Artists Rights Society (ARS), NY.

3.87, Museum of Modern Art, Purchase. Photo © 2002 Museum of Modern Art, NY.

3.88, Syracuse University Library, Department of Special Collections. Syracuse, NY.

3.89, Photofest.

Profile, Walton Arts Center, Fayetteville, AR, permission of the artist.

Chapter 4

Page 4-9, Georgiana Nehl © 1996. Photo: David Browne.

4.2, 2002 Cordon Art B. V. Baarn, Holland. All rights reserved.

Profile, © Nancy Callahan and Diane Gallo.

Chapter 5

5.1, Cooper-Hewitt, National Design Museum, Smithsonian Institution/Art Resource, NY, gift of Gary Laredo, 1956-10-1. Photo: Dave King.

5.2, Museum of Modern Art, NY. Gift of Edgar Kaufman, Jr. Photo © 2002 Museum of Modern Art, NY.

5.5, Museum of Modern Art, NY. Gift of Herman Miller Furniture Company. Photo © 2002 Museum of Modern Art, NY.

5.6, Photo courtesy of Knoll, Inc.

5.8, Photo: Peter Colville

5.9, Corning Museum of Glass, gift of Vera Lisková.

5.10, Chronicle Books, San Francisco, 1995.

5.11, Museum of Modern Art, NY, Mrs. Simon Guggenheim Fund, © 2001 Yves Tanguy/Artists Rights Society (ARS), NY. Photo © 2002 Museum of Modern Art, NY.

5.12, Private Collection. © 2001 Artists Rights Society (ARS), NY/SIAE, Rome.

5.15A, Photo: Kate Gollings.

5.15B, Photo: John Gollings.

5.17A, Honolulu Academy of Arts, gift of James A. Michener, 1991 (21.971). Photo © Honolulu Academy of Arts.

5.17B, Honolulu Academy of Arts, gift of James A. Michener, 1955 (13,695). Photo © Honolulu Academy of Arts.

5.17C, Honolulu Academy of Arts, gift of James A. Michener, 1991 (21.968). Photo © Honolulu Academy of Arts.

5.18, Photo: Leslie Leupp.

5.19, Left to right, Private collection; Collection Stedelijk Museum, Amsterdam; Private collection. Photo: George Erml.

5.20, Copyright 1999 Iomega Corporation.

5.21, Museo Nacional Centro de Arte Reina Sofia, Madrid/Bridgeman Art Library. © 2001 Estate of Pablo Picasso/Artists Rights Society (ARS), NY.

Chapter 6

6.1, Art Institute of Chicago, Charles H. and Mary F. S. Worcester Collection. Photo © 2001 Art Institute of Chicago. All rights reserved.

6.2, Stanza della Segnatura, Vatican, Rome. Photo: Copyright Scala/Art Resource, NY.

6.10, South facade of the Nelson-Atkins Museum of Art and the Kansas City Sculpture Park. Aluminum, fiberglass-reinforced plastic, urethane paint, approx. 19.2 ft h × 16 ft diameter (5.9 × 4.8 m). Nelson-Atkins Museum of Art, Purchase, acquired through the generosity of the Sosland Family (F94-1/2-4) © Claes Oldenburg and Coosje van Bruggen. Photo: E. G. Schempf.

6.15, Collection: Moderna Museet, Stockholm. © Robert Rauschenberg/Licensed by VAGA, NY.

6.16, © Robert Rauschenberg/Licensed by VAGA, NY. Photo: Harry Shunk.

photo credits

7.51, Photo: Dirk Bakker.

7.52, Collection: Staatliches Museum fur Volkerkunde, Munich. Photo: S. Autrum-Rulzer.

7.53, Los Angeles County Museum of Art, Gift of Howard and Gwen Laurie Smits. Photo © 2002 Museum Associates/LACMA.

7.54, Edition of Six. Courtesy Alexander and Bonin, NY. Photo: Orcutt & Van Der Putten

7.55, Courtesy of Gallery Nii, Ginza, Tokyo.

7.56, Private collection. Courtesy of the artist.

7.58, Courtesy Fisher-Price.

7.59, Courtesy of Toshiyuki Kita/IDK Design Laboratory, LTD, Japan.

7.60, Courtesy George J. Sowden/Milan Pacific.

7.61, Courtesy Michael Graves & Associates. Photo: William Taylor.

7.64, Collection, Whitney Museum of American Art, NY. Purchase, with funds from the Louis and Bessie Adler Foundation, Inc., Seymour M. Klein, President, the Gilman Foundation, Inc., the Howard and Jean Lipman Foundation, Inc., and the National Endowment for the Arts (79.4). © The George and Helen Segal Foundation /Licensed by VAGA, NY. Photo: Duane Preble.

7.65, Museo del Templo Mayor, Mexico City. Instituto Nacional de Antropologia e Historia (INAH). Photo: Gabriel Figueroa Flores.

7.67, Corning Museum of Glass, Corning, NY (84.3.234).

7.69, Photo courtesy Inuit Gallery of Vancouver Ltd. Photo: Kenji Nagai.

7.71A–B, Chesterwood Museum Archives. Chesterwood, a National Trust Historic Site, Stockbridge, MA. Photo: De Witt Ward, by order of the sculptor in 1922, to demonstrate lighting problems in the memorial.

7.72, Designers: Bill Cannan, Tony Ortiz, H. Kurt Heinz. Design Firm: Bill Cannan & Co. Client/Mfr: NASA Public Affairs.

7.73, Busch Lobby, MIT Permanent Collection, gift of the Albert and Vera List Family Collection. Photo: Julia Fahey.

7.74, Courtesy Lance Fung Gallery, NY.

7.75, Courtesy Barbara Gladstone.

Chapter 8

8.1, Solomon R. Guggenheim Museum, NY, purchased with funds contributed by the Louis and Bessie Adler Foundation, Inc., Seymour M. Klein, President, 1985 (85.3276). Photo: David Heald, © Solomon R. Guggenheim Museum Foundation, NY.

8.3, Courtesy of Humanscale, NY.

8.4, St. Peter's, Rome. Canali Photobank, Milano, Italy.

8.5, Santa Maria degli Angeli, Rome. © Mauro Magliani/SuperStock, Inc.

8.6, Transparency 2104(2) Courtesy Department of Library Services, American Museum of Natural History.

8.7, Collection Kröller-Müller, Otterlo, The Netherlands.

8.8, Client/Mfr: Corona Clipper Co.

8.9, Collection: Hokkaido Asahikawa Museum of Art, Asahikawa City, Hokkaido, Japan. Photo: Yasunori Ookura.

8.10, Solomon R. Guggenheim Foundation, NY, Peggy Guggenheim, Venice (76.2553.50). © 2001 Artists Rights Society (ARS), NY/ADAGP, Paris. Photo: David Heald, © Solomon R. Guggenheim Museum Foundation, NY.

8.11, Partial gift of the Arts Club of Chicago; restricted gift of various donors, through prior bequest of Arthur Rubloff; through prior restricted gift of William Hartmann; through prior gifts of Mr. and Mrs. Carter H. Harrison, Mr. and Mrs. Arnold H. Maremont through the Kate Maremont Foundation, Woodruff J. Parker, Art Institute of Chicago. © 2001 Artists Rights Society (ARS), NY/ADAGP, Paris. Photo © 2001 Art Institute of Chicago. All rights reserved.

8.12, Museum of Modern Art, NY, given anonymously. © 2001 Artists Rights Society (ARS), NY/ADAGP, Paris. Photo © 2002 Museum of Modern Art, NY.

8.13, Photo © Fratelli Alinari/SuperStock, Inc.

8.14, Museum of Modern Art, NY. Purchase. © 2001 Artists Rights Society (ARS), NY/ADAGP, Paris. Digital image © 2001 Museum of Modern Art, NY.

8.15, Collection: Edition 1, Museo Nacional Centro de Arte Reina Sofia, Madrid. Edition 2, Los Angeles County Museum of Art; Modern and Contemporary Art Council Fund. Photo: Gary McKinnis.

8.16, Commissioned by the port city of Algeciras, Spain.

8.17, Ministero degli Esteri, Rome. © Canali Photobank.

8.18, Courtesy the National Ornamental Metal Museum, Memphis, TN. Collection of the artist. Photo: Seth Tice-Lewis.

8.19, © 2001 Artists Rights Society (ARS), NY/ADAGP, Paris. Photo © CNAP Command Publique, Ministère de la Culture, Paris.

8.20, © 2001 Artists Rights Society (ARS), NY/ADAGP, Paris/FLC. Photo: Ezra Stoller © Esto Photographics.

8.21, Nelson Atkins Museum of Art, Kansas City, MO, gift of the Hall Family Foundation (F99-33/1 a-dd). © Magdalena Abakanowicz/Licensed by VAGA, NY/Marlborough Gallery, NY. Photo: E. G. Schempf.

8.22, Photo: Don Hamilton, Spokane, WA.

8.23, Installation: San Francisco Museum of Modern Art. Courtesy Paula Cooper Gallery, NY.

8.24, Courtesy Mary Boone Gallery.

8.25, Installation: Capp Street Project, S. F. Courtesy Alexander and Bonin, NY. Photo: Ben Blackwell.

8.26, © 2001 Artists Rights Society (ARS), NY/ADAGP, Paris. Photo © Bernard Bansee/SuperStock, Inc.

8.27, Private collection.

8.28, Museum fur Kunst und Gewerbe, Hamburg.

8.30, Musée d'Orsay, Paris. Reunion des Musees Nationaux/Art Resource, NY. Photo: Herve Lewandowski.

8.31, Collection Walker Art Center, Minneapolis. Acquired with Lannan Foundation support in conjunction with the exhibition *Sculpture Inside Outside*, 1991.

8.32, Solomon R. Guggenheim Museum, NY, gift, Mr. and Mrs. Sidney Singer, 1977 (77.2325.a-.bbbb) © 2001 Estate of Louise Nevelson/Artists Rights Society (ARS), NY. Photo: Robert E. Mates, © Solomon R. Guggenheim Museum Foundation, NY.

8.33, Courtesy Agnes Gund Collection. © The Joseph and Robert Cornell Memorial Foundation/Licensed by VAGA, NY.

8.34, Museo National de Antropologia y Arqueologia, Lima. Photo: © 1991 Dirk Bakker

8.35, Photo: © 1996 Don Pitcher/Alaska Stock.com.

8.37A, Wright State University, Dayton, OH. Photo: Susan Zurcher.

8.38, Product: Cleret™ Glass Cleaner. Client/Mfr: Hanco

8.39, Courtesy Artimede.

8.41, Collection Majorie & Arnold Platzker. Photo: Tom Vinetz.

8.42, Kunstindustrimuseet I Oslo, (Museum of Decorative Arts & Design) Norway. Photo: Teigens Fotoatelier AS.

8.43, Art Institute of Chicago, Grant J. Pick Purchase Fund (1967.386). © 2001 Artists Rights Society (ARS), NY/VEGAP, Madrid. Photo © 2001, Art Institute of Chicago. All rights reserved. Photo: Michael Tropea, Chicago.

8.44, Courtesy of the Artist and Spacetime C. C.

8.46, Collection: Detroit Institute of Arts, Detroit, MI. Courtesy of the artist. © 2001 Sol LeWitt/Artists Rights Society (ARS), NY.

8.47, Albright-Knox Art Gallery, Buffalo.

8.48, Raymond Loewy International Group Ltd., London.

8.49, UCLA Fowler Museum of Cultural History (X64-395a-c). Photo: Don Cole.

8.50, Photo: Timothy Hursley/The Arkansas Office.

Chapter 9

9.1, © George Glod/SuperStock, Inc.

9.2, Photo: Shigeo Anzai, Tokyo.

9.3, Temporary Installation, New York Public Library, 1998. Courtesy Ronald Feldman Fine Arts, NY. Photo: Dennis Cowley.

9.4, Saint Peter's Basilica, Vatican, Rome. Photo: Copyright Alinari/Art Resource, NY.

9.5, Left to right: Private collection, Collection Martha Schwartz; Collection Oakland Museum of Art. Photo: Mark Johann.

9.6, Private collection. Photo: M. Mimlitsch-Gray

9.7, Courtesy of Michele Oka Doner. Collection of the Art Institute of Chicago.

9.8, With permission Gianfranco Frattini. Courtesy Acerbis International SPA, Milan, Italy.

9.9, University of California, Berkeley Art Museum. Photo: Benjamin Blackwell.

9.10, Kukje Gallery, Chrong Ku, Seoul, Korea.

9.11, Near Charlotte, NC. Copyright Maya Lin. Landscape Architect and Photo: Henry Arnold.

9.12, Private collection. © The George and Helen Segal Foundation /Licensed by VAGA, NY.

9.13, Courtesy of the artists and New Langton Arts.

9.14, BLUE SKIES 1990 (installation view) © Susan Trangmar.

9.15, Photo: Yoshiki Nakano.

9.16, On loan to The Philadelphia Museum of Art, Philadelphia, PA.

9.17, Metropolitan Museum of Art, Bequest of Mrs. H. O. Havemeyer, 1929. The H.O. Havemeyer Collection. Photo © Metropolitan Museum of Art.

9.18, Giovanni e Paolo, Venice. Bridgeman Art Library.

9.19, Philadelphia Museum of Art, the Louise and Walter Arensberg Collection (50-134-18). © 2001 Artists Rights Society (ARS), NY/ADAGP, Paris. Photo: Graydon Wood, 1994.

9.20, Museum of Modern Art, NY, Acquired through the Lillie P. Bliss Bequest. Photo © 2002 Museum of Modern Art, NY.

Chapter 11

Chapter 12

12.2, Saint Louis Art Museum, funds given by Mr. and Mrs. George Schlapp, Mrs. Francis A. Mesker, Henry L. & Natalie Edison Freund Charitable Trust, Helen & Arthur Baer Charitable Foundation, Marilyn & Sam Fox, Mrs. Eleanor J, Moore, Mr. & Mrs. John Wooten Moore, Donna & William Nussbaum, Mr. and Mrs. James E. Schneithorst, Jain and Richard Shaikewitz, Mark Twain Bancshares, Inc. Mr. & Mrs. Gary Wolff, Mr. & Mrs. Lester P. Ackerman, Jr., Hon. & Mrs. Thomas F. Eagleton, Alison & John Ferring, Mrs. Gail K. Fischmann, Mr. and Mrs. Solon Gershman, Dr. and Mrs. Gary Hansen, Mr. & Mrs. Kenneth Kranzberg, Mr. & Mrs. Gyo Obata, Warren & Jane Shapleigh, Lee & Barbara Wagman, Mr. John Weil, Museum Shop Fund, Contemporary Art Society, and Museum Purchase; Dr. & Mrs. Harold J. Joseph, Estate of Alice P. Francis, Fine Arts Associates, J. Lionberger Davis, Mr. & Mrs. Samuel B. Edison, Mr. & Mrs. Morton D. May, Estate of Louise H. Franciscus, Anonymous Gift, Miss Ella M. Boedeker, and Museum Purchase, by exchange.

12.6, Photo: Brad Freeman.

12.10A, Copyright © 1963 and renewed 1991 by Edward Gorey, reprinted by permission of Harcourt, Inc.

12.10B, Copyright © 1963 and renewed 1991 by Edward Gorey, reprinted by permission of Harcourt, Inc.

12.11, Reprinted with the permission of Little Simon, an imprint of Simon & Schuster Children's Publishing Division, from *The 12 Days of Christmas, a Pop-up Celebration*, by Robert Sabuda. © 1996 by Robert Sabuda.

12.16, Holding Together–Images, design and poem by Judite dos Santos (limited edition artist book). Published by Visual Studies Workshop Press.

12.26, © 2001 Robert Irwin/Artists Rights Society (ARS), NY. Courtesy Dia Center for the Arts and Robert Irwin. Photo: Thibault Jeanson.

12.27, Collection: Edition 1, Collection of Marion Stroud Swingle. Edition 2, Collection of the artist; courtesy Anthony d'Offay Gallery. Photo: Roman Mensing

12.28, Collection of the artist. Photo: Roman Mensing.

12.29, © 1997 Sandy Skoglund.

12.30, © Nancy Callahan and Diane Gallo.

12.31, © 2001 Jenny Holzer/Artists Rights Society (ARS), NY. Sponsored by the Public Art Fund Inc. Photo: Lisa Kahane.

12.32, Photo © Dan Rest/Courtesy B.A.M.

12.33, Photo © 1983 Paula Court.

12.34, Courtesy The Rachel Rosenthal Company. Photo: Lothar Schmitz.

12.35, © 2001 Yoko Ono Lennon. Photo courtesy Lenono Photo Archive.

index